Heart of Lightness

HEART OF LIGHTNESS
The Life Story of an Anthropologist

Edith Turner

Berghahn Books
New York • Oxford

First published in 2005 by

Berghahn Books

www.berghahnbooks.com

©2006 Edith Turner

Library of Congress Cataloging-in-Publication Data

British Library Cataloguing in Publication Data

A catalogue record for this book is available from the British Library
Printed in the United States on acid-free paper

ISBN 1-84545-126-0 hardback
ISBN 1-84545-127-9 paperback

CONTENTS

For
Chester Michael

LIST OF ILLUSTRATIONS

ACKNOWLEDGMENTS

Many thanks to the friends who have encouraged me to write this book, especially the late Barbara Myerhoff, whose last words to me were, "write, write." Also I pay tribute to Vic Turner, my late husband, still there in the dreams of myself and my children. Before he died he said he would never leave me, neither in this world nor afterwards, and he did not. As regards the living, I owe more than I can say to the wise people who have instructed me in the anthropological field; also much thanks for the friendship of the woman I call Mary in the Small Group, to Roy Wagner the anthropologist, and to Chester Michael. I thank those who have financially sponsored my efforts in anthropology: the University of Virginia; Mary and James McConnell, the Carter G. Woodson Institute for African-American and African Studies, and the Wenner-Gren Foundation for Anthropological Research. There are many in the Church of the Incarnation at Charlottesville whose love has fed me like manna; and I am also grateful to David Stang for much encouragement and help. Thanks above all to Fiona Bowie, who gave me the chance to go on with this book. Gratitude also goes to my family for waking up my ideas; I thank them for their love. Finally I thank the source of the moments of joy described in the book.

FOREWORD
Ronald Frankenberg

Cultural Anthropology: Edith and Victor Turner, The Poetics of Discovery of Self and Other.

Edith Turner, developing her joint work with her late partner Victor (Vic and Edie), is already among the most influential researchers and teachers of social and cultural anthropology in the twentieth century on both sides of the Atlantic and in the wider world. Her autobiography stands alongside and even surpasses in its long-term significance, those of Levi-Strauss and Margaret Mead. Readers will find in it both an adventure story and the story of adventures across the world.

Vic and Edie were also amongst the earliest of the small group of anthropologists who aim successfully at *knowing* rather than merely *knowing about* the people with whom they lived and studied, as well as having genuinely shared in their daily lives. Above all they showed through their creative partnership that learning about others goes hand in hand with learning about oneself. Anthropologists studying their own home societies in Europe and in the U.S.A. adopted the slogan of *making the normal, strange*. Vic and Edie, not without a struggle, accepted the practices of those they studied—strange as they might seem to outsiders—as at once normal and valid as well as deserving of respect. They took them as seriously as those of anyone else, a far cry from the dismissive diaries of Malinowski. Edie here charts the shared life of herself and Vic's development from a premature hippie style with links to the British artistic and literary *Bohemia* of the thirties, through anthropological training and radical communism, to orthodox Roman Catholicism, and then on to a humanist Catholicism—the acknowledgment of diverse spirituality. This becomes for Edie a small "c"—catholicism in the broadest sense that follows the spirit where it moves. Edie, once converted and received lovingly, but loyally, like many other thoughtful intellectual Catholics and pragmatically alert lay people, became critical of the politics of Vatican and Church Catholicism while still deeply embedded in the practice of the faith in a wider, yet more basic, context. She does not hesitate to condemn the adoption of patriarchal and hierarchical techniques by various Popes, historical and contemporaneous, by the Vatican and the organized Church at the expense of the poor and the peaceful, and not least, of women. Although she was critical of some pronouncements of former Cardinal Ratzinger, she will surely take more kindly to his first Encyclical as Benedict XVIth on the subject of love—"Deus Caritas Est"—and on its opening statements (see below) which in an important sense Vic and Edie prefigured in the trajectory of their own lives.

The book chronicles how the Turners formed, with their parents and their offspring, their friends in many societies across the world, their colleagues, and their students, an ever dynamic and always changing but perduring team. They, within this one, intimate, but often widely dispersed human milieu, and in many diverse cultural environments, produced for themselves and made available for others, constructive escapes from bureaucratic and oppressive communism, from hierarchical alienating churchiness, as well as from dehumanizing formalistic scholarship within academia, social science in general, and anthropology in particular.

First, however, as Edie explicates, they had to experience, like the protagonists of *The Magic Flute* and Dante's *Divine Comedy*, not merely dark days of the intellect but also dark nights of the soul. Edie chronicles these and even illustrates the journey with a wealth of expressive photographs (as we know and enjoyed Vic doing elsewhere with poems and lectures, literally dancing and singing to share experience of spirit, mind, and body). She does not disown the experience, the example, or the goodwill of either the comrades who shared with them the frustrating bureaucratic distortions of mid-twentieth-century communism, (see page 66) nor the Cathedral and Church status-obsessed formality of class-organized ceremonial, rather than the true rituals of shared faith. That includes the sometimes disembodied, even body-rejecting, Anglicanism in which she was, however lovingly, raised. The book begins and ends with visions of the English town of Ely and its cathedral that, as she reveals in the final chapter, provided a lifelong backdrop to her dreams, waking and sleeping, achieved and frustrated.

Together Vic and Edie, a partnership continuing to this day long after Vic's passing, raised the idea of participant observation (and indeed of team learning) to heights and depths that most anthropologists never achieve. Even before they came together, they were both people of broad religious and literary culture in their own right. They gradually, as their studies progressed across the world, became literate in several world languages. Victor died of a second heart attack in December 1983 at a relatively early age of sixty-three.

For more than 20 years into the beginning of the twenty-first century, Edie has carried on, sustained by colleagues and friends as well as interlocutors and co-participants in rituals who became friends and colleagues themselves. She has never been totally alone but always also in the spirit of, and with inspiration from, her abiding love for her family and friends, and her memories and dreams of Vic. This is as evident in the grand hotels of academic conferences as it is in humble homes whether huts, igloos, tents, or villas.

The book is titled in reaction to Joseph Conrad's ambiguously pessimistic projection of his own darkness onto a supposedly mysterious other. It acknowledges that Africa, while not necessarily the ultimate source of the Turners' enlightenment, was the continent in which their shared experiences crystallized into their mature key concepts of liminality and communitas. It was there that the material and spiritual shape of their future analyses of their own and others' ritual and their feelings and experiences took shape and was confirmed by Edie's return in 1985 to an independent Zambia, thirty years later. Key moments in Africa are condensed in Edie's account of a literal meeting of hands across the bounds of race that leads to the possibility of meeting of minds (on page 62) and the prediscovery of "actuality" (see page 71).

The book is a very personal but theoretically and empirically informed memoir centered on the life of Edie herself, alongside her family and close friends and collaborators. In its wholehearted embracing of both spiritual and dramatic experience as real and legitimate, and indeed often overlapping, it is part of an important and possibly expanding trend in American, and hopefully world, anthropology, centered on, but not confined to, the Society of Humanistic Anthropology within the AAA. It has its parallel also in other AAA sections including, not least, medical as well as critical anthropologies to my direct knowledge, and no doubt elsewhere.

It is not, however the kind of autobiography based on diaries or letters and other documents that aims to tell it historically, exactly, in strict chronological order as it was. She realises that her truth might vanish if she did not recognise, if she had not at the time, a particular present as embodied in several pasts and the future, however uncertainly it is glimpsed.

One biographical note of a more formal kind has been published (and exists in greater detail in a dissertation) with Edie's collaboration and that of many of her friends and colleagues (see Matthew Engelke 2004 in Volume 10 of *History of Anthropology*, pp. 6-49). It is rather Edie's own interpretation of her life, as she sees it looking back from the time of writing, self-consciously and, I believe totally honestly, seeking to make sense of her experience.

It is legitimate for a reader, who like myself, shared a miniscule proportion of her life events (mainly in Manchester UK), to feel from time to time, "it was not like that at all" but that is not to say she is wrong, merely that the same events had a different impact on me or on other participants. Such differences of view, stimulatingly lively and conflict-producing, kept all of us, despite partial gender segregation, awake and alert to novelty especially in the intellectual (and sporting) milieu of Manchester. In fact, they paradoxically confirm the aptness of her overall intellectual and emotional stance.

Atheist anthropologists are on the whole surprisingly (or at least, it seems so to me as, archetypically, a virtual-secularist but somewhat observant Jew) and considerably less tolerant of the religious in the modern era than the religious are of the secular. I feel after long association and interaction with Catholics and Jews, that both categories allow themselves an almost but not quite authorized, questioning agnosticism despite the fulminations of priests and rabbis. It is only the totally *EX-* of both religions that enjoy at once both their new-found undogma and, negatively and often inaccurately, the dogma they have deserted.

Although, at the time when I first met Vic and Edie, I had long since refused the personal invitation of Raji Palme Dutt, president and Comintern representative of the Communist party, to join the party, I was already committed to the left through pre–WWI Bundist and pre–WWII communist family tradition and had been a recent member of the Zionist Ma'pam Party that I had joined at Cambridge. Vic and Edie had just returned from Africa and I had returned from rural Wales to work on our Ph.D. degrees. I had in fact, earlier been excluded from the West Indies on suspicion of being a security risk. I shared reading Mgr. Ronald Knox's newly published translation of the Vulgate Bible with Vic during the Suez and Hungarian crises of 1956, went with Vic to the cinema to see—and being Vic, to analyze—the film on the Coronation of the Pope. I also accompanied Vic on visits to Moss Side to try, against party policy and the personally communicated directives of the same Palme Dutt, to get black comrades to organize their own branch to escape the embarrassment of tea and sherry party-branch meetings in white middle-class intellectual Didsbury, with their policy urgings which often seemed irrelevant to the working class as a whole, let alone to its "black and colored" sections.

The general thesis of the book will perhaps not at first appeal to many, perhaps even most, anthropologists. But any who start reading it will be gripped by the well-told story, and the genuine and shared experiences recounted will, at least for many, open new vistas.

Edie considers her (upper?) middle-class childhood in Ely (creatively revisited with her poet daughter, Rene, in the last chapter 16), weaving together recollected and reinterpreted experiences of inclusion and exclusion at home and at various boarding schools, with the older generation and with servants and the "lower" orders. She recalls discrimination against her in the family and especially the cutting short of her education compared with that accorded to her relatives. She discusses the dynamics of rebellions and rejections, and the well-meaning avoidance of genuinely experienced religion by the religious who tried to make her accept a morality based on God's will. She now recalls its presentation, modified perhaps, in the days before the impact of modern mass communication, by their class and educational status. She remembers the occasional experience of communitas and the experiential characteristic of liminality, which she sees as the central concepts of Vic's and her own thinking. Later she traces her part in the discovery of this to the actual and felt warmth of her family's kitchen. Without excessive nostalgia she recaptures the paradoxical unity of families and servants and the sense of communitas based on difference that it engendered which, despite its popularity in film, museum display, and television reads so strangely today even to literate British and Americans (pages 25-26). She begins also to sketch out the links between this and Wordsworth's and other Romantic poetic insights about nature and the way that spirits are perceived in many different cultures. In later chapters George Herbert becomes a greater influence. She was also influenced by Bernard Shaw's feminism, Bergson, and Blake.

(In Jewish North London and at an Anglican, so called "public" Highgate School, I shared all these influences plus D.H. Lawrence, four or five years later, thanks to an inspired English teacher and Sir Allen Lane's Penguin Books!) At the age of eighteen Edie fled to London and her communist elder sister Helen, and helped work for the revolution, as she now sees, ironically supported by her Conservative party councillor mother and physician father. Then in 1940, at the time of Dunkirk she found herself in the Woman's Land Army joyfully working on the land with animals. Like Lucy in Wordsworth's poems (but still alive) Edie "Rolled round in earth's diurnal course with rocks and stones and trees."

When her brother Charlie, a conscientious objector at Keble College, Oxford, was drafted into a non-combatant section of the army stationed nearby in Berkshire, she moved to Oxford to be near him. She worked as an under-gardener at Lady Margaret Hall turning flowerbeds into vegetable patches. Perhaps this was good training for her later activity as an anthropologist when she and Vic turned earthy material Rhodes-Livingstone vegetable patches into flowerbeds of sociological spiritual understanding (a transition from Daryll Forde and W. Allan, agronomist cooperator with the Rhodes-Livingston Istitute, to the Celtic Romantic, Alwyn Rees), without their ever losing their awareness of the intimate connection between them.

The same brother introduced her to his "hippie" bohemian mates including fellow communist, poet, and "conchie" (draft objector) Vic, who was literally an immediate hit, *un coup de foudre*, even before they had touched each other. The relationship developed rapidly and soon involved life long friend, John Bate, and both their circles, including Vic's mother (and even through visiting his old church, Vic's boyhood mentor, an Anglican mystic known as "Padre"). As a teenager, Vic had an "actuality" vision of the death of the old man as it was taking place far away. Edie is reunited with her siblings and her own mother. They are all politically and poetically active and their earthy occupations, as well as their literary and spiritual leanings, make them feel linked to both working class and intellectuals. Blake's roaring spirit and Burns's rich bluntness (like Vic he was a "heathen of the heather"), replace Wordsworth's *intimations*. This is reinforced by Violet, Vic's actress mother with an enthusiasm for Ibsen and Shakespeare. Vic himself had read Jung and Freud and already had a considerable poetic output which he declaimed to his lover, soon to be wife, and the mother of Freddie and then Bobby. After describing Vic's dark but "anti-wastelander" (his own term for his rejection of Eliot, Pound, and their ilk) poems, Edie writes "he himself was a flat-out character; in a sense he was out of control, his consciousness had escaped from him, it was there ahead of him like the *arutam* souls of the Jivaro Indians flying out ahead of their bodies over the battlefield. Vic had no side, no 'dignity,' no 'manner,' no self-consciousness or masking of his real self, although he loved acting. I don't think calculating types ever realised this about Vic as long as he lived." (46)

The story of their early love, like good wine, needs no verbal bush to be displayed on its behalf in this introduction. Like their whole life together, before as well as after Vic's early death, and like the aspirations of the embodied faith they both espouse, it is a dynamic blend of tears and laughter, poetry and prose, the earthbound and the sublime. It emerges as the united essence of their lives and their works.

Before the birth of their first child, they briefly shared a cottage until Vic was "posted" 80 miles to the North, had an accident and was hospitalized and then sent to Rugby, where they had a meagre cottage. Freddy was laboriously carried on foot but *in utero* to, and eventually born in, an Emergency Medical Service Maternity hospital. After the newborn had spent his early months in chests of drawers in several hired rooms, Edie reluctantly gave in and moved to share the drawing room in her mother's house at Ely with her sister Helen and her baby. Helen spotted a gypsy caravan (shades of Augustus John!) for sale for £25 in the *Ely Standard* and Edie had nearly enough money from her Land Army savings to buy it. With the help of "liberated" navy rum, the price was reduced and after hair-raising near calamities the caravan came to permanent rest minus one wheel on the banks of a canal where, with the help of Vic's army mates, it provided Vic and Edie with a shared home and a birthplace for Bobby in February 1945. Meanwhile Vic read the life of Toulouse Lautrec and Edie looked at the pictures. Edie had a prolapsed uterus which made for difficulty in the four mile walk to Rugby for shopping with Bobby in the pram, while Freddie, because she could not carry him, had to struggle behind.

A major change in their outlook came when they discovered Margaret Mead's two Pelican books *Coming of Age in Samoa* and *Growing up in New Guinea* by chance in a Rugby bookshop, followed by Radcliffe-Brown's *The Andaman Islanders*. They realised that anthropology might offer them, if not poetry, at least close contact with living ordinary people, whom they wouldn't be required, as many other social scientists seemed to them to be, to look down on from a great height. This led them to a decision to live in what seemed the nearest thing in Britain, the Scottish highlands and islands with which Vic had ancestral ties. Vic visited Raasay, which he soon felt he understood and where it was possible to find a farm but which Edie's health was not up to. This project ended in Edie's terms as a "mere proto-hippy dream."

After the war, Vic decided to abandon his part-completed degree in comparative literature at UCL as too academic. He negotiated, with the Registrar, a fellow Scot (*and* whisky drinker!), to change to a full three-year undergraduate course in anthropology with Daryll Forde. This was to be followed by a year of archaeology and hopefully a Ph.D. in Africa. Daryll was, of course, as she says, an "argy-bargy down-to-earth Welsh materialist geographer (like H.J. Fleure before him and Emrys Bowen after him at Aberystwyth)."

The idea "that ritual arose from social structures" characteristic of "the British School" introduced a break from the interaction of earth and spirit in favor of the earthy, and did not appeal to Vic and Edie, despite the fact that they were, of course, active communists. Worsening conditions of life in London and the birth of their daughter Rene forced Edie to live near Vic's mother in St Leonards-on-Sea. Vic wrote endless essays but Edie was then not able in either training or opportunity to write. "My hands were not for that, though my ears were for listening." Political systems were seen as central but Max Gluckman, who offered Vic a studentship in Manchester and eventual field research in Africa, was moving towards process rather than structure. [He had already shown this tendency in 1942, before even going to the Rhodes-Livingstone Institute, in his Zulu Bridge Study (see my and other papers in Evens and Mandelbaum 2006).]

Their African adventures begin dramatically. In Edie's own words, "Nothing went according to plan." (83) Not the least failure of plan was that Vic had at first to go on his own to Africa, leaving Edie and the children behind to follow. Edie describes provisioning and her mother's help. Vic arrived in Capetown and was met by Max's "party friends" [all RLI fellows were met by Jack Simons and his wife, Ray, who were indeed CP members but also, respectively an academic lawyer (later Manchester's Simon Professor and Professor of Sociology at the University of Zambia) and a distinguished historian. They were both recognised as experts on so-called native affairs in Southern Africa]. Edie read Doris Lessing and realistically considered the extent to which she and Vic would be able, as they wished, to escape the standard Southern African household pattern (for example, with domestic servants, who often in towns lived either in township squalor or in a hut at the bottom of their employers' garden) and live like Africans. She achieved a lot in this direction but still realistically doubts their more than partial success.

Max suggested a change of research area in Zambia by cable to Vic in order to facilitate an eventual change to the analysis of ritual. Most British anthropologists following Durkheim, as interpreted by Radcliffe-Brown, were in fact interested in ritual but in a way that suggested its secondary status to structure and even economy. The difference between the final position of earlier scholars and Vic and Edie, is that the former, although they respected the ritual of others, and often came to understand it in some depth, nearly always saw it as totally other to themselves. These predecessors observed it deeply and sympathetically but from without. This was, perhaps especially true for many Jewish anthropologists who either adopted a deeply-held cultural secularism or a loosely-worn cultural religious observance of their own. Welsh Methodists or orthodox Roman Catholics, especially converts, also took this approach. The French scholars Marcel Griaule and Germaine Dieterlein, however, were culture heroes to both Gluckman and Daryll Forde. Their long and detailed study of West African Dogon cosmology, as Malinowski's initial experience in the Trobriand Islands had been in WW1, was made possible by wartime internment in their territory. The International African Institute under Forde's direction instituted a major project to build on Griaule's work throughout Africa, which the present author, encouraged by Gluckman who appointed Forde as his doctoral examiner, sought unsuccessfully to join.

Edie and the children eventually reached Cape Town and were blissfully reunited at Lusaka railway station, where the lateness of trains was then and later often measured in days rather than hours. They met Clyde Mitchell and collected the famous RLI census forms, They set off to meet the Ndembu, still with the perception from Max that social structure came first, a view that they were to show to be oversimplified in the extreme. Indeed they turned it on its head first in Africa and then, as Edie graphically describes among many different people, in many languages and above all, in their own lives.

When they arrived back in England, they found Manchester at the peak of its most dynamic period. The idea of social process had vanquished its more staid and stolid structural legacy and life was exciting but fraught politically, emotionally, and intellectually. As Engelke points out in his chapter referred to above, the wives of the department were not much included in its proceedings at the center even on social occasions, let alone in seminars, or rather the almost continuous seminar which went on in Max's office and other offices in the Dover Street building, in local "Caffs," and in the informally annexed TV room of the academic staff club across Oxford Road. The early mid-fifties were also a time of national and political turmoil with fears of nuclear war.

Edie was still trying to come to terms with the emotional, spiritual, and intellectual impact of her Kajima spiritual experiences that was enhanced by a dream in Manchester at this time, and she managed, although in partial isolation, the first draft of what was, decades later, to become *The Spirit and the Drum*.

She also became involved again with the Communist party which pressed her to accept her choice by the local left-wing business tycoon, Lord Simon of Wythenshawe, to lead the Campaign for Nuclear Disarmament organization of a major Manchester regional rally. This was frustrated by a breakdown in her health accentuated by problems concerning the oppressive nature of the local schools to which she was obliged to send her children. She suffered a deep depression, not helped by Vic's increasing, obsessive concern with African ritual. He was trying to link his analysis with his own past mystical experiences and still satisfy the demands of Max and his down-to-earth colleagues and friends. He flirted conscientiously with an attempt to use Freud as a way of achieving this but settled on a dramaturgic performance approach.

"Okay, Freud could show the polarization of a symbol—but that too was Marxist: the idea was that the sensory part of a symbol gave driving force to the socially-required duty of virtue whose commands were embedded in the object, an object like a cross or a flag or an eagle clutching arrows." Vic and Edie characteristically embarked as a possibly productive distancing device, on a local experiment of looking at the varieties of religion available nearby their home suburb. They explored it in Stockport, a smaller industrial city next to Manchester. After going to Anglican and Presbyterian churches and a Quaker meeting house, they set out to attend a Unitarian church that unexpectedly turned out not to be in session. They had engaged in much soul-searching and textual reading including Roman Catholicism, so when they found a Catholic church Mass nearby, they went there instead and were struck by its similarity in feeling to their African experience.

They soon decided to take instruction. "This wasn't research any more, this was serious." The whole family was received after six months, their instruction reinforced by Vic's reading of Catholic novels and other imaginative and scholarly writings and the discovery that his army comrade in bomb disposal, who was to become a lifelong friend, John Bate, had also recently become Catholic.

I too remember and was naively surprised at the resentment that arose in the department; close colleagues who had worked closely with them for months, even years, turned aside when they encountered Vic and bitterly blamed and criticised them, both in their presence, and behind their backs. Two of the critics, in fairness, came from and were marked by communities riven by sectarianism (one had also studied one such) in Holland and Scotland respectively. Paradoxically and unsurprisingly, Vic and Edie's conversion, followed by hostile semi-isolation and especially the joyful birth but tragically very early death of their child Lucy, greatly restored their closeness to each other and added to its depth. Abandonment of birth control had led to the birth of Lucy, who had Downs Syndrome, and who only lived for five months. Edie, controversially but not unreasonably attributes both the disability and death of her child to the Sellafield nuclear disaster since there were indeed "many thousands of abnormal births in Manchester during the period of the late fifties" although the causes remain unproven and may well be multiple.

In the first of what were to be their many experiences of pilgrimage (especially for Edie after Vic's death), they journeyed to Aylesford, the ancient monastery of St. Simon Stock, the earliest English Carmelite House in Cobtree, Kent, said to be the oldest village in England. The Priory had recently been restored by Father Malachy Lynch. Their visit seems to have been another turning point to an improvement in their lives marked by the normal birth of Alex nine months later. Intellectually they began to restudy Kierkegard together and especially his study of the "Sacrifice of Isaac." "It was the opening of one of the doors." Its paradoxes enabled intellectual development and the deepening of the concepts of liminality and communitas, just as the study of St. Augustine's *City of God* later led to the key discussion of Edie's concept of Power 1 and Power 11. These books focused their discussion (118-123) of what religion in general and Catholicism in particular meant to them at that time. They now moved into their own liminal state in Hastings, betwixt and between the U.K. and the U.S.A.. In the course of time they transferred to Cornell in the U.S.A., paid a return visit to Africa (Uganda), and started a new partnership in the study of pilgrimage. Edie graphically describes in the "Hairpin Bend" how their intellectual, religious, philosophical and even geographical lives coalesce in their move to Cornell and the United States. Their apprenticeship, and their trials by fire and water, were to an extent surviving. Their poetic muse was now Gerard Manley Hopkins and they emerged into the light, through lived, not merely observed, liminality as the master/mistress of their craft to continue to learn, like other mature scholars (and artists), by doing and teaching and above all by conscientious submission to the explanatory power of theoretical concepts. (See Power I and Power II, 93)

At Aylesford they had been on pilgrimage primarily to consolidate their learning. They now began their study of pilgrimages where they could still learn but also focus on the research that would bring understanding to pass on to students. They started at the most visited Christian pilgrimage site in the world, Villa du Guadalupe in Mexico, and its story about how the Blessed Mother and a simple peasant made the haughty bishop take notice. Edie describes how, on her insistence, they became determined to study the living religious practice of ordinary people which they felt most scholarly anthropologists ignored out of a kind of intellectual snobbery.

This they pursued to Ireland inspired by Vic's admiration for the Welsh Celtic scholar, Alwyn Rees. "Again," writes Edie, "the trip turned out to be a quest for spirit consciousness, though at the time, we thought we were researching ritual." Visiting Knock, the place of an apparition of the Blessed Mother during the potato famine, Edie vividly imagines herself as contemporary witness of the historic event and visualizes and reports her experiences as if she were present (as in a sense she was) at the contemporary conversation around the apparition of the Lady and St John. She comes down reluctantly from this high, which reminds her of her experiences in Africa, to describe the modern scene and moves on to discussion of miracles over the years. After her first two visits, she notes that the list of miracles was hidden away by the Church "for fear of fraud." The conflict between the feelings of the people and official reactions of the organized church were very apparent and unpleasing to her.

Having relived in vividly imagined actuality and described the original events in Knock, Edie describes over several pages her own physically lived experiences with the companion she made in 1971, Bridget (Bidgy), how they met, and their shared experiences. She discovered that by taking communion before confession, she has departed from local custom.

"When I went into the [confession] cubicle I confessed to having pandered to the scientific coldness that accompanies anthropology. I have not had to do this since, [!] though I confessed to attacking the church." She also put herself up as a representative penitent for English behavior in Ireland over the centuries. She describes many more of her experiences in Ireland and how she and Vic over the years struggled to make sense of Knock and their other Irish experiences in order to understand the spirit and significance of music, femininity, and ultimately the Eucharist.

After moving from Chicago to Virginia, Edie took a Master's degree in English with a focus on symbolism. They moved into a period of intense experience and traveling, intellectually and often spiritually, with a group listed (p. 125), and all of whose names, Edie writes, "glow for me." From this communitas many books emerged. She adds the culminating name of "Roy Wagner, strange and visionary." During these years, lasting until Vic's passing in 1983, they experienced in depth, four religions, and became aware of more. They went to Anuradhapurna, a region sacred to Buddha in Ceylon, with Ranji Obeyesekere. Edie was able through eighteenth century and her own poetic imagination to compare the Bo tree sacred to Buddhism with the English ash, pagan and Christian. They visited Israel in 1980 where she was reunited with the foster brother who as Jewish refugee had shared some of his life with Edie as a child. Edie deepened her knowledge of the Hebrew Bible and especially the poetry of the Psalms, and the spiritual role of trees within them. They met and talked with Coptic Christians and Edie observed, from the women's gallery, ultra-orthodox Jewish students chanting the Talmud and studying its meaning. On a second visit to Israel, with Barbara Myerhoff in 1983, the latter advanced the anthropology of shared experience that has been the mission of Edie's and her own later work. On their return Edie even struggled with the Zohar, the mysticism of which she sees in the context of several other forms of mystical spirituality within and outside Catholicism. Finally she visits a family of Sufi Palestinians and prays and chants with their womenfolk, while the boys learn Koran in school and the men chant the Koran in the mosque next door. She summarizes this chapter as a collection of grains of certitude amidst confusion. "The little grains rest but never go away, and they have become part of a map of the directions in which my wandering path is going."

A short but intensely moving chapter follows the four religions discussion called: "The Loss of my Life Mate: I was broken in half but had to become a whole person." It describes Vic's death and that of their close friend Barbara Myerhoff as well as their funerals and the symbolization of death and eternity in the context of funerals in other cultures.

When Edie returns to Africa eighteen months after Vic's death, 31 years after they worked in Kajima together, the grains arrange themselves into a pattern and, as she puts it, "another door opens to the soul."

She gives as usual a more personal account but less detailed formalized argument about the experiences she had described and analysed in a more formal framework in her book with William Blodgett, Singleton Kahona, and Fideli Benwa, *Experiencing Ritual: A New Interpretation of African Healing,* published by Pennsylvania University Press in 1992. She does what anthropologists unfortunately rarely do, and supplements the scholastic analysis published elsewhere with her presentation of the total experience from letting her hair grow in white, acknowledging her father's name of Brocklesby: the badger, and appearing to be, as well as actually being an "elder," worthy to participate in serious rituals. She worked for the first time alone through "the business of threading her way through official channels" before setting out, by means of renewing old acquaintance and making new friends and co-celebrants to the Ihamba ceremony in both its commonplace and miraculous aspects. The outcome reaches its climax (on page 173) where she recognizes it as a turning point in her life comparable with meeting Vic in 1942, her conversion in 1958 and, still to come, her sense of communitas in the small group (see page 224). She describes it, using a 17th century philosophical term used by Husserl, as an *apodìctic* experience—necessary, clearly established, and beyond doubt. She now regarded herself as a guinea pig of the soul, echoing the crew of the starship *Enterprise* by boldly going "where no anthropologist has gone before, "seeking new experiences and states of consciousness."

Following this star, she sets off, encouraged by a graduate student and Roy Wagner to experience and study Inuit healing in Arctic Alaska by participating with the healer and scholar, Claire. As usual she brings her vividly to life. in a way which experienced anthropologists will envy and tyros struggle to emulate. There is a description of the "four-day shaman syndrome," a kind of "dark night of the soul," preceding moments of power and illumination. (The shamanistic scholar/healer, Claire, sees the moments as coming not from within her but from God, and Edie compares the situation with Vic's four-day "black" periods that preceded his "Aha!" periods when he first wrestled with and then resolved an intellectual or a personal problem.)

There is much else in this crowded chapter that pulls together Edie's world-wide experiences. For example, she relates the exotic topics of seal-skinning and whale-killing with religious experience in English cathedrals as well as the nature of death, the Passion, and Near Death Experiences, then to the beginnings of a coherent personal theology. It is summarised in a key passage: "… they were living in a fully-experienced syncretism of indigenous spirituality and Christianity, in which the people sensed their church, that double-natured church, as one of the two sources of all good power. The other was the whale." (p.195)

The chapter closes with George Herbert's sonnet on prayer and a summary/summery sentence by Edie herself. After her year in Alaska, and becoming an American citizen, Edie returned once more to Ireland in 1995, 1998, and 2001, accompanied at different times by different members of the family.

Revisitings and productive rethinkings are a feature of Edie's work throughout her life and enable her to overcome the snapshot impression of their field that the exigencies of finance and academic life today impose on many struggling young anthropologists. This is especially so in the US and the UK where priority is given to often shallow journal articles, over long thought out books written with maturity and depth. In these visits Edie explores other aspects of "unconventional" healing in Ireland, as well as reengaging with old arguments about the rift between Church and people both in the depth of their participation in the most rigorous pilgrimages, actual on the ground, and personal throughout the life course. She draws a distinction, to Jung's disadvantage, between the merely psychic healing that he advocates and the phenomenological concept of embodied experience. She notes the similarities across culture of embodied symbols from the pricking of thumbs (201) ascribed by Shakespeare to the witches in *Macbeth* and also evident in the practice of the Irish healer. Edie has also become more conscious of her own bodily sensations in critical situations. She is splendidly angry about the rebuilding and modernization of Knock (perhaps one should say postmodernization in the sense of the pilgrimage being transformed into a media event) including the masculinization of its presentation. (205-214) She shares in Irish rage at the depredations of the English over the centuries and she involves herself in fierce arguments with inevitably *male* clergy, some found to be even worse than anthropologists in the one-sidedness of their vision!

Knock is said to attract 1.5 million pilgrims each year, whereas the Purgatory of Lough Derg, only fifteen thousand. Edie's graphic account of its hardships explains why and also how both pilgrim and anthropologist (and indeed feminist scholars) may painfully gain more, including humility, by participating in it. It ends, "the purgatory simply and directly showed me my limits and made me fail, and I accepted that this was where the matter stood."

In the closing section of the book, the last third, Edie takes stock and draws conclusions about her life so far, in all its complexity of combined professional anthropologist, centers of friendship and kinship networks; conscious and unconscious, felt unity and division of mind, body and spirit.

She finally finds and reconciles her two homes in the mind and spirit first in church choirs, then in a small Christian Group, and in the Spiritual Direction Group directed by Chester Michael to whom the book is dedicated. And at the last there is a symbolic return to Ely for a final, or at least first final, stocktaking.

There is a short but key chapter describing how Edie came to join and to experience a life-changing—because communitas-inducing—liminal rite of passage in a church weekend group centering on individual and group confession (practice of reconciliation) in a community context. All this last is, as we have come to expect, intensely experienced and written in lively and polemical style, facing both ways, against church formalism on the one hand and materialism on the other. It also includes cross references to popular culture, science-fiction and the poet. George Herbert is an enduring influence. She makes a similar distinction to her earlier discussion of Power I & II for Social I & II, social rules as against communitas.

The last chapter is a poetic and religious meditation (not in verse) on her life's pilgrimage seen through a visit to Ely cathedral with her daughter Rene in 1999. It gives readers an opportunity to ponder on her experiences as an anthropologist, as a woman, as a wife, a mother, and as a person and thereby adds to identification with her experiences, even if the readers have not had similar ones.

Her life story, set alongside Vic's and that of her close family, seems even perhaps, to begin to answer the question that Pope Benedict

XVIth (who as Cardinal Ratzinger often dismayed Edie) poses at the outset of his first encyclical:

"Let us first of all bring to mind the vast semantic range of the word 'love': we speak of love of country, love of one's profession, love between friends, love of work, love between parents and children, love between family members, love of neighbor, and love of God. Amid this multiplicity of meanings, however, one in particular stands out: love between man and woman, where body and soul are inseparably joined and human beings glimpse an apparently irresistible promise of happiness. This would seem to be the very epitome of love: all other kinds of love immediately seem to fade in comparison. So we need to ask: are all these forms of love basically one, so that love, in its many and varied manifestations, is ultimately a single reality, or are we merely using the same word to designate totally different realities?"

She may still feel the need, alongside the rest of us, to wait to see what might be concealed, albeit with goodwill, behind this text, in addition to what appears on the surface.

At a more general level the work that she records reflects an approach to anthropology that is not based, like modernism, on capturing and explicating the culture of the other. Nor is it based, as at least some postmodernism seems to be, on the reflection of the (usually Western) self, as seen through a glass darkly. What it describes and analyses is the processes of interaction between the actors as they mutually learn about and come to understand one another, not as subject to object, but oscillating passive/active and always, and as directly as possible, subject-to-subject; auto-anthropology squared, or even raised to the power of the infinite.

Ronald Frankenberg
Newcastle-under-Lyme
February 2006

INTRODUCTION
A Strangely Directed Path

I will give you the end of a golden string
Only wind it into a ball
It will lead you into Heaven's gate
Set in Jerusalem's wall.
— Blake's *Jerusalem*[1]

I have learnt something in anthropology which I can in no way unlearn,
that it is wrong to attempt to take away the religion of another culture
and substitute one's own.
— From an essay for a spiritual direction class, 1997

My life has followed a strangely directed path, and its documentation
has become the story of a spiritual journey, one that took a whole lifetime. The story was written on the advice of Monsignor Chester Michael
of the Diocese of Virginia, and I wrote it frankly, just as things fell out. It
is more an account of an involuntary journey than an autobiography.

Here at the start the reader deserves to know what the beginning
and end are going to be like. Something was drawing me along this
path, and to this day I don't know how to name that something. I am
going to try to name it, though. I grew to understand the search as it
proceeded. The path was long and puzzling and had many details,
and it eventually turned into a search for connectedness, communitas,
and the magic moment. Life for me has consisted of an unconscious
search for these things, even in childhood.

The book of memory opens at my learning to read, being taught
that letters connect to make words; the scene changes to children digging to find a secret passage; stories of brother Jimmie, who later committed suicide; the politics of 1926, the rich and the poor; boarding

Notes for this section can be found on page 7.

school at eight and its tears; being deprived of education at age sixteen; and working on a farm and discovering Wordsworth's "presences." This latter was an opening of the path.

In the next chapter the wild life force of early adulthood prevails.
World War II was with us and I dug potatoes in the playing fields of
Oxford, and avidly read Henri Bergson on the life force. I met Victor
Turner and fell in love. He dug holes, his job in the army. Vic is shown
and his mystic mentors; a moment befell on Magdalene Bridge fol-
lowed by an elopement; next came babies in a gypsy caravan.

After the war Vic and I experienced our first brush with anthropology, Margaret Mead and Radcliffe-Brown (chapter 3). We both developed a yearning for anthropology; for Vic, this meant University
College London; for me, diapering babies. Through the habit of social
science analysis we began to adopt positivism and materialism. There
was no path here, but a lot of work.

For research we went to Africa, and found ourselves head over
heels into ritual (chapter 4). We were mysteriously pushed toward a
spirit-aware tribe. The story shows my first contact with Africa, the
picture of black hands and white hands on a store counter; then there
were the "drums"—no small matter: healing, initiations, sorcery, the
thunder god. A strange African elephant path was showing itself.
However, anthropology was at a loss about mysticism and called
it "mystification."

It was when we came back that the path gave a sudden hairpin
bend, described in chapter 5. We were in England writing a thesis for
a PhD. We gave up positivism and Marxism, and I fell into a deep
depression. We saw no way through to life via positivist anthropology. Suddenly a door opened to a highly ritualized church, the
Catholics, and I had an actual experience of the chalice. We became
Catholics. Our thinking changed, and we grasped the concept of the
liminal, limen, the door to change. The family moved to the USA, a
rite of passage indeed.

With religious people, their rite of passage often occurs at a center
"out there, "a pilgrimage center. So in our next research (chapter 6) we
followed the Mexican pilgrim's instinct and journeyed to the place of
the vision of Our Lady of Guadalupe in Mexico City, an event that
befell in 1531. We researched much in Mexico's extraordinary history.
On 21 December, 1970, we came upon a pyramid exactly built for the
winter solstice, and at the sight of that geographic sunset we had to
honor it.

Still wandering far into the path of visions we came upon Knock
Shrine in County Mayo, Ireland; there a vision had occurred in 1879.
Chapter 7 shows how in 1971 I made a pilgrimage to Knock with old

Bidgy, who taught me to be a good pilgrim. I began to understand something about the "Mother of God."

Chapter 8 tells how Vic and I we wandered back and forth among four religions, loving them all: the Sri Lankan Bo tree; also Israel and its Psalms. We knew we were on the path because of the great love found at Jesus's Coptic tomb; and we also saw Jewish mysticism at work at BarYohai's tomb and found happiness worshiping Allah with the Sufis.

But in 1983 Vic died. This was the loss of my life mate: from being broken in half I had somehow to become a whole person again. Chapter 9 tells how Vic had a heart attack; how we heard tales of near-death experiences; how Roy Wagner, myself, and the anthropology students practiced shamanism. While he was in his sickness Vic and I experienced an idyllic interval. But death came, and an African funeral.

Here, some fieldwork came to hand which served as therapy; I joined the Holy Saturday celebrations among the Yaqui of Arizona and saw their great deer dance, and this began my cure.

The next scene shifts to Africa again. In chapter 10, another door opened to my soul. Kabwita, a psychic African medicine man in Zambia, was working cures, and the Ihamba ritual proved to be a revelation of the existence of African spirits. I seriously began to study the soul. Here was Edie as the guinea pig of soul research.

In a further search for healing, chapter 11, I went to the Arctic to live among the shamans of the region. An Iñupiat healer in northern Alaska befriended me and showed me how spirit visitations provide greater power to healers. I experienced a prophetic shaman journey, and began to understand the spirit of the whale.

Ever hungry for more I jumped from the Inuit to the Celtic, finding myself back again in Ireland (chapter 12). There I met with Croine, a Celtic healer. I saw Knock Shrine once more in 1995 and looked at different theories about the Knock miracle; I went to St. Patrick's Purgatory and had a chastening experience.

Back home at the Catholic church I contacted a small spiritual prayer group and found their initiation ritual so profound I was on cloud nine (chapter 13). They really knew the fellow-feeling of communitas, the ultimate sense of togetherness. I went further and took a class on spiritual direction (chapter 14). Half the time I was out front and arguing, seventy-seven years old and still questioning. I studied discernment; Carl Jung and the collective unconscious; the Shadow; dialoguing with the dead; and engaging the multicorporations with the power of unconditional love, the other power.

In chapter 15 I try to understand the unknown realms in which I had been wandering. I attempt a sketch of the world where the spirits are seen; the collective unconscious as a reservoir; presences; the idea of the holy; flowing and the sense of oneness; power; energy. I describe being healed by energy; I experience spirits of the dead and divine visitors; I talk about reincarnation.

In the last chapter I make a journey full circle to my childhood home, Ely; I am left full of wonder at the story of the lantern tower of Ely cathedral.

Joseph Conrad called his book *Heart of Darkness*. This one is called *Heart of Lightness*. I have been impelled uphill, not downhill like the dreadful Kurt in *Heart of Darkness*, and this is not from my doing, any more than it was Kurt's own doing that led him downhill. The nature of the path along which I am continually nudged is what I am interested in as I am dragged forward. My path has actually been a joy ride in the style of a certain Disneyland ride in California, when you go "upriver" in a jungle made to look like Africa, with juju poles and other fun horrors that curiously hint of Kurt's final apocalypse, his truly felt word, "THE HORROR." Poor Marlon Brando, the actor of the part, is himself gone now. As for me, I seem to go upstream into the actual veins and arteries of dear human beings, hearing their grudges and sorrows, as I heard them once in a ritual recounted below in chapter 10. I saw the bad feeling come out in a softened and pitiful ghost form, and all of us gathered there did indeed feel suddenly lighter. *Heart of Lightness*.

It is obvious when reading the book that it does not follow an undeviating timeline from 1921 to 2005: one sees the incursion of flashbacks and "fast-forwards." What happens in the telling is that I find myself placing certain connecting threads from one era of my life side by side with connecting threads from another. Yet I necessarily write from the viewpoint of my "now" in 2005. The whole book is therefore a flashback. Memory tries to do all sorts of comparing as it make the venture backwards. It cannot help it. The results actually help to illuminate the episodes.

There are two other things to note: one, that I have had an unusually erratic life path; and two, that the path—one that still puzzles me—seems to lead to a sort of find. I know that many people have experienced something similar and that the discovery at the end may be a conversion or seeing the light within a religious framework of some kind. However, the path I found myself taking has been more twisty than most and seems to lead to a find that resists any type of framework or corralling into the usual religious folds. The find consists of sights that expand the heart with love, sightings found in all kinds of places and in all kinds of religions, sightings—as people call them—of "spiritual" things.[2]

The story has emerged from an anthropological viewpoint because I have been an anthropologist for most of my working life. Anthropology stuck with me because of its lightsome touch with everybody in the world—"I think that nothing human is alien to me" is our motto—"I am kin to it all." It will be seen how Vic, my great collaborator, was first a mystic—at twelve years old. However, in young adulthood both he and I went through a stage of dryness, sheer positivism, the politicization of our lives. That discipline walled off poetry, magic, and religion from us. For instance, during the dry time, the poet Rilke meant nothing to us. All such matters as poetry and the arts were to be regarded as social constructions of reality. But how could they be? Yes, they could, in those days. In the 1970s to the 1990s, much of anthropology taught that religion was "an expression of the social structure"—therefore in some way or other, "constructed" or "fabricated."[3]

Anthropology has gone through a number of stages since Vic's first training. He himself set up the proposition that rites of passage, that is, transition rituals, bore a peculiar characteristic, that of signally *not* giving expression to the social structure and the ranking of persons in the economic and power structure, but breathing an odd and inverted message that he called "liminality," from the word "limen," a threshold. We saw that the betwixt-and-between nature of a rite of passage cracks the structures of society open and lets people through to what it really is to be human, and to the spiritual things that go with it. This notion was hardly out in the open before French structuralism hit it a fearful blow—apparently—claiming that the structures of the mind shaped all human thought—hard wired structures such as binary discriminations. Politics entered anthropology again with Foucault, a valiant fighter against the hypocrisy, greed, and power of "the State." Then came interpretive anthropology that could sideline Vic's curious findings by highlighting the interpretation of the best minds in the discipline on the meaning of ritual symbols. "Academics know more than the indigenous sages," they claimed, not openly, but in indecipherable academese, with western psychology and the deep structures they detected in the people's religious behavior to aid them. Some of them felt they were only following after Vic's important work on the analysis of symbols. But before Victor Turner died he co-chaired an important conference panel on the anthropology of experience.[4] This turned the viewpoint of anthropologists of religion around toward a much simpler matter. What does the anthropologist actually experience? Anything, there in the field? Oh, too much, was the reply, we shouldn't try using *our* experience. Where would objectivity be then? To which Colin Turnbull in 1990 valiantly replied, "The subjective approach is an absolute requirement if we are to come to any full understanding of the social process."[5]

The result has been that today many anthropological studies have come out in which the authors frankly state they *were* emotionally involved in their people's religions. This is, of course, not a dictum for all, because great humanists and better anthropologists than ourselves have been content with a good range of religious feelings without specializing in religion. Our own thirst, though, has been for ultimate and real participation with those who experience religion.

I quote Rene, my daughter. On 14 August, 1999, she and I and her daughter Rose were in her apartment in America talking over a cup of tea. Rene was looking pretty as usual. She's a great hug and is an unusually affectionate person. She was reminiscing about the sense of community she and I had encountered in Africa when I took her with me to do anthropological research. She was five years old when I took her to Africa; I was thirty-two.

"As a child in Africa—and I think children usually have this— there's a sense of mystical participation of everything with everything, but it's taken for granted. I still feel it's really going on at the moment, and I hold to it, whatever else is happening."

She continued: "And I think that sense inspires my poetry. It's the creative force, as in Robert Graves's *The White Goddess*. It's particularly there in a poet—I see it because I'm a poet. There's always that sense of connection at the root of things—and I want to bring it into everyday life. I want to make everyday life more like that. My friend Tara knows about these connections too. Tara and I are trying to find a way to make connections in a male world that disconnects.

"'Male-plus-female' equals 'connection.' It means 'to connect,' not to separate. I understand that from having grown up in Africa. When I'm being more myself and more human I'm making connections."

This describes what the book is about. Rene's tender time in Africa was one of those times of mystical participation.

Notes

1. William Blake, "I Will Give You the End of a Golden String." In *Jerusalem*, ed. Morton Paley (Princeton, NJ, 1991 [1804]), 77.
2. This note concerns practical matters. It should be pointed out that the endnotes accompanying each chapter will give book references, in other words, clues to the connections of Vic and myself to the world of knowledge, according to our stage in life at the time. The collected bibliography at the end gives full details of these publications. Also I have occasionally changed names of people in the stories to protect their privacy.
3. See Roy Rappaport, *Ritual and Religion in the Making of Humanity* (Cambridge, 1999), passim.
4. The panel papers were published in *The Anthropology of Experience*, a symposium edited by Victor Turner and Edward Bruner (Urbana, IL, 1986).
5. Colin Turnbull, "Liminality: A Synthesis of Subjective and Objective Experience," in *By Means of Performance*, ed. R. Schechner and W. Appel (New York, 1990), 51.

1

CHILDHOOD, LEADING TO
WORDSWORTH'S PRESENCES

Let us go back in reverse matrilineal steps from the introduction with its scene of grand-daughter and daughter, to a distant picture of myself in Ely, England, sitting on my own mother's ample lap going through page after page of *Reading Without Tears*, a Victorian book now unobtainable, based on what is currently called "phonics." The book sets out a method well-adjusted and graded to ease a child into reading. I can see the pages now.

The first picture showed, "A is a house with a window upstairs." Mummy said, "'A.' Look, there's a house like an A!" My finger went onto the picture. There was a whole page of different letters which were drawn like pictures. "'B' is a house with two windows."

Mummy always pronounced the letters in a style like this: "A" (as in Ann, not "Ay"), "Buh" (as in bun, not "Bee"), and "Cuh" (as in cup, not "Cee"), and so on with all of them. Then on the next page I saw a picture of a simple furry beast I knew well. Mummy pointed and said, "Cuh—A—Tuh. C-A-T." The sounds connected. CAT. It was easy.

This was the process of connectedness itself. My body was already connected with my mother's body, and at the same time my understanding was led by hers toward what it eagerly seized on. She was putting out the help-lines which to my delight I saw did lead somewhere. I learned; and so I always loved reading.

Going back even further, I remember something that upset me, something very vivid. It was in 1923 when I was two, before my sister Josie was born. I was standing outside Mummy and Daddy's bedroom door, locked out and left by myself, looking down at the brown

---

Notes for this section can be found on page 33.

interweaving pattern on the linoleum, and I howled and screamed at the abandonment of it. Shut out!

Meanwhile under the door seeped the *smell* of the bedroom, a smell of very strong mushrooms or something—acrid, a familiar smell that was especially fresh that day. What did I know about that smell until twenty years later? Later I would laugh and call it the smell of apples.

So I knew the deprivation of communitas, that is, good fellowship, oneness. The locking of a door against me hurt, and it hurt again later at boarding school when I was locked out by bullies. This was why, much later, when my husband Vic and I were married, we never locked the kids out when we might have wanted to have sex undisturbed.

Next: I am three (see figure 1.1). I sit at the bottom of a five-foot-square hole dug in the earth by my brothers. Georgie, Charlie, and Jimmie are digging to find the secret passage from Ely Cathedral to our back garden. The monks of Ely used to sneak down the passage, we were told. If only we could find it where it was, under the ground! A long time later I realized what it was the monks were probably after: wine, women, and song. Ely could have been the Abbey of Thélème, with many Rabelaisian goings-on. Indeed, there was a vineyard at Ely. We used to walk down into the lane called "The Vineyards" and found it lush with orchards, but the vines were all gone.

Figure 1.1: Baby Edie with her hair curled. Ely, 1923 (photo in the possession of Edith Turner)

I sat in the hole in the garden, and can even now see in my mind the worms half protruding from the sides of the walls. I liked that a lot. A blue thing stuck out too. It was a two-inch piece of broken blue pottery, from some dinner plate. I liked that as well, but my brothers didn't regard it as a find. I could also smell the rough rooty smell of the earth, and I can smell it now. Whenever I smell damp earth, back comes the link with that happy hole.

I don't remember being lifted out. I do remember asking to go down in the hole in the first place.

My brothers dug in many places in that large back garden, especially under the lilac bushes that grew in the hedge at the back of the lawn. The boys were digging on the house side of the hedge. On the back side of this tall hedge, the side that faced the kitchen garden, there were always snowdrops growing in February, clustered bravely and thick around the roots of the lilac. Those snowdrops were the reason I hung around home so much when all the brothers and sisters had gone to school elsewhere. And there was another reason, as if I were supposed to hang around for something else. Beside the garage stood a wooden tub into which the garage roof downspout emptied its rainwater. The tub was full of dark water. This was my favorite spot when I was four or five. The black water was always full of bugs. The tub had a water tap, too, which I used to turn on to make the tub overflow, letting waterfalls cascade down its sides. My shoes used to squelch in the puddles, which I liked. The black depths of the tub fascinated me. I turned up my sleeve and felt with my hand far down into the water, bringing out one black leaf preserved in the depths, drooling with some interesting black slime, smelling strong. Now a different but familiar smell became evident behind me. I smelt hops. I saw out of the corner of my eye boots and gaiters. It was Mr. Goodroom, the old man who looked after the car in which Daddy made his medical visits to the farms. Mr. Goodroom was also the gardener. He saw me peering at the leaf in my hand. "You're a rum'un," he growled. He repeated the phrase: "A rum'un." He liked the words. I danced around, pleased with myself, and skipped out of his grasp. I liked his bleary face a lot.

Years afterward, in my late teens, returning home after working in the Women's Land Army in 1940, I went down the path to the garage. As I drew level with the tub, I stopped, puzzled. The path had caved in, right there in front of the tub. I saw broken grit and soil sunk in a hole two or three feet wide, quite deep, and when I peered down I could see that the hole extended underground under the path at my feet. I saw masonry down there. Now I was excited. I could see bricks that formed an arched roof of some sort, reaching back under the earth in a long cylindrical roof. Some of the structure of bricks had fallen away with the other subsidence, and I could see the hollow area inside.

I stood back. It was the secret passage.

But I never went to fetch a spade to dig away at it, and don't remember why not. The boys weren't there. The urge had gone. I must have been in the middle of reading a book or something. I could at least have written an imaginary kid's story in which I was a younger girl and we kids did explore the place. At the moment of writing in 2005 I would rather keep such a thing secret from people like archeologists, because I would hate to see their little rope fences there—so obsessive—their square plots, the geometrical layout of the dig, so different from the drunken monks and their arched "culvert," as the antiquarians would have called it. As for the antiquarians, they would have been too nice to admit to the monks' cavortings.

But bricks and mortar cannot lie and do not go away.

When we were little and used to inhabit the day nursery at the back of the big house, I used to pick holes in the plaster walls. I made the excuse to myself that someone else had started this hole, so I was free to carry it on. I liked the smell of the old plaster. The house must have been built in about 1800 and looked rather like a Virginian plantation house with pillars by the front porch. The smell of the plaster in the nursery wall was lime, limey earth; bits of wood stuck out of the flaky plaster too. The sticks must have been the wattles to support the plaster. Bits of plaster kept falling to the floor. I think I sometimes sucked the chalky stuff off my fingers. It tasted good. You could get your whole hand in the hole after a bit. I still feel the satisfaction of getting inside there. It was rather like what I'm doing now, probing my memory and its smells.

I don't remember being evil, just obstinate, and I fought my elder brothers when they annoyed me. There were four of them. What do I remember of evil? There was this: I screamed unstoppably, hating everyone. I began to hate my mother. This was just the usual battle of wills. "Shan't," was a favorite word of mine. I don't think I felt guilty, just deeply chagrined at being forced to obey. I wasn't afraid of hellfire; that must have been a fear from which my mother preserved me. Fear of "prison" got through to us, though. Still, I see that we had everything before us if we could only get around our times of trouble. "Edie, it's a sin to disobey your mother," said Miss Blakeman, the lady help, a large old woman with a long Roman nose and an impressive pompous voice. I know I put her admonishments into the category of "the enemy," though I would forget and laugh at her jokes. I had to keep a good look out for her, that's all. I would go on fighting. I'd go along when my elder sisters Anna and Helen summoned me at din-nertime, because I liked their company. There would be ten around the table: Mummy at the head of the table serving out tea, and Daddy at the foot under the picture of *The Last Supper*, serving out the food; Josie under the table playing tigers; Jim in a passion because he had been told off. I couldn't understand why he didn't play-act his pas-sions like I did, why he got really miserable. Even so, I got into the same real passions sometimes, ending with prolonged and stormy crying and being locked into my room with nothing but porridge; after an hour calming involuntarily into an underground swell of sobs, sobs that were almost a relief. What energy it gave me!

Did anybody hug me and love me? The idea of unconditional love was unknown—except from Mr. Goodroom who smelt of drink, and the maids, none of whom had any kind of bad relationship with me. Why was that? It takes some thinking about. The difference was due to the middle-class British philosophy of child-upbringing and the Christianity of the time: discipline came first; expressed love was unnecessary and too much of it was bad for the child.

There were times when Mummy would hug us, in a kind of hug-ging binge. She would be back from some duty, and we would hug all together, "like bees in a bunch." She was a professional teacher after all, rather advanced in her thinking. Her actual philosophy of educa-tion was one of her own invention. She let us do far more adventur-ous things than other mothers. Still, she was full of bad criticism of all of us, full of prevention and rules. Nicky, our nanny, was in contact with my body much more, and I simply loved her.

The so-called Christianity we were taught didn't seem to take, except in certain action scenes in Ely such as when we visited the workhouse. It was just "stuck on," as a matter of principle. There was too much of it; anyone could see that the doctrine was a set of rules that *had* to be applied—never mind love or anything else—because it was God's will (not "law" of course because "Jesus had surpassed the law"). But I didn't believe in this "God's will." People invented it—so I came to realize. It was words coming out of their mouths for fear of what would happen to them if they didn't say that kind of thing. Kids can see this. Nobody reached my soul by doing that. The adults only reached it in spite of themselves, and one occasion was when they took us to sing in the workhouse—a story I will tell later.

In 1925, when I was four, lying sick with mumps, I had a dream. I spoke in my sleep, "You won't let me say my prayers." *Who* wouldn't let me? Who? Was it that I wanted plenty of time to say my prayers? Or did I want a way open without distraction? Something wasn't let-ting me have it.

I remember going to sit in a mushroom ring in the fields because I wanted to be taken away by the fairies; and in a different field, many times I experienced smelling a cowslip bell, many cowslip bells, yellow, little, clustered, and heady in perfume, each like a miniature version of angels' lilies hanging their heads. I also remember feeling awe under the Octagon at Ely Cathedral—looking way up high at the "lantern," a space in the ceiling like a high tiny palace of angels perched upon great dividing stone fans suspended over unthinkable space.

I was nested in the family order between Jimmie and Josie, Josie being the youngest and Jimmie, just older (see figure 1.2). The whole family used to take the dog and go down to the River Ouse to bathe and learn to swim. I remember going in 1926, in the bright weather of my home town, Ely. We went past Barton Square and Mr. Martin's at Barton Farm. We walked in our family group of eight children and the dog Roly, with Josie and Jim in the middle of us. We named Jimmie "Sunny Jim," when he was little. "High in the air goes Sunny Jim, Force is the food that raises him"—so went the ad printed on the packet of Force, the breakfast cereal. Jimmie was seven. He had lots of golden hair and was cuddly. I myself had short brown hair at that time and used to loll my head on one side. I had my mother's brown watching eyes and was very obstinate.

Figure 1.2: Edie, the seventh of eight children. Bob, Helen, Anna, George, Charlie, Jimmy, Edie, Josie. Ely, 1925 (photo in the possession of Edith Turner)

We walked around the sunny sides of Barton Square, passing the stile to the right that led into a field we knew as the Roman Encampment, a place where we often played. I remember sitting between the grassy hillocks that had for centuries obliterated the ancient walls, and I picked the daisies that grew everywhere. I made a daisy chain, joined the ends, and put it on Josie's head for a daisy crown. She put one on me. We looked at each other, both wearing daisy crowns. I loved that place—the smell of the grass, the warmth, and the smell of the white crushy little daisies with their long stalks.

I had a momentary interest in the Romans as I saw them in my picture books. Decades later, not surprisingly, the place became an archeological site.

Once past Barton Farm you could see if you peered to the left along an ancient street, the enormous tower of Ely Cathedral. Continuing on our way down to the river we reached the bottom of the hill and passed the Angel Inn, then up onto Ely High Bridge, where we stopped in the middle of the bridge and looked over the parapet. You could follow the river with your eyes as it stretched far away between grassy fields, with the bathing shed a mile beyond on the right bank.

Once on the other side of the bridge we climbed a stile to the right. The grass in the field was long and tussocky, with a herd of cows actively grazing. The cows looked up, backing and lowering when they saw the dog.

"Quiet," we shouted to the dog. Accordingly, Roly set her head bowed down toward the narrow pathway, clenched her ears down, drooped her tail, and obeyed, trotting swiftly along, looking neither to the right nor to the left at the cows.

The bathing place was far along the path and the opposite side of the river. When we arrived level with the sheds, Mr. Broad the boat-man was waiting for us with his punt. We embarked, dog and all, and he punted us slowly across. Then for the swimming.

As I undressed in the wooden cabin I could see the sun's reflection from the water underneath coming up through the gaps in the floor boards, its light dancing on the wall, and I could hear the occasional splashes of the divers outside. The smell of waterweed and damp wood was strong around me. I heard somebody speaking outside: "Not a *claou—ud*. Not a claou—ud!" It was the old man, who must have been looking up at the sky.

I came out dressed in my swimsuit and went to Mr. Broad. He placed a wide belt around my waist and buckled it on. A rope was attached to the belt behind so that he could hold me up while I was learning to swim. Now belted, with the rope in Mr. Broad's hands, I gingerly stepped down the ladder beside the diving board until the water came up to my waist. Mr. Broad was there. I spread out my arms and let go. The belt held me up. I was swimming. He walked around with me out to the end of the diving board (I was then four or five). He shouted to me, "Breathe! Breathe!" because I kept my mouth shut and didn't appear to be breathing. I liked learning in the cool green water that smelt of water weed and reeds and river mud. After a time I realized it was my own swimming that was keeping me up; it was no longer the belt that was keeping me up.

One day Roly the dog had a bad moment. She caught sight of the entire family swimming off down the river toward Ely and she went in after them, dog-paddling, to save them. This endeared her to us all over again.

Roly had thirty-six puppies by the time she was done. My sister Anna used to make a bowl of Bengers food for her on every occasion she gave birth. Nevertheless, after 13 years Roly developed cancer of the stomach and finally died.

Anna said, "It was always me who had to take the animal to be put down. I had to do it for the cat too. Before I went to the SPCA I gave the cat a lovely meal of fish. Then she bowed her little head, got into the basket, and curled up, clearly saying, '*I know.*' I took her along in my bicycle basket. It was the same with Roly's puppy Jerry. I had to do it."

"Once," continued Anna, "when I was little, bathing in the sea at St. Leonards, I spent quite a time under the water. I simply liked being under the water for a long time." Anna laughed. "Cousin Mary had to pull me out. I was furious because I didn't want to be pulled out. I liked looking up through the water." This was like my own grandson Benjamin when he was three, under the lake near Kenyon College. We had forgotten about him, but he was quite happy down there until we realized where he was and we hauled him out, showing how worried we were. And it was like me at the age of six, all by myself on Exeter Station, happy up to the moment when they began to make a fuss, all because I had been left behind and lost. Why are kids like that? And they are.

On the way back from the river, tired from the swim, first of all we had to pass the Angel Inn with its smell of beer and its drunks, and had to dodge the raucous remarks of the men standing outside. Then we labored up the hill—which slowed us to an aching trudge—then past Barton Square, then Silver Street with the Green King pub halfway along. Then home to hot cocoa made with milk and sugar.

I can see the view from the bridge now. All through time, quietly on its own, the river stretches forty miles north and south, and beside it on either side lies the fertile black miracle of the fen country.

There is a pathetic connection here with Jim, who now sleeps happily in death, and whom I still see in my inward vision as a curly-haired little child. In 1935, when Jim was sixteen, he had been continually raped by older boys at his prep school and was in a badly disturbed state of mind. One night he committed suicide with cyanide, an event that was carefully hushed up. Decades later, at Cardiff in January 1994 at a shaman conference—this was when I had reached the age of 73—I undertook a curious shaman spirit journey along with the conferees. I suddenly felt I had to reach Jim because of what happened so long ago. In my journey I "saw" my poor brother, sixteen years old, his head for some reason hiding in a black crevice. Nevertheless at last I could speak to him.

"I love you, Jim. Bless you. Be happy. I remember you, I'm here." After that he has often blessed me too, as his persona as the little fellow of seven.

For some curious reason, after leaving the shaman conference in Cardiff my train stopped dead for half an hour before reaching the Severn tunnel because a man had thrown himself in front of the wheels and had been killed. After the long wait the train finally resumed the journey, passed through the tunnel, and emerged in the flooded lands of Somerset and Devon where I was to meet my elder brother George who was slowly dying of prostate cancer. While I telephoned George at my destination the wind tore my umbrella inside out. I marked the surrealist train of events.

Jim had been raped at prep school by a certain schoolboy who later became close to the highest in the land. These were dark things. Jim said to me out of the past, "Light in our darkness"—my boy of seven.

Yes, things go backwards. And now Ely is all light and it opened itself to me, as I relate in chapter 16 at the end of the book. What I had seen was a bit of the peculiarly twisted path of my life.

I climbed trees at six years old, and once, when I was up the favorite family chestnut tree, I fell down and gashed my knee. My father the good doctor bandaged the wound, but they forgot to change the bandage and the wound became infected. On the fourth night after the accident my fever rose dangerously high due to the infection. I remember crying that night, on and on, until the grownups came in and started bustling about. If Daddy's partner Dr. Slade hadn't excised the infected portion of the knee I'd have died or lost my leg.

The nursery had one bed in it and a nightlight and, importantly, a coal fire, which was kept continually burning while I was recovering. The trouble kept me in bed three months, during which time I was never once allowed on my feet; but I recovered completely. The accident was a temporary obstacle to my adventurousness. When I came back into action I was fierce as ever—the reason for my next experience, boarding school.

I was eight when Mummy sent me to boarding school. Why did my wandering path go this way? The school was a small one, on the gravelly coastline of Suffolk at Aldeburgh. When I arrived for the September term I found I was the only one in the school who was eight years old. All the rest were eleven or older. The older inhabitants maintained a club in their classroom in the evenings.

"What's a club?" I asked—something for old men, private?

"You're not in it," said the eleven year old head of the club, fair-haired Lady Caroline. This was a school for aristocrats. "Let's get her out of here."

They yanked me by the hair, grabbing my ponytail. I fell. "Ow, Ow!" I yelped. They pulled me out of the room, dragging me out by the ponytail, and they locked the door on the inside. I fled in utter misery.

Instead of socializing at that school I became a great reader, escaping after each bullying to lose myself in G. A. Henty's stories of sea adventure. That's how I became round-shouldered and shy, cursed with styes in my eyes that necessitated vitamin B yeast drinks.

All through my striving boarding-school days it was the holidays with my brothers and sisters that were the all-in-all, these were the times when I *lived*. My family called me Edie at home. But at school they called me Ee-DEATH.

"Ee-DEATH! You're anti-SOCIAL! You're a BOOKWORM." They compared their clothes and possessions with mine. My parents, having borne eight children, had no money for expensive clothes and extra riding classes like the other more wealthy girls at the boarding school.

"Do you ride?" the girls would ask in later years. "Do you do point-to-point"—these were the local horse races of the upper class. Of course I didn't. I had no riding habit.

"I was due for the Curse at the last point-to-point," said Lady Caroline. "I just had to race. And you can't race with the Curse. They took me to the doctor's and he—did something to me, you know, so that I didn't have the Curse while the race was on."

We listened, impressed. We younger ones were expecting menstruation any time. What Lady Caroline was talking about was probably a D and C, dilating and curetting, a procedure performed as a convenience in cases such as this.

The girls used to talk about me. "She doesn't know about boys," they said, pulling away from me to gossip in a corner.

Lady Caroline was the worst bully; I heard later that she was unhappy in her life. The Barclay daughters of the bank, Fiona Campbell, and Joan Chivers of the marmalade manufacturer's family, weren't so bad.

But I learned envy. The rich girls liked to see my raw envy. Nevertheless I and one other girl were top of the class. I was never class prefect because I wasn't "the type." This was always the case.

Much later I learned something about chickens and the pecking order, about captive rats in crowded conditions, about caged monkeys and the boss monkey. Where was communitas, the sense of good fellowship, in those cages? Why did the biologists choose the bossing species, chickens, rats, and caged monkeys, to put forward their theories of social behavior, and not the fishes? Milton saw the beauty of the fishes: "The sounds and seas with all their finny trove, now to the moon in wavering morris move." What about the chimpanzees in their joyous rain dance, the beluga whales leaping in silver glory a thousand strong along the horizon of the Bering Straits; geese honking in swift, soon-vanished V-formation? There has been a grim, science-decided selection of what was typical.

In the twenties at boarding school, church was meaningless except for the singing—and except for funerals. Often there were funerals of fishermen, drowned in the North Sea storms while fishing in times of known danger, because at such times fish were in short supply and prices were high. Many of the men took dangerous risks merely to live during the depression. One late November in 1928 on a Sunday morning there was a terrible sea disaster and the parish church at Aldeburgh was packed. The widows were out there in the front of the nave, bent over, the cries bursting out, and my own homesickness was also coming out in terrible relieved gouts at last, watering the prayer book. I was helpless.

> Eternal Father strong to save
> Whose arm doth bind the restless wave. . . .
> From rock and tempest, fire and foe
> Protect them wheresoe'er they go. . . .
> O hear us when we cry to thee
> For those in peril on the sea.[1]

At home in Ely my crippled uncle died, also my grandfather in Cambridge and another uncle in India. The services at the Cambridge church where my grandfather was vicar were heavy, mournful, wonderful affairs, with much weeping. I resonated and resonated with the mood. We sang "Jerusalem the Golden" and my eyes were solemn with love.

Jerusalem the golden
With milk and honey blest,
Beneath thy contemplation
Set heart and mind at rest.

I know not, ah, I know not
What joys await us there,
What radiancy of glory,
What bliss beyond compare.[2]

"And bright with many an angel, and all the martyr throng"—I loved those words. My mother saw her crippled brother in a dream after he died, and he was with Jesus. Yes, her eyes glowed as she told me. I've heard this kind of disclosure many times since, and I've *"got"* it, got the experience myself, whole cloth. My mother became real for me for a moment and not just a town councilor. That conversation with Mummy showed me a little of the path my life might take.

There was another time of total experience. The workhouse was one of them: this was the poorhouse, or the Union as it was euphemistically called, or Tower House, from its stark skyscraper appearance sticking up in a field outside the town. A tall chimney like a factory smoke-stack arose from the building. Groaning noises, wails, and the sounds of dementia came out of it. It was built of a dirty yellowish brick. It was shameful to have to live in it.

Daddy was the medical officer they called if need arose. Because of this connection, on Christmas Eve Mummy made us eight children take sweets in little baskets, and our hymnals with musical parts, and go and sing carols to the "inmates"—people with no real personality, one supposed.

When we arrived at the entrance, the matron met us, aproned and official, busying herself with her reports to the doctor, our Daddy. She lit a candle and led us all trooping around and around a long passage which circled inside the walls. It was cold. The walls bore dull green paint over bare brick. We went on and on, branching at last inwards to a candle lit ward—a place that smelt funny, not so much of urine as mustiness, old skin, and beds. We saw many iron bedsteads in rows against the wall, with an old crone tucked into each of them. One crone painfully reared herself up a little. Her iron gray hair was cut straight and looked ugly. Her neck was scraggy like a plucked hen. She had a harelip and I couldn't make out what she said as I bent toward her. We had to shift back, line up, and sing. "God Rest Ye Merry Gentlemen." Was that appropriate? "In his master's steps he trod." Never mind, once the eight of us got going on a carol we began belting out the parts in fine style. We loved our own singing. We had been practicing under the tuition of fifteen-year-old Charlie with the brown tag of hair and the pointy handsome nose and the voice going bass. Jim was still treble, I was alto, Anna and Helen soprano and so was Josie, the other boys tenor, Daddy bass, Mummy alto. We made a really fine sound in that poorhouse with the crazy people in front of us tucked in their beds. "Ti-i-idings of comfort and joy," we ended. Then we would go forward to each bed and offer sweets from the small baskets. Some of the old hands were crippled and couldn't take them. So we had to take a sweet and put it into the toothless mouth opening, and see the eyes flicker with the nice taste. Ahhhh.

Another woman sat bolt upright and grabbed a whole handful of sweets. I retreated in order to leave enough for the rest of the women. This behavior seemed to be just that particular woman's way; it wasn't the same as being bad mannered at table.

One sweet old lady had a tear rolling down one eye and grabbed my hand for a minute. Why, they liked children! I gave this one another soft center.

Then off to a new ward, where one horrible old woman was wailing and muttering. Still we sang and gave out sweets in the golden candlelight. We went up stone spiral staircases to higher levels, where some of the people were sitting around on hard straight-backed chairs. Then to the men, with prickly gray faces and lambent eyes; they were even weaker than the women. Why was it that most of them were in bed—and it wasn't even our own bedtime yet? I couldn't make it out. None of them had any possessions, I remember. That bed was their whole world—and had been since they were born in the case of "mongol idiots" suffering from "mongolism" (now called Downs Syndrome). These you could recognize by the odd flatness of their heads at the back, their pathetically piggy eyes and slobbering mouths—and their hopeless vagueness. And so it went on in the golden light, with "While Shepherds Watched their Flocks," and "Away in a Manger," delicious in harmony—more delicious even than the sweets. My father felt the communitas, the brotherhood of the scene: I remember his eyes over his white moustache shining with true benevolence and delight. He had a rich bass, BOMP-bomp, BOMP-bomp, while my alto played patterns in and out of the trebles.

So the baby was to be born tomorrow, in quietness and candlelight in a stable, a magical place of long ago, and here in the workhouse as well, tomorrow. All the presents we were giving added up to it, too— and why did they have that effect? Because the presents were magical too. Our little hearts were quivering with the love of it.

Meanwhile Mummy ("Mrs. Davis") was campaigning in Ely for improved workers' conditions, largely in housing and sanitation. She was a town councilor. She had been elected by a big majority to the Ely Urban District Council. She would bustle off to the meetings after a strong cup of tea, dressed in her Sunday go-to-meeting black dress and hat, her hair in a graying bun, her blunt nose determined, her small eyes sharp and grim. When she came back she would tell us tales of the council meeting, of arguments and terrible words with fat farmers across the table, the topic being raising the taxes. Mrs. Davis had proposed a housing scheme by which the new homes for the poor were to have a large kitchen-cum-living-room and a tiny formal parlor, and also she had a scheme for better sanitation. These proposals enraged the council. Now at home, with her children as audience, she parodied the farmers.

"'It's a wicked business,' said Mr. Clark."

"'It's a blooming shame,' said Mr. Covill." She looked fat and pompous, imitating him.

We laughed delightedly.

From political era to political era all eight of us children helped with Mummy's election posters and leaflets. Her help for the poor came supposedly under the auspices of the Conservative party. Later she voted Labor.

Was I at all aware of religion? Hardly at all of the religion I was taught as a duty by the adults. Christianity came as stories—about someone else—and as boring church services. What I loved was Mummy getting carried away playing the piano at "hymn singing," when she pressed the loud pedal of the piano. I can hear it now, "—of that great love which like a fire/is always burning in His Heart." I would sit on the floor by the red mahogany front panel of the piano and set my ear to the wood. The thrum of all those released strings thrilled through and through me. It seemed to me that somehow inside the piano was the free half of my mother, playing without mufflers.

Otherwise we were supposed to live in the goodness of a decent English countryside—"Glad that I live am I /That the sky is blue"—patient in that kind of humble quietism. I did feel that quietism, I felt it too.

My father taught me a rich panorama of science. I read *The Mysterious Universe*[3] by James Jeans, and I absorbed contemporary history from my elder brothers and my sister Helen: I heard tales of the Snyder Trophy air race; of the great dirigible hydrogen air ship R101 and its disaster; of strange foreigners seen skulking about in England with snow on their boots, the Russian Bolsheviks in disguise. They were supposed to be carrying bombs. Then I came across Norman Angell's book on peace, *The Great Illusion*,[4] which stimulated the peace movement of the 1930s. I was in awe. We all felt there might be a chance of the nations learning peace. But the movement was short-lived.

My parents were conservatives. They had returned from missionary work in India in 1919 before I was born and never saw what the war looked like in the eyes of the English people. I felt they didn't intuit it and suffer with the people. As Christians my parents were vowed to live a Christian life in Ely and to practice good works, and they did. The middle class—sometimes without meaning to—knew how to shut itself off beautifully. Its members were brought up that way. My elder brothers and sisters were off to high-class boarding schools: Cheam prep school for the younger boys, then the two eldest boys at the "public" schools of Marlborough and Stowe. Helen and Anna were taught by Mummy and a high-class neighbor at first, then went to the Perse High School in Cambridge, and then Wycombe Abbey School in the Cotswolds. At home we learned about the Romans, King John and the Magna Carta, medieval music and architecture, and the English Civil War. Later we children went by ourselves to town, two by two, exploring the museums in London and frequenting the Regents Park Open-air Theatre, where they were playing *As You Like It* and *A Midsummer Night's Dream*. Behind the culture, all the sufferings of the English poor continued, but that was "just how things were."

Seventy years later I and my daughter Rene walked down St. Mary's Street to find the old house site. It was gone. We found instead a new low modern house, built sideways on, in supposedly-pleasing local yellow brick and modern trimmings. I walked blindly ahead, trying not to look at the place, recalling only the copper-leaved tree on the left which was no more, and the gate where Mummy, Daddy, Maud the cook, we children, and the dog Roly between us used to come out to hear the chimes of St. Mary's Church, where the human—not machine—bellringers went through the changes on some great occasion. I can see Maud in her apron now, red-faced and little, and Roly the dog lifting up her throat and singing with the bells. How we loved to see Roly do that.

But in 1999 the gates were gone.

Rene and I found the lane to the back garden. The lane itself was still there. I walked well ahead now, from curiosity, and found that the actual old garden wall was still there. The top of it used to bristle with broken glass to foil intruders, but there was no glass now. The weathered yellow-gray bricks were still there, now under a canopy of ivy. The wall had been part of the approach to the entrance gates leading to where the old back garden used to be.

I stood in the middle of the entrance.

"Rene," I said, "It's just here," gesturing with my foot. "I remember in the Depression. 1926, I think. Just on this spot." I inched up a bit and looked down at the dull tarmac. "I saw kids playing, little poor boys. Just here. They were small for their age, in rags—barefoot, I remember—with thin legs all bowed outward, and swollen tummies. I'd have liked to have played with them but I wasn't allowed. They had rickets. That's why their legs were bent." I looked up at Rene, blooming in her health. "It was lack of calcium and vitamin D, lack of milk."

Way back in time I had asked old Miss Blakeman—the lady help with the Roman nose and commanding voice—about the poor boys. "Why can't I play with them? Why do we have enough money and they don't?"

"It's a good thing we have enough money," she told us firmly. "What we spend makes work. It makes work for the poor." Fifty years later we heard President Reagan announce his discovery of a new economic law that he called the trickle-down theory.

In the interim my communist elder sister Helen was telling us otherwise. In 1933 she was a wise nineteen-year-old with a trick of raising one eyebrow and looking at you with a solemn slightly humorous eye. She became a Stalinist, painted her bedroom wall red, and put up a huge poster of Stalin. At about that time she went to South Wales with a Communist Party group and lived with the miners, and saw for herself how they were exploited.

One day, Daddy, with his moustache bristling, tore down the Stalin picture, whereupon Helen in a rage ran down the stairs to the front door and seized the front door handle—a battered yellow brass handle with eight sides—I can see it now. Helen was in floods of tears, screaming at Mummy. She wrenched the door open, stormed out, and slammed the door behind her. (This was the classic slammed-door scene from Ibsen's feminist play *A Doll's House*, which none of us had read.)

I never knew what happened after that. Bless Helen for that scene.

Fast-forwarding to 1940 in World War II, I helped Mummy delouse children evacuated from the bombed-out east end of London, the slums. We worked hard on that job of delousing. Mummy was the billeting officer at Ely, in charge of finding homes for bombed-out children from the east end. Down by Ely's river, the Ouse, stood a large Georgian home, the beer manufacturer's residence, full of objets d'art and occupied by Mrs. Porlack, a voluminous lady with a delicate double chin and face powder. None of the officials seemed to be able to enforce the billeting law upon her—she flatly refused evacuees. Mummy put on her full officer uniform and effected entrance with two policemen and some children from the east end of London. Mrs. Porlack was forced to take them in. We loved that gesture of Mummy's. Mummy was actually the communist in this picture, meting out justice to the rich.

The Porlack episode with the east-enders occurred seven years after the front door scene; by that time, Mummy had learned something from Helen. I still can't feel sorry for Mrs. Porlack. She loved her pet dog more than kids. Meanwhile, confusing though it was to us, the wonderful Soviet Union and its Stalin had aspects of hellishness that were no answer to the problem either. Russia never learned the right way to defend those at the mercy of the powerful. I still feel pain to this day when I realize what a chance Russia lost.

All this came back to me in 1999 while I lingered by that now nonexistent back gate. I couldn't resist venturing some steps inside the back driveway. It was home, after all. Another smart new brick house stood fifty yards along the way; the driveway could be seen continuing around to the right to the back of the first new block we had seen already, built on the site of the demolished Victorian house that had been our home. The driveway was neater than it had ever been, but at least in the old position. I could see the same old wall on the right, curving around, just where Daddy used to set out to visit his patients from the now non-existent garage. I remembered it, and I remembered the tub and the secret passage. The driveway, now concreted over—secret passage and all—led to the neat back door of the house of the author of the history of St. Etheldreda who was the founder of Ely Cathedral.

On the left of the new house facing Rene and me stood a large chestnut tree I knew well, one that used to have pink flowers—the same tree as in the long ago. This I knew for sure because half of its top had fallen down when I was fifteen and I had gotten myself a backache cutting up the huge fallen boughs and dragging them away. There the tree stood, grown again with a big new top. It was perfectly all right, sixty-three years later. So was I.

I walked this way and that, trying to get a view of something else. I spotted it.

I said to Rene, "Look, look! It's the sycamore!" There it was indeed, soaring high at the back of the new house: our sycamore, the tallest tree in Ely, which we used to climb to its very summit in order to see Ely Cathedral. We discovered that once we were up aloft the cathedral looked actually close to us across the gap of space. Close. It was a strange feeling.

Now I felt that maybe if I peered around to the left I could see into what used to be the back garden. Maybe I could spot the other chestnut which was the scene of my gashed knee. By now I was standing on the grass right up by the front door of the new house. The house was marked with a plaque: Archdeacon.

Just then out came the archdeacon in his black garb and gaiters and his English educated face onto the lawn at the front.

I introduced myself and apologized for intruding.

He said, "No, no, not at all." I told him my story and he was quite interested. We got to talking about what Rene and I had been looking at in Ely. He turned out to be the archdeacon of the whole bishopric. He was middle-aged, so he must have taken up his position after the time of our family of Davises. I got a hint just from the way he talked—the sense, all over again, of Mummy's Christianity, her good works, the Porlack episode, Mummy's justice—actually—at a time of great injustice. Certainly more injustice would have been threatened if Hitler had come. There was a flicker of the memory of my brother Charlie dead in Burma, a country that had been occupied by the imperialist Japanese but which was now known as Myanmar, in the control of a deadly national socialist regime, socialism gone rabid. And it is from this rabidity that Russia had just recently escaped—but the Serbs had not yet escaped it. "Ah, ah, I cry for all those poor and oppressed," I felt. It was no use being angry with the old ladies of Ely and Mrs. Porlack. But couldn't they have seen, as Mummy did?

I realized that the archdeacon was carrying out the Christianity of the good Anglican church, many of whose members must have been on the forgive-the-debt holding-hands demonstration carried out in London that very summer on 12 June, 1999, on Westminster Bridge, in which my son, grandson, and nephews had just taken part.

So there has been much soreness, and also even forgiveness.

Standing there with the archdeacon on the exact spot where I used to be able to see the old kitchen window, I was back there again in time. The troubles with politics somehow used to be balanced by the warm red-tiled kitchen with the big scrubbed table and the tiny red-faced cook smelling of pee. The maids were spotty, smelling of sweat, sitting for their "camp coffee" at eleven a.m. at their window seats, looking out onto bushes and drains and down the driveway toward the old garage, dreaming of their young men. Maud the cook played the Newmarket races and took in the racing news. Everyone in that part of the house was just affectionate and ordinary. The fact was, I didn't miss the high-class world when I was in the kitchen. I don't think I have ever missed it—except once in World War II when working at Bidnett's farm where the farmer was a go-getter, and criticized me for being a bookworm and not being a go-getter like himself.

"My own kid of twelve is better at feeding the cows than you," he said bluntly. I quailed.

But the kitchen at Ely! This indeed was a kitchen, with its big black coal cooking-range, and old Maud with her brilliantly red face and nose and black hair dragged back in a bun, stoking up the fire.

"Old 'itler's in this stove," she said, giving it a dig. She grinned at her own wit. Hitler deserved the canard for sure. She took the cake out of the oven—which had undergone a miracle change from cold wet dough to crumbly toothsome hot brown sweetness. Cake: dripping, flour, sugar, cake spice, baking powder, raisins; the light hands distribute it all together in the big yellow and white china mixing bowl; then add eggs and milk; then slow rich heat.

That kitchen was a place of communitas. It was communitas with all of us brothers and sisters when we got together. In winter in the large eleven-room house we'd play a hilarious game called kickapeg. One of us would be the "He." The He would grasp the banister knob at the bottom of the stairs while all the others hid. After a count of 100 the He would rove abroad to find some victims. The He only had to *see* players for them to be caught and sent to the banister knob to hold on. Quite a number of prisoners would accumulate and had to hold hands in a string. But, the prisoners could be saved by a free player dashing toward the knob while the He was elsewhere hunting. One touch at the end of the string of tugging children was enough to set the whole string free. (And thus we learned the ubiquity of electricity in a wire, and only now I realize that this was the way I learned the collective nature of consciousness.) The He would return in horror to find all his prisoners fled, and would have to start again. Or he might return to "see" the heroic rescuer and some of the victims, and victimize them all over again.

"Seen George, Jim, Anna, Edie!" And we would return to the string and start to cunningly deceive the He about where the rescuers were likely to come from, while leading our string yearningly in the opposite direction.

The laughs and excitement of kickapeg were intense. Charlie was the best He and we loved him for it, the dark-haired handsome boy with the cowlick. In this way, love and admiration and the glorious process of the game welded us into a communitas of pure happiness—through a process of saving each other.

It wasn't until sixty years later that I came across a game of helping which was as good as this. It was the "Game of Transformation" created by the Findhorn Institute of Aberdeen, Scotland. Findhorn is a kind of New Age nature institution that teaches about the spirits of nature which the facilitators call "divas." The facilitators showed us community games based on helping each other. "Transformation" is a board game with dice and packs of shuffled cards. The players do not share the same course on the board. You could see that, because each person had her own course, called "life path." There ensued drastic ups and downs in the life path depending on how the dice fell, necessitating the taking of "insight" cards and "setback" cards. The object was to reach one's goal at the center of the board where an angel figure awaited the player. Somehow one seemed to accumulate bad cards that, with horrible aptness, showed up one's inmost faults. Mine were always "arrogance." Dammit: arrogance. Would I ever live that one down? Yet there was an unusual aspect to the game. One was allowed to help others by giving them one's own good cards, and they could give you some of theirs, to help you along.

I learned the game and bought a set, then tried it on the family at Christmas 1990. Two members, Don my son-in-law and Fred my eldest son, were total agnostics and joked all the time. By the end of it we were all in fits, though the instructions wanted you to be very holy and to meditate as you played. We had a rambunctious time with a lot of communitas, and Fred got "home" all right, although his professed aim was "money." He had to be ceaselessly helped by other people's cards. Roy Wagner, who was also playing, kept getting the card "impeccability," which corresponded exactly with what he was teaching in his Castaneda lectures. All in all, for mind-boggling shamanic divination and near-hysterical communitas, the game was a wow.

What is this "communitas"? In the 1960s Victor Turner came across the term[5] and used it for a phenomenon found in his anthropological research. Most people have experienced it. Communitas is the togetherness that seeks the whole universe as its boundary. If there are limits they are simply at the boundaries—if any—of the whole universe, whether visible or invisible. Communitas is exactly in all places where unconditional love can be, that is, everywhere; not in the style of *us* apart from *them* or *against* them. Wherever communitas appears, it is the path again.

Going back to my time in boarding school, even there the path began to be clear. I had had some inkling of presences before, if only in the snowdrops under the lilac bushes, and now they were coming back, those presences, not only to me, but to a group of us. We were doing the Romantic poets in our English class, and we girls reveled in them— Pamela Pedley, blonde and intelligent, Rosamund Back, a bit proper but okay, Fiona Campbell, a great sport, Betty, Joan Chivers, Anne Gilfinnan, Anne Heffernan, the last of whom had frizzy hair and marvelous energy. We knew all the Romantics: the Wordsworth *Intimations of Immortality from Recollections of Early Childhood*; Shelley's *Ode to the West Wind*; Keats.[6] It makes me cry just to think of the *West Wind*.

What, what is crying? Why did I feel cold chills, feel my hair lifted, feel the tingle, at "Make me thy Lyre, even as the forest is"? At the "incantation of this verse," as Shelley called it? This isn't literature, it's prayer. Outright, self-confessed prayer. The man went through a membrane or door, somewhere. And they told us it was "poetry." Rubbish.

Communitas reigned, too, at the girl scouts' camp with Fiona, Pamela, Joan, Anne, Rosi, and many others, around a campfire in the darkness near the edge of a sea cliff, bellowing out familiar old songs, "Old Macdonald," "One More River," it didn't matter what. We knew perfectly well this was Friendship with a capital F, and talked about it eagerly.

"It doesn't happen in the dorm, it only happens in camp," we whispered to each other in our sleeping bags under the canvas.

Nowadays I recognize that camp scene as a liminal, true betwixt-and-between experience: not home, not school; we weren't children, we weren't grown up. Years later I learned more about the nature of the rite of passage. Then, the phrase would have meant nothing to me.

Around the time I was thirteen I left boarding school and went to the Perse High School, Cambridge. There I learned eye-opening facts called social history about the nineteenth century corn laws. Meanwhile at home I took the politics of social history seriously and opposed every conservative or religious move of my parents. I became known as "impossible" and was sent away to live at the Perse School boarding house. There I suffered once again what one could only term "anti-communitas" in the form of in-group/out-group bullying. We were given to know from the boss-girls that we were supposed to compete about boys, and that we should give homage to the most adept of the boss-girls. I hated them all and instead began to develop a strong personal conscious philosophy of selfishness. I proceeded to proclaim this argumentatively around my Christian family.

When I was just sixteen, in the back corridor upstairs at home leading to the maids' room, by the bathroom door with its corroded geyser—I can see it now—Mummy informed me that, unlike my other brothers and sisters, I was not going to move up into the "sixth form" in school (intended for those destined for the university), in spite of the fact that I had already gained enough points in the school certificate examination for university entry at sixteen. I had become known as the naughty one of the family. The grown-ups took my harsh words to mean that I wanted nothing to do with them. They were right; I did feel that. Therefore Mummy had decided to give me one year's training in something and let me go.

I was in a rage. "Be *nice*," Mummy said. No, she didn't plead. She said it as if she was commanding a weary impossibility. I couldn't tell if she meant her remark. She was imagining a fantasy, a nice Edie.

I chose to do domestic science for that year of training. "Science?" Whatever its name, it consisted of cooking, cleaning, laundry, and dressmaking. I deliberately chose it because it was the least intellectual, the least classy of studies. Where was my power of relating that I had enjoyed with Anna, Josie, Helen, and Charlie? And stranger still, where was the me I am now, the person writing? Down inside me there still exists the me that was angry, but by god, now I can see the sweet love in people and know it will come out if I give my own love—if only in the form of a flashing grin. Then I had no idea that there was anything in the enthusiastic person I was, the person who dug and planted a private garden with Hans, the small pale bright-eyed Jewish refugee boy who lived with us; me, the person who told Josie and Hans my dream of a Maharajah's Palace. Mummy knew a maharajah, through her mission work.

It was down by the lemon verbena and along the box hedge walk-ways in the kitchen garden that the idea of the palace came to me. I said to Josie and Hans, "Yes, the Maharajah's palace. It'd be a huge place. A palace with hundreds of rooms. Huge grounds—they'd include mountains to climb. There'd be hockey and lacrosse fields—and a big gym with acrobatics you could actually do, rooms for art, special rooms for oil painting—and for carving really big sculptures—and play acting. Magic rooms. Children's rooms with lots of cushions just for romping. And we'd have huge rooms for singing, and an orchestra with trumpets. Processions. The lot." Josie dreamed with her eyes of the art studio, of humungous blazing canvases and zillions of paints. Hans had halls of scientific apparatus. Everything. Electronics, telescopes, microscopes, sun-harnessing machines. I think there was a perpetual motion machine (I don't remember mention of splitting the atom). But definitely a space port. Probably antigravity. We just let rip. A wealthy maharajah would have uncountable money. It could happen.

How we loved one another. No one praised us. We just were.

I had a dream, I think it was after a visit to Birmingham, or was it Bristol? Bristol. I dreamed I was in some big town on a hillside, and there was a high wall all down one side. The wall had a large oak door. One day I went by the door and it was ajar. Beyond was the country consisting of open hillside, where I very much wanted to go. I could even smell the oak of the door, peppery and fresh. I had this dream at other times too. Also a sense—a sense that brought tears to my eyes—of people who were in a marvelous circle of comradeship, totally at ease, all fond of one another—"communitas," as Vic Turner, my husband to be, came to call it later.

I had no idea that this was the door to the path toward which I was being invited. I was reading Coleridge on "The Imagination." I began to worship "The Imagination."

And I grew to hate the church; all its teachings were mere strictures, all of it was a war of conditional obedience, not unconditional love. I was always the naughty girl, beyond the pale of any consideration, not well-dressed either in clothes or in virtue, not praised. I found a lot of pleasure in rebellion.

Bagging a place in my father's armchair and straddling my legs on the arm, I said to everyone, "When I grow up I'm going into space in a space clipper, for women only." By then it was World War II, and evacuated teachers and high school students were sitting around, bombed out of London. There was a derisive laugh, even from Hans.

"What's that you said? Space kipper?"

"Hee-hee-hee-hee," said the others.

I used to rest in that armchair to "save my strength." I remember telling them that.

All this time up to the age of twenty I was never in love, I just had good times playing with a family called Armstrong and one of their sons called Charlie. It was pure idle fun. I was a little titillated by the fact that Charlie was around so much. The other kids tried to make me feel it was important and teased me about it. I thought it was silly.

It was my knowledge of science, the physical strength I possessed, my rebellion, and the comparative weakness (except for money) of the adults who were religious and bland—these things made me arrogant and to feel powerful. At that stage of my life I had a strong face, was round-shouldered from reading, and didn't think I was at all pretty. Who cared? I liked my brown hair which I gathered in a big kind of squirrel-tail in a slide at the back of my neck.

I said to Josie in front of the mirror, "See, look at our different faces. My cheeks are pink. Your complexion—they call it olive, don't they? Look, I've got full lips. You've got thin ones." I stuck out my lower lip. I bent my long nose toward my chin. "I'm a witch. I'm a witch," I said. Never a truer word. Josie tried to be a witch too, pulling her chin toward her nose.

Nevertheless, in later years Josie dressed better than me, carried herself better, was kinder and more beautiful. Looking back I could kill myself for my cruel words. Yet Josie still loves me. It's beyond understanding.

Again, where was the path?

I read Bernard Shaw,[7] both on politics and on the "life force," and later I read Henri Bergson[8] on his version of the life force and creative evolution. I *related* to that life force, I felt it all the time, burning away as in the heady draft of a furnace. There was no way of knowing whether it was within me or was suffusing everything around. In the case of Bernard Shaw I felt his version of it to be rather tinny, metallic, verging on fascism, and resembling a charisma trip; I couldn't put my finger on what was wrong. However, his humor detoxified some of his fascism.

I was proud. I knew I had pride in me. I felt I was well rid of the cruel "Holy Spirit's" insidious weakening of the will. I read *Thus Spake Zarathustra*,[9] and glowed. The words thrummed. When I look back now I think of fascism. I wonder what Europe had got itself into in the nineteen-forties, inflicted with the German nation and its possessive heady sense of power; Germany walking as by right over other nations, a power that was avid, cannibal, rejoicing in its own violence. For me, the trouble was that I knew the pull of that vortex. There existed a power from below grown out of control, latching on to the greedy ego, a one-way process, taking egos under its power but not their true connections with each other. How could that be?

I admired the idea of social forces with their iron laws: I began to admire communism, wrung clean of religion, acting in the spirit of science and its cool calculations.

I was in sheer rebellion—but against what, and why? I really think it was to do with love. I was greedy to be loved and love. My parents and mentors could never love—so I believed. They wouldn't give love. What had faded from my childhood had turned, not into the light of common day (Wordsworth's phrase), but into proud and secessionist anger. I had no honor—I the egotist. I had indeed worked hard at school but nobody recognized it. I probably had an evil genius in me—they said I had a "poisonous personality." The Africans would have called it witchcraft.

What if I had happened to die just then? Now from this vantage point one can see a little how the logic of the ancients might have worked. The Me would have been totally unformed, its path aborted, the energy abruptly leaked out. The soul I do think would have hung around, angry as hell. If one person had understood and guarded me as the lamas did their sinners in *The Tibetan Book of the Dead*, or—what is very similar—as in the shaman religions around Asia and the Arctic, I would have felt the benefit. My teenage friends didn't know a thing about such matters. As for the Hindus' idea of death—kinder than the once-only "hell " of the Anglicans—as a Hindu I would have been reborn, hopefully as some kind of dog, and would be given

another go-around—not a bad fate. Looked at yet another way, perhaps someone was praying for me in the future and it has worked
retroactively to save me from death at age 18.

So I went to London and became a communist like my sister Helen,
my upkeep paid for by my conservative parents without my being
conscious of the irony of it, and in 1940 in the war I joined the
Women's Land Army—again choosing the low job, the war unit that
was the lowest of the low, even lower in status than domestic science,
and I chose it for similar studied reasons, and in addition, for its noncombatant character.

So it was cows and the smell of dairy milk, green grass, mud, gate
posts, and callused hands. Cows were warm and peaceful to milk at
5:30 a.m. In the reality of the farmyard my Bernard Shaw phase and
feminism began to settle down; and instead, my memory of the
painter Constable, the equivalent of Wordsworth in art, revived as I
brooded over picture postcards showing his magical canvasses. The
scenes themselves appeared up the hedgerows around me, particularly in the form of an ash tree that grew a little north of the farm, its
leaf clusters waving in hypnotic beauty just as forty years later I saw
the clusters of the Bo tree in Ceylon wave. I would walk past this ash
tree and then come back and stand and look at it again. It practically
spoke. It was a presence. "I saw it in my joy," as Wordsworth would
have put it. Another Wordsworth passage told in unconscious exacti-
tude what I found happening to me:

Ye Presences of Nature in the sky
And on the earth! Ye Visions of the hills!
And Souls of lonely places! Can I think
A vulgar hope was yours when ye employed
Such ministry, when ye, through many a year
Haunting me thus among my boyish sports,
On caves and trees, upon the woods and hills,
Impressed upon all forms the characters
Of danger and desire; and thus did make
The surface of the universal earth
With triumph and delight, with hope and fear
Work like a sea?

                            Not uselessly employed
Might I pursue this theme through every change.[10]

Those Presences are, as I now know, real spirits: *kami* in Japan, *inua*
in the Arctic, *akishi* in Africa, and so on in many other languages. They
had purposes for the young soul. Wordsworth saw them too. I saw
them in my ash tree; Constable saw them in his tree. Matisse kept see-

ing them. What did I know of those beings except for Constable and Wordsworth? And now in this book: "not uselessly employed might I [too] pursue this theme through every change." How accurately in many poems Wordsworth recorded his "now-you-see-it-now-you-don't" effect, faithfully, almost clinically, like an anthropologist, but expressed in that musical writing. The spirit rolls away from him and rolls back, in a regular tidal effect. The seeing phase actualizes the full spirit union; these are the times when he sees "into the heart of things." The common day effect returns and fills him with despair; then back rolls the vision, every time. My own course was just as unseeing, just as vagrant, as we shall see.

The summer of 1940 came upon us in blazing sunshine in the hay fields of Northamptonshire. We were working until 10:00 at night. My favorite brother Charlie Davis stayed at the farm to help for a bit. Both of us were soon stuck all over with prickly hayseeds, so that afterwards we had to swim in the stream to get the seeds out—a heavenly feeling—and then there was the joy of going to the pub together. I can smell the beer now.

"Look at my arms, Charlie." They were deeply tanned, just from the work.

The evacuation of Dunkirk was in full progress. "We shall never surrender," said Churchill on the radio. We all heard it in the farmhouse that night. Later, Charlie, then at Keble College, Oxford, was drafted into the army. He was a conscientious objector and was therefore stationed as a private in a noncombatant corps near Oxford. So I asked to be shifted to be near Oxford.

Notes

1. W. Whiting, "Eternal Father, Strong to Save," in *Hymns Old and New*, ed. Kevin Mayhew (Bury St. Edmunds, UK, 1989), no. 127.
2. Bernard of Cluny, "Jerusalem the Golden," in *Hymns Old and New, no. 273.*
3. James Jeans, *The Mysterious Universe* (Cambridge, 1930).
4. Norman Angell, *The Great Illusion* (London, 1913).
5. In Paul Goodman, *Communitas* (New York, 1960).
6. Wordsworth, Shelley, and Keats, available in *The Norton Anthology of Poetry*, eds. A. Allison et al. (New York, 1975).
7. Bernard Shaw, *The Intelligent Woman's Guide* (London, 1929).
8. Henri Bergson, *Creative Evolution* (New York, 1931).
9. Friedrich Nietzsche, *Thus Spake Zarathustra* (London, 1932).
10. William Wordsworth, "The Prelude, Book 1," in *The Norton Anthology of Poetry*, eds. A. Allison et al. 586.

2

COURTSHIP AND MARRIAGE
Wild Life Force

I was given a war job turning flower beds into vegetable plots at Lady Margaret Hall, a women's college in Oxford. I knew Oxford a little from the underside, and privately used to laugh at the "studentesses," so nice and la-di-da compared to farming people. Even so, my brother Charlie and I and an intellectual woman friend called Margaret met up and talked in a free way about the recent appearance of the New Writing literary group. Madrigals were the thing among medical students. I was impressed. I was just exploring around, often quite shy and out of communication with people in my environment. I had joined the Young Communist League, yet the office workers who were communist members looked askance at the ingrained dirt on my hands. I became ironic. Wasn't it supposed to be honorable to have worker's hands?

Our main job as young communists was to distribute *The Daily Worker* and study Stalin's handbook, *The History of the Communist Party of the Soviet Union Bolshevik*.[1] From my point of view the whole enterprise of communism looked good. This was on paper. Communists were in favor of sharing wealth—what could that do but good? I wonder now, did I see the Party this way because I had no experience of life? Could evil really be altered by "force, the midwife of progress," as the communists put it? Force, as this chapter will show, is a bad thing in childbirth. The exit tissues split and the womb sags. With entire societies, the method is even worse. I had no idea of what nature really was, how complicated.

I was actually a hippie like many others, well before the 1960s. "Bohemian" was the word used in the 1940s. I wrote poems about

---

nature arising from feelings of my own free consciousness, poems expressing nature's wild emotion, about wild play and laughter. The poems were deliberately non-studied. I showed them to Charlie and the others. Poems about nature notwithstanding, ours was an intellectual world, along with Charlie and Margaret and Jo my sister who was at the Slade College of Art, and my sister Helen in London keeping the newspaper library of *The Daily Worker*. I know now that thoughts such as ours were in existence on a world scale, in Australia, Vienna, Germany itself with Brecht, the young Picasso in France, and certainly in the US with Howard Fast and the like. These thoughts were all developing in parallel. So I was no naive farm girl. The break with the workers was there.

I was sunk thus, somewhere in the lower reaches of academia, when I met Vic, my future husband. The meeting was engineered by my brother Charlie. Charlie was in a work gang of conscientious objectors in a noncombatant unit that included John Bate—a man who became my lifelong friend—and his friend Vic Turner, a man who was also proud to belong with the others of the unit, all of them private soldiers, including many artists, writers, and saints; it was a curious circumstance that Vic had read the poets and mystics at twelve years old and therefore regarded his new friends as great finds. The noncombatant members knew of Vic's favorite poets, Wilfred Owen, James Elroy Flecker, and Matthew Arnold, so he was not alone; and in music they listened to Claude Debussy and Benjamin Britten, not madrigals—no, they cared nothing for the medieval and Tudor aristocratic graces, but for those lush French symbolists, Baudelaire, Rimbaud, and Proust. For the symbolists, poetry was a matter of beauty, the shudder that was stimulated by the drugs of the pitiful civilized addict, not by the empathy of Wordsworth, nature's priest. Also included were Thomas Mann and the golden fire of D. H. Lawrence. Violet, Vic's literary actress mother, had taught the young Victor her own beloved playwrights, Ibsen and Shakespeare; not the Romantics.

Violet was divorced. She was a super-civilized being, with gray Marcel-waved hair. She had turned herself into a small controlled performer, a true actress. She was highly trained which I was not. She was a spiritualist and a vegetarian.

Vic himself was caught up with William Blake, the visionary.[2] Blake was a kind of Celtic shaman and saw things direct. Blake once saw Milton in a vision as a spirit being. He had visitations from Swedenborg and Homer, and received inspiration from Boehme and Paracelsus. Where Wordsworth had "intimations," Blake roared. I could see in later years that the visions of all these writers were intensely idiosyncratic; none of them could produce a genuine collective ritual in which the whole people participated, although any humble group of peasants or hunter-gatherers knew well how to accomplish this. After the Enlightenment the "whole people" had no common thread. It would take such star figures as saints and prophets to bring back the sense of glory.

Vic in his thinking had already gone beyond his mother, who was preoccupied with spiritualism, dabbling in table-turning and drawing-room spooks, and serving delicately thin brown bread sandwiches and China tea to the other mediums. As a boy Vic cheated on his vegetarian school lunch money and bought meat pies on the quiet. Much of him was Celtic Scots—he was a "heathen" of the heather as he proudly said. He was a pacifist, yet he often dreamed of murdering people. He had read a bit of Freud, a little Jung—but one could not connect Jung with anything to do with the existence of spirits.

Did Vic have the sense of presences as his son Rory now has? Did he see through to one's very soul? He knew he had the gift of poetry. Many of the words in his poems, meticulously handwritten in neat lowercase print, reached through the membrane that somehow separates ordinary reality from the visionary world. Some of his poems, like his *Knight, Death, and the Devil* series, were written as in a land of despair; others were like Wordsworth's *Intimations of Immortality* but in Vic Turner fashion. They were dark poems. Yet he called himself an "anti-wastelander," that is, he couldn't stand the despair running through T.S. Eliot's *The Waste Land*, and also prevalent in the upper middle classes. He himself was a flat-out character; in a sense, he was out of control, his consciousness had escaped from him, it was there ahead of him, like the *arutam*-souls of the Jivaro Indians flying out ahead of their bodies over the battlefield. Vic had no side, no "dignity," no "manner," no self-consciousness or masking of his real self, although he loved acting. I don't think calculating types ever realized this about Vic as long as he lived.

What had I woken up into? What kind of world was this in which I had suddenly opened my eyes?

Our first meeting came about like this. It was June 12, 1942. Charlie told me, "There's a man in my unit, Vic Turner. You must meet him. He's an interesting man. In a way he's dangerous, a dangerous man."

Aha! That was enough for me.

Charlie and Vic turned up at the rendezvous, which was the central crossroads of Oxford, called Carfax. They were wearing their rough army uniforms. I looked at this new stocky dark-haired character: he was wearing a badge on his arm depicting a red bomb. Vic was in the bomb disposal unit of the noncombatant corps, and was helping to dig up unexploded bombs.

Vic's ear tips pointed outward like a pixie's. His hair grew to a little downward point in the exact center of his brow. He was a gnome. He had a snub nose and was much like a handsome burly pixie with a Scottish accent. Okay, that started something in my lower regions. Where did this boy come from? Apparently none of his parents or relatives looked like that. Maybe he came from outer space.

But he had ventured within the epicenter of my ego. The "I" in me was ionized, tingling. You might say bells rang. I found I was being broken down and reconstituted all over again differently, which was an understatement. No, I would never be the same again.

All of us chatted around and went to eat savory toast at a cheap café. I was happy, talking of anything; we laughed a lot. A huge part of me that I had never known about and that had been absent came and took up its place where it was designed to fit; a big pole, if you like, that had been missing from the construction set. There it was, unmistakably. Vic apparently hadn't realized this himself, but he had come within my epicenter. The effect also began to work on him. After two weeks it was obvious. We were both pregnant with love before we had touched each other.

I was so excited that at the next meeting I played games with him, running away in the parkland toward the river, hiding in the trees, so that he came after me, puzzled. It was midsummer and it did not get dark until eleven o'clock, double daylight saving time.

We met and we met. He showed me the poems he'd written about a mulatto beauty, Gloria Delgado, with whom he'd been in love. We went to see *Mrs. Miniver*. We liked movies because they weren't high class. Vic had also been in the Young Communist League. We talked and talked. The whole literary movement came before us and resolved into focus. But the natural courtship was evolving so fast we were unable to think of much else. Electricity hummed between us, but we hadn't touched. It was October 1942.

We met at Carfax in Oxford and found ourselves walking down to the river. We had to cross the trafficky road by Magdalene Bridge, and I started across. Vic came after me—and he put his hand firmly through my arm. He had taken me. We were one. We felt it like sound waves running through a bell. This I remember more than the first kiss. It was a man's act. This was a man.

We went into a fish-and-chip shop and got white cod, fried to flakiness within its soft crust of batter, sweet and salt, along with luscious chips, like French fries only soft and potato-fresh inside. No one can do them like the British. The man wrapped them in greaseproof paper, then in newspaper. We held the packages open like a horn and sprinkled salt and vinegar into them. Once outside, we picked out tasty bits for the hungry mouth, walking along the darkening street, picking out good flakes of cod. We finished, and wadded up the masses of paper and threw them in a bin.

After that night we always walked arm in arm; we had been fed and put together in a funny kind of joy.

The spot on the road where we crossed is still sacred for me, and last year in Oxford I gazed on it again as John Bate and I swept by in the car, on toward Cowley where John lived.

Way back in the year 1942 things warmed up considerably. Early in January 1943 Vic and I took a trip to Reading where we spent time courting under the walls of the ruins of Reading Abbey. At last in the cold night we had to give up and look for the train home. When we got settled into the crowded wartime seat Vic muttered to me sideways, "I suppose we'll have to get married."

"I suppose so," I said with great casualness. But that was what I wanted. He said something about getting a special license because you could get one quickly, in two weeks. That was also what I wanted.

"We'll get a ring."

"I've got £2 saved," I said.

"Good."

We met at a jewelers and bought an 8-carat ring for £2, not exactly deep gold and a little tinny. But it was fine.

"We can't have all those awful relatives around," said Vic.

"Don't let's tell them—at least, not till the last moment, so they can't come."

"We'll have John Bate."

"And Jo."

"And Charlie."

"Anna won't approve." (Anna my sister was a hospital nurse in Oxford and had become a fundamentalist.)

Two weeks later as I pedaled down St. Giles Street from my lodging, it appeared that Anna had twigged what was about to happen. I saw her following me on her bicycle, out of breath.

She came up beside me.

I thought I remembered her saying, "Don't do it, Edie, huh, huh, stop, stop a minute. What about Mummy?" Since then Anna has told me that, no, she never said that. In fact she rather wanted it to happen because she likes babies.

I didn't stop. We simply went on together and she went in with me to the registry office. I had sent a telegram to Mummy half an hour earlier telling her what I was going to do, too late for her to appear with her hordes of respectables to bag the occasion for the society types.

There was one other man there, a friend of John and Vic; also my housemate Joyce Trinder. Anna and my sister Jo were present, both in a good mood. After the registry office sign-up we went to Lyons and had sausages and French fries, plus orangeade. My memory told me that this unknown friend of Vic's, a jolly guy, had smuggled in a bottle of vodka which we privately poured into Anna's glass along with her orange juice. She loved it without having any idea why, and became quite human. Perhaps that's how God became man.

"This orange juice is so good."

There were happy smiles all down the long table at Lyons. I can see them now, the secret smiles. This was communitas, in spite of the fact that Anna told me later that the vodka-spiking episode happened at another celebration, and that she wasn't fooled. Also, unbeknown to me, she had paid for the meal at Lyons.

Vic and I rode away on our bikes to Abingdon, a small town halfway between Oxford and the village of Wantage 16 miles south of Oxford where Vic was stationed. We signed into a bed-and-breakfast for an attic room with one double bed. The night was wild and stormy. It was Saturday, 30 January, 1943. Vic taught me how to make love there in the attic—a "beginner's course in Love," as he called it, and I found my homework rather pleasant, homework which became intolerably essential in a short time. Meanwhile the chimney cowl on the roof of the bed-and-breakfast just above the double bed made a perpetual whirling creaking sound all the wild night long.

The next day we wandered around Abingdon in the gusty daylight eating fish and chips and watching the sparrows sitting on the telephone wires, some in groups. One couple was just alone.

"We're like that," we said. "Only they have a nest."

They were just birds out in the cold air, unconnected with anything. We felt lonely, and walked with our arms linked, Vic's khaki touching my coat, both of us wondering about the future.

It was time to part, Vic to the south and myself to the north. The wind and rain howled down the road from the north, nevertheless I had to face the trip in order to be back to my job on Monday morning as under-gardener at Lady Margaret Hall. Soaking wet, my legs aching, I toiled up those hills in the darkness with no bicycle lamp and no gears on the bike. That satisfied my nature. All was in place.

So we kept meeting—even venturing to Ely and Bournemouth to pay our after-wedding respects to the respective in-laws. I did not satisfy Vic's mother. Her old mother Jeanie, Vic's grandmother, presented me with a large wicker basket with a gesture as if it were a gift. In it I found a quantity of Vic's undarned socks, all of which she had knitted herself but which now had holes in them. I understood the symbolic gesture. Darning was supposed to be my life. I did it, I obsessively darned them all.

As for Violet the mother, she had given her life to Vic, her only child, she had educated him and refined him, and he had gone and married a Bohemian, one who knew nothing of the poet Swinburne and French romantic music, and who stumbled about likely to break her porcelain.

It was on that trip to Bournemouth when Vic and I were walking down a street of grim respectable Victorian houses with high gray garden walls that I noticed something move on the path beside me. It was a rat. It was wounded, I thought, because it was dragging itself along.

"Oh, oh, poor thing. I'd better put it out of its misery," I said, and I went over thinking to grind my shoe upon its head.

"Don't, don't," said Vic, drawing me back. "Just let it live. Perhaps it'll recover and be all right."

I never forgot that scene. Vic was more merciful than I was, he was indeed against killing. I was ashamed and tried to learn the lesson he taught me. Furthermore, Vic was consistent. Not once in my experience did he ever physically hurt anyone.

On the same visit, in the sunshine around the sandy corners of Bournemouth's suburbs, Vic showed me a red-brick Anglican church. It was closed when we tried the door.

"That's where my padre was the minister."

"Padre?"

"That's what everyone called him. We were good friends when I was twelve."

This was when Vic's parents had broken up, his father an electronics scientist in Glasgow, his mother a classical actress. At the divorce Violet left Glasgow and moved in with her own mother in Bournemouth. How did the padre come to meet with the fatherless boy? I never knew. Way back in Vic's lonely days the padre had shown him—had spread out before him—all the mystics of Christianity and many from the rest of the world: the Rhineland mystics, the Silesians, Santa Teresa of Avila and St. John of the Cross, Blake himself, St. Francis and his counterparts, Rumi and al Ghazali in the world of Islam, the *Mahabharata* and "Bhagavad Gita," and faintly far off, hints of Buddhism and Zen. (Never had I heard of such an Anglican mystic as the Padre until three decades later when I met the father of my son Bob's wife, Brian Dupré, the rector of Landbeach, Cambridgeshire. Why hadn't I met such people before?)

From the padre Vic had caught the desire to learn Greek, but there were no classes at his school. Vic persuaded the headmaster himself to teach him Greek. Later this accomplishment helped Vic win a scholarship.

Vic told me a story about the padre while we were walking along the sandy pine-fringed avenues of Bournemouth beyond the church.

"When I was about twelve years old the padre fell ill with some complaint.

"I was asleep in my bed, must have been about three o'clock in the morning. I didn't know much, I was just a kid. I awoke and saw a big oval light at the end of my bed. Oval. This light was like nothing I'd ever seen, it was warm, full of love, it was alive, *mild*. I looked and looked. I knew everything was all right."

I could see the light in my mind's eye. I loved it too.

"It went away after a time. Next day they told me that the padre had died at about 3 in the morning. So I knew it was him, telling me something."

Decades later I knew this event as an "actuality," an empirical presence, not originating in Vic's head, not a symbol, but somehow from "out there." Vic wrote many poems about the experience of the light, sensing that only the words of poetry would truly catch the moment. His was not the only story of its kind: in the course of time I heard many similar accounts.

As Vic walked along telling the story I felt in myself what he had seen, and the consciousness of it never went away. But for all that, in the intervening years much water of a different kind flowed under the bridge.

As for the duty visit to my mother at Ely, we found that Mummy approved of Vic because he was a scholar and a gentleman, but as for being Christian, her third requirement, you could see she couldn't tell whether he was. Did William Blake and Meister Eckhart count as Christians? However, Mummy told me she liked Vic very much. Somehow my own stock with her had risen now that I was married.

One day Vic and I went to Woodstock near Oxford and wandered in the public park at Blenheim. We lay on the grass all alone under the sky in a place filled with wildflowers. The flowers seemed special that day and I was astonished. Vic went among them here and there on impulse. He was picking the flowers, and he gave me the bunch with emotion.

"I've never done that before—never wanted to, for anyone." He kissed me with those lips that were outlined like a seer's. I looked up at him against the blue sky behind, at his eyes where love stood, and gazed on love with love. His brown eyes with their fresh bluish whites and long rich lashes were like two souls of angels; the deep black hair was live and radiating, with thoughts within the head, and passion there. He and I stayed a long time running into each other through the eyes and we couldn't stop.

I was then pregnant, and he said later that it was on this occasion that the fact came home to him. "Now I know you. I didn't before," he said. "I came alive."

He was creating his own life by his own acts of choice, step by step—our first touching, on Magdalene Bridge: a determined act. Our wedding: a determined act. He was shy, male, and determined. That was decisive for me, overwhelming.

I had become pregnant at Violet's house in a storm of inspiration, partly due to the spirit of Blake and his *Prophetic Works* and partly in rebellion against Violet. Blake knew how it was: "Sex . . . on which the soul expands its wing." This new little being was Freddie, nine months before his birthday.

When Violet my mother-in-law heard that I was pregnant she told me, "Now you have to come down and live with your relatives and conform. You have to accept what's sensible and safe as I did."

"NO!"

We hardly communicated with any of the parents. We had no home. Vic found me a tiny empty cottage near him, through his poet and artist friends. Across the empty mantelpiece we pasted the pictures of Dostoyevsky, Verlaine, Rimbaud, Blake, Mao Zedong, Proust, Baudelaire, Mallarmé, and Yacob Boehme. We also read Rilke.

We were scarcely in the cottage for three weeks before the army posted Vic away, eighty miles north in the midlands, and I was alone.

At Vic's new center he had an accident and had to go to the hospital: thing upon thing. I went to stay in a cottage near the hospital to be within visiting distance to him. After he was discharged from the hospital he was sent to work on a food dump near Rugby, and had to find me a place to live nearby. This room was even worse than the cottage because it was a pauper's place, just within our means. We were receiving thirty-six shillings a week for the two of us, today about $50.

There existed in the area an emergency wartime maternity hospital where I could register for the confinement. We weren't fools. We would do that, and though we were poor we were free from obligations. However, I had no money for new shoes and there were holes in the soles of the only ones I had, so I was walking on bare ground. I always wore the same long brown voluminous cotton dress, an old one of my mother's. I was walking slower. On one occasion I had to walk eight miles to the office where they issued free milk coupons and vitamins, and I was tired on the eight miles back.

All this time we were reading Blake's *Prophetic Works*. We loved Blake so much we had practically married him into our line, in a manner of speaking. In the army Vic had a friend called Fred Taylor, a young Northumbrian working-man poet who acted with a kind of prophetic Biblical seriousness in everything he did. We loved him and held him in awe. Fred always wore freshly whitened leggings, which symbolized something for him—sacredness. He had wild craggy features, and he was a visionary. He wrote us a poem at Freddie's birth. Vic himself wrote poem after poem of his own visionary kind, his "poems of uncertainty," of "being" and not "doing." He wanted nothing to be cut-and-dried. How could there anything cut-and-dried for us, just then?

Was my body flexible, for a start? Being flexible mattered, sure enough, when the contractions started. I went in to the maternity hospital and howled the place down for eight hours—I simply couldn't help it. The nurse told me again and again to keep quiet. The baby emerged like an express train, screeching. He had purple skin, red hair, and a furious body. After a minute he got his thumb up and stuck it back into his mouth where it had obviously resided many times before.

Two weeks later when I was ready to leave the hospital after the required stay, the question was, could we go back to that hole-in-the-corner lodging? But there was no room anywhere else. Vic was a conchie (conscientious objector) and nobody would take us in. But it turned out that the local Presbyterian minister's wife had a nice new villa-type house, and in the spirit of Christianity she offered me a room for a couple of weeks. I slept under a beautiful down quilt and ate well, enfolded with much friendship. The baby slept in a drawer that we pulled out from the dressing chest. We placed the drawer on the floor and padded it with cushions. Freddie was fine. He fed and fed from my breasts, and I changed and rechanged his wet and dirty bottom, and washed his nappies.

We moved to a thatched cottage at Kilsby, a good bicycle ride from Vic's food dump, but a feasible place. Mrs. Hirons and her old dying husband possessed a spare room, a room that like the previous one contained a pull-out drawer for the baby. There was no water-closet sanitation, only a garden privy. We had to empty the toilet bucket into trenches in the vegetable garden and cover the contents over with dirt. Next door, however, the inhabitants did not dig the stuff in at all but just heaped it up in a pile against their garden wall, and by the time Freddie was four months old I developed a kind of dysentery from the flies around that heap. I was getting thin. Then I did go back with the baby to Mummy, an act I had long resisted, and I lived in the drawing room at the doctor's house at Ely, a grand salon of a room, now gutted of its Chippendale and converted to a nursery for my sister Helen and her baby Paulie. These two had been evacuated from London during the bombing. The drawing room was big enough to accommodate Freddie and me as well. Now, the various people in the large house, including myself, had to learn civil human interaction just to be able to live together.

"Look at this advert," said Helen one day, peering intelligently at the *Ely Standard* and sticking up an eyebrow. "Gypsy caravan for sale, Littleport. £25. How about that? You'd be mobile if you had a caravan, and when Vic moved, you could move the caravan too." She grinned, thinking about it.

"Let's have a look." Yes, it was for sale. When working in the Land Army I had saved £22, a little short of the sum required. A home of our own for Vic and me!

Helen and I didn't hesitate. We took the babies plus the prams on the train and went to Littleport. There in a field stood a dark red dingy enclosed cart with a roof like an old-fashioned passenger train car, with a half-door and top door, even boasting dull gilt arabesque ornamentation on the side wings. Perhaps it had been a circus caravan. It stood on four large painted wooden wheels with iron tires and gracefully turned spokes, while the other end of the caravan bore horse shafts for when there might be need of a horse. We returned to the back where the door was and peeped inside. On the left we saw a minuscule cast iron coal stove on curvy legs with a stovepipe going up through the roof. At the far end appeared a slatted bunk, barely wide enough for two. A plain wooden box with a lid stood on the right side for use as a seat and as a food container.

We told Vic about the caravan and he turned up. He liked the idea and he was able to complete the purchase money in his own way. At the food dump back on his work site near Rugby he and his workmates had been handling crates of navy rum for the British fleet. The men had loaded thousands of these onto freight wagons, and just sometimes they "accidentally" dropped a crate on its corner. This they did for Vic.

Crash. Tinkle.

A man was ready with an empty bottle, and the others raised the whole crate up. The precious fluid poured unsteadily into the bottle until it was full. Vic corked the bottle and came over to Ely on weekend leave.

We went to the gypsy in Littleport and did some bargaining.

"All right. Twenty-two pounds down, here's the money, and this." Vic uncorked the bottle and let the man smell.

The man's hand went out. He took the bottle and the money. "The van's yours."

Now to transport it to Rugby. At Littleport station the railway men did not seem to regard the consignment as a problem. The gypsy's horse would pull the caravan to the station for us, it would be loaded onto a flatbed, and off it would go. At the Rugby end Vic was arranging things. A Mr. Evans, a farmer near the food dump, agreed to have the caravan parked on his land for five shillings a week, plus free milk and eggs. As for the business of bringing the caravan to the spot from the railway station, Mr. Evans was willing to take a horse to Rugby station to pull it the four miles to the farm.

It can be seen how we were following whatever opportunities we could for the sake of a home. We were *in* this little life completely. I confess I liked these oddities of arrangement and found them interesting.

The moving day was arranged. I packed nappies, a mackintosh, and a tin saucepan in the luggage space of the pram—it was about all I possessed. I plumped Freddie into the pram, said goodbye to Helen and Mummy, and took the train to Rugby, where Vic met me to take me to the farm.

"Something happened. The caravan wheel broke," he said.

"What? What's that? Broken!"

Vic explained. This was the scene. The land of Mr. Evans, called Barby Wood Farm, extended up a hill from fields that lay beside the Manchester-Birmingham barge canal, a stretch of water that ran quietly down on the right. When you looked along the canal to the other end of the first field you saw a pretty little stone bridge leading to the far side of the water. Beyond that could be seen the army food dump, crowded with railway sidings and Nissen huts.

When traveling to the farm from the Rugby end, one leaves Rugby, walks a mile along the Rugby-Cambridge road, and then takes a track to the right. This track winds downward for three miles to a farm gate that opens onto Mr. Evans's main field that borders the canal. The track continues through the field parallel to the canal for fifty yards, then makes a sharp turn to the left up the hill toward the farm buildings.

What had happened that afternoon was this. The horse pulling the caravan had patiently plodded all the way from Rugby, along the three mile track, and up to the field gate. One gathers that once the horse was through the gate and approaching the turn up to the left it scented home and rushed the turn—but in doing so it yanked itself out of the traces. The caravan spun off on its own toward the canal. But before the careening vehicle reached the canal it swiveled around again, broke a wheel, and collapsed at an awful angle onto what appeared to be nothing on the side where the wheel had been smashed. Vic was there and saw it happen.

He never told me his feelings. What he actually did was to go back over the little bridge to the army dump and gather all his workmates in the unit. They first scouted around the railway sidings in the dump area and found about twenty spare railroad ties, "sleepers," which they carried away over the bridge into the field to the site of the mishap. (All this happened before I was due to arrive on the train with the baby.) The group of men set to work beside the caravan creating a bastion out of the sleepers, then they got their hands below the caravan, lifted it up, and eased it level and onto the wall of sleepers. It was upright again and solid as a rock. There it sat in its self-appointed place, positioned parallel to the canal and about thirty yards away from it, facing a fenced-in cow pond about twenty yards downhill from the field gate.

It was evening when Vic and I arrived on foot from Rugby station pushing the pram. Vic had brought a candle and some food. In the darkness we mounted the steps of the caravan and entered our tiny new home. The first thing we did was light the candle; then we lit a fire in the iron stove and I breast-fed the baby. We drank hot cocoa and ate bread and butter, and stowed little Freddie on slats under the bunk bed, first putting down the pram mattress, then covering him with the pram blanket. The bed above was still spread with the gypsy's dingy flock mattress. Vic had brought gray donkey-type army blankets with him from his billet in the dump. We climbed up to the high bunk and we slept.

I remember the matter of getting a blacksmith to repair the wheel, and the triumph when they brought the wheel and fitted it back onto the axle, fastening it with a stout cotter pin. We were complete.

Looking over the picture after the passage of time I am amazed at the frequency of ordinary charitable acts—how often people did what there was no call to do—such as the Presbyterian minister's wife's hospitality, my mother giving up her drawing room after I had been such a bitchy daughter, Helen, always ready with ideas and help, the men on the dump with their rum, the railway men dealing with the tricky transportation of the caravan, and Vic's dump mates with their railway sleepers. For decades I have never thought about the generosity aspect of it. But the facts remain in my memory. In the old days I looked at those things as routine, they just happened.

Every evening Vic came over the little bridge and we had supper. He sometimes brought spare rations with him, Soya sausage and occasionally even real sausages. There was always canned mackerel to be had. Everyone was on war rations which I went to fetch from the shop, trudging along the four miles to Rugby with Freddie in the pram. On our return we'd boil chicory-and-coffee in the candlelit caravan and look at the books from Rugby Public Library.

At first we read about organic farming as practiced by the Chinese since 2000 BC, and also learned about soil from the organic farming advocate Howard.[3] In our own little area in the field we learned how to do organic vegetable-growing ourselves. The small fenced-in patch of nettles and high grass on the far side of the cow pond served as a garden plot. We dug it up and layered it underneath with our chamber-pot material, then sowed carrots, potatoes, and cabbage. The carrots were huge until the farm pigs broke in and ate them. Then the farmer put the pigs in another field. After that the rest of the crops did well.

Chickens laid their eggs in the hedge and I gathered them for the farmer, receiving some for ourselves. Freddie at eight months learned to walk, run, and climb fences. He was intrigued by the way the roosters climbed up on the hens from behind, and he tried the same thing on the roosters. He came back running and crying, with peck marks on him.

When we were digging fresh soil he'd find a worm, and we caught him popping one into his mouth.

"Uurm *snuggle!*" he'd say, swallowing it. Ah, well, it was all extra protein.

Time went on. "I've missed a period again," I said to Vic. "I *thought* our hanging around in that gorgeous buttercup field in May meant something."

"Good."

"Look, there's that willow tree with osiers near the cow pond. We could make the new baby a basket cradle." We gathered the long whippy stems, soaked them, and started a long basket with two lengthy bunches of withies crisscrossed as its base. The method worked after a fashion, the way I had learned at school. I built the weaving in and out, up the sides, and finished the top with a braided and woven rim.

"It's a bit rough. I'll line it with padding and scraps of cloth." The cradle was quite good once we had set it on a box and tied it to the post of the bunk.

Little Bobby pushed his way into the world on 18 February, 1945. He was the most contented peaceful child, born in the caravan with a midwife in attendance. Vic was present at the birth, which was not a common experience for a father in those days.

The birth itself had been a peaceful process. While we were waiting for the contractions to develop Vic picked up a book, the life of Toulouse-Lautrec.

"Toulouse-Lautrec? Let's look at the pictures," I said, and saw those scenes of the night club at the Moulin Rouge, women with enormous bosoms and upturned noses like Jean Avril, all physically blessed, in scenes of sexual paradise. We loved the French impressionists. Still, we hoped the kid wouldn't be born a dwarf like Lautrec—but that was just our joke. We were still Bohemians, later known as hippies. It is true of me still, although now I might be labeled New Age and that also might be true.

The baby had not yet arrived. As nothing seemed to be happening to me with Lautrec, Vic read from the life and poems of Rabbie (Robert) Burns, the Scots poet of "A man's a man for 'a that." Ah, that had an effect. Now I was staggering about, large in the tiny caravan, feeling the familiar rich sickening catastrophic gripes of childbirth. I lay down and Vic put his hand in mine. I knew how to let it happen, feeling "Let it be." The contraction passed, and he resumed the book. Very shortly afterwards other contractions overcame me in waves, and finally the express train effect occurred and little dark-haired Robert showed up. The name was aptly given.

But the midwife failed to give me stitches, so that I developed a fallen uterus, otherwise known as prolapsed womb, which caused an unpleasant saggy feeling that made me artificially tired. Then, when I walked my four miles to Rugby for the shopping and had to push the pram with Bobby in it, I couldn't carry much because of my prolapse. So Freddie, who was two and a half, had to walk most of the way, crying. The picture of his little crying figure struggling some way behind the pram still haunts me.

Nevertheless, we were in the caravan: we had a home.

Notes

1 . Joseph Stalin, *The History of the Communist Party of the Soviet Union (Bolsheviks)* (New York, 1939).
2. William Blake (1757-1827), *The Poetry and Prose of William Blake* (Garden City, NY, 1970).
3. Albert Howard, *Soil and Health* (London, 1946); Franklin Hiram King, *Farmers of Forty Centuries: Permanent Agriculture in China, Korea, and Japan* (New York, 1911).

3

THE FIRST BRUSH WITH ANTHROPOLOGY

During that time we were also getting interested in the farm on which we were living, in natural food, in forestry, in the connected way of life, also in what we were reading about mycorrhiza organisms that function in natural soil as catalysts enabling roots to pick up nutriments—in fact, acting as connectors. The rural character of the place, and the life of dealing with babies, and our own constant interactions and discussions were directing our attention to nature's general organic connectedness. Not far from us, Mr. Evans ran the farm with his twin sons, an elder son, and his wife and daughter. This unit existed as a skilled, knowledgeable, and operating community, out there near the canal. I had worked in such a unit before and appreciated the common sense of it.

All of a sudden we happened to pick up from a bookshop in Rugby a paperback copy of *Coming of Age in Samoa* by Margaret Mead.[1] Here we read about a different way that humans relate to one other. You could see the differences again in Mead's other book, *Growing up in New Guinea*,[2] and again in the Andaman Islands in the Indian Ocean where the anthropologist Radcliffe-Brown[3] shows a very neat social system among the indigenous islanders, operating like an organism within its own social structural laws.

We said to each other, we could live in a community like that; we knew they existed in northern Britain. We started planning to buy a sheep farm on the Island of Skye in Northern Scotland. Land would be cheap, and we could live and farm in those simple pastoral communities, some of which happened to be located on islands near Barra, the island of Vic's forebears. On one of his army leaves Vic traveled up to the island of Raasay, a more likely spot than the

---

Notes for this section can be found on page 56.

romantic island of Skye. He quickly identified the social system there. It showed itself as one of almost total interdependency, yet with patrilineal succession and at the same time much power in the hands of the women. However, because of modern conditions out-side of the island, many of the young were emigrating in search of jobs, leaving one end of the island in the doldrums, an area that became known as the "land of bachelors." Vic came to understand the people and their lives.

Farms were indeed to be had in the area. Still, it so turned out that we couldn't fulfill our plan because of the prolapse I had suffered dur-ing childbirth and my resulting lack of physical strength, so it all came to nothing, a mere proto-hippie dream.

The war was coming to an end. Vic could have been demobilized from the army earlier if he had agreed to become a schoolteacher, but he wanted to do research. His war-aborted studies in University College London had entitled him under army law to a grant to con-tinue with his degree after demobilization. So he was considering what his research was to be. Should he change to anthropology? He had previously done English, Old Icelandic, Old Norse, Middle English, then his own explorations up and down the literatures. Did he really want to take up a career in English—after our experience in a caravan world? How limiting it would be, writing papers on books that discussed books of literary criticism about the books of play-wrights, poets, and novelists, that is, of writers who had invented a literature coming out of themselves as individuals, based in a literary world with its own canons and its own purposes. These purposes seemed to consist of style, the philosophy of art, mimesis, poiesis—in fact, invention. So the English discipline consisted of writing papers on books on books on books? Fiction was something—it might be fun to make up a story, that part could be interesting, but it was *events* that were the real thing. Events happened all around us, actual people act-ing in relation to one another, often passionately. Didn't the high-up literati see? Now in our new interest in anthropology we had discov-ered there were direct studies being made of actual people across the globe, much in their lives being startlingly different. They were actu-ally alive: this was the raw, raw material.

Vic came to a conclusion. He aimed for what he wanted at University College London and got it. It was a reassignment to anthropology instead of English. The registrar was a Scotsman named Robertson. It appeared he and Vic had a great conversation about Raasay and the highlands generally, and about what Vic was pursuing: the raw mate-rial. Mr. Robertson gave Victor Turner permission to join Daryll Forde's department of social anthropology at University College

London, to take the full three year course for a BA, with a year of archeology to follow, and if hopes were realized, do research in Africa for his PhD. Africa was Britain's major anthropological field. There was no more need for literary criticism.

Daryll Forde offered what was actually human geography, from his down-to-earth Welsh materialist book, *Habitat, Economy, and Society.*[4] The title tells it all. Daryll was an "argie-bargie" guy and loved an argument. So did the students. So did Vic and I. Vic relayed all his lecture courses to me in every detail. We received the Yoruba system in Nigeria parceled down to us from Daryll. We saw how patriliny arose from cattle-keeping and plow agriculture because men were essential in the handling of cattle, how descent was likely to be segmentary in such scattered communities, how a primary matter like soil conditions caused a fan-out of particularized customs and relationships among strongly localized tribes. From Meyer Fortes[5] we found out about the Tallensi's complex overlayerings of customs and obligations, all mutely understood, causing little nodal points in the overlaps where ritual mattered greatly. We learned that immense subtleties existed among this obscure tribe in Ghana and Burkina Faso. Ritual arose from social structures, said the British school. This conclusion arose from the general assumptions of positivist materialism.

To implement Vic's complete training period we moved to the town of Vic's mother Violet, St. Leonard's-on-Sea, where Violet had retired with her old mother. I needed an operation for my prolapse, which I endured in the usual way, other than being troubled by an Irish hospital nurse who used to come off with "turrible" fatal jokes which stretched my new stitches dangerously. Luckily the advantage was equal to the disadvantage, and I finally came out to the world again marvelously grateful, back to my two little boys. In a couple more years I gave birth to baby Rene, Irene, which means "peace," at a time when there was a hopeful rapprochement with the eastern powers of Europe, at least a rapprochement at the Olympic Games starring the popular Zapotec, the Czechoslovakian runner.

Vic commuted in to the university on the train. One frosty winter's night when Vic was traveling home the fire in the locomotive broke down. There was no heating in the train and everyone was stranded for four hours. Vic came home at midnight sick with flu, which kept him at home for two weeks.

While I was washing nappies, breast-feeding, making clothes, cooking, and washing dishes Vic used to convey to me all the anthropology he learned. I had heard there were women university students in existence. I knew from the bottom of my soul they would never wash dishes or breast-feed babies. These intellectual women were ladies with exquisitely kept fingernails and hairdos, whereas my tasks were those of the lower orders. I was of the lower orders, and I was aggressively proud of it as usual. It wasn't until 1995 that I discovered that many university women, especially those with families, actually felt and experienced as I did;[6] but they must have hidden their real lives away to give the appearance of being career women. However, there are two sides to this. They were anthropologists, supposed to be studying people. Why were they forced to distinguish themselves so radically from the ordinary people they studied? Intellectual academic control by means of the job selection process has ruled the discipline from way back, and it still does—which is a reason why anthropology has drifted so far from contact with the ordinary public.

In 1948 times were hard for us, living as a family under the governance of urbanism. We were living in a built-up environment, and there wasn't a tree or a patch of grass in sight. Big hotels and expensive shops surrounded us, where those with money could buy any amount of the goods they wanted, while much was rationed for the ordinary folk. Again, ironically, much later in 1993 and 1999, I saw the same injustices in Russia after fifty decades of communism had ended, and these injustices were due to the existence of an enormous oppressive Mafia. In the 1940s, though, Vic and I again took to communism, which we still thought to be the cure, joining a small group who studied Marxism, learned and urged working-class tactics, and sold *The Daily Worker*. We adopted democratic meeting procedure. That was as far as our efforts went: no bomb throwing, no stealing atomic secrets. We learned—concerning matters of colonialism in Africa which was sure to be our own political concern—that the local Party was not particularly interested in what happened to Africans and the colonies. It was for the Africans out there to organize, create their own revolution, and enter the world struggle using the same political methods as in the metropolitan countries. There should be no sentimentality about the beauty of their pristine systems. Such peoples should cast off their own religions, which were only opium, and clear their heads for action. So we obediently forgot the sentiment and poetry; indeed it went so far that we could no longer remember why it was that the poetry of Rilke had seemed so profound.

Still, the UCL courses went on. Africa grew in fascination for us both. A fire lived on in Vic beneath the cold iron, the iron march of the proletariat. Meanwhile the Party remained as our moral stance, and its rebellious character suited my mood.

It keeps coming home to me how Vic and I grew together, influencing each other, in a mutual dance, a dialogue of sensitiveness, well-practiced and loved, present in every little act and spontaneous decision. Now that he has gone, that sense always remains as a little sob of heartache when I cease writing and stop to think.

Vic toiled through the UCL requirements, producing essay after essay in his well-formed sloping handwriting. I meanwhile wrote not a thing. I couldn't have written as a scholar; I had left school at just sixteen. My hands were not for that, though my ears were for listening. Vic wrote on West African market women (pure economics); leopard-skin chiefs (a structural anomaly); ecology (on the Barotse floodplain of the Zambezi and the Nuer floodplain of the Nile, almost pure geography); the marvels of Ashanti kingship written by Rattray; ancestor worship—which was taken to be the collective representation of the power of the elders ("Africans mistakenly fancy the ancestors are around them"; this mental glitch of theirs, we learned, arose from the psychological effects of the cruelty of the superego). Vic wrote skilled papers on political systems where custom was king, a state of things persisting in what, we gathered, were quietistic untouched communities living through unvarying cycles; or alternatively, custom was king in stagnant systems perpetuated by power-greedy potentates, you take your pick. We learned that the colonial system was present just to hold the peace—oh yes, hadn't you heard of the Pax Britannica?

The conversion to Marxist anthropology brought about a conversion away from an element—a faculty—of listening, of hearing true tales of the spirit, of resonating with the beauty of human ritual. Yet there also existed Evans-Pritchard the shaken positivist, the osmotic man, who saw a spirit among the witch-bound Azande of the Sudan and who wrote what I think is the greatest book of anthropology of his time, perhaps of the century, honestly showing the blood-red paths of fear in an African village and the Azande consciousness of the spirit's force.[7]

Vic went on and on, getting first-class grades. He had three children to feed. We were "in the mesh," as Sartre was beginning to put it. Nowadays I compare the controls on us with those of Violet in her time, at her divorce. Violet, to give her credit, had realized when divorce struck her she would have to come down to practicalities and appear to agree with the respectables—and so did we now, with the minimal proviso of our private communism.

Towards the end of Vic's training at UCL Max Gluckman, a great progressive Africanist and newly appointed to the professorship at Manchester,[8] came to London and spotted Vic as an upcoming man. Max had power. He was right up there in the British system of grant-giving and he gave Vic a grant. He had already headed the Rhodes-Livingstone Institute for African Research, based in Lusaka and

Luanshya, Northern Rhodesia, funded by the Anglo-American Copper Corporation, the Northern Rhodesian Colonial Government, and the Beit Trust, the diamond corporation. Max's brilliant "down-to-earth" anthropology looked like practical common sense to the gentlemen of business; and as the discipline of anthropology universally praised Max's genius, that was all right: the experts knew best. Max actually was very fond of Africans and deeply respected the Barotse judicial system that he studied (he and his father had been trained in law). Max taught us to understand the difference between law among on-the-ground communities such as the Barotse, and the bureaucratic systems that the metropolitan countries have invented and forced themselves to obey.

The unlettered Africans knew very well what law was, and judged what "the reasonable man" would be expected to do. The humanism of those thatch-shelter judges in the Zambezi villages was a thing Max admired very much. We were seeing the reality of Africa through Max's eyes before we ever went there. We were happy to be under the wing of this tall, warm-eyed Jewish man who was balding; and we found him to be a man of great imagination.

Thus we anthropologists in those days were romantics, that is to say, we looked for and described those humanistic interactions that one can still find plentifully wherever human beings exist. Warmth toward Africans used to escape from our Manchester group from time to time and it would sweeten the kitchen stories of researchers when they got home. Also this warmth did in fact power the carefulness of the researchers in portraying the Africans' complex lives coherently and well. They had tried to refrain from altering the lives of Africans while doing research so as to leave the African culture as they found it (an ethic that Star Trek later called the prime directive). The tone of their books gives evidence to how they eliminated themselves from the picture. In point of fact their lives make good stories, as shown on a video made on the life of Evans-Pritchard.[9] I fantasize that the stories could be even richer, developing into a humanistic and fascinating documentary series, a series at last educating the public about themselves and about the nature of humanity as we see it operating in alien societies.

The grant that Max cornered for Vic was modest but it lasted for five years: a year's postgraduate training in Manchester, 1950-1951, while working as a research assistant, on about £600 (of which about £250 went to rent); funded research (including family fares) from 1951 to 1954, consisting of one year in the field, one year back home for checking up and consulting, another year in the field, and one year to write the thesis (dissertation) for the doctorate. This rate would be at about £700 a year.

So we moved to Manchester. There, much of our life had to do with the Communist party. In the party at that time we experienced something like communitas. It resembled the communitas of the Girl Guide camps in which I had participated at thirteen—a sense of great love for our fellows. We felt that the whole world was going to benefit from socialism, and all humanity might well end up happy. At first the present rich/poor divide didn't occupy the forefront of the picture. We saw only the grand vision. In contrast, up there in the Party headquarters in London sat leaders who were iron planners. Even that idea gave some kind of thrill, but we had no desire to make that iron world our life's work. What was that thrill? Now, I think, it was the thrill of power, "Power I, material power." It was thrilling to be anywhere connected with it. How was it that this faulty thing put its touch on us, conveying such exciting harmless-looking messages?

Ethics and morality ruled our family; religion and poetry were out. We intended to go to Northern Rhodesia and study political systems. We would gauge how human beings reacted in a world of hardships, jealousies, power struggles, and colonialism. Many of our colleagues were of the same mind and had the same plans: Bill Epstein would do copperbelt politics, the fight that preceded the independence struggle;[10] Dick Werbner followed the sad stories of sufferers under the whites and later wrote how they suffered under their own tyrants in Southern Rhodesia, later Zimbabwe;[11] Elizabeth Colson, the reaction of the tribes whose land had been used for the Kariba Dam.[12] Vic was planning to study social change and chieftainship politics among the Mambwe (which Bill Watson later did instead, emphasizing colonialism and the ladder of command among the Mambwe). None of us got to head any revolution in those places, we were just the writers. But one could see where our sympathies lay. Max remained in the background. For some time he had been mulling a breakthrough. This was a break with the "structure" world of theory, to look at human life as *process*, things moving, not static. He was a humanist of the best sort, but nervous, because the only way he could see to implement humanism was by means of the progressive way. But this was the era of McCarthyism and the antisubversive government group, "MI5," in England, and progressives were suspect. Max didn't want a witch hunt.

My father died. My mother, unusually white-faced, walked behind his coffin to the cemetery. My father left me £20. Ten years later, when my mother died, she left me nothing, but she left £2,000 each to the only children out of the remaining six who had retained their Christianity—Anna and George. I got a grisly satisfaction out of that arrangement. Helen, who had taught me communism, was furious at the injustice and wanted to go to law. She needed to educate her son

Henry better than she could when trapped in a low-paying teaching job in India. We told Helen we could have Henry with us in Manchester and give him the kind of education our children were getting. So in the fullness of time he joined us.

Meanwhile back in time for the adventure of Africa.

Notes

1. Margaret Mead, *Coming of Age in Samoa* (New York, 1928).
2. Margaret Mead, *Growing Up in New Guinea* (New York, 1930).
3. Alfred Radcliffe-Brown, *The Andaman Islanders* (Cambridge, 1922).
4. Daryll Forde, *Habitat, Economy, and Society* (London, 1950).
5. Meyer Fortes and Edward Evans-Pritchard, eds., *African Political Systems* (London, 1940).
6. See Edith Turner, "Changes in the Status of Senior Women Anthropologists after Feminist Revision," paper presented at the Society for Feminist Anthropology's session entitled *Through a Gendered Looking Glass: Women Doing Ethnography, Before and After 1974* (American Anthropological Association Annual Meetings, Washington, November 1995).
7. Edward E. Evans-Pritchard, *Witchcraft, Oracles, and Magic among the Azande* (Oxford, 1976 [1937]).
8. See Max Gluckman's classic study of human ecology, *The Economy of the Central Barotse Plain* (Manchester, UK, 1941).
9. Bruce Dakowski, video recording, *Strange Beliefs* (Princeton, 1990).
10. Arnold L. Epstein, *Politics in an Urban African Community* (Manchester, UK, 1958).
11. Richard Werbner, *Tears of the Dead: The Social Biography of an African Family* (Edinburgh, 1991).
12. Elizabeth Colson, *The Social Consequences of Resettlement: The Impact of the Kariba Resettlement upon the Gwembe Tonga* (Manchester, UK, 1971).

4

AFRICA
Head Over Heels Into Ritual

Nothing went according to plan.

Vic tried to book passages for the family on a Cunard liner to Cape Town, and discovered there was a seamen's strike in progress. Owing to the shortage of berths he could book only his own passage. I and the children would have to wait until the strike was over and then look for berths.

I took it phlegmatically. I would reach Africa a little later, that's all. Before Vic left we paid a farewell visit to Mummy who had retired to a suburb of Cambridge, and there we found her limping around with her arthritis in a small house, all on her own. While we were there Vic looked for a portable typewriter, a requirement in the field. He had never possessed a typewriter before. As we were hard up Vic bought a secondhand one from a dealer in Cambridge. He brought it home to Mummy's house but it didn't work. Mummy was angry on behalf of Vic, whom she was now backing up with all her might. She went off in her wheelchair with the typewriter, her eyes glittering, and came back with the money Vic had paid. Now Vic bought a new Olivetti from a proper store, and practiced on it using only the forefinger of each hand, peck, peck, peck. Soon he could do it, peck, peck, peck, with no mistakes.

That act of Mummy's I remember.

I myself was to do the purchasing of the fieldwork camera and also undertake the photography. Vic packed his spare flannel bags (pants) and some underwear in a heavy suitcase, planning to wear his Harris tweed jacket en voyage. He intended to buy cheap bush shirts from African stores when he reached the field. He filled up the suitcase with

Notes for this section can be found on page 82.

new unused notebooks and a number of other books, plus an introduction from Max to some party friends in Cape Town. Vic was planning to reach the Rhodes-Livingstone Institute and its director, Clyde
Mitchell, in Luanshya, Zambia (then Northern Rhodesia), and afterward travel to the Mambwe in eastern Northern Rhodesia and study
social change and local-level politics. He departed with the suitcase
and typewriter and I was left on my own in St. Leonards-on-Sea, with
Violet and her mother as my neighbors. I occupied myself with busy-
work, planning and packing for my coming February trip. This was
January 1951. My mind was on the tropics. I was sewing underwear
out of cotton to avoid the sweaty and ubiquitous rayon that everyone
wore in England. For a time I was under the advice of experienced
colonial officials and various ladies who had been "out there" and who
"knew" how to run a comfortable western home in the land of mud
huts. Later I was interested to read Doris Lessing's autobiography[1] in
which she describes her Southern Rhodesia childhood home, a place of
furniture and "boys" cooking in the kitchen, a world in which Africans
always gave great respect to whites. The Lessing house was a white
environment. Looking back, I have been wondering if Vic and I ever
escaped the same thing. After all, we too were white. We were to
employ Africans to fetch water and wash clothes, though we never
called them "boys." We had tables and stools, although we were poor.
We tried hard to live the way Africans did but didn't dare to do so fully
because of possible health problems, and to this day all I can do is wish
other researchers better success in the attempt. Right away our color
gave us higher status, and that engendered in me the same radical
anti-white anger as it had in Doris Lessing—let alone the anger such
inequality engendered in the Africans.

From the very first, even while preparing for the trip, I intended to
bide my time. I was *not* going to be like the colonial ladies. NO. In this
way my uncertain path was creeping through the underbrush.

Vic sent me a cable from Northern Rhodesia. He was quoting a
cable from Max Gluckman in Manchester, England, who had come up
with an idea. Max knew that in spite of Vic's Marxism he was interested in ritual.

"SUGGEST YOU CHANGE PLANS FROM MAMBWE AREA TO
LUNDA NDEMBU IN MWINILUNGA WESTERN PROVINCE.
MUCH YELLOW FEVER BUT ALSO MUCH RITUAL. GLUCKMAN"

I cabled Vic that it was okay by me. We would all need to have a
good many shots anyway, and another for yellow fever would make
no difference. Vic cabled Max giving him the go-ahead.

But ritual? In the study of Africa that both Vic and I had been
undertaking we found not only reports of differing social structures

but tales of arcane initiation ceremonies, funerary rites with masked dancers, rites of ancestor worship, and drumming to dispel evil spirits. The anthropological analyses as usual related these to social structure. They turned out to be highly colorful events, and indeed, in the course of time I witnessed examples of all the Lunda Ndembu ones except the inner rites of the boys' initiation. The work of Vic and myself became focused on a detailed elucidation of their meaning.[2]

The time came for the trip. I sent ahead some large, oddly-shaped packages containing mosquito nets, camp beds, plain crockery, and bulk medicines, all consigned to the boat dock in London. I omitted the now unneeded pram. I packed suitcases and then dressed the three children, age three, five, and seven, for the trip. We took the train to London, then a taxi to the dock.

All four of us sat in the taxi, jerking around the corners of industrial London to the docks, my last sight of England for a while.

Rene, age three, suddenly said, "I feel sick."

"Quick, a window"—but it was too late. She threw up on the floor of the taxi.

Freddie and I surreptitiously tried to clear up the mess, but by now we had arrived. The taxi man opened the door.

"Wot's this 'ere?" he growled. "Now I've got to clean up that there. Yer gonna 'ave to pay me ten bob."

It was a lot of money. I meekly paid. We got our things together. In the dock in front of us rose the boat, ten thousand tons, small, named the *Umtali*—the name of a place in South Africa. They put us in the steerage in a cabin for four.

The children slept. Late in the night I heard a rumbling. It was the engines starting: we were leaving England. Good. I got out of bed and peeped out of the porthole. Yes, we were slowly moving. You could see the water moving away from the side of the ship, and the reflection of the lights, moving. The lights of the embankment passed us backwards in slow procession, dipping and disappearing. Rumble, rumble. Distances were lengthening now; dark water stretched before me, with lights showing far away. How I loved to be moving away! May this never end, I said to myself.

Time passed. Once I saw a lighted buoy. The boat rocked a little, and after that there were no more lights.

We were going to Africa and I had never been outside Britain in my life. Happily I climbed into my bunk, feeling this was what I had been born for.

The journey was hard enough. As it so happened we experienced the worst storm for four years in the Bay of Biscay, and I learned what seasickness really was.

Fourteen days later, in the early morning, we were on deck in tropical clothes, the small boys in shorts and sandals and Rene and myself in summer dresses. A fellow traveler said, "Look!"

"Where, where?"

"Up there." She pointed high in the misty air. There appeared to be a ridge of rocks suspended high in the air, far away.

"That's the top of Table Mountain," she said. "We've arrived at Cape Town."

"Huh?"

We could see no coastline, no city, nothing but mist and those suspended rocks. The view gradually cleared as we watched, and we saw that it was true; a large city lay spread out before us, gleaming white, framed by the mountains.

Here at Cape Town lived the Dutch and English. Cape Town was a city of traffic and police like every other city I knew. Soon we were on a train winding up among the neat Dutch-Mediterranean-type crops, across fertile fields. The Dutch possessed none of the joy and arts of the Mediterranean Italians in a climate similar to the Italians', nor the craziness of the Californians. The Dutch brought with them ox-plowing with its terminology. They were adamant and righteous. Why did such a country of nobility and song and color belong to the Dutch? The English spoken there was a Dutch-ified version of English, clipped and precise to make the Kaffirs understand. English people took on the values of the Dutch.

Being colonists was very bad for the Dutch. Their country folk at home in Holland were good quiet people, real Boers, "Bo-ers," people of the earth like the Frisians, like the folk of old Ely—not these adamant lords of the superior race. A break had happened between human being and human being. At this point the cancer of racism had crept in.

The train passed the fields and rose among the Karoo wilds, which was a region of frighteningly bare mountains with no heather in sight, as fascinating as a damned region of hell. I got a real lift out of this. I was *really there*, looking out of the train window at a sight different from anything I had ever seen. I snapped photographs. I thought I was doing something stupendous by taking those pictures—just as those heights were stupendous. The pictures turned out afterwards to be simply the scenes I had taken, harsh and unlovely; in fact those first pictures were just a collection of oddities.

We slept nights on the train and came out to flat-topped trees with black people waiting at the stations. Then eventually we arrived at our destination, Luanshya—a copperbelt town to the north of Lusaka, the capital of Northern Rhodesia. The train stopped.

We looked out onto this strange world. There on the platform stood Vic himself. I grinned. Vic! We were quickly reunited, the children crowding around and hugging. He took us to the station yard to his pick-up truck, then known as a vanette. This was nice; we had never had a car before. We drove off to the home of the good Clyde Mitchell, the director of the Rhodes-Livingstone Institute for Social Research, who was going to put all of us up for a day or two while we laid in flour and stores for our year in the field.

In the interim Clyde had been training Vic in fieldwork methods among the Lamba people. Afterwards Vic had done some preliminary fieldwork among the Ndembu of the north-western province, which was our final goal. Clyde provided us with census forms suitable for African villages. We also bought camera film, lots of it, and extra gas and oil. Vic was supplied with directions, and with information about rest houses and about the mailing system, given pay in advance, and was officially enrolled as research officer of the Rhodes-Livingstone Institute.

It must have been March toward the end of the rainy season when we set out. Rene, age three, and I were seated in the cab of the pickup with Vic, and the two boys, five and seven, were perched among the luggage on the back. We started off, first toward Chingola, the most westerly copperbelt town, and then out further west still beyond Chingola into what seemed nothing, along an insignificant dirt road that wound for 350 miles toward the Ndembu people of Mwinilunga, ending up in a corner of Northern Rhodesia in a high forested area where the borders of Portuguese Angola, the Belgian Congo, and Northern Rhodesia joined. This was in 1951. We understood that the neighboring Portuguese bastinadoed the feet of Africans in punishment, that is, they beat them on the soles, while the Belgians ruled a tropical rain forest of an enormous size about which not much was known. Pygmies lived in the east of the Congo. Our people, the Ndembu, were hoe agriculturists, Bantu in language, with a loose chieftainship system that the British were in process of trying to make firmer. The British policy was always to turn chieftainships into civil service institutions authorized to collect taxes under the crown. The British were "fair" and "benevolent" to their tribes, we were given to understand.

Vic had studied African political systems and was interested in seeing for himself how they worked. Although Max had given Vic a mandate to study ritual, he also made the stern proviso that nothing should be ventured until he had mastered the social structure of the Ndembu to which all symbolism referred and from which it was derived.[3] In other words, ritual was a social construction of reality, a fabrication made by human society, as anthropologists put it later.[4] We were supposed to have learned how social structures themselves were derived: the correct answer was, they were derived from the means of production. We found the opposite. I now see all forms deriving from people keying into the spiritual world.

Necessity had been nudging us into a false philosophical position, but as we set out on that dirt road we were free—free in a wide land of thinly scattered flat-topped trees, sometimes joining together in thick forests. The trees were *leguminosae*, pod-bearers, able to fix nitrogen from the poor, rain-leached, reddish, laterite soil. I gazed at the trees and the blue distances over the brow of the hills and found them beautiful.

I was full of delight, on the out-trail along with Vic. My own attitude had come so adrift from English life that latrines, dirt, even malaria, were preferable to the police-and-traffic worlds, or for that matter the world of China tea and beautiful porcelain. How was I likely to conjure up a critical attitude to Africa when the door had been opened, the life waiting and ahead of me for which I felt I had been groomed, prepared for if only by my own horridness and arrogance? I was to come down, in my deliberate and rebellious humility, not even to the level of mud huts, but to *grass* huts, the lowest of the low, and I was happy.

As the pick-up bumped along I could see for myself that the grass on each side was indeed 8 or 10 feet tall, not in the least like English grass. We passed Africans walking those 350 miles to and from town, jiving as they walked, or playing on their tiny Kaffir pianos, five-inch hollow gourds set with flexible prongs that would play like musical tuning forks. At last we reached the inhabited woods of Mwinilunga that sheltered small mud-hut villages three to a mile, a dozen huts to a village. Their food crop, cassava, was everywhere to be seen. This was a wide-spreading plant ten feet tall, with roots underneath measuring one or two feet long, *makamba*. Everyone lived on *nshima*, a white, stomach-filling pudding made from the large roots.

Vic drove the pickup over a rough wooden bridge and we stopped at a store. This was the township of Mwinilunga. Vic already knew the storekeeper, and warm greetings ensued. A couple of black women were leaning on the counter spreading out their hands in conversation. Vic showed me how to greet them by passing my palms along their palms. I did so and then smiled. I laid my own hands on the counter, hands devoid of keratin, white like egrets' skins are white under the feathers. But they were human hands, useful enough to me, like the black ones also resting on the counter. The black hands showed veins threading over the backs and between the knuckles. So did mine. I pointed to the black veins before me, and traced mine too, smiling at the faces with their recognizing eyes and curved everted lips, which were now grinning. We laughed.

"How do you say, 'the same?'" I asked Vic.

"*A hama, afwana yami.*"

"*A hama, afwana yami,*" I said.

"*Ey-YO! Ku-twesa nehi.*" The women laughed, slapping their sides. "Would you believe it?"

Meanwhile my kids were in a little group, silently watching another little group of kids who were watching them.

Everyone sprang to attention when our purchases were finished, then helpers passed the goods into the pickup truck. We were off to the village (see figure 4.1).

We had a glorious reception, because the village had already grown to like Vic. Now he had come back with his family. I didn't expect what I got. The villagers suddenly gathered and sang a welcome song, simply, "You've arrived, you've arrived!" They began to harmonize it, clapping in rhythm, crowding around, giving us seats in the shelter, presenting us with a chicken. I loved the rich harmonizing. I told myself I would learn it too. But what had I done to deserve this? Why would one lot of people so value another lot? In the non-Christian village I was learning about love. Later I saw the Ndembu do the welcome for their own surgery patients returning from the hospital alive and well. The scene is etched on my mind as a blueprint for

Figure 4.1: Village of Vic and Edie's first fieldwork: Kajima in Zambia in 1951 (photo by Edith Turner)

all welcomes, for all true sociality. How can I argue this? I did learn: in my life since, I myself have given and received these welcomes. I experienced much later (see chapter 14) the total warmth of the Closing of the Small Group Weekend. It showed me and the others what the heavenly kingdom might be like. How could I possibly document the Ndembu's welcome in social science parlance, underplaying it? It was like the "Hallelujah Chorus," Beethoven's "Song of Joy," the "Marseillaise," the ending of the song "For All the Saints," "When the Saints Come Marching In," many wonderful anthems of praise. It was unconditionally intended. It is the song of communitas, and it is the essence of this book.

We had to move on. We had rented a rural rest house, and now we were able to work on our living arrangements, put the children under the day care of a benevolent young man called Zachariah, and organize a work system so that the initial research load panned out. We had a batch of Clyde Mitchell's census forms to fill up, six hundred of them, which for us was the first labor of Hercules. We set out to the villages. Vic completed about 400 of the forms, I did 150, and Isaac the literate assistant, learning the job, did about 50. We discovered that the divorce rate was about three times the English divorce rate.

That census made the basis of a very dull first section of Vic's dissertation and later book. We were supposed to see some great meaning in the divorce finding. Sure, we found there was frequent divorce, which was natural in a system where at the least thing you could run back to mama. Mama was someone important in the village because of "matriliny," descent through the mother. It wasn't surprising. But Vic had five mouths to feed so it was important. I helped him all the time; I, too, wanted to feed my children's mouths as well as possible. The truth was I liked any sort of work that appeared to be needed. I gave the children their lessons in the mornings; in the afternoons they played mud pies with their friends or learned to hunt or dance (see figure 4.2). After the preliminary trip we eventually moved to new grass huts in the village, and it became a grass home we loved.

Vic read children's classics to the young ones at night. The nighttime storytelling developed into a time of thrills and hugs and, at that season, a time of thunderstorms. The children were completely happy and it set them up for happiness for the rest of their lives. I was with Vic all the time and I too was happy, though my cheeks had changed from pink to a sallow tan so that my face seemed dominated by enlarged pores and a long nose. I could still grin, and did. I worked hard and found each day fascinating.

We were living in a rich brew of people. I had a Ndembu friend, Fatima, who took me around to girls' puberty ceremonies, and

Figure 4.2: My daughter Rene and Monica Kajima dancing. Kajima, Zambia 1953 (photo by Edith Turner)

gradually the entire initiation scenario grew clear to me. This came about simply because Vic and I, among the crowd at the coming-out dances, were just extra crowd members, slightly unusual in color but that's all. Vic made friendships among the men just as they made friendships with each other; he was not there as an "investigator" of the place in the sense of "conducting" research (as if it were an orchestra, or a police search). No, we enjoyed the rituals as the others did, only they were newer to us. Apparently they were never stale to the others either, any more than Christmas is stale to us. (I still ask, *why* isn't it?)

How can I describe Vic going off with Musona for a walk up the road to see Sanganyi or some other jolly headman, probably in search of millet beer? Vic called into the kitchen, just as he used to call his friend on the soccer team in Bournemouth to come out to practice—with a kind of beckoning with the head. Musona rapidly wiped his hands on a bit of rag and smoothed his shorts, his knotty smile crinkling up his face. Then he positively leapt out of the kitchen on his spider legs, and the two would be off, Vic "tanking" from side to side (like a tank over rough ground). Vic's black hair would float up in wings on each side as he talked nineteen to the dozen to Musona who was gay and joking. Vic's slightly upturned nose gave nobody, ever, any cause to call him snotty. *He* was snotted on, like the working class. But he was conscious and gay, resistant and tough. He identified with everybody in Kajima, including old Sakazao the sly one, who glowed a little when Vic was around, like an old dog. Vic would give out cigarettes, shooting them out to everybody like bullets.

But for the work: we were supposed to follow the effects of modernization, so we could not stay for long in the "backward" regions but had to move again and make a camp in the serpent's nest of the modern trading chiefdom of Ikeleng'e. Serpents' nests were "good" material for anthropology, it seemed. But even after the move in 1951, when we made visits back to the rural area we saw healing ceremonies, for example, the Ihamba, which we studied in detail. We actually saw trance, yet we reckoned that all we were watching was some woman we didn't know out of control and in an odd mental state. I pointed the camera and the scene came out in sinister light. In spite of the sinister light we later supplied the caption in cold matter-of-fact style: "Ihembi 'catching' an *ihamba* tooth. The patient is quite dissociated." In vain the people had tried to tell us: "This *is* the spirit, man. It *is*." But no, it was a psychological condition we had seen, "dissociation," expressed in "symbols." Symbolism.

Dear god, let me calm down and tell the story. Because later still, in 1975, Vic did see through the lie. He wrote down everything; in 1975 he managed to write down the true spirituality of an even greater ritual, the Chihamba ritual, for he had been reading the mystics again. But at the time of experiencing Ihamba and the Chihamba ritual in 1953 he was supposed to be a party member.

Now I am proud to maintain that the party did an indispensable job for Vic and me. Without knowing it, it had nudged us both through the membrane of the elite into the really beloved world of the non-elite, the ordinary people, and that for good. Neither of us could ever renege on these folk. We *knew* the superior moneyed classes, their wealth-loaded camels jammed in the eye of the needle. They were done for. Also, it was through the party that Vic's eyes were opened to the very precious "thing-mysticism" of the Ndembu, something that could also be termed *spiritual* materialism, the sense that everything is holy. Thank the party for that too, though the members would have no idea what it was. When we returned to England Vic was forced to translate mystical matters into academic terminology to gain his Ph.D. As for Party officials, as distinct from the genuine leaders of the ordinary people, they would tear their garments at the very notion of thing-mysticism. They were pure positivist materialists without a crack in their armor. We had escaped the structures of their hidebound system by slipping down a crack in it—a crack they had not noticed. This crack dwelt in the very nature of things. What we saw was this. A crack is given to humankind in its very biology, in the chrysalis stage of puberty, when the child becomes something quite different for a time, before finally unfolding into adulthood. There is no such thing as gradual development. There is a time of apparent stasis during the rite of passage where in Africa the individual is secluded; but far from being a time of stasis, things are happening off-stage which verge upon the eerie.

I became very familiar with the girl's rite of passage. The first one in which I joined was for the girl Ikubi. My older friend, Fatima, was her midwife. "Midwife" implies the one to bring her into the world of adulthood, or a facilitator of biological change. First Ikubi was a "baby," and a "dead" person too. The women laid her passive body down on an antelope skin in the woods, in the bosom of nature. The place was important. It was at the foot of a young tree that exuded milk from its leaves, and there she lay, curled up like a fetus, and the women covered her from head to foot with a blanket. The milk, just by its presence, exuded its benison upon the "dead" body, fertilizing it, electrifying it with a new sexuality. She could not help but sleep, she was enchanted. In full daylight she lay asleep while high festival raged around her, with folk drumming, dancing, leaping from side to side, clapping, chanting boisterous and salacious songs (see figure 4.3). She was asleep. Was it trance?

Not until sunset did they come back to her body in the *ifwilu*, the death place, to bear her body like a corpse and also like a womb-enclosed baby into its new dwelling, far from its real mother. Ikubi the puberty girl woke from her trance with twenty new mothers, who were the entire band of village women. Into the rafters of the new grass hut the women placed a small string of white beads.

Figure 4.3: Initiation girl lying in the place of death or trance (photo by Edith Turner)

"*Diyi mukishi*; this is the spirit of the mothers," they said. This was about thirty beads on a string. The idea was, any one of them could be your future child, you can have your pick. But you mustn't look at them.

What is this mystery initiation in the middle of ordinary life?

It goes on. In the privacy of the seclusion hut during her three months' stay, the midwife and the women again take her and lay her down on her side. The midwife herself lies down facing her closely. The girl's elbow is crooked out, and the midwife's head rests comfortably on the crook. They begin. The heat in the two bodies on the floor grows. This can be as hot as it likes. Both bodies are moving stomach to stomach, a belly dance for two, they cannot help it, woman to woman. Very soon the midwife causes the young girl to flower open like a lily; the eyes of both feminine beings faint and the eyeballs rise to heaven, this is it. Meanwhile the sister-women gather all around crooning an African jive in rhythm, with beauty in their voices and sheer delight in their souls.

I watch, sighing. They call it the dance on the bed: a bride trained like this is guaranteed to make the shyest bridegroom grant his arrow, his bride price for such a paragon.

This is only the seclusion as yet. After three months of training in the art of eros and in the supreme coming-out dance of the moving breasts, the coming-out day dawns. The women enter the hut and bear the girl away to a secluded spot to be anointed and garbed for her final display. First they hide the white beads in the part of her hair. Then, dressed like a queen, breasts bare, enswathed with beads, she flits again into the bush to emerge suddenly into the midst of the entire population of the region that has gathered with drums in the plaza for her moment of annunciation. She charges in, strikes the drum, rises in triumph and—look, she is fully-teated, naked to the gift of her swelling domes, fearless as a hunter with a gun—which she actually carries—a gun; she's black, in ecstasy, all a-dance from head to foot, and she's harnessed on her back and calves with susurrating rattles (see figure 4.4). Who can bear not to do this dance, not to ride through this rite of passage?

As I watched the girl's initiation I saw how they literally hid her in the seclusion hut, and hid the things they did to celebrate her majority. The things they hid were anomalies. There is a huge anomaly in human life to start with. One's daughter grows up and is surely going to have her own ménage. "But she is *my* daughter," says the mother. "That person is *mine*, I gave birth to her. She'll always be mine. What are you saying?"

I was disturbed when the mother of a tuberculosis girl patient of eighteen tried (in vain) to prevent me and another helper from taking

Figure 4.4: She's in ecstasy, all a-dance from head to foot. The final initiation dance (photo by Edith Turner)

the sick girl to the sanitarium. The mother reckoned the girl was supposed to stay and dig for her, even though the girl was dying. The girl had been too sick to escape into marriage. The mother feels: "Break from me? That cannot be!"

"Look at the way I was when I was a kid," I told myself. I had been engorged with the spirit of independence. For a girl at that age, nothing is stable, nobody belongs to anybody. A process almost akin to flying is taking place with adolescents, there is no other way to describe it, like a bird learning to fly. But we are heavy humans, and with what big aches and wanderings inside us!

No, among these people from way back in Africa, young girls had a surprise coming up, the surprise of that great display.

I failed at the time to trace *how* this initiation came to be in the first place. Later I found I could trace the secret origin of most ritual.

Certain people were instructed by spirits what to perform and how to do it. There is plenty of documentation for this, including the prime case of the rituals in *Black Elk Speaks*.[5] Then I wondered what was the origin of laying the girl on the ground in front of a milk tree and covering her with skins, then calling it death. This "death" was like stumbling into a deep hole, lost, yet in the hands of all the women. Now this is very sexy. Sex—which happens in spite of one, just as sleep does and the restorative processes—comes up under negative capability, like art, like the shaman touched by the wild animal which comes of its own free will as a helper. The girl, flung down as it were in a dark hole, still cared for, in a womb of burning beauty and ecstasy, the colors roiling inside her, knows she must stay still or—or else, as with inspiration, you could blink your eye and the ability would be gone. And what was this all about?

One sees anomaly after anomaly in the initiation world: a super-attractive world that is like nothing else, not like hut-building, cooking, digging. Not like quarreling with your sister. Just a matter of this: stay still and it will come. Now there you get the sense again!

Is sex just a physical thing? Is its awakening comprehensible to the psychologist? Biggest question of all, are the customs of initiation those of "Power I," that is, obedience to the mores, serving the men—in a word, social structures?

How could they be? Something else was going on, and Vic and I later called the phenomenon, whatever it was, "liminality," found in the liminal or threshold stage in the rite of passage. We documented both the girls'[6] and the boys' rites and, item after item, we identified the points that were not part of the "structure" picture, that were off the chart: for the girls these were: taking her away from her mother; the public indecency of the songs; the hidden white beads which they called the spirit; her mentor chosen from a generation not her mother's; the defiance of the women; her identity as dead, as a baby, and as a mother all in one; her disappearance like a spirit just before her public dance; the testing of her husband on their first night together—all was in contradiction to the structures of society. These were "spirit" characteristics, not structural ones.

Primarily one is confronted with the death feature. You die to the old life and are born into the new. "Die" is a rather strong word, not used in graduation ceremonies in the United States. Were these Africans mad, or morbid-minded? Incidentally, why was this "die to live" feature also a favorite of Christianity?

"Death" here is the membrane from one recognizable world into another. The idea of something beyond death, and the consciousness of sometimes being in a different world, is to be found everywhere.

The spirit beads involved in initiation, the white beads, were very secret. Didn't they represent the matrilineage, though? Weren't they just a fancy of the people so that the girl would respect her mother and grandmother better? Charms, fetishes, magic; weren't they merely that?

Try following down those beads and the sense of recognition in those who kept them clean and safe from one generation to another. "This is the spirit of the mothers, from generation to generation"— "*Diyi mukishi*." They kept saying it plainly, like "This is my body." They recognized the beads as what I now, in 2005, translate by the word, "an actuality."

For decades after the fifties I had been looking for such a word—a word for a symbol which meant "the thing itself is holy, not just what it means"—in other words, a sacrament. At last, at the big national anthropology meetings in December 1988 Michael Harner and I had breakfast together and came up with a word for "sacrament" that might cover all religions and not just Christianity, when used in the same kind of context. This was the word, "actuality"—meaning the actual thing, an actuality. The Africans sometimes had sacramental objects which *were* the spirit, "*diyi mukishi*," with an understanding of the holiness of them, and that they were *the spirit itself*, just as in Christianity. Native Americans know animals with this character. Vic Turner wrote briefly about the matter in *Revelation and Divination*.[7] I now see a little better what the sacredness of an object implies as compared with what symbols and metaphors are doing. I recognize that what we are dealing with in ritual are often different from symbols.

Vic and I knew of other African initiations, among the Yao, Bemba,[8] Thonga, and Nyakyusa. We simply couldn't see them as straight representations of respect for the customs. They were hung about with indications of spirituality, here, there, and everywhere.

However, at this stage in 1951 we were writing down straight ethnography and had merely developed a fondness for and wonder at "the drums," *ngoma*, a word meaning both "drum" and "ritual healing." I remember that at lesser moments we thought the rituals constituted a kind of overplus of culture, a version of play, something people did to add to the interest of life. We tended to think they were mumbo jumbo, mere custom. Even so, when looked at closely, girl's initiation was a complex mysterious performance, more like the chrysalis stage of a butterfly than anything else; in 1951 a theoretical way to handle such a phenomenon was yet to be found. We never compared those rituals to church services. In my memory the Anglican services consisted of a series of reminders to be good, an hour in a lordly arched place, and a period mildly enhanced with hymns with a moral meaning. They were not primarily a "perfor-mance," nor were they effective in their own right. The Jesus story was a bit of heroic history like many other bits. However, the Jesus story was surrounded with dread and awe, scary, for a reason no one seemed to understand; one's heart was supposed to beat faster at the thought, and it did, as if one had done something wrong. I think I was instilled with a hidden feeling I had murdered Jesus and was likely to murder him all the time. I grew to avoid the idea of Jesus above all things: religion was false, and wrongfully made you afraid, suborning the will. It was like being stalked by someone who wanted to stir you up sexually, someone you dreaded, who wanted to control you. Someone was out to hook you, obsess you; and there was that holy accusing stare of the religious. So I steered clear of it.

Whatever that memory was, the trip to Africa cleared out all traces of it. Meanwhile Vic was busy with his own social anthropological agenda, intimately social, a kind of anthropology that came to be called "local level politics."[9] He was filling up bits and pieces of a notable ongoing feud between an able man who was a sorcerer and the village respectables. Vic liked the sorcerer personally. He liked him better than the others.

Let's look with emotional sympathy at the story of the sorcerer in its deep past. Samatamba was a man who had real charisma. Way back in the past he began to exploit the attraction of his own particu-lar personality. He was handsome with a kind of thrawn Humphrey Bogart or Han Solo charm, a propensity to grin and to show a bit of extra power, to fix things for his friends, to rollick around and get things done. As several decades passed he became accustomed to using these gifts for the sake of power. Anything but a shy man, he was ebullient, a leader. He went to the copperbelt and got a job, suc-ceeded, and enjoyed his beer. Anything went, on the copperbelt, so he took up with a woman he didn't know. Then he found he had devel-oped gonorrhea, a disease of yellow pus in the semen. He must have endured this trouble for thirty years. He came home after a decade on the copperbelt, now well-experienced in the white man's world, and walked into the chief road man's job at Mwinilunga, called *capitaõ*. He married two wives from his local major lineage, one of whom was linked to the power structure of the village of Kajima. She was the headman's daughter. Samatamba, whom we ourselves loved and in whom, somehow, we felt no evil, used to get drunk and badmouth the whole village. The most human of Ndembu, he was the worst. He killed by witchcraft, by the power of his anger. I know this is possible. I have been ill through people's anger, and have myself caused bad things to happen by my own anger, which I truly regret.

The Africans said Samatamba bewitched his favorite aunt to death, so they drove him out of the village. The shouting must have been terrible—the gathering of men, the positive danger from blows and thrown weapons. He must have rushed home and grabbed his hunting gun, his ax, his knife, and one or two oddments—medicine horns, it was thought—in a shoulder basket. He went raging north up the road to the trading chief at Ikeleng'e.

But the village performed a reconciliation for Samatamba. I now find the reconciliation episode more interesting than I did formerly. The dead aunt was now an ancestor spirit; she had been a good woman. Her name, Nyamwaha, actually meant "good woman," just that. What those people felt was this: that the spirit of this dead person Nyamwaha wanted to "come out" in another person. So people watched for it. Whoever felt that something of the kind was going on inside them was beginning to take notice. This was close to the idea of reincarnation; it was the metempsychosis of a spirit into an already living person. The Ndembu called it "the inheritance of a name" or "becoming the dead person," *ku-swanika ijina.*

It was my dear, spiritually minded friend Manyosa, the daughter of Nyamwaha, who was affected by this compelling spirit. She felt that her mother was near, asking again and again for her spirit to be taken into her own daughter. Now, much later, I can see the contrast with the earlier interpretation made by Vic and myself, which was that the ritual was merely a renaming. Much later I realized from my own various experiences of the dead that the Africans were right about these intimations: one can indeed sense the ancestors. Back in the 1950s—whether or not I had any insight—when I saw the ritual of Naming I particularly saw its beauty. It featured a section of a tree sapling planted as a shrine, its bark stripped at the top like a circumcised penis, its wood running with clear sap like semen; while the two principal women, Manyosa and her friend Yana, sat near the shrine-tree wearing white cloth headbands. Drumming and a keening chant broke forth, then the medicine man poured white maize beer on the ground at the foot of the planted tree. This kind of tree was the ancestor tree itself, able to quicken and send out shoots when planted, even though it had been brutally cut off at both ends. *Muyombu* was its name, a holy thing that one might call the "tear tree" because it wept (see figure 4.5).

Now that the songs had called the spirit, the two women drank the white beer and were sprinkled with medicine; and forthwith the spirit jumped over from the ancestor into them.

This wiped the slate of that trouble, even though Samatamba was not the principal figure in the rite. Nyamwaha was now back with them, empowering the fertility of the village, spreading goodness as

Figure 4.5: Connecting with the ancestors in front of the weeping tree. The Ndembu Naming ritual, Zambia (photo by Edith Turner)

before. Vic and I wrote down notes on the rite as an ethnographic exercise of close observation and were therefore never to forget it. However, it took me forty-eight years to even partially understand it.

We have to note that the story of Samatamba did not come to an end after the name inheritance, but continued in a way typical of him. He was back in the village and trouble began again. It was to do with Samatamba's wife Zuliyana, the daughter of the headman. The worst effect of being abandoned by the ancestors is sterility, and Zuliyana was not giving birth. Samatamba had no children because of his gonorrhea, and that only made him drink more. Both Zuliyana and her mother Nyamukola, the headman's wife, were in deep misfortune, Zuliyana from childlessness, and Nyamukola from leprosy. It was December, the time of high storms, terrible heat, and malaria-inducing chills. Bad times had come again. In the swamp-like miasma of the people's depression, could anyone find hope?

At night we could hear Samatamba's bellowing voice cursing the village, "*Wa-a-a-anza wey-ey-yi!* Dirt under your foreskin!"

The story of Samatamba portrayed a people on its own path—the Ndembu in their own saga, a saga we should treat with deepest sympathy. This was no mere story, but their own pitifully destined path, down from conflict, from anomaly, from the rift in the system between descent through a woman and marriage in the husband's house, down, down, down, step by step.

It was *their* path. For Samatamba it was a helpless social fall, fate itself, becoming transformed into a dreaded path, down to the terrors that form when many things go wrong, caused by who knows what witchcraft, what disgust and abandonment by the ancestors. Then indeed one asks in reality, what spirit it was that finally took up Kajima Village in its misery and fears and set it going once more to perform the ritual of Chihamba, in which the village ventured along the woodland path to the Isoli revelation shrine of the thunder god himself? Now in this ritual, the villagers were going to have to "kill" the thunder god to reverse the whole process, for this is what he himself, the thunder god, commanded them to do.

There were medicine men living in the vicinity whose job it was to lay an ear to the people's troubles, not as a doctor might begin to combat measles, but more like the way the prophets in the Old Testament received messages from their spiritual entity and started listening to the people floundering in their mess, finally leading them out of it. The growth of healing would be mutual, in this case a kind of simultaneous stirring by some of the Kajima lineage who had been given spirit help before, and the spirit masters, Lambakasa, Itota, and the diviner, those who were gifted to hear the spirits quite plainly. It is said that the villagers asked the diviner for his instructions. And the diviner said, "Go to Chihamba. Go to the Grandfather. He will help you."

So the greatest of the Ndembu rituals was set afoot, with Vic and me like little mirrored buzz flies with cameras hovering around everywhere taking things in. Additional patients volunteered from the outlying villages. I lined up among the patients, Vic joined the medicine men. The rituals began.

We patients were chased in and out of the forest for twelve hours, further and further in, and out and out again, until finally on the inward path we were drawn close to what we began to see as some sort of goal out there in the forest. We were tired, persecuted, and humiliated by the adepts. Yet we were excited. The adepts talked about "The Grandfather," nobody's particular grandfather, but the grandfather of all.

By now we patients had come to know each other well. Also each of us had a "friend of the bosom," a sponsor, from among the adepts; I had Manyosa. The column of patients, led by the leper Nyamukola, and after her, the childless Zuliyana, went forward to the end of the path, attended by a fringe of adepts around us. Everyone was excited. What we saw in front of us was something blazing white in the dim forest light. Something that moved; and we heard music, the drums, a keening harmony, syncopation. The white thing became clear now, it was an *Isoli*, a Sighting, something unexpected, quite strange. It was moving back and forth, dancing to the off-beat rhythm, a round dome rising from the earth, vibrating voluptuously to the rhythm of the drums, filling our eyes with whiteness (see figure 4.6).

"It is the spirit! It is the Grandfather," chanted Lambakasa the medicine man beside us, susurrating loud with his two-chambered rattle. All our toes were twitching with the rhythm. We sang and sang in praise of the Grandfather.

But it was time for the killing which we knew had to be done. First, each patient in turn went forward, crouched to the ground, and hailed Him, "*Karombo vrai*, Chief!" and the women milked their breasts before Him.

Figure 4.6: Something blazing white, moving back and forth. The thunder god of the Ndembu (photo by Edith Turner)

Figure 4.7: Healing a wounded tree root (photo by Edith Turner)

Then Lambakasa placed the rattle in Nyamukola's hand. "Kill," he said. "You must kill your Grandfather."

She leaned over and struck the jiving Thing with the butt of the rattle. Crack. There was something very solid beneath the white. It shook, convulsed, and died.

Each of us, including me, came forward in turn and struck it. "You have killed the Grandfather," chanted Lambakasa.

I had only just learned to love the Grandfather when I had to kill Him. But the blow seemed to cause things to jump a notch. As soon as I had done it I had a foolish grin on my face. Every one of us came alight—we were full of glee, in fact our eyes were sprung open with happiness. Why was this? Why? Somehow we had set the spirit free from what was a white cloth with a wooden mortar beneath, and the spirit was now with all of us. "*Diyi mukishi*, it is the spirit. And now you are all innocent," came the words of Lambakasa.

Figure 4.8: Samatamba and his fertility shrine (photo by Edith Turner)

The finale was coming. We each took rattles and paired off with our bosom friends, I with Manyosa, Vic with Samatamba, all the others in company with their bosom friends, two by two. We walked back along a wide alley of the forest to the village, singing and happy in the setting sun. Even now I remember that moment as one of the four great happy moments of my life, and it was the happiest for the Ndembu too. All were cured. They had come down the woodland path. The path had literally led them to the *njila*, the way; *chinjila* means holiness.

That path was clear, that time. But as for my life-path as a white person, it was still a twisted path through which I was jostled, not by my own will. How could I know then that the Africans were right? These were pagans, animists. In 1953 no one in the West believed in African animism, no one. Yet as our fieldwork progressed, as the scene in Africa rose for us more and more, in ritual after ritual, we realized that not only had I escaped the old cruel hypocritical Christianity, but that even

Figure 4.9: Home in Africa, 1951. Our mud hut in Zambia (photo by Edith Turner)

Figure 4.10: Home in Africa. Children Bob and Rene with flowers (photo by Edith Turner)

Figure 4.11: Home in Africa. Children Fred, Bob, and Rene, in the Zambezi rapids (photo by Edith Turner)

the positivist "means-of-production" determinism was falling behind, that we had eaten up Marxism already, it was a thing of the past.

Still, what Vic and I were supposed to do was to see and hear all we could and to simply go on recording. We harvested rich material; and attended to the family (see figures 4.9-4.12). We were working in the dark except for that one flash of communitas at the big village ritual, Chihamba. We just plowed on.

In our dull consciousnesses a certain fact jiggled into focus and resolved itself: that we weren't studying political structures, and that we had been encouraged by Max Gluckman to study the Ndembu because of the plentiful ritual.

"If so, I may to be able to change my dissertation topic," said Vic, when we realized what rich material we were looking at. "I'll write to Max, he's my chairman. I'd better discuss it."

Figure 4.12: Home in Africa. Edie in the bush (photo in the possession of Edith Turner)

Max wrote back saying it was okay to study ritual. But he reminded Vic that in his dissertation he was primarily required to set out the ecology, social structure, and political system, and to use the proper anthropological way to relate them. When Vic brought the Chihamba ritual into the dissertation he would need to show how it was related to the social structure. Furthermore, Chihamba should be shown as part of the social process. Process was the putting into motion of structures and forms, the switching on of the machine as it were and seeing it in operation. Max felt that this kind of dissertation was a necessary preliminary for further explorations (see figure 4.13).

Figure 4.13: Victor Turner's Ph.D. graduation, Vic Turner (left), with Derek Allcorn, 1955 (photo by Edith Turner)

Vic loved social process and was working deeply in it already. But he also held in his hand the complete documentation of the Chihamba ritual with its curious consciousness of a demigod—this was shining like a light. Yes, he would do what Max suggested for the sake of the children, but after that, let academia see![10]

Notes

1. Doris Lessing, *Under My Skin: Volume One of my Autobiography* (London, 1995).
2. See Victor Turner, *The Forest of Symbols: Aspects of Ndembu Ritual* (Ithaca, NY, 1967). Later in the Manchester department an interest developed in the curious way rituals managed to "cloak" [sic] the troubles that accrued from the underlying faulty psychology of the people, due to what one might call dysfunctional social structures. As regards the party, before I went to the field in 1951 I understood that as a party member it was my duty to set ritual on one side, or record it as opium for the people.
3. In the manner of Meyer Fortes, *The Dynamics of Clanship among the Tallensi* (London, 1945), and Meyer Fortes and E. E. Evans-Pritchard, eds., *African Political Systems* (London, 1940).
4. A recent influential example of this theory is Roy Rappaport, *Religion and Ritual in the Making of Humanity* (Cambridge, 1999).
5. John Neihardt, *Black Elk Speaks: Being the Life Story of a Holy Man of the Oglala Sioux.* As told through John G. Neihardt (New York, 1932).
6. Victor Turner, *The Drums of Affliction* (Oxford, 1968).
7. Victor Turner, *Revelation and Divination* (Ithaca, NY, 1975) chapter 3.
8. Audrey Richards, *Chisungu: A Girl's Initiation Ceremony among the Bemba of Zambia* (London, 1982 [1956]).
9. See Victor Turner, *Schism and Continuity in an African Society* (Manchester, UK, 1957).
10. The section on revelation, called "Chihamba, the White Spirit," appeared in Victor Turner, *Revelation and Divination* (Ithaca, NY, 1975).

5

HAIRPIN BEND

Here I have to hunt in my memory for the trail. In 1954 we wandered back from the field to Manchester, England, with the three kids alive and well. Perforce—according to English law—they would have to be shoved into school. I felt it as shoving because their experience in Africa would mean little to the teachers and the children would surely forget all about it once school started. I mourned the loss of Africa for them, as I mourned the loss myself.[1]

Yet I had a dream. I dreamed I was back in Kajima. My heart quivered at the sight of the overgrown track at the entrance and then the plaza opening out as I moved toward the center meeting hut. I saw the people there—Manyosa, who did not look at me; all the others. Everything was taken for granted. The women fell behind as I walked on. I put out a hand to greet someone; no hand touched mine, but everyone was present, their faces relaxed. My heart expanded with happiness. I was actually back. Joy and certainty spread until my range of sight opened out to the entire village. I seemed to glide into the whole of it. I was it, lifted from touch and tread. I was home.

From the perspective of 2005, far in the future of those days, I mourn still more. For me when I look back on Africa I see in my mind an unfillable gap resting permanently over Kajima village, starting in 1954 when we left. Now the gap is worse than ever. This is because I have been playing, or in a sense, conversing in my conscious soul with those dead ancestors, and by all that's holy they are not dead. Come, my dear friends, Manyosa and Yana and Yana's flowering son, comfort your friend here. That hand on my shoulder, please, a puff of your African kiss, your breath in my ear. Thanks. I shiver.

Notes for this section can be found on page 100.

Back in the decade of 1955 in Manchester I set to work to write what I had seen and done in Kajima, what I actually experienced. I wrote it out on one hundred single-spaced pages in pencil, on extra-long paper. Then other things intervened and I put away the sheaf of pages in a drawer. From time to time I pulled them out again and worked on them. Thirty years later to my surprise the manuscript was accepted, by that time enlarged and edited. How was I to know, at my crude level of writing in 1955, whether it might actually be published? My only comment now is, there is nothing like letting black marks go onto paper, they do last somewhat.

My "Kajima" piece consisted of just the "living moment" material. Such a style was not used in anthropological writing at the time, so the purpose of writing the piece was for me alone, confirming in me— anchoring firmly in me—the understanding that the living moment is precious. It was my private opinion that it was the basic stuff of anthropology. I didn't mind that there was no audience for my tales. I felt the method was a natural fact. At least I knew that living moments had been experienced by others—such as the Africanists who attended the Manchester department seminars with Vic and me.

A general atmosphere of "social process" theory in that department always lent it warmth. It was remarkable how innocent and free from ingrown theory that department was, compared to Cambridge anthro-pology with its high-class systematizing and particularly Oxford with its abstract symbolism and fanatical worship of "structure." We in Manchester were busy telling stories to each other, relating extended cases of conflict, laying out law cases, and tracing social dramas (see figure 5.1). Of necessity when using such a method, much of the time we looked at events from the grass-roots up. I was involved with every-thing anthropological and worked on large sectors of Vic's dissertation.

There was also another agenda going on in my life. It was a pity that it happened at all, but after the dissertation was finished the Communist party secretly got hold of me again and thrust me into the thriving Campaign for Nuclear Disarmament, undoubtedly a good thing in itself. However, this was in 1957, in the notorious 1950s, one of the worst decades of the century across the world. Other bad eras were those of the wars, the 1919 flu epidemic, and the economic cata-strophe of the late 1920s. In 1957 everything was unstuck from every-thing. The working class was certainly unstuck from communism; why shouldn't it be? International politics were crammed with poi-son. I suddenly dropped the movement like a hot brick. It happened like this.

A monster peace meeting which I was supposed to have led turned out to be full of little corruptions and it was depressing me. Just one

Figure 5.1: Manchester anthropology department members, 1956. From left to right, front line, Professor Max Gluckman, Bill Watson, Ian Cunnison, Sheila Cunnison, Tom Lupton. Back line Mary Gluckman, Thelma Lupton, Vic Turner (photo by Edith Turner)

day before it was scheduled my body crashed on me—which my hard-working mind wouldn't have let happen. I got a total migraine, exactly covering the last planning sessions and the meeting itself, a meeting which therefore had to be run by someone else. It was the end of my alliance with the left wing because I recognized what was happening.

The physical attack of migraine was reflected at other levels too. Though the black predicament was finished, my life wasn't finished with blackness. I was damaged in some way. The ending of the party era went searing deep in me—not just because of the fall of an idol but a kind of amputation of something, a lack of comprehension of what was going on and where I actually was in the world. Now indeed was the time when "At length the Man perceives it die away / And fade into the light of common day," as Wordsworth said of the light that brightens the time of childhood.[2] It was no use saying that I went into a classical depression. I did indeed, but that is just a clinical term. Vic was busy teaching as a junior lecturer. The children were at school. I was wandering in a dark limbo, not having tried anything properly, not even having failed in any art, never really wanting to be a politician, having lost the fragile sense of community of Kajima Village which was now hopelessly out of my reach. Vic drank wine and seemed absent from the problem. I felt, "bully for him"; I myself was a nothing.

I really cannot understand how women who have given beautiful-ly manufactured blood to the fetuses of their children, who made the supreme effort to expel those babies out of their bodies, who gave them the very milk from their breasts—then are supposed to hand them all over, to lose their children, to schoolteachers! In what way does that follow? Someone's enslaving us and as it were getting us to build a house without our understanding what is going on, then because the system had it all planned, taking the house right away, along with much humiliation. What did we do wrong? We've been farmed, like cows. Now we moo pitifully for our lost calves. All quite correct, that's farming.

Yet was even this picture the right one?

The blackness persisted. Day after day it was bad. I've had bad times, but this was the worst. I would go into the front room by the glass cabinet and moan, mourn, keen, the tears pouring down. I can see that black-lacquered glass cabinet now. What was it that I was going on about? I didn't know.

Something else was going on.

Vic had been pondering deeply on the rituals he had experienced—especially Chihamba: the ritual of the absent god; the running; the ordeals. Vic was a man who had once truly felt with the mystics, Meister Eckhart, Yacob Boehme, St. John of the Cross. Now in 1958 Vic and I were facing a crisis; the party had come to pieces in our hands. Both of us kept thinking of Africa. Vic had written his dissertation as required, bringing the ritual of Chihamba into it merely to show how the organizing of a ritual could unite a shattered community, an argument he gave in the last chapter of the book of the dissertation, *Schism and Continuity*. He knew very well what the ritual was actually saying, but that was not destined for the dissertation. Vic's flooding speculations about how to deal with the ritual had had to wait. But the analysis of ritual and symbol was taking form in spite of all, alive and branching before him like the medicine man's quickset tree-shrine. Was the clue to Chihamba to be found in the analysis of its symbols according to the Freudian way Vic had garnered from psychology? Or was the clue somehow in the very fact of the active *performance* of the ritual? But how could that be? There were only more questions instead of answers.

As for me, I was slowly going mad, crammed between the materialist world views of anthropology and left-wing politics, and stuck in the matter-of-fact Manchester city attitude to life. Sex might be all right for the enlightened to talk about, but any idea that the rituals of the Africans really mattered to us was taboo. That would be treating them as religion. So all that fluid warmth was closed off, and there was nothing in life but back kitchens and gas cookers. So I thought in my loneliness. But Vic was starting his own Chihamba analysis, weighing whether to use Marxist guidelines or his own developing theory of ritual. He was beginning to see that the means of production and their resulting social structures were not sufficient as an explanation of the phenomenon of religion as a cultural manifestation. That was a negative way to put it. There was more. Okay, Freud could show the polarization of a symbol—but that too was materialistic: the idea was that the sensory part of a symbol gave driving force to the socially required duty of virtue whose commands were embedded in the object, an object like a cross or a flag or an eagle clutching arrows.

Yet a jump from Freud was necessary in order to understand the desperate seeking of spirit help during human quarrels and sickness, situations in which people somehow found themselves projected through the membrane that separated their ordinary brittleness from some great experience of ambient oneness. Vic had been beyond that membrane before. The Africans knew about it. One gets flashes, quite unconnected with rational theory—of an influx of something, an ingress from without.

Perhaps, we thought, it would help us if we tried some comparative research in the religions—actual fieldwork in religion, not textual analysis. Maybe there was something in Western religion that paralleled the beauty, seriousness, and effectiveness of what we had seen in Africa, unlike the flat moralism and cruelty and sheer deadness of what I had seen as a child. Here we were, settled in Manchester. We could look at religion in modern everyday industrial England, in Manchester, or even better, in Stockport, its adjoining cotton city. Vic and I discussed it. I leapt at the idea. I always delighted in research.

So we started in the industrial town of Stockport, near Manchester and near our home. We went first to an Anglican service in a old Gothic church that was beautiful but dead. The vicar surprised us by instructing the congregation that to fight the devil you had to use the devil's weapons. We gathered he was talking about the hydrogen bomb. We left and went to a Quaker meeting, and sat for an hour in silence and nothing happened. (It was enough to make one laugh, but of course that was not the whole story about Quakerism.) We went to the Presbyterians' service, and dutifully sang hymns among respectable people; then left. Somehow no.

There was a drift, a pull, a weakening of the membrane. In the field Vic had read St. John of the Cross's mystic poetry. Vic's own poetry had been pouring out of him: "I cry and cry on the salt sea verge ... for yesteryear." He was making an invocation. He kept writing this kind of poetry, it's all down there in black and white. Crying. Africa had opened him up and he had become far too much for the Communist Party to cope with, with its hideous rationality and moralism.

We both of us broke through, and this is how it happened.

We were considering going to the Unitarian church. Its imposing spire dominated a dingy crossroads near the ancient and blackened medieval marketplace of Stockport where I used to buy my children's pajamas as seconds. But we had come at the wrong time that Sunday; the Unitarian church door was locked. A sign said, "Service at 12 A.M."

Hesitating at the crossroads, we looked around in case there were other churches. We didn't quite know what to do. On the right was an alleyway, and the moment we glanced that way it became crowded with people pouring out of a church at the far end. They were mostly Irish cotton-mill girls in shirtwaist dresses. A very pretty lot they seemed to be, chattering gaily with the men.

"'Tis the Catholic Church," said one of the girls.

H'm. Those image-worshipers? Papists? However, I liked the girls and their young men. They passed, and then in the empty street I felt a hand take my shoulder and propel me down the alley toward the church. Vic felt this too. I looked around, but there was no one doing any shoving. Interesting. We grinned at each other as we felt ourselves propelled along. We approached the grimy church along with other people and followed inside along with them. Then we gaped. We were in a different world. Saints in red and blue looked down in blessing; a haze of something like wood smoke filled the air, giving the stained-glass windows a dim beauty. Symbols were painted on the ceiling, while tones of plainchant sounded softly. Way down in front we saw an altar, which was obviously used. There were candles everywhere, forests of candles before each saint, golden candlesticks, much gold everywhere. We sat down, enchanted. Old women pushed by us dangling black rosaries, which they proceeded to mutter over and click.

"Vic! It's like Africa!"

"Quiet."

People crossed themselves—which I'd never seen done before. Was this some kind of self-immolation? Cutting themselves into four pieces? (I laughed later at the thought.) I was nervous of doing such a thing. If I did it to myself I'd never be the same again, I'd be for it. I flubbed the gesture somehow.

A young priest came out clad in white and embroidered robes. He stood swaying with the prayers, chanting Latin, which Vic and I knew. My hair began to rise. This was ancient.

"*Introibo* ..." "I shall enter," the future tense. "*Kwingisha*," in Ndembu, the "going-in" stage of a rite of passage.

The rite proceeded. It was all there, the going in, and then the strange liminal world. At last came the moment of sacrifice. With an almost terrifying obeisance the priest bowed into the hollow cup and uttered words, *"Hoc est enim Calix Sanguinis mei* (this is the cup of my blood),"* knelt, rose, and lifted the big chalice. I looked up. Down from the stained-glass windows I saw a broad stream of sunlight descending right into the chalice. Why, this was the Holy Grail, wasn't it, evanescent, the same, seen by King Arthur? My skin prickled and I shivered. "Oh, yes! Yes!" It was.

Vic and I looked at each other. We smiled.

Then the shared meal as in Africa.

Afterwards we came out and stood on the corner again, quite fulfilled, not merely in our anthropological hunger. Why, this was it.

We went to see the priest to take instruction. This wasn't research any more, this was serious. The result was that every Tuesday evening for six months in the cold church we and the three children listened to the old priest teaching us. We were finally received.

Meanwhile Vic got hold of a heap of books by Catholic writers, which he read aloud to me and sometimes to the children: Evelyn Waugh, G.K. Chesterton, Louis de Wohl, *The Shoes of the Fisherman*, Graham Greene, Péguy, Gilson, Butterfield, Knox, and even a book by Baron Corvo called *Hadrian VII*, which I now see as a little crazy and extremely right wing. But it thrilled me then. These books contained writing that was not purely missionary and moralistic in purpose but was rich with the visionary content for which we had been starving.

Vic discovered that his old army friend, John Bate, had long since become a Catholic. He was now an ally. We saw the gentleness of John's good wife with their children, and saw how they prayed. I began to like praying now, if it was to be with friends like that. Now my heart beat again. I knew for a fact this was not the old guilt-ridden Bible world in which I had suffered, but the Celtic world of grail and vision. What was the difference between this church and the punishing Bible-Christians? Was it just a matter of what suited us? What I experienced was that a heavy old oak door had swung open, just the reverse of a prison clanging shut.

I knew I had to accept the gift and follow its implications. Things weren't easy after this event. Our socialist agnostic colleague Bill Watson said, "You've betrayed us. You've let us down. We were strong, and now you've given in—to the Papists!" He saw the anthropological fight against illusion and bigotry as weakened—by us.

"It's better to be free," said his beautiful enlightened wife, Pamela. "I'd far rather be out on the windy heights and free. Religion!" she said in disgust.

They had no notion that we'd suddenly become very happy. Anthropologists were still too close to the age of bigotry from which they had fought to free their students for them to believe that we could see something they couldn't. And in the discipline of anthropology in those days no one spoke of it if they had such experiences themselves.

We did have each other. We had to go on in life; even so we were literally helped by the good spirit flitting with us wherever we went. If anyone wanted to wrest the word "literal" away from us they wouldn't have been able to do it. For there was such a sense of "apodicticity" in us, the sense of the absolute certainty of this religious experience, that we were more alive than ever before.[3] It was experience that gave us certainty, the experiences included in radical empiricism—experience of real events, the certainty of ordinary ones *and* those beyond the usual limits. Among many, this misunderstood sense of certainty has been kept alive as an actual human faculty, one that is on the "endangered species" list as a faculty. So far the faculty has refused to go away. It is the sense of the soul.

It was 1958. Now that I was a Catholic I was not using birth control. Then came a stage in my unwitting journey that led me into the very valley of the shadow of death. In Manchester, there occurred an accident at an experimental atomic pile called Windscale, about 11 miles from the city. The containment began to leak radioactivity. At the time, the British government assured the public that the danger was very slight. In 1959 I gave birth to a Downs Syndrome baby, Lucy, who died after five months. I was told by the doctors that women in later life were more likely to have Downs Syndrome babies, so I never associated the tragedy with Windscale. It was only after sixteen years that the true facts about the leak were dragged out to the public view: there had been many thousands of abnormal births in Manchester during the period of the late fifties. The event is now known as the Sellafield Disaster, worse than Three Mile Island, perhaps second only to Chernobyl. At the time, the terrible danger and vast number of deaths were known to the doctors but nothing was told to the public. I myself did not know that the Windscale event was regarded as a disaster until the 1990s. Then I came to the inevitable conclusion that what was far the most likely thing to have caused the trouble with little Lucy was the large amount of radioactivity in Manchester, not my age.

A similar thing happened in a very different place. In the late 1990s the anthropologist Henry Stephen Sharp revealed that when he was stationed at army bases at Fairbanks and Fort Wainwright, Alaska, in 1971-1972, talk of the existence of a supposedly secret and illegal government nuclear dump made in 1964 was commonplace among the men. The work was undertaken by the Army Corps of Engineers near the same Eskimo village where I later did fieldwork in the 1980s and

1990s. The radioactive material was not in containers and caused much cancer in the village. Steve Sharp was stationed in the middle of damning evidence, unable to help, and feeling uneasy. In the 1990s I helped the Eskimos to persuade the US government to move the dump, and thus I was learning more about the history of nuclear disasters.

These two cases of illegality are ones that are known to me personally. There are many others.

Back in 1960, during this trouble with the baby and at her death, the department of anthropology at Manchester University put out their richest humanistic kindness to us, blessed us with as heavenly a love as from any church across the world. I say this now because I have had much experience, one way or the other. Native peoples have got anthropologists wrong. They are not really cold-blooded analysts. We have not seen anything yet of what good they can do.

After a few months, Vic and I, knowing little of the cause of Lucy's death, went on pilgrimage to Aylesford, the ancient monastery of St. Simon Stock, who was the first English Carmelite. The monastery had been destroyed during the Reformation and was now rebuilt by Father Malachy Lynch, who welcomed us and showed us a jocund image of Our Lady of Fatima, almost Gaelic in style, as was appropriate in Portugal and Galicia. Then we sat down to supper with Father Malachy in the middle of a long table. The good prior kept pressing on me lettuce from the salad bowl. I thought for a little. Vitamin E for fertility?

Nine months afterwards I gave birth to a normal boy, Alex. Father Malachy was known for his miracles. I lived through all these doings in a generalized sort of way, bathed in our ongoing Catholicism.

As for anthropology at the time, Vic was ranging among different classes of facts, social facts with respect to Durkheim, psychological facts with respect to Freud, and nonrational facts encompassing paradoxical experiences with respect to Kierkegaard. I remember how Vic read Kierkegaard's book on paradox as long ago as 1944. Kierkegaard had boldly faced the accounts of God's irrationality in the Old Testament, particularly over the question of God's requirement that Abraham should slay his son Isaac.[4] For Vic and me the gap between plain rationality and something divine, shown when one is in the hands of a spirit who was taking the initiative, began just there. The path of my life had now been swung in another direction, and I was companioned with the courage of Kierkegaard's ideas imparted from another world.

Kierkegaard's paradoxes about "paradox" came back to Vic when he finally wrote the full account of the Chihamba ritual—which Max had advised him not to make the theme of his dissertation. For the first publication of the book Vic gave the title *Chihamba the White Spirit*, and when it was published again with a long discussion section he gave it the title *Revelation*.⁵ It was a book that surfaced irrepressibly like the subject of that "revelation," the white hump of Kavula himself, the Ndembu thunder god, who had surfaced from the earth in the African forest. We realized we were facing paradoxes again, the manifestations of antistructure: the god Kavula was both good and savage. His image was constructed by adepts, yet this was, *was* the thunder god; the neophytes "killed" him with their rattles in an act of sacrifice, yet they were "innocent" of murder, and the god grew up again in the cassava. The nature of the godhead is pure paradox, said Kierkegaard, and these paradoxes had to remain in their strength as paradoxes; and for Vic they were not analyzable according to social-structural principles.

If one cannot analyze, what can one do with this material? Just give up and change one's career? Jung asks whether, when one "reaches the bounds of scientific understanding [and crosses over into] the transcendental … no further scientific statements can be made." Yet Jung himself was determined to include as scientific facts much that we would call occult. Jung always had trouble with his own resolve; even though he said in one passage⁶ that the contents of psychic experience were "real," in another he said, "The great advantage of the concepts 'daimon' and 'God' lies in making possible a much better objectification of the *vis-a-vis*, namely, a *personification* of it" (p. 337).⁷ Are experiences of God real, or invented in the mind and by society? Are they clothed in "personifications"?

The fact was, in the book *Revelation and Divination*, our restrictions loosened and opened up at the same time as we became Catholic. Then we interpreted the unnamed Ndembu demigod as an appearance of the divine unknowable. It was an opening of one of the doors.

Soon afterwards we began to develop the concept of liminality. "Liminality" arose out of Vic's ponderings on Van Gennep's *The Rites of Passage*.⁸ Van Gennep had conned the large numbers of world rituals to do with change. In those rituals one can see a kind of celebration of in-between-ness itself—the rituals we now know as initiations. In-between-ness, the stage in the middle of change, has a very strange character, out of this ordinary world. I had seen the strange acts within the Ndembu girl's initiation. When Vic applied Van Gennep's passage theory to the rituals and symbols of the boys' circumcision camps among the Ndembu, he noted the figure of the anomalous spirit dancer from ancient times who appeared in the seclusion period. The masked figure was liminal, nobody's relative, slightly mad, huge, and with the appearance of a lord of spirits. We saw that the circumcised novices were secluded in a world full of spirits. Their own acts were spiritual acts: for instance, even their reentry back into the world of the everyday was sudden and unexpected, like the coming of spirits.

The other great feature of most ritual, "communitas" between people, is a phenomenon anthropologists themselves experience in the field, often around a log fire, and they see it manifesting itself in others. Communitas is a very simple thing but an enormously important part of social life. It does not often find its way into the social sciences because scholars do not know what to do with it. I now see it as unconditional love, outside any differentiated respect for rank, moral status, and social structures. It flourishes best in those precious in-between times when stress about status is low and nobody bothers about rank.

We realized we had stumbled upon an anomaly, a flaw in the theory of society held by the leading sociologist of the century, Emile Durkheim.[9] Durkheim had no sense of in-between times and particularly the betwixt-and-between liminal phase within rites of passage— no sense of its paradoxical nature. We realized that liminality and communitas were social facts that were not his kind of social facts.

More closed areas of thought gave way once the process had started. Now Vic was reading St. Augustine's *City of God*,[10] about the two cities, the city of God and the city of man. The city of man was the world, with its dominations, powers, structures, laws, force, violence, business cares, and family troubles: a world of "Power I." The city of God was that oneness that Vic had known through Eckhart; it was love; the last shall be first; communitas; beyond alienation (what Karl Marx first thought of and lost); strange ancestor figures; a state betwixt-and-between the ordinary business world; of the world and yet not of it; and thus, the now-you-see-it-now-you-don't effect, what one might term "Power II." It was what happened in the so-called "liminal" or threshold period in a rite of passage and it was its own thing and had its own meaning in its own right.

Here I have to discuss religion. What was really going on with us? I have to explain what religion's power is and that is very hard. I have referred to Power I and Power II. Power I is what we all know, physical force, the military, the power of money over human survival. Power II is the power of love, but it is more than that. It is a spiritual thing, not hurting, but has its own character; it is nonlogical. The postmoderns make a god of ambiguity itself in order to label it and thus dispense with the mysteries of the nonlogical. They would say, don't go the way of religion. You'll expect to find absolute certainty and there's no such thing. You'll find ambiguity and *that's it*. They say, "Keep talking," but then they won't let you talk.

There's a difference between the postmoderns and Blake, who was a mystic and non-churchgoer. He knew about the contraries and contradiction before the postmoderns did. Yet he didn't betray, for one thing, his love of human energy—and for another, his human experience. So he had his vision. These things need attention, the second attention described by Castaneda and the Buddhists. We're very lucky to have these in our age. At the time of the conversion of Vic and myself in 1958, what we were seeing were cracks leading into the vision—cracks we couldn't locate elsewhere in the modern world.

Then I have to discuss the church's continual fall into structure and Power I, which is where its central organization stands at the moment of writing, 2005, for all its protestations to the contrary. The central organization largely operates in the city of man (literally, the male sex). Meanwhile, nobody has taken seriously the ritual of folk Catholicism, and also that of other societies, ritual that has been in continuous and effective operation from primeval times right up to the present. A serious reconsideration of religion itself by religionists has rarely been made, with the exception of Rudolf Otto, Tom Driver, and a very few others.[11] In my search I have heard only vague philosophical or personal discussions concerned with moral stance. The labor of anthropologists in researching vast amounts of ritual seems in vain. Now, researchers like me have found that the handling of spirit events and experiencing them ourselves is quite surprising, heartwarming, and strangely effective, never mind if the critics call it "mystification" or "magic." So it is possible that we have got religion all wrong. These ordinary folk *are* dealing with spirit entities. Yet how can I say what religion truly is? I haven't reached the end of the path yet and it keeps twisting.

But there have already been some strange things on the way. One of the oddest is this: at the time of this church's origin its leader got himself killed in a mysterious way to give us his anti-power, his power II. Vic came across the word "immolate" for what was done to the communion bread and wine. It appears that humanity has been endowed with this ritual trick of sacrifice. And when we do it, things jump a notch, as in Chihamba, and as I saw later, in the Yaqui deer dance and the Samaritan Passover sacrifice. These last, the Samaritans, sacrifice real lambs at their Passover, in a ritual located high on their own holy mountain, Gerusim. A paradoxical effect takes place when you actually do the sacrifice. René Girard, who wrote *Violence and the Sacred*[12] has not understood sacrifice aright. He called sacrifice the "sublimation" of violent impulses, and praised Western religions for this beneficial use of sacrifice. He did not appreciate the "reversal," the "inversion" effect of it, the paradoxical effect. Sacrifice is entirely precious; there is a sense of love in it which is quite over-whelming, that doubles you around and sets you off running at 180 degrees. Try celebrating the immolation of a sacred object with the Samaritans at their Passover sacrifice of lambs, or during the Hopi's act of immolation of a sand painting at the finale of their ritual, or the similar act of the Bemba women of Zambia after their painstaking modeling of a sacred serpent, or the Yaqui Indians in the deer dance at the stage of the death, or the Iñupiat when a whale gives itself to them. Some inexplicable things are going on. Joy, for one thing. Sacrifice is an actualization of identification, connection, and unity. It is only one of the characteristics of Power II.

So, joining the Catholic church was fieldwork for us after all, the best we could get at the time. I wonder now what exactly happened. The anthropologist might have let herself be corralled into a hide-bound religion that had apparently been corrupted into political power. She glides into its cells and arteries, gets the smell of it, won-ders how the heart chambers behave. She becomes deafened by the pounding, the will that is in it. Yet that is what she's interested in. The pounding effect.

Yet flip it around, and something much bigger than the church and all its theologies seems to have arranged this damned entrapment. Though even here one wonders. "Take the Borg's eye-enhancer, if you won't look at things for yourself. You'll be enslaved, but you'll 'see'"—a horrible temptation.

So it seemed. Vic and I complied—we obeyed all the command-ments. We threw away the condoms. A Down's syndrome baby was born and died. Two more children were born, one of whom says he had a miserable childhood and has taken a long time to become happy. Vic died at sixty-three, not having looked after himself. I would have been better off totally unconscious of myself, like a Borg. But as it happened I was still alive after he died, feeling blankly igno-rant again, stuffed with heavy weary anthropology and needing yet another leg up.

But I haven't flipped the dial around far enough for my friend the reader. Once flipped into a further dimension, one which is actually, truly, literally, palpably out of this rational world, what happens? Why,

> morning, at the brown brink eastward, springs,
> because the Holy Ghost over the bent world broods
> with warm breast and with ah! bright wings.[13]

Just that extra tilt and you can see it, the way that Gerald Manley Hopkins saw it. Back there at our conversion in 1958 Vic and I were walking about in a different world. Another faculty had sprung up before us for the taking. A kind of communitas was everywhere. John Bate, the laughing comrade-in-no-arms of the war, was our guide, he who had had a vision in Bala Cave in Wales. For us in 1958 the saints stood out in 3D and we prayed to them (they were like ancestor spirits). We knew exactly why the saints had downed tools and gone for this "useless" treasure.

Vic's mysticism poked its head above the soil and opened into a sweet-smelling flower. Then he saw his Africa notes and got to work. It suddenly struck him that what he had been through in Chihamba showed an understanding of religion that was no longer just a matter of orectic symbols representing a need in the unconscious, but had shown him the possibility of ritual as a serious, existential, effective entry into the world of spirit powers. He said that the particularities of the entry could not be reduced to laws, they flowered in the realm of antistructure, which realm seems to be an analogue of the "other reality" of shamanistic curing rituals. Vic wrote that the Ihamba pole shrine (*chishinga*), sacred to the power of Wubinda, ritual huntsmanship,

> is regarded by Ndembu not so much as an object of cognition, a mere set of referents to known phenomena, but rather as a unitary power, conflating all the powers inherent in the activities, objects, relationships, and ideas it represents. What Ndembu see in a chishing'a, made visible for them in its forked and awe-inspiring nakedness, is the slaughterous power of Wubinda itself.[14]

Symbols are thus more than ritual markers or representations or statements about the ritual world, but powers themselves, effectors, triggers of the "set-aside" condition, openers through the barrier that encloses a secret, or they may be the god itself.

Meanwhile in England, life sprang up again for me; I felt I could put an arm out into another world where feeding would actually come through, a feeding that I unconsciously knew was natural to me. "Of course communitas is available to you," said my unconscious. Not all the time, but it was safely there. A human being is biologically endowed with a power to reach for it. One has a predisposition for it.

This was immeasurably better than what went before. Now, I was able to experience those faculties and I knew they were available for anyone. I could not access half of them yet and might never have known any of them. But the route leading to them, the path, had reared up of itself and hit me.

Just the same, I was back in the world doing ordinary things again, looking after a handicapped baby, living the kind of life that that task involved. The energy and style of my life was linked up with many

Figure 5.2: The family arrives in the US. The Capitol, 1961. From left to right, Edie, Rene, Vic, nephew Henry Barnard, Bob, and Fred (photo in the possession of Edith Turner)

new and different customs and odd traditions: statues, eating wafers, lighting candles: a religion of objects and acts, as in most religions.

Vic's work was causing him to swerve into the orbit of American academia across the Atlantic. Margaret Mead invited him over for a year's position, but he refused, since he was looking for a permanent job, not being inclined to take on a temporary one along with all the children. Soon after that, he landed a full professorship at Cornell. We moved near Vic's mother at Hastings to await the final arrangements of the move.

While still in England, over the New Year 1963 to 1964, just after the assassination of President Kennedy, the lives of Vic and myself in Hastings had been growing step by step more liminal, "betwixt and between." We were the subjects of our own theory that was developing right there. For instance, we were no longer in Manchester, Vic having been appointed to Cornell; our visas were in question because we had been Communist party members (a membership we now felt had been crazy); we were awaiting special defectors' visas and therefore were neither here nor there, feeling the uncertainty of it; we were renting a house in the ancient port of Hastings, a house beside the Bourne, a stream that joined land to sea; our one daughter Rene was a teenager, neither a child nor an adult; and both Vic and I were in the middle of a complex change in our entire anthropological philosophy. This was threshold living at every moment. We finally made the trip to America in February 1964 (see figure 5.2). Very soon after we

Figure 5.3: The knee-leaping dance during Bagisu boy's initiation in Uganda, 1966 (photo by Edith Turner)

arrived Vic gave a lecture that emerged from the experience of waiting. It was entitled, "Betwixt and Between: The Liminal Period in *Rites de Passage*."[15] He had learned on his pulses what liminality was.

However, even the church was busy going the way of Durkheim[16] and the sociologists. Why this hardening process had to go alongside the widening of the church at Vatican Two I do not know. By 1968 we found ourselves in the age of the hippie priests and liturgiologists who were determined to get rid of various rites within the Mass. You can guess our reaction. We had fallen in love with the physicality, the materiality of the Mass, and found deep spirituality in it, sensing how the spirit informed material symbols, both things and people. Instead we found a generalized ethic being taught in Sunday schools—"Be nice to Johnny next door"—and soon nobody had the least idea what the consecration was all about, nor the effect of sacrifice; blood became white wine, the body was lifted up flat on a plate so you couldn't see it, and so on. No amount of explaining by laity such as ourselves could get anywhere with the new liturgiologists.

Once during this period, on a return trip to Africa, to Uganda, I saw what the focusing of "things" could do at a moment of great suffering. Teenage boys were being circumcised, in public. The boys used a myriad of ritual things, costume, colors painted on themselves, performances, song. They wore the hippopotamus's tusk, for steadiness; the reckless colobus monkey's plumes for aggressiveness and courage and for the beauty of his knob-shaped penis, apparently naturally circumcised; the frothing chyme in the upper stomach of a goat that the boy rubbed on his head for the froth of courage, as in frothing at the mouth—"a froth of a boy," as we say; the plump fresh internal organs of a goat, viewed to divine the outcome of the operation (horispicy); white mud from the swamp on the face, to get close to the ancestors and their help; the knee-leaping dance (see figure 5.3), which is the leaping penis—for manhood after healing; knee bands and arm bands for control; shell bangles for their whiteness. This was a cultural laser beam of organized light, producing a hologram of courage. And as such, because culture objects are also power objects, the hippopotamus strength lay *in its tusk*, not just imagined; its power and energy were actually generated this way. Indeed, on one occasion I personally experienced intense energy that was given to heal me—which it did. That lesson on focused symbols was a lesson we were given early in our research.

In the house at Cornell with our grown son Bob, daughter Rene, and our two little boys born in the early 1960s, Vic and I became a working team. Our collaboration continued when we moved to Chicago in 1968, especially as regards the running of a large home seminar, sometimes with 60 or 70 anthropology graduate students crammed into our living room and spilling into the dining room and on the stairs. We researched many topics other than the usual Durkheim, the prince of collective representations—for instance, Dante, William Blake, and Kierkegaard. We performed ritual. The student David Blanchard enacted the Iroquois False Face ceremony in our living room and people went into trance. The Chicago decade was marked by the fertile ideas of students, particularly the idea of flow, the communitas and magic of work itself, what may now be called being in the "Zone."[17]

We sent the children to school and both of us worked full-time on research, writing, and teaching. In the vacations and in the fall of 1969 we took the two small boys with us on a new research project on pilgrimage, and we set them to work alongside us. The youngest, Rory, at seven years old, was good at snapping the interiors of Mexican churches with his Brownie camera. One of his pictures became the cover of Vic's book *Dramas, Fields, and Metaphors.* In Mexico City we lived in an apartment above a cheerful street busy with market stalls, street cries, and neighbors. "Gaaaas!" shouted the seller of propane gas cylinders. Soccer was the rage. All of us delighted in the Chipultapec anthropology museum.

Notes

1. All three, Fred, Bob, and Rene, visited Africa again in later years.
2. Wordsworth, "Intimations," 602.
3. Apodicticity is a term used by Edmund Husserl, meaning the sense of absolute certainty.
4. Søren Kierkegaard, *Fear and Trembling* (Garden City, NY, 1954 [1843])
5. Victor Turner, *Revelation and Divination* (Ithaca, NY, 1975).
6. Carl Jung, *Two Essays in Analytical Psychology* (New York, 1928), 194.
7. Carl Jung, *Two Essays in Analytical Psychology,* 337.
8. Arnold van Gennep, *The Rites of Passage* (London, 1960 [1909]).
9. Emile Durkheim, *The Elementary Forms of the Religious Life* (New York, 1965 [1915]).
10. Augustine of Hippo, *The City of God* (New York, 1950 [A.D. 427])
11. Rudolf Otto, *The Idea of the Holy* (London, 1928); Tom Driver, *The Magic of Ritual* (San Francisco, 1991).
12. René Girard, *Violence and the Sacred* (Baltimore, 1977).
13. Gerard Manley Hopkins, "God's Grandeur," in *The Norton Anthology of Poetry,* eds. A. Allison et al. (New York, 1975 [1877]), 900.
14. Victor Turner, *The Forest of Symbols* (Ithaca, NY, 1967), 298.
15. Victor Turner, *The Forest of Symbols,* 93-111.
16. Emile Durkheim, *The Elementary Forms of the Religious Life.* Durkheim's book became a kind of encyclopedia for how to explain away religious thinking and actions in sociological terms. In his passage on "soul," after showing a masterly grasp of what people appear to feel about the soul, the author teaches that it is a metaphor for ordinary human interactions, a social construction of reality to give people a way of talking about human communication.
17. See also Mihali Csikszentmihalyi, *Flow: The Psychology of Optimal Experience* (New York, 1990). The concept was originally mooted by John MacAloon.

6

A CENTER OUT THERE

Following the Mexican Pilgrim's Instinct

Vic and I stood in the Villa de Guadalupe, the greatest pilgrimage center in all the Americas, before a glass-framed picture three feet wide. It was a highly enlarged picture of a woman's eye, an eye with a natural epicanthic fold in the corner of the lid like a Mexican Indian's, a feature that Vic outlined with his finger. I noticed something else about the eye.

"Come over this side, Vic. Look from this angle."

He came over and peered against the light.

I said, "It's on the outside of the glass."

He and I could see a wide patch of smearing on the glass, right over the place in the photograph where the eye peeked out from under the enormous eyelid.

"The pilgrims have been touching it. The eye is something holy."

"I believe you're right." He touched the spot on the glass and you could feel from its slight greasiness that many hands had been there.

"Right over the eyeball," I said. It was a photograph of the eye of Our Lady of Guadalupe. "Aren't people supposed to see Bishop Zumarraga and his two servants in the reflection in the eyeball?"

We peered at the grainy blacks and whites in the exact spot in the photograph where you could see the iris. There were indeed three vague dark knobs reared up in what you could see of the iris hidden beneath the drooping lid.

"Hmm." I took a photo of the photo and its smear.

We were making a study of the Villa de Guadalupe, the most visited pilgrimage shrine in the world (fifteen million pilgrims yearly). In

1531 an Indian named Juan Diego, a respectful practical little man, had a vision of a beautiful lady surrounded by sunbeams. This took place on the hill beside which the basilica was later built, with its gallery and the enlarged picture before which we stood. Everyone in Mexico knows the story, and so does practically every northern and southern Latin-American in the two continents. In contrast, few white academics know the story.

Tradition says the event took place in 1531, shortly after the Spanish conquest. Juan Diego, a dark-faced convert, was coming home over the hill of Tepeyac on his way back from Tlatelolco, the palace of Zumarraga, Spanish Bishop of Mexico City, the former Tenochtitlan. Like all Indians Juan Diego was dressed in a tilma, that is, a long jerkin made of rough cactus cloth. He had just reached the summit when he heard a musical voice, like a flock of birds singing.

"Come here, Juan Diego, I want you to do something for me."

He saw a beautiful lady, glowing in the air above the ground, haloed in an oval world of her own, so bright that she made everything around her glow and cause roses to spring up, although it was December and the hill was seven thousand feet above sea level. When Juan Diego looked at her he saw that the crescent moon was positioned just under her feet as if to cradle her, and that a small angel was hanging on underneath too, supporting the moon. The lady bent a fond look downward at Juan Diego. Her eyes were curved in a delicate line. Why, they were Indian eyes and they were black and shining.

She hitched her rebozo robe over her arm. She was real. "Look, little Juan, I've got this big shawl, see, there's lots of space in it. You didn't know it but I'm your mom, and I'm the mother of all the Indians. I have you safe in my shawl."

He loved her.

She said, "You've got to do this thing for me. I have a message for old Zumarraga. I want him to come here, and I want him to show the Indians what kind of mother they really have. You tell him ... ."

Juan Diego was worried. He shifted from one foot to the other. "I don't think I can manage it today, little daughter" ("little daughter" was a Nahuatl term of respect). He started to make off.

"Ah-ah. Come back here. At least have a try, for my sake."

Enough to say, Juan did do what she said, and he went to see the bishop. But he was chased out of the courts of Tlatelolco by the bishop's servants. He said to himself, "That's a difficult visionary woman I've gone and got myself entangled with."

The next time when he had to go by the hill of Tepeyac he sneaked along by a different path so he wouldn't meet her. But dammit, she met him on the new path just the same.

"Juaa-aan. Gotcher! What about the message?"

"They wouldn't hear and wouldn't stop. Littlest of my daughters, I just can't do this. I'm nothing but the tail end of this show, I'm a nobody."

"Just GO!" Her words rang through him; this was an indignant mother. The story tells how he agreed to go a second time and the same thing happened.

The third time she had something for him. "As you seem to be having trouble, I'll give you something to prove I'm real." She went around picking the roses that were blooming all over the hill.

"Spread out the front of your tilma-jerkin, Juan," she said. "It'll make a convenient bag. I'll put the roses in there." He spread out the front of his tilma-jerkin into an apron and she heaped the roses on it.

"There. Pick it up by the corners and take it to my lord bishop and see what happens."

Juan closed the folds and went off, smelling the nice flowers. When he arrived at the stately Spanish halls he crept around for a bit until he found a chance to slip inside. He saw the bishop and his servants holding court. Squeezing through the crowd he managed to get right to the front.

"Now's my chance," he said, and broke out facing the bishop himself. "Y-your l-lordship, a present from our mother, the lady of Guadalupe!"

The servants reached forward to arrest him but he let go the corners of the tilma-jerkin, spilling the roses all down the front and to the feet of the bishop. He gave a breath of relief. He'd done it.

Everyone was staring at him. Zumarraga was looking straight at Juan's rough old tilma-jerkin, fascinated.

"What you staring at?" Juan asked and looked down at himself.

"Whoooo!" He saw the roses in the act of arranging themselves in glowing colors all over the cloth, and as he looked they somehow disappeared into the cloth in the form of a beautiful picture. It was a picture of the lady herself, with her surrounding oval of sunbeams, her Indian eyes—so fond—her turquoise blue shawl with the fold in it, the Mexican-pink gown, the moon, the angel, all of it. His tilma-jerkin had become a picture the length of a person, depicting his lady.

So that was what she had planned.

Meanwhile the poor old bishop was in a mystical ecstasy. "Holy Mary Mother of God, pray for us sinners now, and in the hour of our death, Amen."

Never mind that the lady had never mentioned Mary. That's what Zumarraga took the miracle to mean, Indian epicanthic fold or no Indian epicanthic fold. And so things turned out as the lady wanted. The old man did go to Tepeyac, they did build a chapel and, in time, there were three great basilicas one after the other, because the old ones got shaken by earthquakes. The two entire continents of America now know her as the *"Virgen Morena,"* the Black Virgin (*"Morena"* meaning "Moorish," "native"). She was the Indian's Lady. In 1810, the Indians fought the war of independence against the Spaniards under the colorful banner of Our Lady of Guadalupe, especially chosen by the priest Hidalgo, their heroic captain. After many failures and successes the Indians won. The only political doctrine that religions seem to possess is this: the humble and poor *know*, the rich who keep their riches cannot.

Vic and I stood gazing at the enlarged photograph in the side gallery, a study taken in the nineteen-sixties as part of an accurate photographic documentation of the tilma picture itself. The tilma itself is now enshrined in the basilica for all to see. Tradition says it is the actual tilma-jerkin that Juan Diego wore and that was transformed into a painting. Down the centuries this treasure first hung over the altar of the chapel and then that of the successive basilicas; and now in 2005 it is ensconced above the altar of a new glass and concrete basilica, in the midst of a mural giving a modern artist's sense of the lights of heaven.

Pilgrims had always circulated in the side galleries where ex-votos were kept. By the time we visited in 1969 and saw the enlargement, many pilgrims had been coming that way to revere the three dark objects in the "eye" of the enlarged photo, which were the reflections of Zumarraga and his two servants at the split second when the lady herself became incorporated into the tilma and was able to take one look at what faced her, those three men.

There the men were before us, now.

I too put up my hand and touched the spot on the glass.

"It's holy," I said.

What Vic and I had been chasing after at this stage was the material world of the ordinary people's religion, whatever religion. When we first pondered where to find such a religion in the West that was truly in action, not performed by rote, not possessed by bureaucracies, we thought we were stumped. The monotony of everyday life patterns that had crept into religion was not what we had in mind; there had not been an iota of such monotony in African religion.

Where did we get the idea of pilgrimage from? Vic had already propounded the concept of liminality: it was found in rites of passage. First came the separation stage, then the threshold or liminal stage of seclusion, and then the return stage. Would a good example of the liminal phase in Christianity be the vigil of a knight in armor before his knighting ceremony? That was medieval. Would confirmation rituals in the church constitute rites of passage? But they were boring. Were we unconsciously referring to the Carmelite pilgrimage to Aylesford that we ourselves had made in 1960, curiously resulting in the birth of Alex? Possibly. Was the Chihamba shrine deep in the bush, toward which we had run so impatiently, an example of liminality? Oh yes, that was the start of our understanding of it.

Something was drawing us, having hooked us by way of liminality. A big kind of amorphous "Uuuu-hu" was there pushing, in whichever direction a passage might open before us. We had no idea where we would arrive but we went with the pressure.

Originally it was I who had proposed the pilgrimage study and pressed it into action, because I could see at the time that anthropologists and scholars of religion were too intellectualized to study such a dubious phenomenon, one so drenched in the superstitions of the high middle ages, representing practices which, if you had any intelligence, you would abhor—surely humanity should have shaken itself free of them by now. However, it was obviously my kind of thing. Also it was good social anthropology, whose motto is, "I think that nothing human is alien to me," or "In my reckoning, as long as it's human in any way at all, it comes under my bailiwick."

Pilgrimages kept happening. The ordinary people in the religions often made journeys to the site of an ancient holy event or one connected with a holy person. It was these journeys that corresponded to the great spirit rituals of indigenous Africa. Pilgrimages are undertaken because of some personal need, often an illness of one's own or of a relative, sometimes because of a call to the holiness that people perceive in such places.[1] As for us, we dearly needed to be where ritual mattered, where it was alive. And so these places turned out to be. We entered a world of joking, sharing where need be, even enduring the deliberate self-chosen kind of suffering that I myself had often sought—in my case suffering undertaken just to defy the rich or for some such reason. For the pilgrims, it was a matter of true love and awe for the wonder they were seeking.

Going into the basilica of Guadalupe one festival day, I found myself jammed in the doorway in a huge crowd.

A woman next to me grinned and gasped, "No eglesia miraculosa sed eglesia peligrosa!" (This ain't no church of miracle, it's a church of pericle [peril]).

Hearing this ironic semi-pun I laughed, tightly crushed as I was. We both gave an extra push and were through. When I entered I went to sit in a pew near the front. A high Mass was proceeding. I was excited and touched by the sense of thrill going through all who were there. I watched. At the consecration of the chalice I turned around

Figure 6.1: The Lady of Guadalupe creates her robe (photo by Edith Turner).

and took in the scene behind me just as everyone raised their eyes to the transubstantiation. I will never forget the faces I saw. It was like looking upon hundreds of planets simultaneously lit up by the dawning of the sun after a long time of darkness. More than that: each one was flatly, completely, and helplessly touched and taken over by the spirit that had been given them.

What I was doing in this research was going from point to point, recording the touch of the spirit as much as I could. In the small chapel on the historic hill of Tepeyac nearby I saw Indians in shawls kneeling for a long time on the stone floor at the very spot where Juan Diego saw the lady poised in the air. Afterwards the Indians made their way to a side panel in the chapel where a picture was displayed. They paused before it and then moved on. Vic and I went to have a look at the picture. It was a seventeenth century composition depicting the scene in 1531 when Juan Diego emptied his tilma before the bishop. There was the bishop in red wearing a big crown-like hat. There was a servant fussing around with a surprised moon-face and El Greco-like expression. Juan Diego was leaning forward, his apron outspread and the roses tumbling. The artist had painted the roses blurring into the cloth (see figure 6.1). The image was already there upon the sloping cloth: the robed lady was there in her dark starry-blue shawl, its fold full and free, the sunbeams rising out of her all around. The bishop is kissing the tilma.

As I looked, I saw a little living hand creep up the edge of the glass and touch the picture. The hand belonged to a small Indian woman at my side. I leaned over and touched the picture myself. I was again hoping that if something could rub off on the Indians, it might rub off on me. This might then be real fieldwork and I myself might know a little bit of what the Indians were feeling. I would see.

In Mexico we discovered an intricate network of pilgrimage routes to thousands of pilgrimage centers. Most of the fifty million inhabitants seem to have had a natural gift for religion, especially when what is offered was powerful ritual and a strong awareness of death and the soul. The *Semana Sagrada* (Holy Week), the *Tres Reyes* (Three Kings), and the *Dias de los Muertos* (Day of the Dead) all feed the idea of the soul and of a divine spirit. We were seeing here the many variations that our own religion of conversion was taking.

The "Indians," of course, were those left behind from the ancient civilization of Meso-America. During our stay in Mexico Vic was delighted with the massive scholarship on the ancients available everywhere in the country. We honored the genius that built Teotihuacan. Where is the link with the past now? It is seen in fiestas, in village street layouts, in the arts, in the strong importance of the directions, in the Huichol Indians and the Yaqui, the Maya and their still sacred cob-bearing stands of corn placed in the church at the Assumption—there are many remnants of the culture.[2] During that first winter of 1969 in Mexico Vic and I took a trip down to the Gulf of Mexico to Tuxpan and along the left to Tamiahua, to a pyramid near the coast. Our assistant, Jorge Serrano, wanted to show us the pyramid. Jorge was a Chicago graduate student of Vic's and also a priest, a friendly, serious person.

It was late afternoon toward the end of December. We parked the car and came to the foot of the structure. It was the low wide-topped type of pyramid, among trees. We climbed the usual close-set stairs to the exposed flat summit. Laid into the stone were two tombs, side by side.

"Shamans' tombs," said Jorge. The tombs lay parallel to each other, pointing off into the hinterland, which by now was shadowy with the approaching sunset. We saw the sun slowly moving down along the crest of mountains on the horizon. As we looked in the direction to which the tombs were pointing we saw a notch on the horizon that the sun had not yet reached.

Sun? Notch? "What's the date?"

"Twenty-first of December," said Vic, quick, sharp, "and look at that!"

"Ah-h-h-h." The sun slipped neatly into the notch, then was gone. Between the notch and the pyramid on which we were standing, halfway across the shadowy land, rose two mounds, neatly paired on each side of an exact line from the notch to us. I traced the view with my finger and let my arm fall to my side.

Later I knew them as lines of power, seen also in the form of the Nazco lines of the Andes, at Stonehenge, in Drakensberg cave art, at the Ayre Rock in Australia, in Chinese geomancy, in the five-thousand-year-old New Grange mound in Ireland, and in much universal consciousness of the land of Earth as the bearer of a power of its own. On the Gulf of Mexico, when we were beginning to understand the placing of the pyramid in relation to so many miles of the earth's surface, in relation to that particular date, the shortest day of the year, and in relation to the tombs of two visionary people, we saw that those two shamans' deaths had been treated very seriously indeed. That burying was the anchoring of the dead permanently into the landscape, for one thing. It was also an act of honoring the sun, "our father." It was recognizing as sacred the very unseen line itself from the tombs to the horizon. The honoring took place much as a cathedral rises in recognition of the sacredness of a saintly Christian figure, or like the Black Pagoda, and many other monuments. The Gulf pyramid gave honor to something that we call "natural," parts of nature, the sun, mountains. In Mexico, as with native Americans and circumpacific peoples generally, all *things* as well as all people have souls. For the Inuit they are called *inua*; for the Japanese, *kami*. No, this wasn't just geomancy. Even the word "geomancy" might give too much of the idea of manipulation: these peoples did not mess with the earth, they respected it, they experienced its power.

Whence had this earth lore fled when it left the Indians in the Guadalupe era of conversions? It emerged in many Christian forms, such as in the moments of the touching of the pictures, connecting with the time of vision. It was even there in the recognition of the Transubstantiation in the church—a different kind of wonder but related.

For me I felt an education was going on. I myself have gazed at the Host, and, from discussions between Vic and myself, knew and was familiar with the occasions when a thing like bread is not a symbol but an actuality. *"Diyi mukishi." "It is* the spirit." We were getting used to coming across places and circumstances where the presence of a spirit was self-evident and was actually experienced. I did not put my hand on the holy images for fun. During all those years of the pilgrimage studies I wanted to trace spirituality and "get" what different societies were "getting at" by way of this odd kind of communication.

As I have noted, we were plunged into pilgrimage studies because of an undefined pressure on us, and beyond and after that, plunged into a whole mass of experiences that have kept rippling from a continuing energy center up to the present moment. As the story continued on, our interest led us to Ireland, to Lourdes, to Brazil and the Umbanda trancers, to Buddhists in Sri Lanka, to lovers of Hanuman the monkey god in India, to temples and shrines in Japan, to the Sufis and Orthodox of Israel, to the deer dancer of the southwestern desert of America, and, in general studies of religion, to ritual as performance, and the ritual faculty in the brain.

When Vic died my hunt went on through shamanism, healing in Africa, healing in northern Alaska, healing in Ireland, and the land ritual of Marae among the Maoris. Meanwhile all kinds of studies carried out by other anthropologists of religion came into view, and these built up into a considerable body of mostly non-Christian material, documenting spirit and soul consciousness.

This corpus of material will be unfolded in the course of the book. My own story has, as it were, disappeared into them all, and anything of value comes fleeting and oozing out of this mass of material. To get at the "me" in there someone would have to haul me out, like the Thing from the Lost Lagoon, dripping and obscene. Perhaps best not, because the chances are I would just stand there and laugh at the oddity of the situation.

Notes

1. Victor Turner and Edith Turner, *Image and Pilgrimage in Christian Culture: Anthropological Perspectives* (New York, 1978).
2. See the masterpiece on the material symbolism of the Cuicatec of Chiapas, Eva Hunt's *The Transformation of the Hummingbird* (Ithaca, NY, 1977).

7
WANDERING IN THE PATH OF A VISION
Ireland

Almost at once we changed our main venue of research to Ireland. The change simply transpired, nobody planned it. Manchester in England had been full of Irish laity, Irish priests, Irish intellectuals, the very poor Irish—but important factors in our change of orientation were Vic's love of Celtic culture that was for him linked to the work of Alwyn Rees, the great scholar of the Celtic whom he had known at Aberystwyth University in the war, and also those countless Irish Catholics who confidentially advised us to "go to Knock," wherever and whatever that might be. We decided to go where we were directed and do fieldwork in Ireland, a country that had certain similarities to Mexico, both possessing a deep past scarred with the results of colonizers' cruelties.

Quickly we got our plans together and left for Ireland, settling in a rented house about twenty-five miles from the pilgrimage center of Knock. Again, the trip turned out to be a quest for spirit consciousness, though at the time we thought we were researching ritual.

I found Knock to be a small village in County Mayo with an ordinary Catholic church (see figure 7.1). Much fame is attached to the place because in 1879 a very bright light appeared one evening with a beautiful woman at its center. The church terms this sort of event an "apparition"—rather a frightening word, but no Catholics seem to think so. Everyone was convinced it was Our Lady who had come. The story was something like the Guadalupe tale. The accounts were well documented.

Notes for this section can be found on page 124.

Figure 7.1: The most attended pilgrimage center in Ireland. Knock church and shrine (photo in the possession of Edith Turner)

In the summer of 1879, rain had been falling steadily. The whole countryside was sodden. Earlier, in the fine weather, the young potato shoots had been green and firm. Now, in many villages, their leaves turned bronze and started to loll with the potato blight. Soon entire fields were lying black and mushy, every plant dead. The new potatoes underground turned out to be slimy masses of pulp. (I have seen this blight myself and dug up that slime.) As in the great famine of 1845 many people were starving, for potatoes were their only food. The people of Knock were deeply involved in the disaster. They were facing many more years of starvation, hardship, and political oppression, and it was under these circumstances that the apparition occurred.

I started reading the published testimony of the witnesses of the vision.[1] Once into the accounts I felt myself suspending disbelief and taking them seriously. I began to imagine myself walking behind the church in that deadly potatocidal rain at 8.00 p.m. on the evening of Thursday, August 21. That's the place: I can see it, a muddy lane where turf carts have been passing. The meadow grass over the stone wall of the lane is high and lush, growing right up to the back gable of the sanctuary. I'm holding a sack over my head atop my black shawl. My clothes are worn and my feet bare. There's been nothing for supper but a single old remaining potato, boiled in the skin, not the ten pounds necessary for life.

A couple of women, clutching their shawls against the rain, race rapidly past me in the mud, chattering. Suddenly one of them clutches my arm and points to the church. I look up.

"Oh! 'Tis a terrible dazzle!" I shade my eyes. I can see in the dazzle a brilliant scene—people there, glowing, at the back of the church. The one in the middle—why, she looks like the world's mother, with her arms out toward us. A glowing mother, a beautiful dear shining mother. I never knew my mother, she died in the famine of 1846. My uncle and several others are coming to look, and they're busy craning over the stone wall of the lane.

"What can those figures be doing out there in the rain?" No one can make anything of it.

"Look! They're not in any mind to move," says one of the villagers. "Maybe they're statues. Are you thinking the priest ordered new statues? Why should he be putting them there at the back?"

"The light—'tis coming *out* of the people. Look, 'tis everywhere."

"I think I see her," says a villager. Her voice is lowered. "She's the mother of God. Herself." She pauses. "Think of it." The woman of light is right in front of us, facing us, alive, quietly there.

"'Tis Our Lady herself, true enough, look how tall she is—and—and I think I see a crown. See her hands? I can feel what she's after, she's after healing us. Look, that's old St. Joseph with her, see how he loves her. And who's that on the other side, the fellow with the book?"

"Look, he's reading from it," says my uncle. There are about fifteen of us by now, we're quiet like the Lady, we're gazing. "Our mother!" She stands there in the sight of us all, alive, our beautiful lady, with healing pouring out of her hands.

One lad, my nephew, says, "I think I see an altar behind her, something like—" But most of the others can't see it.

"Something on it like a lamb and a cross," says another lad. "With light flickering round it?"

"You've the rights of it," say a couple of men, peering. No one else can see any altar.

Mary Bierne, my auntie, says, "When you come to think of it, the fellow with the book—young-looking—that's St. John. I know that one. I was after seeing his statue in Lecanvy church."

Three children are climbing over the stone wall of the lane. "Lift me up," says the small boy. "I want to see the grand babies!"

"Wait a minute now," says old Mrs. Trench. She waves them down. "I'm coming with ye." She hauls up her skirt and nips over the wall fast. The grass out there is high and soaking wet, but she pushes through, holding her skirt up a bit. The old lady is now in the middle of the dazzle and the children are all around her. She knows that this is as near to heaven as she'll get in this life. She holds the little fellow to her side.

Mrs. Trench gazes up at the lively eyes and at the hands outspread. "A hundred thousand thanks," she bursts out. *"Ceid mille failte! Thanks to the good God, and to you, our glorious lady, for giving us this manifestation."*

It is a marvel to see the figures afloat—dazzling people made of light, hovering two feet above the ground, with their feet scarcely touching the tops of the tall grass. The grass underneath the lady looks dry, so the old lady feels at it with her hands. "Tis dry." The old lady reaches out to the Blessed Mother's feet—she dearly wants to hug them—but her hands go flapping through the light just as if they're passing through a sunbeam. The big boy stands on tiptoe by St. John and tries to catch a sight of what's in the book. The words shine but he can't make out what they're saying.

He whispers to his auntie, "I'm thinking it must be Latin."

After watching the vision for an hour or two, we've all been getting wet, so we go home.

I never wanted to come down off this high, but have to make certain observations. In the first holy pictures in color the scene became standardized showing the lady as almost central, with conventional saints' representations on either side, while the altar shows behind, small, and well to the right. The villagers are shown in the foreground in a friendly attentive line (see figure 7.2).

As to the reports of the witnesses and the sense one gets from the transcriptions, a homey atmosphere was discernible even in the stiff writing of the reports. One can imagine the fifteen peasants, now in their Sunday black, sitting on the edge of their chairs in the bishop's chancery at Tuam, with a secretary in attendance to write down their testimony in nice English. In 1971 Vic and I also sat on the edge of our chairs when we in our turn met the existing bishop at Tuam.

I found myself prepared to run with what the peasants said. How could those villagers have invented such a story and pulled off the consequences of lying about it? There were all sorts of difficulties about the various theories of fraud that were proposed. The real question was, had there been a crack in ordinariness, letting through something which human beings were very lucky to experience, a distinct flash of knowledge about the reality of spirits? That is how the whole of Ireland subsequently took it, and they immediately framed it in Catholic terms.

Then there was the matter of the miracles. At the time of my first visit in 1971 anybody could have access to the voluminous reports of the miracles that followed this event. Now in 2006 the church has

Figure 7.2: Popular holy picture of the Knock vision, 1971, with St. Joseph, Our Lady, and St. John (in the possession of Edith Turner)

clamped down on miracles completely because of its fear of fraud and because of its policy of caution, amounting to a policy of rationalism where possible. Were it not for the strong links between the original event and the people themselves, the church hierarchy might well have ripped the whole phenomenon of Knock away, miracles, controversies, and all—and that would be like a planetary oxygen layer being ripped off by a nuclear meltdown for the people of Ireland.

Back in 1971 I used to visit and revisit the place, hearing the soft and loving tones of the pilgrim poor, and feeling very much at home. Whenever they knew I was open to them I would heard their stories. Out came miracle account after miracle account in running reedy voices—voices extraordinarily similar to that of trancers such as Manyosa in Africa in 1952 and many I was to hear later. These storytellers in Knock were not in full trance while giving their stories but they had been taken over, and were willing to be taken over by what they knew as God running through them. Their mouths were being used by that—and, looked at another way, it may have been the voice of the woman creator-spirit which is the enlivening spirit flooding through all things, speaking through them, the same spirit which appeared in 1879 to some of the most sorely tried, innocent people in history.

I used to stand listening in the big crowd at Knock just as they all did, listening for the miracles which would flash off at random throughout the mass of people. They would move slowly around the church against the sun "as into another realm" as tradition puts it, telling their beads, often pushing a wheelchair with a sick person in it who was also contentedly telling her beads. Then they would gather for the open-air Mass, with the wheelchair patients clustered most closely around the priest, with the general crowd on the outside. The sick were "Christ on the cross," we were told; somehow the sick were the salvation of the people. I and my elderly friend Bidgy made the rounds together and spent one of the best days of our lives at Knock.

This is what befell Bidgy and I on that trip in 1971, starting at the beginning.

At the top of the row of shops in High Street in Castlebar, the county town of Mayo, stood a public house. Its frosted window outside bore a notice showing pilgrimage bus schedules: "Sunday pilgrimage to Knock. Castlebar, 10.30; return 18.30." The notice itself marked the bus stop; there was no bus station in Castlebar. A woman came up and looked at the notice. She wanted to go to Knock, but did not understand "18.30." A man who approached tried to explain it to her but failed, so the woman, after bantering with him, gave up and left. Now a plump woman appeared, a pink-cheeked old body of about seventy-five. This was Bridget Lydon, whom people called Bidgy. She was talkative, and subsequently became a helpful friend to me, explaining what I ought to do on pilgrimage. Like most old women of the time she wore a long black coat of coarse linen, and kept a checked scarf tied over her rough white hair. She wore a pair of black boots, old ones but not down-at-heels, and she carried a dumpy handbag.

Two other women approached. One was a young girl with a kind face, wearing the usual cool, smart European outfit of the young in Castlebar, including a minicoat; this was 1971. Her long hair was smoothed with a headband. The other was a middle-aged woman with permed hair that showed signs of peroxide that had been badly applied; she wore face powder that was much too light for her, also orange lipstick and a pair of glasses. She was friendly, but Bidgy couldn't stand her, and kept alluding to the "flour" on her face and to her pants suit. Two other men came up. The men all wore respectable dark suits and were clean shaven with short hair. Like all Irishmen, their cheeks were marvelously rosy and rough. One of them had a distinct line across his brow above which the skin was white, a line caused by wearing a hat while farming. Everyone joked, and when the bus arrived the seven of us boarded it. Bidgy saved me a seat in front on the right next to the window behind the driver, arranging things like that because her left ear was deaf. She was a spinster, slightly "tongue-tied" as people described her, that is, she spoke in rushes; and sometimes she talked in Gaelic. People regarded her as an "old'un" and rallied her up. She worked at the Castlebar town hall doing dishwashing and taking messages, but had no address. She was one of five children, born in a thatched cottage and orphaned early.

The bus stopped at a hamlet and a woman embarked. "That woman," said Bidgy, "was cured by a miracle at Knock." I watched with interest. The woman was pulling herself up the steps very slowly and laboriously, helped by the driver and ticket inspector. She had a caved-in, strange face (perhaps she had no teeth or dentures), marked with an almost animal determination. There were no lines on her face, just hard fearsome surfaces. Once in, she toiled down the center of the bus to find a seat. Bidgy told me how she had been a helpless cripple, quite unable to stand at all. She had been praying to Our Lady of Knock when she suddenly felt a great weight pressing on her. Then she immediately found she could walk. "There have been four miracles this year," said Bidgy. I was interested, but I was bothered by the woman's incomplete cure. I have found later that this is common with all healing, including, of course, medical ones.

The bus kept stopping to pick up pilgrims. There were now seven men, eight children, and fifteen women in the bus. A nun and a middle-aged woman behind us were discussing the woman's daughter and this girl's future career and desire for independence; the tone was approving. There were a couple of other nuns on the bus. Whenever we passed a church or graveyard, Bidgy crossed herself, and pointed the place out to me. I soon learned to cross myself also.

The bus was going down a pretty, tree-lined road weaving in and out of the little hills towards Knock. All around appeared a wide sweep of small fields, with occasional brown areas where turf was being cut, and clumps of trees which hid the great houses of the former Protestant landlords, along with their accompanying villages. Now, most of the great houses were converted into convents.

Our bus crossed a wide featureless plain and at last made its way into Knock. We passed among a couple of dozen small houses and shops set here and there on each side of the main street, which by now was laced with a constant shift of cars and drifts of people. Pilgrims here are truly transient; few stay the night. The loneliness of the village was distinct through it all. Beyond the houses could be seen sheep in the fields and the high pale blue sky above, which reminded me of the Arctic Ocean. Kitty O'Shane, an old invalid staying a week at the Knock invalid's center and with whom I made friends while I was pushing her wheel chair, felt the loneliness and said, "When they all leave in the evening I could cry."

The bus passed a row of booths selling holy objects, and then we saw the church—a solid building with a square tower—then a glimpse of many people—and the bus was stopping. As it did everyone in the bus gave a deep sigh (one could sometimes hear this sigh at the consecration of the host at Irish church Masses, and much later I heard an African medicine man give it when he was in touch with the spirit). Then the people climbed out, and I exited with Bidgy, trying to do everything she did. We went toward the church. Bidgy entered to say a few beads of her rosary under her breath. So did I. The church was filling up with people also "visiting the Sacrament" as this was called. Inside I got the impression of a plain old village church. Soon Bidgy was out again on her way to the apparition gable, the next visit. She told me that Our Lady had appeared to the poor at Knock, not to the proud, not to educated people. I nodded affirmatively. I found later that this kind of consciousness is extraordinarily general in folk religion. It can hardly be overemphasized that understanding the spirit is not an intellectual gift but is markedly democratic, and is often claimed as such.

At the back of the church on the outside was a large glassed-in altar area called the Oratory, at the apparition gable. It had been built at the actual site of the apparitions. That back wall, which had originally been made of common stone and plaster, was now faced with fine quality marble.

Under the dome lights of the marble shrine stood statues of the three apparition figures, the Lady's being the central one. Already in 1971 this arrangement was deplored by the Knock Shrine authorities and was in the process of being redesigned, with a Lamb of God altar as the centerpiece. The suggested change corresponds clearly to the changes in the church since Vatican II, de-emphasizing the veneration of the saints and particularly of Mary, and emphasizing a single-minded concentration on God, in this case, the male lamb. It is hard to know whether the main hazard to Mary arose from feminists of her own sex or the immense predominance of males at the Vatican. I have been watching the attacks over many decades.

Bidgy prayed happily to the holy figure at the center of the oratory. Mass was being said there, so I received communion. Bidgy and many others did not take communion. It appeared later that they had been waiting to take it after they had been to confession, and Bidgy commented to several people around on my unusual behavior. I remembered too late that in Ireland one should always go to confession before taking communion. This custom is a relic from Jansenist times, when our imperfections were considered a serious bar to a perfect communion and people only "received" once a year, always after confession. It is an interesting fact that Jansenists had an immense reputation as miracle workers. One has to infer that their awed respect for communion and their special purity when taking it must have increased their healing power.

After this Bidgy and I decided to have lunch. (Bidgy must have approved of me, because she kept calling me a "good wumman, a plain wumman," somewhat to my discomfiture.) We ate a passable lunch at O'Brien's Café, costing 60 p.; then she led me toward the confessional chapel.

"We'll meet outside here when we've finished," said Bidgy. One could get lost in the crowd, we both agreed.

The confessional, a wooden shack, was packed with people sitting on rough wooden benches. The people were organized in threes and were proceeding at intervals into the confessionals that lined the walls. The atmosphere was indeed penitential; the poverty of the place and lack of paint reflected the poverty of our souls. When I went into the cubicle I confessed to having pandered to the scientific coldness that accompanies anthropology. I haven't had to confess to this since, though I confessed to attacking the church.

"Tell what's true. You should do that anyway," said the priest. On this occasion I felt bad about being English, and therefore in some way guilty of the wrongs of Ireland, so I confessed it. Here it can be seen how the pilgrimage did matter to me, existentially, to the extent of my putting myself up as a representative penitent on behalf of England's sins, concerned for England's millions of souls in purgatory, just as the Irish were concerned for their own. The historical gap of a hundred years meant nothing here. After confession, Bidgy was waiting for me outside as she had arranged.

The next visit took us back to the church, to a spot on the extreme left of the gable, a part of it that had not been covered up when the new oratory was built. There I saw a group of women and a few men standing in a line and gradually moving along. This was the nearest place to the apparition that the people were able to contact physically, now that the main gable had been covered over. At hand's height on the plaster I saw a place about the size of a hand, rubbed deep down to the grey stone inside. Each person put her hand to the stone, and then rubbed her hand over her face. Finally she would take the cross of her rosary in her hand and rub it into the stone, quite hard. Bidgy uttered a prayer here in a singsong voice. I did the same actions.

The same ritual of touching was done at Lourdes; there was a little runnel of water just below the apparition niche where the people lined up and touched the wet rock, because they were no longer allowed to touch the Lourdes water where it had originally sprung out. At Drom Beg stone circle in County Cork the frontal megalith shows a deep hand-sized impression at hand-height, in which one can place one's hand. As I have told, the Mexican Indians at Guadalupe also touched the picture that reminded them of the tilma picture that was now placed far out of their reach. The scattered quartzes at the New Grange mound near Dublin have even been artificially cemented against a wall to keep them out of the visitors' reach. There is the notable example of Stonehenge, now railed off from the visitors. One continually sees the control of the authorities in these situations. Wherever the people obtain some concrete experience and contact with the divine, the authorities limit what they see as their unseemly destructive responses, and control them. In the process, they often kill the sense of the divine.

Next we filled holy water bottles—blue plastic bottles in the shape of Our Lady that were sold in booths beside the main road. We filled them at the holy water taps in the procession ground. Bidgy drank some immediately. I did too, shyly. We went to make the fourteen stations of the cross in the church grounds, set out in the form of a series of carved upright slabs of stone. Bidgy held her rosary. She prayed at each station in Gaelic, in her keening sing-song voice. The prayer seemed to be the Hail Mary, not the Stations of the Cross prayer sequence. Each carved station bore its own inscription in Gaelic. When Bidgy came to the Fifth Station, "Simon of Cyrene helps Jesus," she fervently grasped the carved leg of Simon. At the Third Fall (Ninth Station), she gently kissed the face of Christ. At the Crucifixion, the Eleventh Station, she knelt on both knees and sighed her prayer. Once I saw a working-class woman standing by the Eleventh Station sobbing and crying. An official Knock handmaid in white comforted her and led her away.

When Bidgy had finished she went to the Knock Shrine Office. It was clear that she could not read. To my surprise Bidgy handed over a donation of a five pound note, which must have been her entire old age pension for the week. As I peered over the list I saw that apart from Bidgy's donation, the handmaid's List of Donations all consisted of one pound notes.

It was now time for the principal Mass of the day. By this time about five thousand people had collected in the main grounds. We found seats in the open air, facing yet another Mass center, a tiny octagonal building in the middle of the grounds. The seats were tightly crammed. After we had sat down two women wanted to cram in as well. One of them managed it. I had to sit somewhat sideways, and Bidgy was obviously cramped. Bishop Conway of Elphin and a procession of priests came out from the church to the altar shelter and started the Mass. The homily included a story about the little boy who had said only three Hail Mary's in his whole life. He died and went up to the gates of heaven. St. Peter threw him out the front door. Later, however, Our Lord found him wandering around in the streets of heaven. "And how did you get in here?" said the Lord. The boy told Him, "I went round the back door and your mither let me in"—laughter in congregation.

Later, in due course, the priest raised the host in the consecration; at that moment there came an audible gasp, an indrawing of breath with a sigh, throughout the crowd and especially from Bidgy.

When the "old'un" went to receive communion, she became confused, joined the wrong line, and when she knelt on the asphalt and received the Host she very nearly failed to make it to her feet afterwards. With great difficulty I hauled her upright.

The Mass concluded. Afterwards the bishop processed around the grounds with the consecrated Host enclosed in its golden Gaelic "monstrance" (golden showing-frame), making his way among the rows of invalids in wheelchairs, blessing them with the Host. Around the Host a very serious attitude developed, a kind of magnetic field, wherever it went. People clasped their hands and prayed with all their might. It must have been a time of their completest being. Bidgy prayed intensely as the procession passed her.

It was 5:30. I suggested to Bidgy that we go to the ambulance shelter to say goodbye to Kitty O'Shane, my invalid friend, who was due to start back to Dublin in a few minutes. The fenced-in ambulance area was choked with buses, ambulances, stretcher parties, wheelchairs, men fetching in canvas shelters, handmaids, and stewards. We were ordered out of the area by a steward. We went out, but looked for an opportunity and got back in under the barrier. Bidgy accomplished this in a dreadful crouching manner, hardly able to struggle up again on the inner side of the fence. Over yonder we found Kitty in her wheelchair, her hands brushing her face, because her eyes were red and tears were pouring out. She grabbed my hands when she saw me, looking up at me woebegone.

"I don't want to leave!" she burst out. She shook hands emotionally with Bidgy. She needed lots of comforting but there was no time at all, for the men were approaching—they immediately grabbed her wheelchair and swung her fearsomely up and into the back of an opened ambulance. There she sat, surprised and waving and smiling and crying, her face all ups and downs, in front of a crammed ambulance-load of stretchers, wheelchairs, poking white faces, and handmaids. The men shut the doors. That was the end of the stay of one batch of invalids at the Center at Knock. The ambulance started to move. We waved, and waved again to the waving hand we saw through the glass. And soon the ambulance was gone.

Kitty hated the tiny little two-room house where she lived, on a poor street in Dublin. She was completely alone there, and heard nothing but traffic and rock music all around her. She was crippled, with only the health visitor to talk to sometimes, who was no company. Bidgy and I were both crying. Trying not to think, we went off and sat by the Sisters of Charity Hostel until our bus turned up.

On the way back in the bus we were seated near the young girl and the old blonde again, who were both very happy, glowing from their visit. At length we were bumping along into Balla, a village with a holy well (the well was used for healing that same year, 1971). As we passed the well, and passed the village statue of Eire with her harp on the square, and the round tower from the days of the Vikings, and negotiated the sharp bend by the long convent wall, all deep in the twilight of trees, Bidgy started telling me a tale about a wild horse at Balla which killed and ate a man. There were other wild animals, she said, badgers and such, which did the same.

Now evening was falling. We were out beyond Balla under the wing of a large lonely hill. Now the road suddenly turned into a private cut-off valley in which lay a little lake, delicately fringed with reeds. The level rays of the sun shot between the slopes from the far away mountain of Croagh Patrick and dazzled upon the brilliant green of the hillside. Hill and high blue sky were taken by the still water and turned upside down in a perfect reflection—a wild and appealing scene. I turned quickly to Bidgy and exclaimed, "Isn't that beautiful!"

But she clutched my arm: I felt her shuddering. "'Tis the lake where the kelpies come from, those wild animals!" Her tongue-tied mouthing grew terrible. "The animals, the animals, they cum' out of ut, they eat us. 'Tis wickud."

We passed the lake safely, and the dull plains and bogs. We soon found ourselves in Castlebar where the men were already standing outside the pubs along the high street. All was well. Bidgy needed help down the last giant step from the bus, which she made in an awful blockish stiff manner. She might have fallen wallop on the road if I had not caught her. She stumped off after many God bless yous and handshakes.

Had the sun done something wrong at Balla? What a contrast to the famous apparition scene at Knock—consisting of rain and a self-made holy light with the old friendly saints in it. At the Kelpie lake there was an inversion that created cold chills, a hint of a world upside down made by something strange in the water—and then those evil tales of death and feral violence. No wonder Bidgy shuddered. This was another side of the spiritual.

The high points of the pilgrimage for Bidgy, from what I saw, were touching her rosary at the gable, which was her material act of union with the saints in heaven and with the old Irish in their suffering, and then the consecration, signaled by the indrawn breath. One concludes from what happened that Bidgy did not often take communion—a circumstance, as I knew, deriving from the old Jansenist diffidence. Clearly the consecration was the center for her. For myself, it was confession in the plank-furnished chapel, and Bidgy's tender care that we should meet each other safely afterwards—also the chaotic and funny scene that eventuated when Bidgy tried to find the communion line amid that crammed crowd of devout and somewhat dissociated people, all wondering, waiting, with an ear to the coming of some angelic event, some miracle of healing under the pearly sky.

Ever since 1972, Vic and I strove to understand Knock. From 1995 to 2001 I tried to manufacture an argument that the lady *was* God. But the thing didn't stick. Not that the male god was jealous and wouldn't let me. That would indeed have been in keeping with the angry mood of my argument. I was trying to say this: the lady, the so-called carpenter's wife, was miraculously far more vast than in life; she was the being that created the creator—thus she was the original creator. Male priests have lately been shutting her right out where they can, literally pushing her statue to one side and pushing their male god to the center. Yet she miraculously appears to children, the poor, and women and nothing can be done about it. The consequence has been, under the mysterious law of Christian power inversion, that the lady's shrines have attracted the vast majority of Christian pilgrims. I had an idea that the male hierarchy might have a problem explaining this and favor hiding it and educating the faithful out of it, as we shall see in chapter 13. What I had forgotten was that nothing lives by argument, only by experience, shared experience. The prime thing in life, I find, is this gift, the spirit, which I feel: a kind of energy, neither male nor female, and very, very kind. It is a spirit all right, and I pray to it frequently, and not in a set prayer. This comes much more easily in the year 2005. From time to time I've known the presence of particular spirits, those of dead close friends, of spirit help in healing, and in the utterly lovely *unio mystica*—which in a sense is the shamanic state of consciousness, the collective unconscious (that is, the fullest consciousness, *najual*, or Augustine's city of God). Gender issues simply pale before this.

Now it is dawning on me that the apparitions given to the folks in Ireland are exactly the same kind of thing as this spirit help, and I have stirrings in my own memory of that special sort of lady-kindness. One twinkling memory is of Sibelius's *Pohjola's Daughter*, the music of the wondrous appearance of the god's daughter weaving at her loom high in the clouds of Finland. I get cold chills remembering the music. Then comes one of those songs, Ave Maria, caressingly there in a true sense of holiness—Mother of God in her own sweet right. There's nothing to compare. And Benjamin Britten's song to the Virgin, rising and pleading and combining with the lady to live in her holiness. Then, when my poor baby Lucy was conceived—the Down's syndrome baby—I had a dream. I was turned upside down by the lady, a powerful divine lady; I was roiled and given to know— that something was trying to form in my body. What was odd was that I was actually aware of the conception in that way. As a result there occurred an event which came to absolutely nothing in the material sense, because Lucy Mary died at five months old. But all was not gone.

Who is this lady, achingly beautiful, beyond all paintings and statues, "love in my heart"? Father Chet, my mentor, says when we take communion we take *her*, because the only material part of Jesus was Mary, he was all female. The Eucharist, being material, is the body and blood of the mother of the creator. This is not just an argument but an eerie fact.

I loved her so much, on one day especially. In the church of St. Thomas the Apostle in Chicago the eyes of her statue, which seemed to have been painted closed for years, unexpectedly came open, and were very much alive. After that I was simply happy and used to look at her during Mass with much satisfaction. These were my gentle experiences. So that when at last in 2000 I went to Knock alone after my half-decade of anger over the ugly changes, alone to think what I liked, I knew the rosary for what it was among those vision-seeing people, and suddenly realized I had "got" Knock after twenty-nine years. Blessedness filled the place.

Note

1. Liam Cadhain, *Cnoc Muire in Picture and Story* (Dublin, 1945); Michael Walsh, The Apparition at Knock: A Survey of Facts and Evidence (Tuam, Ireland, 1959).

8

BACK AND FORTH
Experiencing Four Religions

We moved from Chicago and went to the University of Virginia. There I took a master's degree in English, focusing on symbolism (see figure 8.1). This era, 1977-1983, was full of travel, research, and conference attendance. Vic did not at all like the "high-up" positions into which people pushed him, and would try to break the formality of meetings by making awful puns and spreading communitas. I loved the man totally. He was writing with perception, yet many people mistook him for a dry academic scholar. He taught what communitas was—it is there in print.

A number of researchers in anthropology became our buddies— one can only call them buddies, a bunch of people who were working on ritual and symbol and who often collaborated. We were all mutually fascinated by the rich and complex nature of the material each one of us had explored (see figure 8.2). The siblinghood of all of these, especially when the Wenner-Gren Foundation gave us the treat of meeting together in a bunch, was something beyond all natural siblinghood. All of their names glow for me: Barbara Babcock, Barbara Myerhoff, Don Handelman, Bruce Kapferer, Roberto da Matta, John MacAloon, Richard Schechner, Eva Hunt, Terry Turner, Terry Holmes, Masao Yamaguchi, Ed Bruner, and the Zygon group.

At last there came Roy Wagner, strange and visionary. He had cracked the impossible ritual code of the Daribi of Highland New Guinea,[1] and tells us they are the most intelligent people on earth. All these characters would meet in a bunch from time to time and the talking was electric. Once when I wasn't there lightning literally flew

---

Figure 8.1: Edie. MA degree at the University of Virginia, 1980 (photo in the possession of Edith Turner)

Figure 8.2: Vic, Edie, and Richard Schechner working in tandem together (photo in the possession of Edith Turner)

in and out of the window. The hugging was continuous, the numinous sayings magical. I remember occasions when we all hugged in a bunch. We rejoiced in the communitas while it was on. Many books were written. Many felt our excitement, but the implications of it all didn't register among the anthropological community.

Vic and I traveled often. There were places that kept tallying with other experiences I had had before. For instance, in the north of Ceylon, at Anuradhapura, is a region sacred to Buddha. A friend, Ranji Obeyesekere, took us there and showed us the focus of the sacredness. In the third century BC in Banaras, the emperor Asoka, the Hindu ruler of India, was converted to Buddhism, changing from a warlike conqueror into a man of peace. In his kingdom at Bodgaya, near Patna, there still flourished the Bo tree. This was the very one under which Siddhartha Gautama, the Buddha (meaning "the enlightened one"), experienced his great moment, around the end of the sixth century BC. That same tree exists to this day.

Three hundred years after the Buddha, under Asoka's influence, Buddhism was beginning to reach far south into Sri Lanka. A great journey to Sri Lanka was planned, with many abbots and monks. They took with them a small living shoot from the Bo tree, planted in a flower pot. This they conveyed down the length of India to its southernmost tip. Once there, they sailed by ship to Sri Lanka, and soon were able to transplant the precious tree in the vicinity of Anaradhapura in northern Sri Lanka, where it now flourishes like its parent. In testimony of this one can see in a huge cave hollowed out in a mile-long rock at Dambulla in Sri Lanka an ancient wall frieze depicting the journey of the monks and featuring a procession of holy persons in red, with the tree in its pot held up in the midst of them.

Vic, Ranji, and I arrived at Anuradhapura, and Ranji led us to the tree itself. Nearby stood flower stalls where Ranji advised us to buy a few flowers. Then we approached. Many Sri Lankans in saris and dhotis were approaching the huge trunk of the tree, beside which we saw tables set with water bowls. We looked into the bowls. They were afloat with little petals, so we added our own. All was quiet here. I looked up. The tree spread wide; a slight breeze was blowing. The tree appeared to be a species related to the aspen, because every leaf was moving and quivering. The larger trusses also swayed lightly. One might say the tree was in a sense aerodynamic, lightsome, in motion, swaying this way and that, in a kind of slow quiet dance.

Some of the leaves had fallen. I remember the ground was white and chalky, pleasantly fresh and leaf-strewn. I picked up a leaf. It was indeed in the shape of an aspen leaf, heart shaped; only at the tip, instead of the usual graceful aspen tip there was a greatly elongated point, about an inch or more long, not only making the leaf more beautiful but saying something all of its own. Maybe it was the long tip that made the branches sway so touchingly. Maybe. I looked up again and couldn't help thinking of Siddhartha, there, seeing this sight after all his seeking: there, in a oneness between him and this tree. I realized that this very tree had sprung from his tree. Sway, sway. My head stopped thinking for a while.

Many times after that I have compared the Bo tree to another tree that sways, the English ash, sacred to the druids in Celtic lore. Constable caught its power in a famous picture. You need to *address* the ash tree, synchronize your sway with it, because it has the same movement that enlightened the Buddha. So, paradoxically, is it not that *things* have souls? (See figure 8.3.)

Figure 8.3: The living universe surrounding the Buddhist lotus. A half-circle step in a stone entryway near Anuradhapura, northern Sri Lanka (photo by Edith Turner)

Figure 8.4: In Israel, 1980. Edie's old foster brother Hannan Jarosch. Vic, and Hannan's wife (photo in the possession of Edith Turner)

We left India and Ceylon, and shortly afterwards, in 1980, visited Israel (see figure 8.4). So now we plunge into the two most monotheistic of the religions, Judaism and Islam. After Ceylon, one may ask, what was likely to be the shape of any unified field theory of religion that we might be able to comprehend? That is to say, are there universals in ways of thinking that cover monotheisms, the no-mind-no-god doctrine of Buddhism, and also pantheisms of the deistic or nature kind? Must one read each of them in a fixed theological way?

For a start, we are allowed to see right into Judaism, "the wonders of our God." This began with me recently through a sudden appreciation of the Psalms when I picked up a Gideon Bible while in the hospital for gallbladder surgery. I seemed to hear the voice of the singer of them, someone who lived nearly three millennia ago. Surely that person must somehow be around now.

16:11. You will show me the path of life.
23:2.   You will guide me along the right path for the sake of your name.
29:5.   The voice of the Lord breaks the cedars. [Compare this with Shelley's, "The Cloud":[2]]

I sift my snow on the mountains below
And the great pines groan aghast.

Shelley heard the cloud with its snow breaking the pines. What Shelley and Wordsworth saw was an enormous power in the creation, acting now; this is what the Psalms singer saw, much like those visionary Native Americans and Japanese who see spirit in all things. The Psalms singer experiences the great spirit. We do not have to regard the spirit of God as a barbaric monarch, as many Christians unconsciously do. That very wind that breaks the cedars is the voice of the spirit, which *is* the wind.]

Also, 19:5-6. God has set a tent there for the sun; it comes forth like a bridegroom from his chamber, and like a strong man joyfully runs its course. [This passage, although it uses simile, resonates in the collective unconscious, a power that floods from person to person, in mystical participation. Thus we are free to hail the sun in its actual personhood, as a visionary being, as Blake did.]

31:6. Into your hand I commit my spirit; you have redeemed me, Lord, God of truth. [The singer had a sense that the spirit of the Lord took the initiative: it gave the gift of redemption *to* him. He accepts. This is illuminating.]

34:3, 7. This poor man cried and the Lord heard him and saved him out of all his troubles. [Compare Jero in her poverty. Jero was a Balinese shaman who recorded her life story on videotape. In her early life she was driven to leave her family because she was starving. She wandered into the jungle and came across a mysterious spirit house, where she found a spirit person, sanctuary, and food. This was a true example of how there *is* a spirit looking out for us, supplying us with miraculous help until our own powers can kick in.]

34:8. Taste and see that the Lord is good: blessed is the man who trusts in him [the way I trust I will get back in touch with the spirit—a trust justified from long experience.]

40:5. Many, O Lord my God, are your wondrous deeds, and your thoughts which are toward us [how could he know anything about God's thoughts? But he did, he *knew*]: they cannot be reckoned up in order: should I wish to declare and speak of them, they are more than can be counted. [This praise and wonder is not about oneself; here is the same old shaman's ethic, which is, don't take credit. Moreover, the singer couldn't put the experience into words.]

139:4-6. For there is not a word on my tongue, but look, Lord, you know it altogether. You encircle me behind and before, and laid your hand upon me. Such knowledge is too wonderful for me; it is high, I cannot attain it.

139:17-18. How precious also are your thoughts toward me, O God! How great is the sum of them! If I should count them, they are more in number than the sand: when I am awake, I am still with you.

Compare 115:1. Not to us, Lord, but to your name give glory for your love and your truth's sake. [All these pieces are concerned with the same shaman ethic, in such poetry as makes your heart break. This singer was a poet of experience.]

42:2. My soul thirsts for God, for the living God. [He totally catches the feeling: "for the living god."]

42:6. Why are you cast down, O my soul? And why are you disquieted in me?

42:7. Deep calls to deep at the noise of your water-spouts: all your waves and your billows have gone over me. [Noise is the shaman's bane. He could go mad. His "deep to deep" is exactly the collective unconscious. What is so interesting is that it is a fruitful madness: it is Jung's "Shadow."]

These passages represent the inner workings of a seemingly contemporary soul. Yet at the same time many of the other utterances in the Psalms are full of horrible politickings and blood and thunder. But the soul is there; the singer has vividly depicted the soul for us. He went the way of the mystic, the way of simplicity and delight in the love of the goodness he saw, much as in the age of peace that reigned in the *huya aniya* prelapsarian "world of wild lands" of the Yaqui Indians in Mexico, in former times when their deer talked, or in the simple unified world of the Andaman islanders before contact, or in the original world of the Eskimos, looking "upside-down" to us, when all was one: in other words, in their era of mystical participation. So the Psalms are alive, live, "on-line."

At the time of my Israel visit it was still early in my knowledge of spirituality. Apart from my conversion twenty-two years previously, I wasn't overwhelmed with awe about Christianity then, just alert to its symbolism and ritual as usual. But I wrote a poem about the place of the resurrection. I couldn't help it.

Closet Christian Visits Israel

What magnet draws us to the City? One atheist Jew
will take us there, so he says. I ask him, "Do you understand?"
His brown eyes in pity tell me so.
What can I do but cry? He does understand.

The atheist Jew, like Jesus, leads us on
in his army fatigues, brown eyes in wonder,
slipped disc, drawn; but Jesus in his face.
I've never seen such faith, not among Christians.

We took him from guard duty at the Wall,
he got permission, round at St. Stephen's Gate.
Now we can't find Pilate's Floor. It's locked.
No one kneels at the Stations of the Cross.

Lump in my throat I photograph everything,
photograph electric wires coiling the Sixth Station,
photograph the Moslems on their way back from prayer.
Can't see a thing above these high walls.

The road is all gravel, very hard to walk; uphill.
"Hard enough without carrying a thing," I mutter.
The others stumble. The atheist limps. On
to the Eighth Station, the Ninth. A door.

He's gone. Why did he go in there? We go through.
There's a sunken courtyard, a great old church.
Can it be—? Glad we're here. Wasn't *he* too?
We follow through to the Tomb by a secret way.

I know this place. It is all as I was told,
exactly, like my fifty-nine years' memory.
Upstairs on the right: two competing shrines. At the very heart
of Christianity structure lays its deadly hand.

Structure kills right hand, left hand. They bleed. My hand opens,
Lets out its knowledge. ... Following a woman in black
I creep forward, ugly like her,
protruding my bottom; reach, touch, kiss my hand.

The hole was deep. That's because it's old.
The blood is dried now. What happened here?
Back comes crashing my ignorance. I'm like them all
who believed everything was over. Wasn't it?

But look, the Tomb of the Anastasis. The atheist
learns what the word means: what can never be structured.
That's religion. As we enter the Tomb,
we see our death, our life, on a small marble bed.

I can't hear the heart beat, though I lay my hand upon it.
Now my candle burns there. Of course, he's gone.
We back out the low door, still turned toward the miracle;
the same place where the Abbot Daniel stole a piece of rock

a thousand years ago. Now pillars stand
trembling from earthquake. Water drips down.
The roof is leaking, like an old railroad station,
familiar, ordinary. We go to the back of the tomb.
In a little cave there sits a priest. Coptic,
funny round cap, twinkling eyes.
An old monk handing out trinkets,
a small cross, a picture of Christ Risen.

I give him only a coin. He takes my hand
and pulls it deep into the back side of the Tomb
beside him. I feel rock,
not marble. Rock, the bedrock.

I'm not quite sure what to say here. It wasn't
any sense of Jesus' resurrection and all that.
I've told the story straight. I'm no saint
or visionary at all. But back came flooding

Here in Jerusalem the old human contact
I knew once and lost a long time ago. Can't tell you what.
Something I used to cry for at night in boarding school:
Lots and lots of happiness through this old man's hand.

* * *

We've left. We've passed the ice of Newfoundland,
the pilgrimage is over. The skyboat shakes.
Will the atheist remember? Will I remember
those points of time in a dot pattern that make the picture?

These were the Copts. More than a millennium after King David, the Copts, too, saw that the hard life of the desert would produce miracles—not that it was miracles that they were after, but this is how things happened. Another millennium after that again, in the mid-eighteenth century, the Jansenists brought into existence the same power, rather, they felt it, got alongside it, steered themselves right into the middle of it, and—it began to click with all sorts of miracles.

During our six months' visit I got to know the Holy Sepulcher quite well (see figure 8.5). That pile of worn and ungraceful stone didn't do

Figure 8.5: Four priests, Coptic, Greek Orthodox, Armenian, and Catholic, at the inner chapel of the Tomb. The Holy Sepulcher, Jerusalem, Easter 1983. (photo by Edith Turner)

much for me in itself; not that my opinion mattered, because it did matter for the black-shawled Greek Orthodox women who gave devotion to the place, and I trusted those women better than I trusted myself. Why? As I keep arguing, they are in the midst of life, they are troubled about their own sick, they have lived in close conjunction with their own living religion all their lives, they haven't ever killed off the sense of the spirit with symbolic analysis or psychological interpretations of the roots of ritual, they were living off those roots themselves. All the tawdriness and mess, the rusty steel scaffolding holding up the dome of the Anastasis which is the holy place where Christ rose from the dead, are okay by me.

It was in Israel that I also observed, as I sat in the women's gallery in a Jewish yeshiva school in Tel Aviv, a scene that as a woman I was not allowed to approach closely: that of the terrible swaying of the ultra-Orthodox students, the ancient leather volumes of the Talmud displayed open in their hands as in many generations past, ritually arguing with one another as they stood before their rows of lecterns in the great school of rabbinic learning. How I loved their pale pink-mauve faces which hardly ever saw the light of day because of their life of learning; their side ringlets, flowing down those flawless cheeks; the clear purpose in these men, their scissoring strides, along streets or up the mountain path of Meron to the shrine of Rabbi Shimon Bar Yohai, their own great second-century mystic. Just the black wide-brimmed hats moved me, and the hats at Bar Yohai, the streimel hats, wide, like the hats worn with Ph.D academic robes. These are made of fine fur and are very honorable; then the black brocade coats, knee-length, archaic, with brilliant white leggings below; black polished shoes. These were the Hasids. Talk of resurrection! This resurrection of Jews was hardly less miraculous than that of Jesus. The miraculous resurrection of the Jews as we saw it in 1980, barely forty years after Hitler, has succeeded: the miracle is, how much Hitler has been shown to have failed in purging the world of this religion. It has risen again in beauty (see also figure 8.6).

Barbara Myerhoff, the scholar who had once described Huichol shamanism, came with us on our second trip in 1983 when we all went on pilgrimage to the tomb of Bar Yohai at Meron. Barbara was an anthropologist with unusually good rapport with people, a small beautiful woman with black curly hair and an impish laugh who became a close friend of mine. Seventeen scholars, anthropologists, sociologists, archeologists, museum curators, historians, psychologists, folklorists, and students gathered that year to study a three hundred thousand strong pilgrimage. We stayed nearby at a field school in a military bunker. I wrote up the material about the pilgrimage in

Figure 8.6: The Samaritans still sacrifice lambs to celebrate their own Passover on the slopes of Mount Gerusim, Israel, 1983 (photo by Edith Turner)

1993,[3] giving the history of the devotion and a view of what it was like as we went along with the people on the pilgrimage. Barbara wrote the true participant's piece,[4] unfolding the Jew's sense of a religious act of pilgrimage, and thereby giving another example of possible perspectives for the experiencing anthropologist of the future. (At that time, the anthropology of experience—that is, the importance of an anthropologist being fully inside the experience of the people she studies—was hardly a consideration in the discipline.)

Vic had a dream while at Meron, as most of the pilgrims did—many of whom we saw huddled as near to the tomb of the rabbi as they could get, fast asleep, so that the saint could come to them in a dream. Vic dreamed that he was coming down the hill and met a young Hasid (was it Bar Yohai himself?) coming up. There was a sense that they were on the roof of a house somewhere.

Barbara tried to discern the meaning of the dream, but neither she nor Vic got to the bottom of it, and now they are both dead. For them now it is surely as plain as daylight. I still ask, what is its meaning?

While we were on the pilgrimage itself, the dream filled us with light which also spread to many of us. A nighttime episode, recalled by Barbara Myerhoff on 1 May, 1984, and written down with my own comments in my diary, runs like this:

Vic was drunk under the stars outside the "flower-surrounded bunker" (which Barbara thought was ironical). We were all around him, Vic standing with his back to the wall on the right of the door, very unsteady; all the others were listening to his wonderful and fantastic talk. High unsteadiness was in the air, anything could happen. What would he say? This country, these people were sensitive (these were my inward thoughts). But Barbara, watching and loving, saw me go into the house and come out with a pillow which I put in front of Vic as he stood, lest he should fall onto the concrete. Barbara said this was the warmest, best, most human thing she had ever seen. (I don't see much in it myself. I've tried and tried always to help and steer things well in these situations. Only, she saw it and told me to write it down.)

(There was no pillow when Vic did fall down on December 18, 1983, against the bedroom door in Charlottesville. Enough of that.)

Later in Charlottesville I thought about the great book that Bar Yohai was said to have written, *The Zohar, The Splendor*,[5] and I tried to read it. It was true, as the indigenous scholars said, you'll not understand it. But once, in a crazy exalted mood, I seemed to get it. The sentences are airy, full of light, spiritual. Some modern Catholic architecture tries to catch a sense of that light. The Catholic chapel at the Holy Sepulcher, for instance, and St. John's Basilica, Montreal, and, I'm told, the church at Nazareth; the new chapel of Reconciliation at Knock Shrine. In *The Zohar* I seem to float from sentence to sentence, hearing words that are like the songs of angels, like a kind of musical gift, like the songs of birds, only in wild and strange words, such as I have heard in the words of those who speak in tongues or in trance. It is like the speech of Philip Kabwita, the African whom I met later, in trance on his mystic telephone. It is like the recounters of the Knock shrine miracles, or the healer Claire telling her magical life story, or a Tlaxcala woman in Mexico telling of the miraculous walking Niño doll, or Manyosa in Kajima telling me about her trance, or Jero, the shaman of Bali, telling about her journey in the spirit, or like Castaneda's voice on his sound-tape; yes, here I have coupled *The Zohar* and modern Catholic spirituality with Castaneda. I'm following connections here. I assure you I'll hold them tight. Yeats first wrote "Innisfree" like that, in a wandering tranced way, but was cruelly reprimanded by Ezra Pound, who made him recast the poem in controlled rhyming verse so that it was charming and nice. But in the first version you could smell the bean flowers and the marsh reeds.

Barbara and Vic were gathering together a sense of Judaism that had come alive. They spoke of the Shekinah, that word with a feminine ending, which is the glory of God, the light, the splendor, that same light which Vic saw as a boy, that Patrick Gaffney once saw at the sepulcher,[6] the light that surrounded Kwanyin in a vision of the bodhisattva at Nachi in Japan. I saw the picture of it, with the rays coming out, and photographed the picture. So the Japanese have seen the splendor too. So have the visionaries at Knock. It comes into the human senses most vividly and unforgettably when it does.

Back in Israel, on the roof of Bar Yohai's tomb, there stands a concrete barrel, and on the greatest night of the pilgrimage, the feast of Lag B'Omer, the Hasids light a fire in the barrel and cast into it innumerable candles and burnt offerings, even streimel hats, it is said. I saw a brocade coat go into it, reverently folded. Old men with beards, black hats, side locks, men greatly revered, were in the midst of the circle, and one of them lit the fire to start it. Then all the men, a black-garbed throng, widened their circle, arms on each other's shoulders all around, and danced slowly, slowly around, chanting a deep simple tune, "Bar Yohoy, Bar Yohoy!" I watched and sang under my breath. No one turned me away. Later in the night and in the early hours, so I was told, they began to look to the east for the Shekinah to arrive, the lady, the glory, the dawn coming, walking over the hills, and then they welcomed her and sang praise. This was the supreme moment of the pilgrimage.

Hidden in the Israel visit was a privileged moment, when on a Friday we visited a family of Sufi Palestinians, fine farmers and good Moslems. I was invited to go and pray with the women when the men went next door to their mosque. The women gave me a white cotton robe, much too small. Nevertheless I put it on and we all knelt down as they chanted. We went down on our knees, then forward with our heads right on the ground. Then up again, more chanting, and down again with our heads on the floor, many times. Again, the place was light and airy, and it was good to be there. Everyone was pleased. Previously, the schoolboys had attended their Koran class, and afterwards in their schoolroom they chanted the Koran in the beautiful accented style they had been learning (see figure 8.7).

In this kind of life, we were drawn on from religion to religion, pushed forward to make obeisances, left with mouths agape and souls a-spin. Did it matter if there seemed to be universals in the performance of ritual? What one saw in each case was simply that each was more than we could cope with, not even counting Brazilian Umbanda and Japanese Shinto: "They cannot be reckoned up in order: should I wish to declare and speak of them, they are more than can be counted." So do you simply give up?

Let us attend very quietly and look again. Something or other waves with the Bo Tree, sways with yeshiva students, sings in shamanic psalms, connects like magic under tombs, quavers in trance voices, burns in a truly mystic light, and bows—what else can one

Figure 8.7: Palestinian boys chanting the Koran (photo by Edith Turner)

do—to the god beyond all likenesses. My poor old brain was being inoculated in many places with little grains of certitude. The little grains rest but never go away, and they have become part of a map of the directions in which my wandering path is going.

Notes

1. Roy Wagner, *Symbols That Stand for Themselves* (Chicago, 1986).
2. Percy Bysshe Shelley, "The Cloud," *The Norton Anthology of Poetry,* eds. A. Allison et al. (New York, 1975 [1820b]), 671.
3. Edith Turner, "Rabbi Shimon Bar Yohai: The Creative Persona and his Pilgrimage," in *Creativity/Anthropology,* ed. Smadar Lavie et al. (Ithaca, NY, 1993), 225-252.
4. Barbara Myerhoff, "Pilgrimage to Meron: Inner and Outer Peregrinations," in *Creativity/Anthropology,* eds. Smadar Lavie et al. (Ithaca, NY, 1993), 212-222.
5. Zohar: *The Book of Enlightenment,* tr. Daniel Chana Matt (New York, 1983 [1286 by Moses de Lyon; 2nd Century CE by Simon Bar Yohai]).
6. Patrick Gaffney, "Fire from Heaven," in *The Nature and Function of Rituals,* ed. Ruth-Inge Heinze (Westport, CT, 2000), 151-178.

9

THE LOSS OF MY LIFE MATE
I Was Broken in Half but Had to Become a Whole Person

I've come to the great disaster, Vic's death. What was Vic like in 1983? Though he is dead now, he came to me again a week ago, in a dream, quite solid and real. I see him, my short stubby man, overweight, with badger-like stripes of black and white where his hair has gone white over the ears but not in front. He's marked with energy; he's just a big, definitely "there" personality. He walks into the room reading out from a book. He's onto some idea nobody's thought of. You add an idea to it and he suddenly builds it into something new, the implications of which go right out of sight. While he's saying all this his mouth shapes the words with fond accuracy and pleasure. His lips are a little everted, beautiful, like an African's. I think the Africans recognized this.

But in 1983 when we returned to America from Israel on the news of the birth of our granddaughter in Boston, he often seemed white-faced and tired. Back in Charlottesville he didn't like taking the necessary exercise because his arthritis hurt him, and so he wouldn't take exercise if he could help it.

It came on to October 17th and the season of board meetings, and he hated board meetings. He'd already had to go to the Smithsonian Council board meeting in Washington. Now the Bayly Museum Council meeting was coming up. I still quail at anything to do with the Bayly Museum because it was just before the council meeting that the event happened: his coronary artery blocked up. His ankles began to swell. He was awake all night. I still wonder what it must feel like to have that happen. At the doctor's office next morning I knew that the game was up, this was it. I think I was numbed.

Notes for this section can be found on page 150.

We went straight on from the doctor's office to the hospital and he was admitted. I sat on a worn vinyl chair in the waiting room all night, unable to bring myself to go home. Everything felt empty. They put him in intensive care, and in the morning I went up to see him. He seemed to have expected his heart attack. Nevertheless we were both frightened and couldn't talk about it.

He was a week in the hospital. During that time the pastor of our church, Father Carl Naro, made the rounds and called at the ward. What was good was that the three of us had a warm and pleasant conversation.

"I'll tell you a story," said Father Naro, who was an Italian American. "When I had my heart attack, a funny thing happened. It was in the church, over on the right side where the choir stands. It got me and I passed out and fell on the floor. When I was lying there I left my body, and you know, I could see my body down on the stone floor. Then I found myself going up, and up, and up. I was going to the Lord! I was very happy. I reached the church roof and I wanted to go through to God. There were rafters all around me. Remember, you can see those rafters when you look up. Well, I was right up among them. Then I noticed a hole in the roof behind one of the rafters. I'm telling you, the church architect and I had been trying to spot that hole for weeks. It was letting the rain in. And there it was! By now I was begging Jesus to let me come to him. But to my great disappointment he said, 'It isn't your time yet. You have work to do. Go back.' And down I went, down, down. Next thing I knew there were people looking at me as I lay on the floor. All the faces were very concerned, you could tell. I was back.

"I made a good recovery. Of course I called up the architect and told him where the hole in the roof was. He went up with a ladder and found it, just where I told him. 'How ever did you know where it was?' he asked. I explained. He could hardly believe my story."

Both Vic and I smiled. We were beginning to hear accounts of near-death experiences, and this was another of them.

The hospital gave Vic a large number of pills and—as I realized afterwards—sent him home to die. That's what it was. He was white and helpless for those two months—actually trembling inside, I think—yet standing firm at the same time, like a good Scotsman. And I—I had to carry on, terrified about what was happening to Vic but not daring to say so.

Many times I walked with him all over the house to give him the needed exercise. Somehow our relationship grew tender and delicate all over again.

I wrote in my diary on April 30, 1984, addressing him after his death:

Where you are now? Do you hear me, my love, like you did last November?.... The love when I walked with you; and in Rene's room you used to catch me as we turned, and kissed me, and we stood embraced, quite absolutely happy? Afterwards, your terror and panic! What was going on? Your poor heart, whose electricity wasn't sure of itself, was giving the body trouble. Nerves need blood too.

My friends and Vic's friends, how will you others continue your work? Very well, but the grand coordinator is gone.

One more story from 1953, long ago: walking over the plain on the north side of Kajima village with Vic. You strode over the plain, Vic, hale and well, thinking in thunderclaps of brilliance, about the Fortes and Lowie controversy: Fortes being the theorist of the inevitable, arguing that the means of production determines social structure and social structure determines culture and ritual (positivism); Lowie, the flowering-culture man, saying that cultures produce far more than needed to satisfy social structural needs and it is from this that structures arise. The tiny crystal flowers of an old village site lay at our feet while we talked—I saw the wide open space, almost a desert, a rain-fed tiny tropic desert, a wilderness—and it was there that Vic *saw* the way of the cross, attained a *sense* of it, the truth of St. John of the Cross the mystic, flaming clear; the unity of all, in silent awe in front of . . . what the soul soars to. And your soul is there, on that African plain now, Vic, and you knew it then, and though April 30, 1984, is not in your calendar and it is in mine, that's not the point. That's when your soul sang, in 1953. It sang with eternity and thus is singing now.

Here it comes. Like a shaft of light. I tell you, this is not to be understood.

That November 1983, the time we were walking around the house, I was calling our love "idyllic." But the word held a hidden irony. How could it be idyllic when he was in such danger?

It needs to be told that during the in-between period between Vic's two heart attacks I had been acting as substitute to head his anthropology seminars at the university. One of the sessions was organized by my friend Roy Wagner. He had acquired a sound cassette of drumming. It was something to do with making a shaman journey, he said. He wanted to experiment along with Vic's considerable class of graduate students and see if they could make a shaman journey in the Michael Harner manner. Harner had written about the strange "soul" system of the Jivaro Indians of South America and their shaman journeys.[1] Roy Wagner was the best scholar in symbolic anthropology, a luminously imaginative character, a German-American of the spiritual kind. It was this man who had managed to crack the meaning of the strange rituals of New Guinea. I was interested in Roy's shaman experiment and agreed to cooperate, ready to try anything once. I remembered how, earlier, when listening to Brazilian music, I myself had had a strange waking dream about a dog-like animal in the rain forest.

So we met at night in the roomy front office of the anthropology department, about sixteen of us. Roy gave us our instructions.

"This method is taken from American Indian shamanism," he said. "Everyone lies on the floor and shuts their eyes. I'll get the drumming tape started, just a plain beat. The idea is to find in your mind a cave in the ground, and go down into it, any kind of cave or tunnel. There you might meet an animal. It might be important to you. The change of the drum to a series of quick beats tells you when to come back."

That was all there was to it. So we put out the lights and lay down, packed in like sardines. The beat—beat—beat—beat—beat started. What I saw in my mind's eye was something like a wide well, a dry well, about eight or ten feet deep and about as wide. Okay, and in it was a largish white dog with round ears and smooth fur, looking away from me to the left. Okay, a dog. In a way the dog resembled the Brazilian rain forest beast, which had been somewhat like a kangaroo for some reason. But this was a regular dog. However, as I watched, it sort of turned into a South American Indian wearing a headband. Now to the left was a kind of sill to the lower part of the well, and over it stretched a rope like a washing line, way to the left again, and I couldn't make out what the rope was fastened to at the far end. Never mind, I could go along it for a little. Then the drumming became fast and I was supposed to come back. No more rope, no more well or dog or Indian. Now I was in the department front office again, with all of us lying on the floor. Roy turned on the lights.

"How did it go? Did anyone make a journey?" Eight or nine of us raised our hands.

Some of the stories were rather vague, some surprisingly definite. Roy was interested that so many had made the journey and met an animal, and I understand that since that time several of the graduate students developed more respect for shamanism. I myself was becoming interested, because I had read and edited Barbara Myerhoff's manuscript[2] about Huichol shamanism, which did not represent quite the same phenomenon as this but had affinities with it. The experience we had just had could be compared with theirs. Later I encountered some of the more complex and extraordinary things this core shamanism could do, such as the extraction of harmful intrusions, finding and restoring the soul in cases of soul loss, the power dance, and the "moving drum" dance. Later still, in the Arctic, I witnessed healing, the finding of lost objects and people, changing the weather, prediction, and a sense of the presence of the dead.[3] I began to understand visiting the homes of the dead and of animals, and the eagle's gift of inventions to humankind, such as the drum with singing and dancing, the dog sled, and trade. It is very likely that all the religions are based on something shamanic. Shamanism has to do with direct encounters with spirits; thus it renders power II and the gift of spirit presence available to us and is truly useful.

The grave did have the victory over Vic as far as I was concerned. At that time I did not believe in an afterlife. I thought that the eternity that people called heaven *was*, simply, the great moments of this life, and that these moments had already happened here on earth, like the times when Vic and I and Barbara Myerhoff used to have our brainstorming sessions. Those moments were so good that for me they existed in eternity anyway—and I could settle for that.

But an odd thing happened first. On Sunday November 20, exactly four weeks before Vic's death, Bob, our scientist son in England who had been keeping in touch about his father's illness, called up, sounding especially anxious.

"How's Dad? Is he all right?"

"All right? I suppose so. He's going to rehabilitation classes."

"Oh." He sounded relieved.

"It looks as if he's over the hill, I mean, over the hump," I said. Silly mistake to come out with. I didn't like it.

"Oh." He sent a hullo message to Vic and rang off.

Four weeks later, on 18 December, 1983, a Sunday, Vic was sitting at the kitchen table over his diet breakfast, reading the *Washington Post*. Bob was also sitting there, having arrived the previous day from his lab in England for his Christmas visit.

Vic had obviously been thinking, and was puzzled. He said, "All my memories are coming back to me. Everything."

"Tell us them, tell us them now," I said.

"No, another time. They're all up here," and he pointed to his head and went on reading the sports news.

"The Redskins are having a day off," he said. He was fed up with them. Then—"I feel funny."

He got to his feet and in a trice lurched toward the bedroom. We followed, but we hadn't reach the end of the passage before Vic went through the bedroom doorway. At once the door crashed shut. Bob tried to open it. It was jammed. Bob pushed, hard, and at last it gave. Vic lay with his head against the door, dead.

Had he slammed the door on me?

Never mind that. I knelt down and started the Cardiac Pulmonary Resuscitation treatment I had been learning. I called into Vic's ear, "Vic! Vic!" Silence. "*Just answer*," I thought hopelessly.

Bob phoned the rescue squad, and they came in ten minutes. They cut open Vic's chest and applied an electric shocker they had brought with them to start his heart. It was no good. Bob and I, and our grandson John, and Charlotte his mom went into the kitchen. Martha the

dog stood with us by the door. After a few minutes the stretcher men
came by with the covered stretcher. Martha was standing between us
with her tail so far between her legs it was curled up under her belly.
Looking at her made me realize what had happened. The stretcher
passed and they took him away. We hugged each other piteously.

That same terrible day we heard the continuation of the strange
telephone story.

"I have to tell you something, Mom," said Bob. "You remember
when I phoned you on November 20th from England? I was worried.
I'd just had a dream. I dreamed that I was at the kitchen table in
Charlottesville. Dad said, 'I feel funny' and ran to the bedroom. Then
I was inside the door with him, only I was somehow floating near the
ceiling in the left corner and saw everything that happened. I saw Dad
slip on the mat. He fell with his head against the door and that made
it slam. I saw his face change when he died. Then I got the sense that
everything was all right with him. And I woke up."

"So that's why you phoned us?"

"Yes. I wondered what it all meant, though you said things were
going on okay. So I thought it was just an anxiety dream."

But it was a prophetic dream, experienced by a science-minded
person. I was in awe.

All the children came home from their whereabouts in America,
they came and took the strain for me. We were at least together.

Fifty people danced in the basement at Vic's funeral, his old buddies
and many more. He would have been there himself if he could, holding arms over shoulders and bellowing out the songs. I chose to sit as
the Ndembu widows did, on something resembling an ash heap, surrounded by other widows. What I sat on was a pile of dark rugs topped
with a black cushion, and I got great comfort from the shoulder beside
me, which belonged to Betty, whose father had just died. Wonderful
Ndembu. I was wearing Eleanor's black dress, but my hair was still
dyed brown over the gray. Moving among the dancers before me I
could see a Ndembu funeral mask constructed by the students and
borne on the head by Roy Wagner as he wove in and out of the circle,
hooting and speaking in a high-pitched wavering voice (see figure 9.1).

The following week Fred's little son Benjamin, aged five, snatched
the shattered Christmas from the hands of the thieving Grinch by
organizing an entertainment, "Courtesy of Santa Claus and Victor
Turner," as his dad put it. He put on plays, drawing, singing, and
mysteries to search for in the basement. To speak the truth, no one
knows quite how Benjamin did it, that tiny boy with the Chinese eyes.

What had Vic done to the world? Why were religious studies people in awe of him? It was because he had shown them communitas

Figure 9.1: The students' African funeral mask, 1983. Rene and Edie (photo in the possession of Edith Turner)

and what its nature was, and what structure could do to it, hardening it off and killing it, and how communitas would always grow again.

Almost at once I was broken and battered with the troubles of a widow. I had to submit to the process of being glued together again by my close friends who gathered around, mainly Barbara Myerhoff and Richard Schechner. It was they who set me on the path to being my own person, a thing that had to happen or nothing would be any good. Nothing was easy and I think that having difficulties was the right thing for me. Richard in his huggable Jewish way heartened me. He told me, "Whatever you get asked to do, say yes." So I did. Barbara said, "You can go it alone, Edie. You, Edie. *You* are something." I had the sense that I had been broken up in order to be put together stronger. I'd been broken away from my welding with Vic, and was also suffering the general fragmentation that overtook the whole group of us at the time of his death, and now, in the hands of people who loved me, I would have to grow in ways I had never done before (see figure 9.2). Vic would have called the process the "sparagmos," or "dismemberment," a term taken from Eliade,[4] who understood and documented the curious spiritual process of breaking-down and re-forming that shamans undergo. But it was hard. Furthermore these processes cruelly affected two of the children,

Figure 9.2: American Anthropological Association memorial panel for Victor Turner, 1984, organized by Edith Turner. From left to right, John MacAloon, Sally Falk Moore, Barbara Babcock, Frank Manning, Ron Grimes, Edie Turner, James Peacock, Kit Roberts, and Don Handelman (photo in the possession of Edith Turner)

Alex and Rory, the college students. Prior to the tragedy they had been feeling they had already lost their Dad, that his work had screened him from them and they couldn't get at him. Now, at the wrong time, they knew they had never gotten to know him as much as they might have done and they had feelings of bitterness and resentment—of painful knowledge. They slowly crawled out of the problem in the course of time.

I was weighed down with many unaccustomed responsibilities, now being main householder, which scared me at first along with the academic visits I had to make. There were also spiritual processes going on inside me, pulling me this way and that, the directions of which I knew little. On the other hand, to my delight I became more aware of something in anthropology that reassured me, something extra—the knowledge that by "pulling out" what people wanted to say, by a strong kind of listening and finding delight in what people said, I could make discoveries. People *wanted* to talk. This had been Vic's fieldwork method and it was mine too. A much greater richness of life and culture showed itself that way. I was consciously thankful for this gift of anthropology.

Barbara Babcock, another in our group of friends, asked me to Tucson at Easter to give a talk in her department and also to witness the Yaqui Holy Week deer dance. During that whole year of 1984 I was very nervous, with an acid stomach, which the Mylanta that the doctor ordered only made worse. I was writing a diary which was full of prayers and woe, consisting of no words about anything real, but it was better than nothing, resembling the art therapy they give to disturbed persons.

But as regards visiting the Yaqui, it was Yes! I agreed, for I was always a sucker for fieldwork.

This would be at Tucson, where in the late 1970s along with Vic I had witnessed the deer dance done as a performance, in which the *chapayeka* jackal figures pull down the deer and kill him.[5] This time the occasion was the *Semana Sagrada*, Holy Week itself.[6] The crucifixion had been enacted the day before, on Good Friday, with Judas and the deer. This Saturday the Bier of Christ stood in the church, a high cradle with bars wound with colored paper. The entrance wall of the church had been entirely rolled open, turning the church into a shed-like shelter, a *ramada*. Indian women in shawls were passing in and out of the church all the time. I sat near to the altar and watched. In came a small *chapayeka*, an insolent jackal figure in a mask. I couldn't take my eyes off the mask, pointy and nasty. The thing approached the bier and started to do something to it. It was trying to desecrate it, pollute it. Its hand went to its own bottom and seemed to pull out some stuff. Its nasty fingers wiped the "stuff" obscenely on the bars of the bier. It turned around and rubbed its bottom along the side of the cradle.

This was the custom. No one rose to drive the *chapayeka* away. After it had finished and left, I felt the need to do something. I rose and went to join the line of Indian women as they made their way to the left and to the front of the altar, where they crossed themselves and prayed. There were many crucifixes on the altar and they prayed to each one. So did I. I began to feel better and to love these women.

In the afternoon the confraternity erected a small cottonwood tree in the middle of the open back of the church. This was the native tree of much ritual. The entire plaza of the pueblo was becoming packed with people and I could see a great number of masked persons assembling at the far end of the plaza. Yaqui men arrived at the church end and started the music of flutes, skin drums, and water drums. Now a company of small boys garbed in white, in what looked like long dresses, gathered in a row at the entrance of the church. They were the angels, bearing switches cut from living trees.

The music began. Along came the maskers in a massed body from the far end. As they advanced in outspread lines you could see they were dressed in long capes with short shoulder-capes over them, all of them in black. They wore black snouted masks under low black hats, and they looked for all the world like a dreaded company of Darth Vaders. They were the Pharisees, *fariseos*, on the march to attack the Christ. In ranks surrounding them on left and right came long lines of *chapayekas* in stupid-looking pig or jackal masks. This formidable army drew nearer and nearer, right to the entrance of the church. There was a scurry among the little boy angels in their dresses. One of them snatched up the church's large crucifix and hurriedly hid it in the cottonwood tree planted at the entrance. Then all of them took wands, went forward, and faced the gesticulating Darth Vaders. The children poked at the enemy, and the black companies were taken aback. The children took a step forward and the ranks retired further, back to a line some twenty yards from the church.

Now came the deer dancer wearing his weird plumed headdress—which was an actual deer's head bound on his head just above his eyes, its antlers adorned with flowers on the points. His Indian face, long and in semi-trance, had *become* the deer. He held rattles in front of his knees; his legs and garments were fringed with rattles. He stamped the deer stamp, and shook, looking this way and that, and advanced. He took possession of the land between the church and the evil host in the name of the ancient Yaqui and the angel children. His to-and-fro work of scouring the territory between the angels and Pharisees gradually cleared the ground, and now we could see the whole company of black and colored invaders retreating to the back of their assembly ground. But soon they came on again, and so the drama was repeated all that afternoon.

At night there was a bonfire of all the accouterments, masks, and costumes of the ritual—a bonfire that was also the enactment of the burning of the body of Judas after he had killed himself in the potter's field. All was now ready for the resurrection, the midnight Mass in the church.

Why do I include this event? I think that the knowledge that there existed a resistant core of old ritual tucked into the lower west corner of the United States was part of what made me strong again. That old communitas, that "world of wild lands," *huya-aniya*, was then possible, still operating here and there. Moreover it existed as a connectedness even between the Darth Vaders, whose enactors were themselves penitents and who undertook the roles as their penance. The existence of an unchoked throughway from the past was a curious relief, greatly reassuring, like tears.

During that year Barbara Myerhoff, too, fell ill with a disease that soon killed her. Here, I look for where my path might have run, but it wasn't in the memorial panel I had to organize for Vic at the meetings, nor in the talks I gave on girls' initiation. It led underground, into the open grave of my friend Barbara, where a serious pile of earth had been thrown on one side, where her box was lowered into the ground, and was then covered up. The line disappeared down into the grave. So where was I to go from there?

In an ancient cave among the San bushmen of South Africa, stick people with rays coming out of their heads are depicted hovering over a path.[7] This path was a line that the ancients had drawn leading on and on over the protuberances on the wall of rock stretching the length of the cave. After a time the line comes to a crack and you don't see it any more. Yet you can look a yard or two further to the right, and there it is again, coming out of another crack. Going through my memories of 1984 and early 1985, I couldn't see anything except the hole in the ground. Was there no path at all after that? Yet the world's an odd place, for the line finally came out of a crack right across the globe in Zambia, Central Africa.

Barbara Myerhoff's dying example had been that of a person who had gone out for fieldwork against all obstacles, even to the point of death. A year or two before her Israel trip her husband told her she was traveling too much, neglecting him and their two teenage sons. She broke down and gave in completely, promising only to give lectures at the university and nothing more. She would be a good wife. She actually complied for a week, and then whatever it was within her said, "No, it's impossible." Her old Jewish friends of her fieldwork needed her to travel to promote the book she had written about them, to lecture and go on TV, to put their special humanity before the public, and there were other tasks calling to her. So the promise was broken. She went to do more fieldwork with us in Japan, and she went to Israel. The inner conflict stood within her and began to take away the living breath from her body, eventually eating into spine and lungs. And so she died.

Notes

1. Michael Harner, *The Jivaro: People of the Sacred Waterfalls* (Garden City, NY, 1972), and *The Way of the Shaman: A Guide to Power and Healing* (San Francisco, 1980).
2. The manuscript was published as Barbara Myerhoff, *Peyote Hunt: The Sacred Journey of the Huichol Indians* (Ithaca, NY, 1974).
3. See Edith Turner, *The Hands Feel It: Healing and Spirit Presence among a Northern Alaskan People* (DeKalb, IL, 1996).
4. Mircea Eliade, *Shamanism: Archaic Techniques of Ecstasy* (Princeton, NJ, 1964).
5. See Edith Turner, "The Yaqui Deer Dance at Pascua Pueblo," in *By Means of Performance*, eds. R. Schechner and W. Appel (New York, 1989), 82-95.
6. For full details of Yaqui ritual life, see Edward Spicer, *The Yaquis: A Cultural History* (Tucson, AZ, 1980).
7. See David Lewis-Williams, *Discovering South African Rock Art* (Cape Town, 1990).

10

RETURNING TO AFRICA

Another Door Opens to the Soul

I came away from these sorrows with my health, if not with academic skills and status. I was sixty-three years old, of unusual determination like the badger. My father's family name was Brocklesby, meaning badger. I'd go back to Africa. I would. I'd let my hair grow in gray
so that the Ndembu would treat me as an elder, with respect. While
Vic had been still around I couldn't go back because he wasn't well
enough for the hardships involved, and showed no inclination to go.
It was now eighteen months after Vic's death. I would do a restudy of
girl's initiation. I'd see what the girls really felt. (Teenage girls? What
was I thinking of? Who in the world can get into the mind of teenage
girls except teenage girls?) That was the idea, and it was the idea that
won me a small grant to go. Bill, the son of my good friend Ceece,
wanted to go with me. So I would have help. Things were shaping up.
I would go back to the very village where Vic and I had lived thirty-
one years previously.

Then followed an interval concerned with the business of threading
through official channels, a task I was learning firsthand, having been
protected from the grosser forms of it all my married life. It was like
cracking a hard nut or pulling teeth. I fought every inch of the way—
with the Zambian telephone system, with visa forms, with the Institute
for African Research, which was a body struggling for survival under
the impoverished Zambian state, and, worst of all, with the problem of
the nonexistence of transportation to the outback. Indeed, Africanist
anthropologists today have even worse stories to tell. We were finally
informed we could hire the institute's only vehicle and driver for the

---

360-mile bush trip if we paid £160 plus all the driver's expenses there and back. It seemed like a lot of money in 1985, but it wasn't.

Arriving back after thirty-one years was a surprise in itself, and hidden in this surprise lay another surprise that came at the end of a ritual. From my present viewpoint I can see my trip to Africa in 1985 as coming upon me unbeknownst. It was part of the vagaries of my life way, part of the life-swerves I had been observing.

I arrived in Kajima village and found there our old assistants of the previous research, Musona and his wife Mangaleshi, and now there was one of their many daughters, Lessie the schoolteacher, whom her mother, Mangaleshi, offered to me as an assistant to work with the women. Lessie was a fundamentalist, a member of the Christian Fellowship, which was derived from the Plymouth Brethren. In 1985 40 percent of the people were Christians compared with 5 percent in the 1950s. I worked with Lessie until I found it was against her religion to translate for me the girls' initiation songs of that era, naughty as ever and even more violent than in the old times. The difficulty got worse when I saw a Christian mother beating her tiny son for taking the milk I had given her for her children. It was supposed to be for her son. What was wrong? Was it because he had sneaked it from where I had placed it beside the mud hut? In the two and a half years between 1951 and 1954 when I had lived among the same communities in the pagan days, I had never seen mothers beat their children. I quickly grew to hate Christianity in Africa, even though I continued going to Mass, said by a priest who had a Nazi mother. I wondered if I was right to do that.

To replace Lessie I obtained help from the niece of Peter Matooka, the old Ndembu scholar and diplomat. Jennifer Matooka was an intelligent and loyal helper and I was grateful. Now Bill and I were able to launch out on a serious study of the rituals of the 1980s, starting with spot censuses in the same way Vic and I had done fieldwork in the 1950s. The censuses were enlightening. Patriliny was setting in and matriliny falling away, due to the advance of property ownership and the greater importance of jobs. The divorce rate had gone down; the infant mortality rate had dropped from 250 per thousand during the 1950s to 140 per thousand. The population had trebled. Children were hungrier because the soil had deteriorated owing to over-cropping, caused in its turn by the high fecundity rate, which had risen to five instead of two per family. Twelve children in a family were quite common. Trees had been cut down for tens of miles around every settlement, and now, owing to general continental deforestation, the weather had changed from a heavy rainfall to a rather light one, worrying to the planters of cassava in November. The cassava roots now measured only four or five inches in length, compared to twelve or eighteen inches in the old days.

I was sickened. I was scared when I thought about it. This was the same era when many thinking people in the metropolitan countries were actually despairing about the survival of the planet as a livable environment. Bill and I were seeing the reason for the danger with our own eyes: the deterioration of the biosphere due to modernization.

Close before us were mud-brick huts in crowded groups extending for eight miles around, with areas of ragged low scrub and weeds, red laterite paths here and there, and patches of white behind the huts where those lucky enough to have cassava pounded it. The women were now using metal, not basketwork, sieves for the cassava flour. The people were active as always except for one or two under the care of a tribal doctor in a seclusion hut. The people were happy to say hullo and tell us who the traditional doctor was in each case so that we could come and witness the next treatment (see figure 10.1).

So we came to the next one offered, and found the traditional doctor, Kabwita, treating a woman who had had many miscarriages and now at last had given birth to a fine live baby. Kabwita had been washing both mother and child with herbal medicine and holding rituals for them, and he had set up a seclusion enclosure for them and decorated it with broad upright leaves in a striking row along the fence. The leaves were actually protection medicine against witchcraft. Kabwita

Figure 10.1: Zachariah and Edie performing the hunters' dance. Zambia 1985 (photo in the possession of Edith Turner)

himself had taken on power with his garb. He was wearing not the usual shirt and pants of the 1950s that would have made him look like an ordinary, rather timid African, but a grass skirt, grass armlets and leg frills, and a tall genet-skin hat. On his bare breast hung a small turtle shell on a string. He was clearly a thinking listening person.

Shortly after welcoming us he gave a gasp. "Hoo-OO!"

He was getting a spirit message. It was like, "You've got mail," but this was live, real. He sat down, reached into the black bag at his feet, and drew out a five-inch conch shell on a cord. He placed the conch to his ear. My eyes followed the cord down. It led into the black bag. I looked up again. Kabwita was speaking in a high fluty voice. He was in trance.

"Good evening, Mary, Louisa, and Jack. It's a little boy. Thanks, thank God. Message to the mining town, by telephone of Africa. Thanks to Abraham, Moses, Joshua, Elijah, the Lord Jesus, President Kaunda, with white clay blessing.

"Message to the white woman here, for singing. Message to the husband in the mining town from this new mother. He's dreaming of what is happening in this enclosure. Thanks for a son. Thanks to the elder chiefs, to the people who began the world. We received the medicines from you. Now we have it ourselves, in our own generation.

"Ngo! Nothing more."

Kabwita gave a great sigh, "Oh-ho-ho-o," and put away the conch.

I had been rapidly writing down the words, full of respect for Kabwita's gift. I had been learning about trance with shamans. Kabwita explained to us that he had been given the power of spirit communication and healing from Casto, his teacher spirit, and that these faculties had always been a possibility from the time of his birth. At his birth he had emerged from the womb in an unusual white covering, called a caul. His daughter possessed the gift of communication too, and they could converse over long distances in the same way whenever Kabwita received warning of a call—which was his own throat making the spontaneous gasp, "HOO-OO." Later, when Kabwita used to sit in our hut telling us his life story he often received these calls, suddenly. Once, oddly, while we sat, I had a picture in my mind of him taking up the shell, just a moment *before* he gasped and took up the "receiver."

His genet skin hat itself was a strange thing. I was impressed how Africans still held fast to their bits of knowledge about certain material things, in this case the skin of the genet cat, one of the *muskelidae* family related to the civet cat and skunk, and similarly endowed with a smell. It is a solitary and evasive beast, avoiding company, like the badger. The skin of the genet had the power, when needed, of making a person invisible. Kabwita was wearing his hat when we first met. Musona and his hunter friend told me how they had escaped from being trampled by angry elephants because of the genet skin apron worn by the hunter companion. When the elephants were about to run them down the hunter told Musona, "Come here and touch me." The two men stood still as the elephants rushed by, and the animals never saw them.

Later Kabwita performed another ritual, this time for the cure of a madman, Noah. On our way to the ritual that evening Bill and I wove along a path among the old mounds of a darkened garden. We could see the fire at the center of the ritual gathering not far ahead. Just before reaching the crowd I happened to pass a tall tree stump on my left—unusually tall. Tree stumps were at most about two feet high. I looked at the stump and then went by. Just as I did so I heard a sound: "HOO-OOoo." I looked back and realized that what I had seen was no stump, but Kabwita himself in his genet skin hat, just coming out of a tranced communication. He had been invisible to me.

Kabwita officiated at the ritual late into the night, with song, drumming, and the washing of the blank-faced mental patient Noah, who sat silent throughout the proceedings. The next morning after it was all over, Noah came around to see me. He was now quite sane and normal.[1]

All the phenomena that I am recording in this book, and not only the ones in Africa, happened in the space of my lifetime, that is, the lifetime of just one person; not all the time, obviously, but they did occur, those events, among the other events and exigencies of my life. I am keeping to this kind of event as I go along in my account, much as if I were being careful to tread on stepping stones over a stream, because I reckon the events accumulate to represent another human faculty we possess that is at serious risk of being endangered, likely to disappear. I want to save it. It's fine by me that it only operates sporadically, for the word "spore" is from the Greek, *sporadikon*, "spread out"; while our word "spore" implies much fertilization over wide distances by tiny living grains. Much grows from those little grains.

A little later I met a medicine man named Fideli who often enacted the Ihamba ritual that Vic and I had witnessed in the 1950s (see chapter 4 above).[2] He asked me to his next ritual because I knew some of the medicines and I might act as a supernumerary doctor along with his other assistants.

The ritual took place on November 27, 1985, on the outskirts of a village called Kahona.[3] By this time I was very much wanting to participate in sympathy with the people and was intrigued by the people's tale of a tooth, called Ihamba, wandering about in a sick person's

veins, something that could be taken out by cupping, using hollow
horns. In the past I had never known quite what to make of that particular ritual. I was determined to go now and pay attention to what
was actually going on, and try to take seriously what the people said.
I didn't know what I was in for. The surprise turned out to be a strange
experience, one that demanded a reorganization of my anthropology.

Singleton and Fideli first decided to schedule the ritual on Thursday, November 28, and began to send out messages to the village
extended family. Then news came through that Princess Anne of
England was to visit the Ndembu on that day on behalf of the Save
the Children Fund. So the date for the Ihamba was rescheduled earlier, on the Wednesday at dawn, thus adding an irregularity which
became important during the event itself, as we shall see.

The night before the ritual I had a curious dream. I dreamed that
down a long hill there was a wall, and in the wall was a door, a very
heavy closed door that I had always wanted to open. I had dreamt
this dream before. Now it was standing slightly open, that solid
wooden door. I pushed hard, and it opened some more, so I was able
to get through to the pleasant hillside beyond. That was good.

Bill and I had to wake early so as to arrive at the village at dawn. We
left, Bill taking his tape-recording equipment. In the twilight village an
apprentice called Vesa approached, followed by Fideli, and the two
gave us their courteous greeting: "*Shikenu mwani*," "Welcome, come."
Vesa set the ritual in motion by fetching the drum, a tall African bongo,
on top of which he placed a flat basket containing various items of
equipment—a long musical rasp, an ax, a small hoe, and two small
bags, one made of mongoose skin. The basket's contact with the drum
dedicated it to ritual—for the word "drum," *ngoma*, also means "ritual." Vesa and Fideli then raised the basket between them high into the
air: its raising was its honoring, with hints of consecration.

At this ritual I found I could retranslate what Vic and I previously
called "symbolism" as actual effect—the basket was now sacred, its
contact was not merely a symbolic one. I could see that this was so,
now that I was intent on experiencing the ritual myself.

The senior medicine man, Singleton, then joined us. He was seventy years old, a tall man with a long lined face—a conscious face, capable of unearthly flashes of irony and mischief, a man who said what
he thought, an elder. He had touches of gray in his hair. He wore old
blue overalls and carried himself with limber ease even though he
was thin and elderly. Our friend Fideli was his nephew. Fideli's face
shone with the health of early middle age. He was an able man, a
thinker with a knowledge of science, carrying himself this morning
with the buoyant air of one looking forward to a procedure in which

he was well versed. His religion was Baha'i, which is tolerant toward other religions. Fideli rested confidently in that fact, and I thank the Baha'is for it.

With Singleton in the lead we set off into the low scrub to look for medicines, "yitumbu," bits of special tree and plant that have powerful effects, spiritually as much as chemically. I knew I must give respect to this mass of vegetable stuff, because although it seemed to be merely a collection of unfamiliar botanical species, yet they were substances of power. None of them as far as I could ascertain later was a mind-altering drug, but I may not have identified them all. I realize now that what the Ndembu people saw in these material things was their inherent mystical character. Until that time I was not fully aware of the depth of discernment that Singleton was accessing, because for the previous thirty years I had tended to translate the effect of the plants as symbolic. It was simply our Western way of thinking about it. By the climax of the ritual treatment I began to realize that the concentrated effect of all the ritual and all of the plants, all the people's acts, those of spiritual beings included, all did indeed produce the extraction of the harmful tooth from the body of the sufferer.

From the following description of the medicine quest one can see a little into the mystical participation of people and plants as the Africans know it.

During our peregrinations in the fields, Vesa followed after Singleton carrying the basket that contained the ritual equipment, then came Fideli with the ax. I came next. Then my friend Bill with his long legs and youthful goodness of expression brought up the rear. In front walked Singleton playing rhythmically on the wooden rasp, singing a plaintive little ditty in which we all joined:

Mukongu, katu-ka-tu ye—
Mukongu, katu-ka-tu ye—
Hunter spirit of the medicine tree, let's go, let's go—

We sang the second line a note below the first, in falling tones, with Fideli's light bass continually sounding the fourth harmonic below, and Singleton's rasp softly sizzling like the shivers of cold chills. We were tuning and repeating, and all the time gradually approaching and focusing on the first medicine tree.

We reached an area blighted with over-cropping. Singleton walked swiftly now, weaving toward a small tree he had spotted among the garden mounds. It was the African oak, the "greeting" tree, the "mother" of the ritual. Inherent in this living thing, this oak, was a power, the power that brings together a herd of animals. It was the tree of herds. Singleton hunkered down before the base of the tree trunk and took out his mongoose skin bag, from which he drew a lump of red clay; he rubbed this clay in a broad vertical line down the west side of the trunk, then in a line from the foot of the tree to himself, and then on the east side of the tree. He drew the lines to call Ihamba to come soon, to direct it along the lines. "Ihamba knows 'I am soon going to be out of the patient.'" (I saw that the tooth-spirit, Ihamba, was a conscious being. The red line had brought the spirit right into contact with Singleton.) Then he took a cup of beer and poured it out at the foot of the tree on both sides, saying loudly and abruptly, "Maheza!"

"Maheza!" we shouted back.

"Ngambu!"

"Yafwa!" we returned—with special emphasis on the last word. I remembered this chant from the old days. It meant, "Friend! Friend! Sudden death! It's dead!"—a hunter's cry. My nostalgia and my affection for the dramatic cry rose within me.

Singleton addressed the tree; his tone was urgent and harsh. "It began with Kamawu, it came from Koshita, from Sambumba, from Chisanji, from Muhelewa Benwa. Today it's in my hands. True! This red clay medicine of yours has reached us. It's bad that we've often had to do without the tooth-removing ritual. We're putting this red clay of yours on the western side of the tree. You deserve a cup of honey beer, you'll be blessed; give us the power to cure this woman well. You others who made things hard for us, you bad guys, here's a drink of beer on the other side. You really screwed up; besides, you failed to shoot animals." Singleton used the pejorative word for having sex, *kusunja*.

In this conjuration Singleton emphasized the name of each of his Ihamba doctor ancestors who had handed down the ritual to him. Here one could trace a kind of apostolic succession of spiritual persons, all members of the spirit-tooth doctors' guild. Singleton was talking to those old healers, even including the bad lots, the *ayikodjikodji* as they used to be called in the old days. I watched, trying to connect with the spirits, although I was not a member of the dynasty as the doctors were. Curiously, I had my own dynasty, a long lineage of medical doctors, the Brocklesbys and Davises.

Fideli said that from that moment onward in the ritual Singleton was informed in his task by the spirit of his father Sambumba and the others. They would guide him to the herbal trees and give him discernment in the course of the ritual.

Singing our song to the gentle rasp of the reed as it swished over the musical bar, we went on to a blessing tree, from which we took some bark to make drinking medicine and leaves for washing the

patient's body. This tree had the power of consecration to the ancestors, as Africans do by blowing on their food as a grace before meals.

We went to a Congo pepper shrub where Vesa squatted down and
proceeded to tear open the whole root, while Singleton addressed the
spirits in a throaty voice, "You are my elders—if you're really underground there, really there underground." He was speaking to those
old hunters, wild man Chisanji, to his father, to his hunter uncles,
there in the disturbed red dirt of Africa in front of us. Then he said to
Vesa, "Chop some medicine." The root was large and plump. He took
the entire system of roots, then replanted the top and filled up the
hole again afterwards until the dirt reached the surface. The root is
bright orange inside; when mixed with beer it makes Ihamba obey.
"The medicine passes into the bloodstream, goes throughout the
body, and kills the germs troubling the patient"—as Fideli explained
it in scientific language.

We came to a huge anthill and found a thorn tree. The power of catching lay all over this tree, in its little thorns. Chikwata was added to the
basket so that it would catch the Ihamba with its thorns. We picked its
branches gingerly. It was a purgative medicine for expelling the trouble.

Off we went singing and sizzing with the rasp to a broom tree,
trusses of which are often used for mystic sweeping. The passing of
the broom over the ground clears witchcraft creatures from the area.
We took leaves and roots which had the power to sweep bad things
out of the blood.

Now we came across another tree of herds. As this was not the
greeting tree, the mother, we could cut medicine from it, so we took
bark and leaves, which possessed a herding power in it and would
call a large gathering of people.

We took bark and leaf medicine from the coco plum. The pit inside
the fruit was ancestorhood itself, ancient and never decaying. The
sweetness of the fruit was drawing power itself, and drew people into
a gathering.

Then Singleton circled around a bed of what looked like bracken
but with broad double leaves. The plant was called the lemon root. It
possessed an underground system of fine wandering black roots, fra-
grant with a lemony scent. Singleton sometimes cured malaria with
these roots by rubbing them into cuts on the left shoulder of the
patient, or he would use them infused in cold water as a poultice. I
wondered if they contained bitter quinine.

There was more to the lemon root. Singleton told us that the
Ihamba might have little children inside the patient's body. The drum
ritual might be successful in bringing out the mother Ihamba, but her
children might remain inside, as indeed the afterbirth might. How-

ever, scraped lemon roots, put into one of the Ihamba cupping horns with certain other ingredients—a mixture called *nsomu*—could kill the afterbirth inside the body and make the entire Ihamba brood come out. So they took several tangles of the long roots.

Singleton circled around another shrub with fixed attention. "This is the tree which I didn't think anyone could find. Go easy on the leaves. Take them from the eastern side, not the west. It is the tree of vision." With tree of vision the Ihamba would appear quickly and would not be able to hide; but the tree was now rare. The leaves and bark contained the power of sighting, the opening of the eyes, the unexpected appearance of figures like antelopes beneath the tree, feeding on its fallen pears. We took a few of the big leaves and some bark from the east side, the side of the sun's revealing, and went on singing—"Mukongu, katu-ka-tu-ye."

Soon we stopped again and looked around. We were on a path above a long derelict garden without a bush in it. "It's all been dug," said Singleton to Vesa disgustedly. "Search carefully in this area. We may never find the tree I've been telling you about. We're back where we started, at the first tree of herds. I think I saw the tree I'm after when we went that way before; I don't want to go all the way over to Mindolu Village for it."

Vesa said, "Look! Over there!"

It was a small tree known as the soap root, a tree which needed extra care in the cutting. Singleton wielded the ax while Fideli held the basket beside the trunk. Singleton very neatly cut grooves into the bark outlining a four-by-six inch vertical rectangle, with Fideli squatting beside him to catch the chips in the basket, careful not to touch any. "If any of them fall to earth you can't have Ihamba," explained Fideli, watchful. Singleton then levered off the rectangle of bark with his ax and let it drop safely onto the basket. "Ihamba will permit us to catch it without running away." We didn't treat the piece of bark lightly. It was the power of "catching" itself and the catching power had to stay in the bark. "Ihamba might fly away so we must be careful to make him honest," said Fideli. Soap root had a strong smell; when they were ready to take the Ihamba tooth out of the patient's body and put it into a tin can, that piece of bark could be used as a lid to keep it in. "Ihamba doesn't like the strong smell, and won't try to come out of the can and escape," said Fideli. This medicine could also be used as a soapy lotion to wash all the bad things from the body.

We continued on our way, now searching for an ironwood tree to provide fuel for the ritual fire. But before we found it Singleton spotted a bitter-bark sapling. He set his legs firmly beside it and with rapid deft strokes of his ax cut it down and made it into a forked shrine pole, sharpening the branches into tines exactly as I had seen done thirty-one years earlier. Bitter-bark has power over the teeth. It sets your teeth on edge with its bitterness: as a result bad teeth drop out, an major desideratum in the case of the Ihamba tooth. The tree has the spiritual quality of the wind, ubiquitous and invisible.

We proceeded onward, singing. The doctors were concerned about the ritual firewood; it had to be ironwood because this wood was strong, tall, and unbending, and had no stringiness in its texture to tie up huntsmanship. At last we came across a felled ironwood tree just as we were turning back home. Fideli got astride the bare trunk and hacked patiently at it with his ax, careful to let none of the firewood fall to the ground. When they collected enough they gave me the wood to carry, which I liked to do. They then searched among young trees until they found a termitary made by a species which produces small mud towers eight inches or so across and about a foot high.

"We're lucky," said Vesa. "Here's a big specimen of small anthill."

"Let me see it," said Singleton. "Yes, that's it. We won't find another one like this."

"We should take it out whole, right from the bottom, " said Fideli.

Vesa cut it off right from the bottom and we lifted it out. I could see the termites flooding the broken bowl below, each grabbing an egg which she bore off to safety. Vesa sheared off the domed top and carved the column into a house shape, a cube, then put the cube into the basket. He respectfully replaced the dome on the broken termite home. The cube would be placed at the foot of the chishinga shrine pole, becoming a grave for Ihamba, that is, for the dead hunter who now existed in the form of Ihamba as a spirit.

We found a plant called "no-reason" by the side of the path. It was a plant barely four inches high, so we took it all, exposing startlingly black roots which when cut showed a brilliant white interior. This with the flaming yellow-orange Congo pepper, and the thorn root, rosy red inside, and the lemon root tangle, sweet and lemon-smelling, and the prickles of the thorn, made a telling collection, more telling than color, scent, or prickles when one includes the coming-out effect of drinking the mixture, whose exact properties were unknown to me—and if one includes the cure.

Singleton said he was going off alone later to collect some "suddenly-falling leaves" from a plant of that name. It has the power of sudden ejection. It can suddenly eject malaria, and also eject the Ihamba from inside the patient. Suddenly-falling leaves, used along with the Congo pepper, call Ihamba to come out. The two comprise a potent dangerous coming-out medicine, used to procure abortions.

They found a true abortifacient, used for expelling placentas, taken from a tree that grew atop an anthill. Singleton wanted the leaves so he could chew them and spit the pulp into a cupping horn to "call Ihamba to enter the horn."

"There are medicines for the below and the above and inside, every medicine to make Ihamba come out," said Singleton. Then he said, "Let's go back to the road."

At this ritual Bill and I were watching and learning. I was eagerly taking in all those properties that referred to "coming out" and child-birth. I was remembering the strong physical contractions of giving birth to my five children.

We returned to the hut of the sick person, a middle-aged woman named Meru who was a kind of sister of Singleton's. We found a shaded spot behind her open-air kitchen to establish the shrine, then Fideli laid an antelope skin on the ground so that Vesa could deposit the basket. First they planted the shrine pole, the forked pole of bitter wood sharpened into horns to attract the hunter's spirit, and they set the squared-off spirit house in front of it. Then they spread the skin as a seat for Meru in front of the shrine. They prepared the medicines, found a can to receive the tooth when it was taken out, and covered the can with a smelly castor oil leaf and on top of that the soap bark lid to keep the tooth in once it was taken. The doctor lit the ironwood fire with matches, not by means of kitchen coals. All was separate and new. A mortar stood near and was filled with medicine leaves. The woman assistant, Etina, got busy and pounded the leaves, then she took a calabash of water and poured some out, first on the ground to the east of the mortar, then to the west, then into the mortar, to make leaf tea medicine. The libations were for the spirits, who must not be forgotten. Remembrance of spirits was growing all around us in that ritual space.

One pan of cold medicine stood by, and one of hot medicine was stewing on the fire. Cupping horns lay ready in the medicine basket. Drums were brought close and people began to assemble.

Now Singleton medicated the five doctors. He, Fideli, Vesa, Luka the second apprentice, and I drank some of the leaf tea. For a moment it made my head swim, then after a minute my senses cleared. Singleton announced to the crowd, "If there are any pregnant women here, go away." The concentrated "coming-out" effect of medicines and objects was so strong that there was a real danger of a woman having a miscarriage.

Singleton inspected the shrine; then said, "Look, we've made a mis-take. We should have had Meru facing east, where the sun comes out from the earth, not the west the way we've got it."

"We did that because of the shade," said Fideli. "But it doesn't matter, we'll leave it as it is." But it did matter, toward the end of the ritual. A small procession was approaching—Vesa leading Meru, the woman with an Ihamba tooth in her body. Where it came from nobody knew as yet. Vesa seated her on the antelope skin. She pulled faces at the sight of the medicines around her, especially at the razor blade lying in the basket. This was a miserable proud haughty suffering woman. They washed her with spongy masses of the leaf medicine, squeezing all the pounded and focused "coming out" plants into her body until it was drenched with the speaking and penetrating way-opening stuff. The medicines now began speaking to the Ihamba inside her, "Come out."

The doctors used red clay to draw a line down her brow and nose, temples and cheekbones, lines to protect her head. They gave her medicine to drink and thus the opening effect went inside too.

The ritual power was accumulating. Now they performed. They took castor oil leaves, laying them over their fists, then with a concerted shout—"Paya!"—smacked the leaves with the other palm— and the leaves fell on Meru in blessing.

"Maheza!"

"Maheza!"

"Ngambu!" shouted Singleton.

"Yafwa!" we all replied. ("Friends! It's dead.")

Then began the drums in an irresistible rhythm heightened by clashing ax irons; and we sang and clapped. Singing, the doctor came close to Meru and shouted, "Come out!" directing his call into Meru's body. He began divining for the Ihamba's name. "If it's you, Nkomba, shake. If not, don't shake." This was using something inside her as a kind of oracle that would show them the truth by the way she acted. I called the address to the spirit a "divinatory proposition."

She hardly shook at all, sitting there with her legs straight out on the antelope skin. "Is it Kadochi? Shake, if it is. Quick now!" Singleton danced the antelope mating dance before her (see figure 10.2). Already the group had increased to a crowd of about thirty persons at least half of whom were children.

They cut tiny slits in Meru's skin at the back, then sucked on cupping horns and blocked the open ends. "Come out!" shouted Singleton at the place where the horns adhered.

Meru suddenly said her first "words." All knew what "words" were. The coming out with your "words," mazu, helps to make the Ihamba come out. Meru said in an oratorical voice, "I don't agree. I have something in my liver, my heart. It's my children; all my children have died. I just want to die because there's no one to look after

Figure 10.2: Singleton performs the antelope in an Ihamba ritual for Nyakanjata, Meru's aunt. Fideli is seated at the back. Note Singleton's musical rasp, the cupping horn marks on the patient's back, shrine pole, medicines, and singers. Zambia 1985 (photo by Edith Turner)

me." The people heard her frankness and were pleased. They continued with their songs.

But Singleton was not satisfied. "I haven't seen you shake happily yet. You're stiff with worries."

Meru's brother said, "I heard how Meru's own younger sister cheated her. When the sister went to sell the beer that Meru brewed, she didn't bring Meru the full price. Her own younger sister cheated her out of her money." By speaking for her the brother helped to unblock more of her "words"—grudges that had to come out. Meru shook violently in corroboration, but she was tired. From the divination they perceived that the spirit inside her was the old hunter Kashinakaji.

More "words" came out: "I don't see Paulos in the crowd. Where is he?" Meru was offended by his absence. Paulos was her well-to-do but distantly related "brother." It was revealed that Paulos had never been told of the change of date for the ritual, owing, as we have seen, to the visit of Princess Anne.

Singleton spoke to her spirit: "If you want Paulos to come to the ritual, shake. If not, don't shake." She shook hard, and they sent a messenger for him.

Worse was to follow. The assistant who was supposed to change our tape-recording cassette had reversed it instead, thus erasing a previously recorded side. Bill was angry and I was disappointed about the loss. The crowd immediately sensed this and turned around in silence hoping to hear Bill's "words."

"Perhaps these foreigners are closing up Ihamba," they said. "They ought to come out with their grudges."

"Bill can't say 'words,'" said Fideli. "He doesn't know our language. Besides, Edie is a doctor. Why should she close up Ihamba?"

Meru broke in with "words" spoken in her high oratorical tone, reiterating all her complaints and ending, "The way things are, I'll die."

Singleton was still for a moment, attentive. He said, "I've seen it. It's the Ihamba, so he's got to come out of her. Her brother has put on his "words." He said things that revealed the bad spirit. It's come. We are now happy, we may say we're very happy. The Ihamba will soon find you've fallen down."

He addressed Kashinakaji in Meru's body: "Forgive us, grandfather Ihamba, I have to take you from the body of my sister so that I can keep you with me." Then he switched his remarks to Meru herself (this switching happened many times—from spirit to human). He said: "The man who's come is your brother, he's coming right now."

Paulos had indeed arrived and was in very ill humor. "You told me Ihamba was to be on Thursday," he said. "And here I find it going on, on Wednesday. Is that good manners?" Everyone tried to explain at once. Then the drums began once more.

The heat was drawing up black clouds above us. Meru fell shaking in the midst of the singing, in the dim light under the shade trees. Singleton again tried to draw out the tooth. Voices broke in, "Yes, let her fall half dead like that. Do you want the witchcraft dancing in her? Yes, you do." The doctors wanted the spirit to show itself so that they could bring it out. Even so there was a tone of horror in the voices. So much was coming out.

It was a long ritual. The horns were reset, drumming began anew, and Singleton repeatedly traced a path on Meru's back to direct the trouble that he could feel under the skin.

Meru spoke from her ritual position, "I feel resentment."

"We've seen the Ihamba," said Fideli. "And you have put on your 'words.'"

Others in the crowd also began "words" of their own, coming out with their own resentments. Now Meru would not even shake.

Meru's pain got to us all; we stood with bitter expressions, gazing at her. Fideli took a leaf bag and dripped medicine on Meru's head. Singleton held his skin bag in front of her face, then brushed her face with it. But Meru would not shake.

I was in trouble myself. We had hired one of Musona's sons to do some translating but to our disappointment he turned out to be an alcoholic. I now saw this man dizzy with gin, talking to Paulos. The man turned to me and said nastily, "Paulos is angry because you never came to see him when you said you would." I was overcome. I was supposed to go to see Paulos the Saturday before. But the old village carpenter had died on Saturday and I was at the funeral. Thing upon thing. I left the translator and went around to the other side of the crowd, mortified; again the crowd sensed anger and waited for my "words," but I would not speak. After thinking a minute I came back and explained the matter of the funeral to Paulos.

I was very upset. How was I to publicly bad-mouth the son of my friend and my landlady? There I was, "stiff with worries." It was stalemate.

But at this very point Singleton remembered that Meru was facing west. Nothing could "come out" with her in that position. He shifted the whole ritual scene into its mirror image, and we all moved around until Meru was facing east to the sunrise. This was quite different. I gazed across the crowd at the drunk translator.

"They want my 'words,'" I thought. "I want to participate, so much. But how can I?" I was forced to accept the impossibility of "words" against Musona's family, and in accepting it tears came into my eyes. The tears came out and I felt the stab of their pain.

And just then, through my tears, the central figure swayed deeply: all leaned forward, this was indeed going to be it. I realized along with them that the barriers were breaking—just as I let go in tears. Something that wanted to be born in the whole group was now going to be born. Then a certain palpable social integument broke and something calved along with me. I felt the spiritual motion, it was a tangible feeling of breakthrough going through the group. Then it was that Meru fell—the spirit event first and the action afterwards. Singleton was very active amid the bellow of the drums, swooping rhythmically with finger horn and skin bag ready to catch the tooth from the prone figure, Bill beating the side of the drum in time to the rhythm, and as for me, I had just found out how to clap. You simply clap along *with* the drums, and clap *hard*. All the rest falls into place. Your own body becomes deeply involved in the rhythm, and all reach unity.

Clap clap clap. Meru's brother was leaning forward and the others were on their feet clapping—this was it. Quite an interval of struggle elapsed while I clapped in total union, crouching beside Bill, while Singleton pressed Meru's back, guiding and leading out the tooth— Meru's face in a grin of tranced passion, her back quivering rapidly. Suddenly Meru raised her arm, stretched it in liberation, and I saw with my own eyes a giant thing emerge out of the flesh of her back. It was a gray blob about six inches across, a sphere. What it was I didn't know—a sort of thick mist?—a kind of plasma? I was amazed, delighted. I still laugh with glee at the realization of having seen it, the Ihamba, and so big! Everyone was hooting, we were all jumping with triumph. The gray thing was actually out there, visible, and you could see Singleton's hands working and scrabbling on the back—and then it was there no more. Singleton had it in his pouch, pressing it in with his other hand as well. The receiving can was ready; he transferred whatever it was into it and capped the castor oil leaf and bark lid over it. It was done.

There was one more thing. Everybody knew they had to go through the last precaution, the divining for the afterbirth. "If the Ihamba afterbirth has not come out, shake, if it has come out, don't shake but be quiet, nzo-o." Meru was quiet. At once there was a huge flash of lightning—the light of a clap of thunder that exploded simultaneously overhead. Meru sat up panting. The longed-for rain poured down, and we all rushed into the kitchen shelter.

"Go to the house, you two," said Fideli, and Bill and I ran on through the curtain of rain to the house door. Bill stumbled before he entered, fell into the mud, and then came in out of breath. Singleton entered with his blue shirt dark with water, carrying the receiving can which he set down on the floor. I wore a big smile.

He held up his hands to us. "See, I have nothing in them," then squatted down and dredged for a long time in the bloody mixture. At length he drew out an old tooth, a molar, natural size, ordinary, with a dark root and one side sheared off as if by an ax. It was the Ihamba.

On the evening of 3 December, Singleton and Fideli visited our hut to discuss Meru's Ihamba. The first thing that Singleton said was, literally, "The thing we saw, we were five." This was his statement that the doctors too had shared my experience of Meru's Ihamba. The doctors were Singleton, Fideli, Vesa, Luka, and myself.

I respectfully described what I saw. Fideli realized that I knew what Ihamba was, as they all did. The conversation in the hut went like this. Fideli translated Singleton's words for Bill, with Singleton interrupting to carry on what he wanted to say even before Fideli had finished translating his previous sentence. Singleton understood a good deal of the English and I understood a good deal of the Ndembu language. Fideli was in his element, knowing we were sharing an important treasure. His voice was rich and generous, while Singleton's was urgent and precise. A rapid swinging flow developed in the conversation and as it went on it became deeply personal and interconnected.

Singleton began, then Fideli said: "I have to explain what his words are."

"Yes?" I said.

This was on practical matters. "We'll kill an antelope for all the five doctors. Then we'll take out the liver for those who saw Ihamba with his or her eyes. We'll take a little piece of the liver and cut a hole in the middle of it, and we'll put the Ihamba tooth into the hole, and put it just like that into a bottle which has maize meal in it. We'll explain it to you so that you know what Ihamba is and so that we may be compared to many others. It's something that's very important. It's right that we should tell you exactly so that we can be seen as different, now, while you're living in Africa. This is your first moment of knowing what Wuyanga is, not from someone who thinks in lies but from me, Fideli Muhelewa, who was given the medicine of Ihamba from Singleton Sangunja." He ended with a gesture of respect to Singleton.

At this everybody clapped in honor of the statement murmuring, "*Mwani, mwani, mwani.*"

Fideli said, "Bill, would you like to get some more beer?"

After Bill had done so and we were settled down again, Fideli said, "The Ihamba has a strange problem. Ihamba always runs like an air. Get me?"

Bill said, "Yes, it's an air, it can fly."

"Yes, it's always flying about. The medicine we collect in the bush prevents Ihamba from getting into her. See? It stops the Ihamba coming out at the wrong place. Every medicine is for that, so Ihamba won't run away. It's a passing air, get me? It's to stop Ihamba coming out of her body and going into someone standing around. We have to catch it in the can."

Singleton said, "My father handed down to me the responsibility for the medicines. Now I possess the right to cure someone and not fail in it. It's true because the thing is from my father. How can I fail to cure a person? I know things from my father—I can't fail with my cures, there's no question about it. Edie, your late husband Mr. Turner—he told you things. Have you failed? Have I failed?"

"No way," I assured him. "I saw it."

"How can I fail?"

I went back to the matter of talking to the spirit inside the woman. I said, "So you're divining all the time, aren't you? At every stage the Ihamba itself is telling you what to do. Like—inside her it's telling her to shake, to answer the question. 'If it is so-and-so, shake. If it isn't, don't.' So you're learning from the Ihamba inside."

Fideli looked from me to Bill in wonder. "She knows, she's on to something. Yes. I think—Mrs. Turner—we've come to the end .... "
And Fideli was ready to wrap up the evening then and there.

Bill broke in, "Can I ask some more questions? I've loads of questions, about Meru and her sister quarreling about money."

"Before we took the Ihamba out of Meru—that's the very Ihamba that bit Meru—it heard the sisters and said to itself, 'Oh, the older and younger sisters are quarreling. The Ihamba came while they were backbiting. It was listening to them. Ihamba is an air person. Even if you're in England Ihamba can hear your "words." You'll turn back to call me—I'm telling you my "words"—you'll turn back and call me, 'Singleton. Come and see me in London.' You'll be the only Ihamba doctor in England."

Later that evening Singleton reenacted some of his own Ihamba utterances with much feeling, keeping his eyes fixed on the microphone as if it were the Ihamba. He stressed again the hunger of the Ihamba tooth, its desire for meat, and, practical as usual, how to satisfy it—which was finally done as follows.

On December 6 at six in the morning, Singleton fed the Ihamba with meat from an antelope. He opened the abdomen of the antelope and cut out a half-inch piece of liver which he trimmed first into a disc, then into a small torus shape with a hole in the center like a Life Saver. He took this disc and a sac of blood into Meru's house, and we followed him.

The winnowing basket lay ready on the dirt floor, with Singleton's mongoose skin pouch on it, also a clean Vaseline jar with a lid, now half full of maize meal made from the grain which is hard "like a tooth." Singleton added to the basket his liver disc and the sac of blood. Now he took out of the pouch some red clay which he crushed with the end of his finger horn and smeared over his fingers, for protection; after which he took up the liver ring and carefully removed from his pouch the Ihamba tooth, then chose a tiny piece of red clay; and holding the tooth and clay together he inserted them into the hole in the liver ring. He put the ring containing the Ihamba into the Vaseline jar, stuffing it in and positioning it with his thumb at the center of the surface of the corn meal. Then he poured over it the blood from the sac, and screwed on the lid. The bottle was now colored brilliant red above and white below, a union of blood and meal. "Marvelous," I wrote in my notes. Bill wrote later: "Subjectively, I felt very strange. Images flashed through my mind ... bread and wine; semen and menstrual blood; solid and liquid; yin and yang; a boulder in the stream and the water; time flowing past; life itself." Apparently we both felt that what had been done was an act of goodness, even of very real justice. Singleton said that when the Ihamba was fed with blood it was satisfied, and so it appeared to be.

Now that the feeding was done Singleton called Meru into the house. She came running, radiant and smiling all over her middle-aged face. Singleton took the blood sac and marked her on her shoulders and beside her eyes. She was now cured and protected.

Looking back now I remember my delight and awe at what I had seen. This was the vindication of what an entire race of people had been trying to tell Westerners: "Spirits do exist, and we Africans possess a good spiritual technology to apply to this level of existence," but Westerners had not believed them. The same vindication can support the existence of the skills of other cultures too. Some of them have experience of angels. Others have knowledge of animal helpers.

I was interested to see that Paul Stoller in Africa made a similar discovery. He relates his own apprenticeship as a healer among the Songhay of Niger and his subsequent experience of freeing himself from the palpable and effective sorcery of a priestess named Dunguri. Consequently he found himself evolving a different attitude toward the current philosophy maintaining in anthropology. He said:

> The discourse of ethnographic realism is no longer completely adequate. When I confronted first hand the powers of Dunguri in Wanzerbe and acted like a Songhay healer, all of my assumptions about the world were uprooted from their foundation on the plain of Western metaphysics. Nothing that I had learned or could learn within the parameters of anthropological theory could have prepared me for Dunguri. Having crossed the threshold into the Songhay world of magic, and having felt the texture of fear and the exaltation of repelling the force of a sorcerer, my view of Songhay culture could no longer be one of a structuralist, a symbolist, or a Marxist. Given my intense experience—and all field experiences are intense whether they involve trance, sorcery or kinship—I will need in future works to seek a different mode of expression. ... Anthropological writers should allow the events of the field—be they extraordinary or mundane—to penetrate them. In this way the world of the field cries out silently for description.[4]

Paul Stoller had had his path changed by something outside of him, just as I had. However, the ordinary public in America still believed that anthropologists were supposed to be impartial observers, scientists, seekers after objectivity. But what about these odd experiences? They may manifest as a hexing, or a mysterious spirit light as in the case of the anthropologist Evans-Pritchard among the Azande, a ghost, and so on. The author of the book *Deadly Words*,[5] about witchcraft in the Bocage region of France where witchcraft is common and possesses real power, maintains that it is necessary for the ethnographer herself to undergo the experience, and thus overcome the difficulty in which anthropologists find themselves when dealing with phenomena on another level of consciousness. Favret-Saada was in fact bewitched and had to learn how to resist it. "To understand the meaning of this discourse [the gift of unwitching, 'seeing everything'] there is no other solution but to practice it oneself, to become one's own informant, to penetrate one's own amnesia, and to try and make explicit what one finds unstateable in oneself." She produced a good ethnography. How was I to follow that up?

Now I would be forced to confront the anthropologists head-on with another experience of a spirit form. The implications were shifting me right over into the world of experienced religion, right onto personal material. Still, I thought, an ethnographer's experience of spirits and witches should count as valid material for anthropology.

I wondered, "Have I left the field of anthropology entirely?" Maybe one might develop an interesting new field to include people who had had experiences; and one might build up an archive of such experience and perhaps come across regularities in these apparently random happenings. One might cross over entirely into another culture, cross into that culture's own field of insights. This might turn out to be a kind of natural history of spirit rituals, performed and documented by anyone, but recognizing the natives to be at the head of the field.

So then, what was actually going on in Ihamba? Among the Ndembu a recognition of the existence of spirits could be seen as a truly parsimonious explanation for what the Ndembu do and what the anthropologist experiences—everything falls into place, as I realized when the implications of my experience dawned on me. The Ndembu perform ritual because spirits exist. For instance the medicines do talk to the Ihamba in their mystic way and say, "come out." Singleton is speaking to the spirit of Kashinakaji inside Meru's body. As Vic showed, the deeds of the Ndembu displayed a coherence and elegance which invites the most complex analysis. Ndembu medicine men said that the spirits had shown them the way. Again this makes sense.

But there was a matter which did not seem to make sense: the tooth. What of the human concrete tooth that Singleton showed Bill and me in Meru's house after the ritual and later when he fed the Ihamba? Which was the disease, the spirit form or the tooth? Did two "things" come out of Meru?

Later in my reading I came across a passage in a chapter entitled "Extracting Harmful Intrusions" in *The Way of a Shaman* by Michael Harner,[6] one of the few descriptions that does not ascribe an extraction to trickery:

> What is happening goes back to the fact that the shaman is aware of two realities. As among the Jivaro, the shaman is pulling out an intrusive power that (in the Shamanic State of Consciousness) has the appearance of a particular creature, such as a spider, and which he also knows is the hidden nature of a particular plant. When a shaman sucks out that power, he captures its spiritual essence in a portion of the same kind of plant that is its ordinary material home. That plant piece is, in other words, a power

object. For example, the shaman may store in his mouth two half-inch-long twigs of the plant that he knows is the material "home" of the dangerous power being sucked out. He captures the power in one of those pieces, while using the other one to help. The fact that the shaman may then bring out the plant power object from his mouth and show it to a patient and audience as "Ordinary State of Consciousness" evidence does not negate the nonordinary reality of what is going on for him in the Shamanic State of Consciousness.

Decades earlier, Vic had made studies of Ihamba too. As he saw the tooth (the concrete one), it was the slaying weapon par excellence, the epitome, the personification of the sudden aggressivity needed to bring down a fleeing animal, a "power object" in Harner's terms, not a simple matter. Vic praised Ihamba for "the mighty synthesizing and focusing capacity of the ritual."[7]

The doctors could indeed "dissolve" from one spirit form to the other. That little hard tooth, bubbled into a big shadowy spirit form invading the veins and arteries, visible, audible, palpable, reminds me of a similar report made by Essie Parrish, a Native American Pomo shaman from northern California:

When that sick man is lying there, I usually see the power. These things seem unbelievable but I, myself, I know, because it is in me .... Way inside of the sick person lying there, there is something. It is just like seeing through something—if you put tissue over something, you could see through it. That is just the way I see it inside. I see what happens there and can feel it with my hand—my middle finger is the one with the power .... The pain sitting somewhere inside the person feels like it is pulling your hand towards itself—you can't miss it.[8]

The skill of Singleton appears to correspond to that of Essie Parrish, who was an English-speaking woman and from an entirely different culture area.

What is important in Ihamba is the moment when Singleton clutches the "thing" in his skin pouch. This is the moment of translation of the Ihamba that was within, into the outward world, following its exit from Meru's body. Singleton then puts it into the receiving can, and later in the house its form is visible to everyday sight as a tooth somehow related to the spirit form. Then it must have meat, then the object that is numinous is a hard concrete tooth, and so the occasion of its feeding with blood produces that palpable feeling of satisfaction that Bill and I sensed at the feeding in Meru's house.

What the Ihamba itself consists of is the biting inside, that difficult spirit which cannot come out without a sudden transformation, effected socially by living people communicating with the spirit, ready for the coalescence and precipitation into existence of what is hard to put into words. It was the final uniting of the power, combined with all the medicines, with our participation, and with the doctor's helping spirits, that liberated into visibility the spirit object that I actually saw.

Thus seeing the matter more broadly, the Ndembu regarded symbols not as matters for thought or metaphor, but as "powers," as Vic said. Looking more carefully at Vic's analyses of symbols, I could see that they traced, not psychological processes, but actual spirit ones, the paths of the spirits' power toward human beings. But this Vic was only able to suggest. At that time anthropology forbade that he overstep its boundaries, and the effect of that taboo lasted into later decades.

As for me in 1985 I remember the glee, the breakthrough effect—which was what the ritual intended. My path had visibly reappeared through its crack. Or one could say the door had opened, as in my dream. This event was a turning point for me, along with my original meeting with Vic in 1942, my conversion in 1958, and, to jump the gun a little, the sense of communitas in the Small Group in 1995. As a result scarcely any writings of mine have come out without mentioning the Ihamba. It is inevitable. I have a sense of absolute certainty about it, a sense that has been termed apodicticity. Because of that event I can stand firm, and often feel truly happy, without a care.

The Soul

On returning from the field I gave papers such as "Carnivalization and Initiation in Zambia" and "Philip Kabwita, Ghost Doctor." I described how Kabwita got rid of the spirit that was making Noah mad, and I also worked on the first versions of *Experiencing Ritual*. I tried some more shamanism in the Harner style, a practice that often worked, which puzzled me.

I hardly dare look back on some of those years. My stock in the discipline seemed low—and shaky. How could such a person as I *write*? But I did.

Meanwhile I was seeking around, relating other rituals in the literature to what I had just seen in Africa, particularly examples of vision and trance. The nearest I could find on trance was Maya Deren's passage on Voudon drumming. Although I had not been in trance in quite the same way as Maya Deren during her experience of the Haitian Voudon dance, yet like her I had the knowledge that I had broken through in Ihamba—we all had, we had gotten our heads above water. Deren's trance was triggered by the drummer.

The drummer ... can "break" to relieve the tension of the monotonous beat and bodily motion, thus interrupting concentration. By withholding this break he can bring the Loa [gods] into the heads of the participants or stop them from coming. He can also use the break in another way by letting the tension build to a point where the break does not release tension, but climaxes in a galvanizing shock. This enormous blow empties the dancer's head, leaving him without a center around which to stabilize. He is buffeted by the strokes as the drummer "beats the Loa into his head." He cringes at the large beats, clutches for support, recapturing his balance just to be hurtled forward by another great beat of the drum. The drummer ... persists until the violence suddenly ceases, and the person lifts his head, seeming to gaze into another world. The Loa has arrived.[9]

I was interested in this drummer of Deren's. Was the consciousness of the approaching spirit in him? Compare my own clapping. It took the "calving" event, coming first, to teach me to clap. As for Singleton, he had prayed to his ancestor spirit to direct him at each turn of the ritual. He was able to listen for the right time, for the moment of "lifting."

There were even examples close to home. Linda Camino and Marcia Gonçalves, graduate students in our department at Virginia, were doing fieldwork among African-American churches and communities around Charlottesville. Marcia asked me out to her church of study, Bibleway. There I saw people allowing themselves to go deep into emotion when the spirit took them. Also in the African American Imani Church run by Archibald Stallings I saw people falling out, "slain in the spirit." In Zambia I had visited the Wapostoli (Apostles) of John Maranke near Kajima with my Ndembu friend Zinia, and had nearly joined the Wapostoli, a movement linked with Pentecostalism. At the Wapastoli meeting one woman fell down with Satan struggling in her. I saw an apostle stand over her, conjuring, abjuring the spirit to come out of her. She writhed on the ground within a tight circle of the other apostles. One could almost wish to be her, able in such strong, good company to let everything hang out: all of one's torturous life, one's desire to do evil—the battleground being oneself; then able to seek the hand of an apostle when the fury got too bad. This woman rose up soon and became quiet and happy, much like the cured Noah.

Again, was it different for Meru in Ihamba? Not very, in fact. Meru's ritual was more elegant, more assured, with a known pharmacy of herbal medicines, with the working techniques of "words" to elicit grudges, the oracle or divinatory proposition to identify the afflicting spirit, and the matter of locating the spirit's gray substance and pouncing on it when it popped up through the skin. Nevertheless the apostles of John Maranke also knew what they were doing and knew about the soul, which they were able strongly to address and admonish. The Bibleway members of Charlottesville also knew how the soul struggled and they valued its free expression (that is, its "words" in the Ihamba sense, as encouraged by the medicine man). The destiny of the souls in the Bibleway and Pentecostal churches needed to be fulfilled and laid open right there in the church, even at the cost of the person being temporarily cast down by the power onto the ground.

I was beginning to teach these mysteries to my university classes. Graduate students would not come, but undergraduates came, and they wanted me to come out with all the stories I could give them.

Meanwhile, what was I thinking, myself, about what was happening in trance?

At this point I was in a sense casting my bread on the waters. The Wapostoli, Bibleway, and Pentecostal examples confirmed what I witnessed in Ihamba.[10] I couldn't help seeing that there were phenomena—entities—out there that had those certain characteristics. These beings were sometimes figures of light or mist, with their own volition. I felt we should take notice of what the field people told us. For me, it really mattered. At this point, when I read other anthropologists I could not understand why most of their explanations of religious phenomena were so reductionist, as if it were not right to take seriously what the people themselves said.

The ordinary public around Charlottesville was much easier with the topic. America has been bursting with small healing techniques and "isms" in the New Age style. In my house I ran a monthly gathering of local healers who worked through a whole gamut of different techniques, each expert taking her turn.[11] What did I make of these techniques? Among some of indifferent quality, others stood out well—they were interesting. There was the dowser, Tom Milleren. He was a retired electrical engineer, and brought with him the kind of divining rods that are made of coat hanger wire, passed loosely through handles, bent over, and shaped like long inverted Ls. These rods are finely balanced and can be held straight out and will stay still if one is careful, but will whirl around uncontrollably at the least thing. So you try someone's aura. You stand near the person, holding out the rods a foot away, and the rod arms whirl. That's the close aura. You retreat a little and the arms stop. You walk backwards to six feet away or more, and the arms whirl again. You have located the further aura. You can go out to the yard and try to spot running water. I did this the day after Tom Milleren's presentation and found a place in my front yard where the rods whirled madly, but that was not a place where there should be any running water at the time. The next month's water bill showed something wrong. The lead-in pipe had indeed burst underground, just at that place, and I had to have it repaired. Those rods were quite interesting.

Trying around with the aura idea drew me toward the idea of therapeutic touch. Could one feel with one's hands the buzz of energy in a person? One can try on oneself. If one puts one's two hands out, a little apart from each other, palms facing, then draws them further away from each other, then nearer, can one feel the difference in one's skin? Is there a kind of tingling? I've felt it; also one can try putting one's hand above somebody else's head, a few inches up. One can feel a faint buzz there too. These are small examples.

Another of the speakers in the healers' series was Gould Hulse,[12] a commercial artist and accountant who had had a most vivid experience and had drawn pictures of it, and there are reasons to believe his story. He had had a sudden knowledge that he was lying on the grass of a battlefield. It was Shiloh in the Civil War, and he was dying. As he lay there, he found that he, that is, his soul, naked and small, was drawn out of him and he was moving up a kind of big tube to somewhere else. His first picture shows this, with other similar souls moving up too. In the next picture the tube has flowered out into a wide bowl or kind of chalice where many souls are resting, crowding around the rim. Out of this bowl pass other tubes, with souls already in them, flying to other destinations. Hulse drew many pictures of this sort. The last one shows a final enclosed globe, with an outlet. Hulse's soul is passing through it. Its destination is into a new human baby, the baby that became the person who was talking to us, showing us the pictures.

From time to time I have come across other attempts to portray the vivid experience of souls. Blake depicts streaming crowds of souls, especially in his Dante's Inferno pictures. Dante himself frequently described them and Gustave Doré also illustrated them. All these souls seem to be the same kind of naked beings, as if various people had seen the same thing. Compare also lines from John Donne:

> arise, arise
> From death, you numberless infinities
> Of souls, and to your scattered bodies go.[13]

A further presentation to the healers' group was made by Justine Owens of the Personality Studies Program at the University of Virginia, on near-death experiences. She had collected about two hundred accounts of near-death experiences (NDEs) from patients at the university hospital. Here the soul, leaving the body at death, looks down from a height on the body it has left, then finds itself drawn up a tunnel rather like the commercial artist's tube, and is aware of the presence of dead relatives. Then it meets with a being of great light, that same light that I have described before. Classically, this being offers the soul a chance to go back because he or she is still needed on earth.

The near-death experience, NDE, as it is termed, has become a feature of spirit experience accepted by New Agers in large numbers. Furthermore, several people from different cultures who experienced NDEs have told me their stories. At this period of my life the stories confirmed the way my thinking was going. However, I had the sense that my attention to this material, because of its association with the New Age, put me further from mainline anthropology. It seemed to be a daring act even to speculate on the reality of such phenomena.

I was now regarding myself as a guinea pig of the soul. My faculties seemed open enough to have a try at most of these phenomena. Like other anthropologists of experience I would dare anything, like the crew of the starship *Enterprise*: "We boldly go where no anthropologist has gone before, seeking new experiences and states of consciousness."

Notes

1. For an account and discussion of Kabwita's work see Edith Turner, "Philip Kabwita, Ghost Doctor: The Ndembu in 1985," *The Drama Review* 30(4) (1986):4-35.
2. See Victor Turner, *The Drums of Affliction: A Study of Religious Processes among the Ndembu of Zambia* (Oxford, 1968).
3. Documented in detail in Edith Turner, *Experiencing Ritual: A New Interpretation of African Healing* (Philadelphia, 1992).
4. Paul Stoller, "Eye, Mind, and Word in Anthropology," *L'Homme* 24(3-4) (1984):110.
5. Jeanne Favret-Saada, *Deadly Words: Witchcraft in the Bocage* (Cambridge, 1980).
6. Michael Harner, *The Way of the Shaman* (San Francisco, 1980), 116-117.
7. Victor Turner, *The Forest of Symbols*, 298.
8. Quoted by Harner, *The Way of the Shaman*, 127-128.
9. Maya Deren, *Divine Horsemen: The Living Gods of Haiti* (London, 1953).
10. A good anthropologist's account is given in Douglas Reinhardt, "With His Stripes We Are Healed: White Pentecostals and Faith Healing," in *Diversities of Gifts: Field Studies in Southern Religion*, eds. Ruel Tyson et al. (Urbana, IL, 1988), 126-142.
11. The sessions are described by Edith Turner in "Taking Seriously the Nature of Religious Healing in America," in *Religious Healing in Urban America*, eds. Susan Sered and Linda Barnes (New York, 2004).
12. Gould Hulse, talk on "Soul and Reincarnation," at Alternatives (Healers' Group), Charlottesville, 1980 (Gould Hulse, 1 Stone St., Staten Island, NY 10304).
13. John Donne, "Holy Sonnets 7," in *The Norton Anthology of Poetry*, eds. A. Allison et al. (New York, 1975 [1633]), 249.

11

SEARCHING FOR HEALING
The Arctic

I had been venturing in a world where healing happens, where spirits are sometimes visible, where people have experiences of spirits that exist outside of their bodies. None of these phenomena happened with unbroken frequency. They were sporadic: their spores appeared to penetrate here and there to keep alive some faculty, keep it in circulation. They seemed to have a function, then, to set off enough of the power—whatever it is—here and there, so there may be enough to meet some kind of emergency, was that it? Or because the entity out there, whatever it is, was giving them foreknowledge—telling them that without the power we would all die? I didn't know.

Because of my work in 1985 in Africa, I began to see the brain as possessing another function that we have not spotted with the scanners, which might be regarded as a kind of radio transmitter and receiver to and from regions with which we would otherwise have no communication: in other words, a spiritual receiver and transmitter. This would account for messages that saints and psychics receive: telepathy, and the like. In addition I reckoned there must also be a power that could heal, a power that could affect solid bodies, that was not concerned solely with communication. However, I couldn't see how there was a place in the brain for that aspect, so kept it in mind as something to look out for.

Other characteristics did exist but up to that time I was ignorant of them. More fieldwork was needed for them to appear, did I but know it early in 1986; for instance, the way spirits take the initiative.

Healing: that I certainly wanted to know more about. A graduate student, Mimi George, had previously been in northern Alaska

---

Figure 11.1: An Iñupiat whaleboat on the beach of the North Slope of Alaska. Subsistence hunting is their traditional way of life (photo by Edith Turner)

studying the way-finding skills of the Iñupiat, an Eskimo people who live on the North Slope facing the Arctic Ocean (see figure 11.1). In the local township of Kotzebue Mimi had chanced upon a huge crowd of Iñupiat at a Presbyterian funeral, that of their famous healer, Della Keats. Mimi learned that healing was recognized by the Iñupiat as their prime gift—at least back then in 1986. Having returned home to the University of Virginia, Mimi discussed the implications of the funeral event with me. She looked at me and said, "It's not difficult to go there, Edie. You could." She knew I liked Eskimos whom I had met from time to time.

I thought. Healing? Their prime gift?

"How do they heal?"

"It's hands on, manipulation, that sort of thing. It's a gift." She couldn't tell me very much about it.

"Is it still going on?"

"Oh yes, Della taught all sorts of people—"

"Hm."

But Eskimos? I knew nothing about their world, and practically nothing about Native American culture generally.

But healing! Might there exist, perhaps, certain universal characteristics of healing that covered all of humanity?

"Do they have shamanism?" I asked.

"Oh no, it's obsolete. Totally obsolete. The missionaries got rid of it. There are no shamans to be found anywhere."

"Oh."

Still. Healing.

I took the bait and worked on the idea. I sounded the possibilities. There were networks I could utilize to obtain connections in a certain sea-hunting village on the North Slope. And I got help. The administration officials of the University of Virginia looked kindly on my project, and I bless them for it. I planned to leave late in August 1987.

That July, on the 19th, while still in Virginia, I participated in another experimental shaman session like the one with Roy Wagner and the graduate students, this time at Madison with Michael Harner, the founder of core shamanism. It turned out to be a useful event under the circumstances. Then I finally got my things together and left for Alaska.[1]

Late August in the Arctic was *cold*. In the eyes of the Iñupiat I was just a stranger grandma who had chosen to live in their own private village, for unknown reasons. But she was harmless, and seemed to be making a brave attempt to take the rough with the smooth like everybody else and never criticized the people's way of thinking. As for me, it was my job to find Claire, the healer, and when I got to know her I found that she healed with the help of her clairvoyance and worked on the principle of the extraction of pain and illness. She was assisted spiritually by the Good Lord. The healing was done by him and not herself. She was aware of her shamanic roots and knew much about the spirituality of her people.

There was indeed a consciousness of shamanism in the village, officially suppressed. But its operations emerged again and again, in wayfinding, altering the weather, bringing the animals, in healing, clairvoyance, speaking with the dead—and it also produced joy. These were good things that people simply did. Claire the healer was a "good shaman"—a term used by Jim Agnasagga, another non-confessed shaman.

I remember Claire, the lady with the oval face and high forehead. She looked out strongly from herself, a known healer, all alive, with a considering expression in her eyes; she moved with an easy walk and big fluid motions. She used to take off her jacket in my house and sit down, ready for anything, with her eyes a little hooded as becomes an Iñupiaq (this is the singular form of the word). Yet Claire was watchful and confident. She was capable. She could look after herself; she asked for what wasn't on the table, such as honey to put in her herb tea. Her voice would wander into great variations in tone, from rasping (during the telling of an uncertainty, along with a note of self-assertion), to sounding a complaint, slump—slump—and very much in "rasp." But when she mused or reminisced her voice softly wandered, musically keyed, her eyes inward, her mind seeing pictures that leapt into existence one on top of the other. Her voice would leap as the memories came. When she was teaching me language pronunciation and I made mistakes, she'd let out a sound full of sorrowful rasping, full of searching and persistence, and she'd be near to despair with a frog in her throat—then came a ray of hope. She'd try me again with "qa-aggaq" ("rough"), and I'd repeat, "kargak," incorrectly, and her hands would flop uselessly by her sides. All she could do was laugh—cackle like the grandmother she was.

While Claire told me stories I would make assenting noises and pour out more tea and honey. Claire's voice and her speaking style were inseparable from the subject matter, and the stories came in a series of vivid pictures. The style itself spoke of great self-confidence such as one encounters in the personal histories of exceptional people. "I dared to visit the crazy old woman"—no one else. She understood speech practically from birth. The subject matter and style were all one with the flow of knowledge: "I just knew," was her constant phrase. It was a life that unfolded by its own dynamic. The unitary principle, her consciousness of herself, was very strong.

I knew a certain thing about her from long ago, though, from the time before I was ever there, and can't bear to think about it even now. It was when she stood before her burning house with her first three children dying inside it, her spirit dead and tortured within her. A screaming impossibility, Claire.

In 1987, with six children more, mainly adopted, and three grandchildren, with an easy job she liked, sitting in City Hall, typing on a computer, running the teleconferences—this was the life (only they went and cut down her hours). She had a telephone and a citizens band radio, so she was in touch to answer sick calls.

I loved that woman.

Once while I was working on language with her, the CB radio spoke: "Claire. Claire. Come in. Claire. Come over and see little Lee, he's hurt." Lee was three years old. Claire went, seizing her jacket and putting it on as she strode out to her ATV three-wheeler, waiting an instant for her seven-year old daughter Jeanie and me to get on behind—and we whirled off. She entered Lee's house, all gentle, already knowing the trouble because she'd been having a preliminary moment of clairvoyance, just as Philip Kabwita did before healing Noah. Inside, the child was screaming. He'd taken a jump off the high-up empty stereo shelf and gone crash on both knees. Now he couldn't stand and couldn't walk and was on his mother's lap crying. Claire brought up a chair and sat opposite Lee with young Jeanie kneeling close by to watch. Like me, Jeanie was very interested. Claire took the child's foot gently and turned up the pants leg. Lee's crying got worse. Claire turned her hand over the throbbing knee, almost not touching it.

"I can't hurt you, I can't hurt you," she told him as an obvious truth, in her most musical voice. "See, I'm making it better." While she spoke she was seeing inside with her hands. It was like an X-ray, as she would say; all inside was as clear as daylight. The mother held Lee and Claire felt both his lower legs. Lee's crying began to give way. She felt down the muscles of each leg, drawing down the legs neatly together. She worked each ankle, the sole of the foot, the toes, bending them gently until they were flexible, showing Lee how good they were. Her hands went back to the knees. The right one bore a bruise and a big swelling below the kneecap. She placed both kneecaps centrally and pressed them gently into position as if they were jigsaw pieces, completing the action by pressing carefully with her palm. She worked the dimpled areas of the good left knee while swiveling the leg back and forth. Then she returned to the swelling on the right knee. I noted that she left the trickiest bit until last. She pressed the swelling slightly here and there and I saw it diminish a little. She left that work alone for a time and turned down Lee's pants legs. He slid off his mother's lap and tried a few steps, using his legs like little sticks. Claire chatted to Lee's mother about this and that. She turned to Lee, "Auntie Claire's going to make some mukluk boots for you. How about that, eh?" Little Lee had been making eyes at Jeanie.

"Come on now," Claire told him, "Auntie's going to feel your knee a bit more." She worked on the swelling again, and showed me. "See? It's going down there, and there. It's simple."

Before my eyes the swelling went away altogether leaving the normal muscle curves visible around the kneecap. I was attending carefully, having experienced under Claire's tutelage the same sense in the hands—the knowledge of a kind of misery and mushiness in the damaged tissues, followed by a gust of compassion for the misery and a sigh of oneness. Then the similar diminution of swelling. When I myself had been sick and had needed healing from others, I remembered how the pain seemed to leak away and just not be there anymore.

Claire drew down Lee's pants legs and let him go. He walked easily. She went to the sink and washed, getting rid of whatever it was. "The pain goes into my own arm," she would tell me. "My hand gets hot. Hot!"

Claire and the mother went on talking. The mother was hard up, awaiting a welfare check. The place was not at all luxurious, lacking a carpet, with torn vinyl chair seats and only a garish rainbow window shade to cheer the place up. Lee was now jumping from the empty stereo shelf to the sofa.

"That's how he did it in the first place," said Claire. "Jumping and falling on his knees. Stop that!" We left before more treatment might become necessary.

Claire kept telling me, "See, it's simple," and it was, it only needed the actual doing. It was healing that was empirical in essence because it was so particularized. The hands knew the details of the inner tissues, they were involved in the tissues, not just laid on the outside. I compare it not so much to Christian laying-on of hands, nor the treatment of the Spiritists of Brazil who pass their hands around the body a couple of inches away from it, nor the work of Umbanda healers with their embrace-like clutches, but to that of Singleton, the old African healer in Zambia, with his mongoose skin bag and horn, stroking and feeling and coaxing the damaging Ihamba tooth out of the back of the sick person into the cupping horn, and aware of the right place to do it. In both Claire's kind of healing and Singleton's, what was at work was the kind of practical consciousness that the Iñupiat meant when they talked about "ordinary" facts. One could term the practitioners themselves, not just their ethnographers, "radical empiricists," because they knew very well what they were doing. I have learned that other types of healers also operate knowing very well what they are doing.

During my acquaintance with Claire a matter came up which had to do with a person's endowment of the gift of shamanism and the urge a person may have to search for it and allow the barriers to it to break. Shamanism is a gift that one cannot concoct out of nothing but which comes to a person. Here I was encountering the phenomenon of the will and the intention of spirits, shown in signs that the spirits were taking the initiative. Claire had had a number of episodes in her life when "the spirit," which was Satan at first and who then turned into Jesus, had come upon her with an intention that at first she could not believe.

Two of the episodes were told to me by others. Two of them I witnessed myself. Claire would be out of things for four days, a state I called "the four-day shaman syndrome." The episode might be connected with the falling off of her healing powers, or with neglect of her practice. Satan would come to her, bringing on a totally black mood. At the end of it a turnaround would occur and Satan would be replaced by Jesus, and then her healing would be better than before.

Psychologists in our culture might term the syndrome "fugue" or even "psychosis"—but these episodes did not derive from psychosis. They appeared to be the classic irruptions of shamanic experience just as the ancient Iñupiat knew them, typically lasting four days. In early times they were characterized by meeting with something fearful, a spirit of the dead or of a dangerous animal, one that first afflicted the incipient shaman and then changed and became a helper.

The account of Claire's first recorded episode was given by a friend of hers, a white woman whom I met in Fairbanks. In about 1978 Claire was in Anchorage in an expensive hotel, alone for four days, for reasons unknown.

"There she had some kind of transformation," Claire's friend told me, looking disturbed. "She said to me on the phone—I was at the airport—she told me she'd had some kind of revelation about me. There were certain things that would happen. A person who didn't know Claire's powers would think she'd gone crazy. What she said was glossolalia. That was a bad time for Claire."

The friend bent over her coffee, thinking. She shook her head. "I don't know what Claire went through in that hotel for four days all by herself."

In 1984 when Claire was not doing much healing she had another episode, a very bad one. Claire would continually see a devil figure in her peripheral vision. At one time in the bad phase Claire uttered a whole lot of blah-blah-blah nonsense words. It was glossolalia again. It greatly upset her relatives. Claire told them irritably, "Don't be like that, you don't think I'm anything, do you? I can't help it, it just comes to me." But at the end of the four-day episode Claire was able to pray to Jesus again, and afterward her healing power was stronger. She appealed to Jesus, the obverse of Satan, to be her helper spirit. The same switch from dangerous to helpful was manifesting itself as in the precontact days.

In the fall term of 1987 Claire and Rebecca, the American Indian school secretary, were studying anthropology together by teleconference. In response to an essay question, Rebecca used Claire's case to illustrate the experiences of shamans. Rebecca told me that because of her studies she was coming to realize that the personality of a healing shaman was not like that of ordinary people and that such episodes as Claire's were not necessarily bad as the Christians taught.

A further episode occurred during my fieldwork. On Thursday, January 14, 1988, I found Claire lying on her couch, very depressed, in what psychiatrists term a state of fugue. She had her eyes shut and would not speak. I was frightened, thinking she was angry. Four days later she was herself again. What I saw had all the hallmarks of a shaman episode.

During a visit in 1991 yet another episode seems to have occurred. I had just arrived to join in the whaling festival and heard that Claire had returned from the hospital, where she had been a patient from May 28 to June 2. I went to her house.

"Where's Claire?"

"Washing dishes," said young Ann.

I approached the kitchen. A small dark figure was at the sink, and she did not turn around.

"Claire, Claire. Look at this. I've brought you something." She still did not turn. Her gray hair was scrawny, her figure thin. I immediately thought, "An episode again? Isn't life in this place pitiful! My dear friend caught up in … something so mysterious. Okay, I have to try to understand it."

Claire peeped into the shopping bag I brought and saw peacock-blue velveteen for a new parka, and a peacock-blue zipper. She turned convulsively and flung herself into my arms. We were crying. I stroked her wild gray hair and haggard face.

"Dear Claire. You've given me everything, my sweet friend." When we recovered she told me the doctor at the hospital had prescribed the wrong medicine. She was really mad at him. "I'll get an attorney," she said. Now she was off all medicines and was feeling better by the minute. I wondered what the doctor thought he had prescribed the medicine for.

Claire had read my article "From Shamans to Healers" before it was published.

"I liked it," she said. "I liked the comparisons"—of shamans and healers. I was delighted to hear it.

Meanwhile the four-day period puzzled me. The same pattern occurred in older Iñupiat accounts of the experiences of shamans. The results of the phenomenon were of great benefit to the community because they provided a heightening of all the healer's shamanic gifts. One old account has survived about a shaman called Kehuq who was the ancestor of Clem, a whaling captain. What the account described was clearly a precontact version of the four-day syndrome.

When Kehuq was a young man, he was out on the tundra when he heard the sound of paddles up in the air. He looked up and saw a boat floating in the sky. It landed and Kehuq saw in it a shaman with one big eye, a figure who danced and gave him pleasure. The boat disappeared, and by the time Kehuq reached home he had forgotten all about it. Late that night Kehuq started up naked and left the tent for no reason. They brought him back, but for four days he was crazy and could not eat. Any loud noise, such as the banging of pots, nearly killed him. But when he recovered, Kehuq could dance. When he danced his spirit left him and he was possessed by the strange shaman's spirit.

Kehuq taught the people the shaman's songs and how to carve the shaman's face in wood. He was now gifted with healing and full shamanic powers.

This is just one of many accounts describing a four-day crazy period, typically followed by a successful hunting period and the gift of healing and other benefits. I noted how it was occurring in the modern village.

Vic Turner himself suffered black periods from time to time. We both used to note that they lasted for four days. I came to believe that the syndrome was related to the general breakthrough effect associated with discoveries (the "Aha" syndrome). Was it also related to the vision quest? Or the Christian "dark night of the soul"? The Jungian notion of the Shadow, often a terrifying dream figure that needed only reconciliation? Perhaps even to the black sense a woman may get while suffering for something like four days from the premenstrual syndrome, later resolved in much creativity? Or to the Way of the Cross, or the three-day death of Christ?

In the accounts, the four-day episodes come at the will of the spirit beings and cut the ordinary person off from ordinary life. They cause the person to reassemble differently inside. It reminds me of what happens inside a chrysalis, because the process concerns not only the brain but the body. Shamans' powers as reported in the "four day" examples are due to the reassembled state of the person. As I have mentioned, Eliade and others have described a stage in a shaman's initiation that consists of an experience of dismemberment,[2] "sparagmos," the breaking up of the person in the course of his or her shaman journey and afterwards the process of being reassembled and endowed with new powers.

To Claire and the others, the perception of these workings was a familiar thing. These healers *knew*, as they were never tired of telling me. I recognized that; I knew a little too, and found that what I have just described was not a hypothesis but an empirical phenomenon, in the category of radical empiricism. I cannot say if I understand exactly what happens, and I have been using personal intuition as much as anything else to probe and guess at it. One can only state that something out there seems to have been arranging these events in the human life story.

Claire went on to describe her near-death experiences (NDEs), three episodes in which she was near death or actually dead and then had an experience of visiting another world and returning again to this one.

"I died three times," said Claire. "The second time I began on a broad road, then I went to a narrow road. There was thunder, and a voice said in Eskimo, 'Go back! Your work is not finished on Earth.' It was hard for me to go back because when I returned I was in pain.

"The third time there was an angel and a bright light. He said, "If you step forward you will not go back. If you go back now, it will be the next time." (She meant, "The next time, you will step forward and go on.") "The angel touched my hands on both sides with the light. The healing is now stronger. I owe it only to God."

She knew about the soul. "You can see if a person's going to die. The person looks like a still boat on a still sea going far away. You have to bring it back and back so that the person doesn't die."

"Just as in Moody's book on near-death experiences," I thought. Again I did not know if Iñupiat near-death experiences were of the same nature as the shaman's four-day episodes. Possibly in one sense they were.

The near-death experience itself shows the experience of the soul after the body has momentarily died.[3] Many shamans in the old days were known to have come back from death after the same classic "four days," having experienced a journey to the abode of the spirits. Perhaps Claire's "person" like a boat going far away is a clue. She does not call this "person" "soul." Nevertheless, the Iñupiat word for "person" is *inuk*, a word to which the word *inua*, "soul," is closely related. Clearly there are two entities, the sick person's *body* and that *person*, leaving and going far away.

The whaling captain Clem Jackson told me about what happened to his grandmother.

"Yes, it's happened before to *Aaka*, Grandma, when she was ill. Her spirit left her three times. The spirit can be seen coming out of the fontanel at the top of the head like a long line of light. It goes fast. The shaman has to go after it—his spirit has to go real fast to catch up with it and bring it back before it's gone too far. Okay? Once Aaka actually died. She told me that she saw people bending over her body. She was up above, see, looking down. Then she came back.

"It happened another time," Clem went on. "Next time she died and went far away, as far as the mountains. And she saw a jade floor spread out, with gold in it, and people walking about on it. They were eating and drinking. She could smell some kind of sweet-scented flowers. She very much wanted to be with the people in that world. But then she remembered her husband, grandfather Kehuq. He would be needing her. So she turned and went back to the world of the living, and came back to life."

I marked these elements: mountains, that is, a beautiful place high up, with people; a place where you would dearly love to be; and the necessity of going back. The Nepalese shamans described the same kind of place full of flowers, up a staircase in their example, a place of whiteness, the house of the supreme deity. Then the return. The story of Jacob's ladder contains the same elements. My pastor in Charlottesville had the same experience. Many examples come to mind.

As I make my path in life in the direction in which I seem to be pushed, and as I write this book, I recognize that a development of a sense of such soul processes is the subject of the book—and is perhaps the purpose of whatever has been pushing me. Spotting what was going on in the apparently random material of everyday life has led me to try to discriminate which were spirit events.

Claire constantly reiterated that her healing was "different." Yet that "different" world is amenable to our understanding, it is open to the inquiries of the scholar of the natural history of the soul; both worlds are within the purview of the researcher—however, such a researcher has to have eyes suitable for what she is researching, and use those eyes.

For instance, I record an odd event that scientifically speaking could not have happened.

It was Wednesday, November 18, 1987, in the Arctic village. Clem Jackson was a hunter in his prime, resistant against any rationaliza- tion of hunting (see figure 11.2). He caught a four-foot ringed seal that was now lying on the floor of his kitchen. He brought a bowl of fresh water and fed it ritually into the dead mouth. Margie his wife told me they were going to skin their seal, so I came to watch.

Figure 11.2: The Iñupiat have a spiritual sense of their hunting, therefore they bring the whaleboat into church to ask for blessings on it. Alaska 1988 (photo by Edith Turner)

Margie, with the aid of the others, managed to turn the seal over. She took the knife and made the first cut into the seal's "parka," into its fleshly envelope, first making a shallow cut into the fat, right down the belly from the neck to the tail, then a cut across the neck making a T. I saw deep white fat inside. Margie started to take off the fine furry skin adorned with faint spots, cutting inside it and gradually alongside it, pulling it off like a garment. Then she took the blubber off, a job with which I helped.

Now Margie bent over the seal and passed her ulu knife in a long line downwards, opening up the chest and belly cavity. A great array of organs sprang into view, very dark red, almost black, glistening. I could make out the huge liver lobes above, at which I gazed, mesmerized: dark red. Then an intricate maze of small intestines twelve inches across, dark brick in color. Then the broad hearty tubing of the large intestine ridged like a vacuum cleaner tube. But all of it was delicate, set glistening and wet in the body cavity, packed neatly and efficiently and comfortably. I looked and looked.

Margie drew out the liver. It was huge. She detached some of it. The round heart, notched at the top, black: she took that. She threw out a knobby object, also the internally located testicles. Then the lungs, which reminded me it was an air-breathing animal. Then they divided the meat. It was finished.

After that it was a matter of plastic bags for the meat distribution.

A few nights later lying awake in my bed in my prefab hut, I felt my cheeks alive and burning warm from the cold. I had not felt my cheeks since I used to work on a farm in 1942. I was wondering how I'd ever be able to leave this place.

Then I suddenly understood the meaning of a curious experience I had had, months before, on July 19, 1987, before coming to Alaska. It had been during Michael Harner's shaman session in which I had taken part at Madison, Virginia.[4] We had been lying on the floor with our eyes closed, while somebody steadily beat a drum. We were seeing if we could go to the "upper world," that is, visualize some tree, mountain, ladder, or tall building, ascend it, then let whatever was out there take over.

The drum sound went before me. I visualized the ancient pile of Salisbury Cathedral in England. I entered the building with its curious inverted arch high above the crossing, then climbed the spiral staircase to where the spire began. I was looking out over the ramparts at this level when I saw a rope extending from the ramparts to … before I knew it I was across the rope and out on a fluffy cloud facing a monk in a long robe. I wasn't dreaming or inventing; these things just happened.

"What the dickens?" I said. This was all very corny. Churches, clouds, monks?

"Be quiet," rapped the monk. "It's not for you to criticize. Do as you're told."

I was somewhat impressed. My "visualization" was reprimanding me—or was it a visualization?

"Go on up a bit further," he instructed. There was another floor about three or four feet up. On this level I saw a whole bank of appliances along a wall. The wall was filled with stereos, VCRs, dials, and an enormous TV screen in which I saw something dark, very dark red. It looked like a sideways image of some kind of internal organs when I peered at it. Unusually dark red ones. They were internal organs all right, but they didn't look ordinary, not like human organs. Elongated. Fatter. I was quite puzzled, but the drumbeat changed and I was supposed to come back. Politely thanking the monk, I returned, opened my eyes, and told the others in the shaman session what had happened. No one could make anything of it.

But now I understood. What I had seen on the TV screen was just what I saw when Margie opened up the innards of the seal on 18 November. Now how could I have foreseen that event? As the memory of the shaman experiment in Madison flooded back to me, there on my bed in the Arctic village on November 24, I put my hand down toward the bed frame to assure myself that this was real. My hand contacted my heating pad, so it must be okay. I was kind of upset. Tears came out from somewhere inside me, seeming to soak as it were the subsoil of my head, my deepest consciousness.

"What am I to do with this material?" I thought.

Such is the cry of many an honest anthropologist. I often tried to encompass it, deal with it. This era of my life was more packed with nonlogical events than any other. Here indeed in the Arctic was the place to learn a different logic.

Then what happens in a shaman journey? The shaman's spirit does go out and it does quest around. It can do so if the aspiring shaman is able to disconnect her spirit from the mental equivalent of the "rattling pans" which distracted and maddened the shaman in the trance described in this chapter. Wearing a fringed hat or cap helps the shaman. Waving a cloth or wide sleeves before the eyes helps to create a kind of strobe light effect that dissociates one from the things of mundane life.

Then the soul pays attention to the drums. The attention *releases* one, it doesn't tie one down. It's simple. You can go, so you think, where you like; but it is where the spirit likes, and that is what is so odd. The spirit leads, and it can do so perfectly well. A person's spirit is like an innocent child who knows perfectly well how to learn to walk and speak and laugh without getting any training. This is the answer to "what is going on?" It is the release of the real person, the inua, soul. It's so easy when one knows how, like riding a bicycle or just walking.

During my stay Clem the whaling captain pulled in a whale. Thinking back over the impact the whale made on me I remembered my first glimpse of a black mound reared high over the ice, visible now that the whole village, including me, had succeeded in hauling it up from the sea. Going near I felt its overshadowing presence, with its life closed down, the body upside down, the eye low on the side, matt and dark; the machinery of baleen all silent like organ pipes without wind (see figure 11.3). This whale was a hill. Its tail flippers were already amputated; there was even a section cut from the side. "Pierced feet and side"? Yes, it was the Pieta scene on the lap of mother ice. Then followed the work, the driving performance with knives and hacking irons and the cooperating rhythm of men leaning on ropes, setting their feet in unison, pulling pieces of fat and flesh off the carcass while others hacked. The groups of men constantly changed, a new group working on another section of the beast, methodically heaving off its immense parka, then dragging each section to its own stash of food. Others performed the different work at the spine which entailed the patient cutting of the gristle between the

Figure 11.3: "A black mound reared high over the ice, its life closed down, the body upside down, the eye low on the side." The whaling, Alaska North Slope 1988 (photo by Edith Turner)

huge vertebrae, a most skilled task. Removing the baleen plates at the mouth was a very hard job indeed because the hardest tissue apart from bone was at the roof of the mouth and lip. The cold wind and sun were always about us, the sound of splashing of feet, the occasional heavy thud of falling segments, the odor of nourishing blood— a reassuring odor; the quietness and warm joy of the men, shown in their willingness, plainly shown in body language, though rarely in their faces (see figure 11.4). Most of the time I was sitting on a block of ice watching. Clem's son Kehuq noticed something in the carcass, went forward, and drew out part of a brass metal tube. It was the bomb that had taken the life of the whale.

Old Annie Kasugaq said, "Poor whale. Poor whale. They feel." I knew they did, self-sacrificing souls, willingly coming to their human brothers to suffer for their sake. We knew what they felt—"We whales do what we must, and we suffer, because of our unity with you. From this comes a greater good"—as I saw later.

"Look," said Clem. He knew I was interested. He had the whale's ear in his hands, its tympanum. It was a conch-like thing on one side and a soft-skinned flat drumskin on the other. It was six inches across.

"This is what has been listening to us," said Clem. The whale knows everything we do.

Figure 11.4: Handing out whale meat (photo by Edith Turner)

The men went on with their work. The last panels of skin and fat came away. The final slabs were hauled free with much pulling this way and that. All the meat was laid in order.

Still the head remained. The huge jawbone, fifteen feet long, still rose from the head in a great arch. I saw that the head was much wider than it was spherical because of the two massive projecting bone processes extending to the eyes on each side. Walking around the mass, I located the nerve endings of the eyes, mere stumps; and midway between the projections, exactly in the middle of the brain case, I saw the hacked-off spinal cord, the nerve cord of the body. All the rest of the nerve world was enclosed in a four-foot-wide bloody lump hiding the complicated bone of the skull. The skull lump was set between those side wings that guarded the eyes, all overtopped by the rearing arch of the jawbone. Inside the skull— what? No one would look. "We never eat that," said Annie. Inside it? I stood facing it as before a wall, wondering.

Next morning I came back to the ice. The head was still there, the only thing remaining on the ice. Clem and his men were standing around the bloody mass. He had told me before that the spirit of the whale was alive inside it, and if the head were released into the water the spirit would be able to grow its parka again and return.

The men drew away for a moment. Clem prepared them for the last task, the return of the head to the sea, the work of *niaquq*, "the head." For the last time they tied ropes onto the jawbone and Clem stationed them along the narrow ice margin between the head and the ocean. They pulled, with a wrenching tug. They came around this side, others steadying the head behind. They wrenched on the rope, rocked, endeavoring to rear the solid mass of the skull out of the pit in the ice that its own heat had melted. They wrenched, and at last the head was free of the hole, standing on ice that was nearer the edge. Now it was a matter of going back to the sea rim on the far side and pulling, then forward to the sea rim on the near side and pulling, edging the head crabwise toward—toward that drop-off into deep ocean. It took half an hour. Steadily they pulled, exchanged sides, pulled, and the head crept toward the edge. When it was right at the edge they detached the ropes and all got behind the skull and pushed, straining with all their might, their gloves wringing with blood. Heave! It moved. Heave! It moved. It teetered. Heave. SPLASH.

(Suddenly Vic was in my mind; the nobility of the animal, the Viking funeral, the crew doing the last honors. My face was streaming, and Clem glanced at me.)

Instantly drawing into a line they howled, "Uu-i, uu-i, uu-i! Yuuuuu!" and rocked with joy. The spirit, inua, was returned. All around there was a sigh of relief, for the ice was clear of it, its red shadow released into the dim water. Everything was quite all right, we had done right. All that was left on the ice were the men and their equipment—material things, ordinary. That great spirit presence was gone. Without the head the stretches of ice looked quite different, a vacant lot. So, a spirit had been there.

Then, as the cries died down one more shout arose, "Come back!"

Now I remembered what the whale wanted, the greater good. Once the head was returned to the water we received a flash of knowledge of the whale's spirit, we did become conscious of it, which was the whale's purpose in coming to us. Absence = presence. Consciousness of absence received its reply, a sense of presence. Some would call this no proof, but that's how it happened. My knowledge deepened. The whale did come; it was somehow in tune with us and we with it. It wanted this. The events were those kinds of events, they had that shape, not any other.

And now our whale went to grow its new parka, to reincarnate, "re-flesh" itself, and once more join the cosmic cycle that rolls forward in continuous replenishment. That cycling was how the world of the oceangoing Iñupiat worked. The whale as a conscious being was for ever their dominant experience.

This was true of a neighboring tribe, the Yupik of central Alaska, as described by Ann Fienup-Riordan.[5] Their dominant being is the seal. It is a spirit, and they give this animal their deepest respect. Hunters have feelings for the seal, so they would never neglect to give it a drink of fresh water. The soul of a living seal has a curious longing to encounter a good hunter because that soul craves that drink of fresh water—because it craves to engage in the cycling of nature. So when the hunter searches the ocean the seal sees him coming in his kayak in the form of a bird, breathing out a soporific mist, a life-giving breath. As the hunter strikes, the seal dives into its own bladder, and there becomes immortal. Its dead body is pulled into the house and is given the fresh water it craved. And when at last the fleshly garment is distributed as food, the people reserve the bladder, the seat of the soul, and return it to the sea. Then, the soul grows a new body and reincarnation takes place, a cycling that is greatly satisfying to animal and person. The seal has experienced the merest "jog" effect, or no effect at all, between this world and the next at that transition point into a world of light and fulfillment. Death is a desirable thing, a crossing point, a way through (see figure 11.5).

We cannot but marvel at the sophisticated sense of the life and death process here. Tradition relates that a festival was instituted by spirits who visited a couple and instructed them in the rites. This became the great Bladder Festival that celebrates the crossing point from death into life. From that time onwards the Yupik have held the Bladder Festival yearly, and it has become the occasion on which the bladders are returned to the sea to be reincarnated.

As regards the soul of the human being as distinct from the seal, death and reincarnation rituals help the human soul as it travels its path after death. Finally the soul arrives safely at the grandmother's happy village of the dead. Once there, the soul has beneficial work to do, principally to return into the body of a new baby—and this is enabled by the relatives' attention to the matter of naming the baby. The name is discovered by a kind of divination search. The moment

Figure 11.5: Edie in the Iñupiat whalebone graveyard (photo in the possession of Edith Turner)

the relatives allow the name of the dead to come to mind and give it to the baby, the baby receives the soul of that person and from then on will thrive.

Death, then, is less an interruption than a way to continue, a way to revivify the spiritual process. Here in an environment on the edge of human survival is found a strong and vivid sense of the soul. I use the term "soul" advisedly. There is an invisibility of the soul itself, like the existence of a glass object in a glass of water.

I spent the whole year in that village until the end of the following August. In the village, spirit matters were all of a piece with everyday life; our conversations often went that way. We all seemed to live it, naturally.

Six years passed. In 1993 I became a US citizen (see figure 11.6) and thus felt more at one with the Alaskan Iñupiat. In 1995 I was in the village for a short visit at the end of April in the sea-hunting season, when the water was normally open for sea mammals to pass through. But it so happened this year that the sea was deeply frozen.

I was in church that Sunday. The Iñupiat had been missionized by Episcopalians, but after many decades of having their own preachers they were living in a fully experienced syncretism of indigenous spirituality and Christianity, in which the people sensed their church, that double-natured church, as one of the two sources of all good power. The other was the whale.

Figure 11.6: In 1993 Edie becomes a U.S. citizen, accompanied by grandson Daniel Turner (photo in the possession of Edith Turner)

When I arrived the village had a dire problem. The settlement lay on a point of land between a navigable beach to the south and a non-navigable beach to the north. Both of these were totally blocked in by sea ice. What everyone was hoping for was a north wind to blow away the ice from the good southern shore. Then they would be able to catch the sea mammals which were their food. But there was no north wind, only a "sultry" south wind of about 26 degrees Fahrenheit, which counted as warm for them.

Accordingly, that Sunday afternoon, the preacher brought his own whaleboat into the church and was joined by the whaling captains and all the people. They left their pews and went up into the sanctuary. There they joined the preacher. They put their hands on the whaleboat and all started to pray for a north wind. I was on the outside of the crowd, with my hands on the parka-dressed woman in front of me, who had her hands on those in front, and so on. We went to it hard. "God send us a north wind, God … " I heard, sometimes in their own language. The sound grew and grew; I was calling and yearning with them. It rose to a great, great, collective cry. I will never forget it—all of us were as one. It seemed that in the midst of the noise we were being collected up and nurtured in some way. At the height of the sound I looked over to Robert the chief of the captains and saw him smile faintly. The calling began to tail off and soon ended. We finished the service and I and my friend Annie made for the door. We negotiated the step outside carefully as usual because of the ice and snow that covered the doorstep. Then we walked together along the side of the church toward Annie's house. We came to the corner of the church. Blowing around it came the north wind, now clearly at about 10 degrees, right from the northern lagoon, from the northern beach, the north pole, crisp and cold. No one said a word but went home to get ready. The water opened, the whales came through, and it was a successful hunt.

Prayer—what was this thing? My memory holds many events, the Sufi prayer when I was in Israel, the restorative prayer among the Yaqui women in Tucson, the Ndembu medicine man, Singleton, praying at his tree of herds, some odd prayer situations later, one at a Christian Group which stopped a member's smoking habit cold, and another at the strange pilgrimage center of St. Patrick's Purgatory in Ireland. A remarkable sonnet was written by George Herbert in 1633, which contains many ritual reversals showing the eerie power of prayer, stronger than God:

Prayer

Prayer, the church's banquet, angels' age,
    God's breath in man returning to his birth
    The soul in paraphrase, heart in pilgrimage,
The Christian plummet sounding heaven and earth;

Engine against th' Almighty, sinner's tower,
    Reverséd thunder, Christ-side-piercing spear,
    The six-days' world transposing in an hour,
A kind of tune, which all things hear and fear;

Softness, and peace, and joy, and love, and bliss,
    Exalted manna, gladness of the best,
    Heaven in ordinary, man well-dressed,
The Milky Way, the bird of Paradise,

    Church bells beyond the stars heard, the soul's blood,
    The land of spices; something understood.[6]

My memory kept resonating with those other events, each so particular, each making music with each. In this respect my path had come out into a flowering land and yet refused to be located along a fixed route. That was all right too.

Notes

1. For a fuller account of this year's research in the Arctic see Edith Turner, *The Hands Feel It* (DeKalb, IL, 1996).
2. Mircea Eliade, *Shamanism: Archaic Techniques of Ecstasy* (Princeton, NJ, 1964), 35, 47-48, and passim; see also a discussion of the "dismemberment" phenomenon in Edith Turner, *The Hands Feel It*, 207, 236 (chap. 8) n.3.
3. See Raymond A. Moody, *Life After Life: The Investigation of a Phenomenon: Survival of Bodily Death* (New York, 1976).
4. For a "How-To" book on shamanism see Michael Harner, *The Way of the Shaman: A Guide to Power and Healing* (San Francisco, 1980).
5. Ann Fienup-Riordan, *Boundaries and Passages: Rule and Ritual in Yup'ik Eskimo Oral Tradition* (Norman, OK, 1994).
6. George Herbert, "Prayer (I)," in *The Norton Anthology of Poetry*, ed. Allison et al. (New York, 1975 [1633]), 287.

12

FROM THE INUIT TO THE CELTS
Returning to Ireland

Now we come to another hairpin bend in the route, back to Ireland; this time to look closer at healing.[1] I was more than ever curious about healing after learning so much from Claire, and I also still had the memory of African ritual cures on me.

In the mid 1990s my friend Em in Ireland asked me over for a visit. She added as an inducement that she knew of a healer named Croine living nearby with whom I might want to work. This was a great opportunity and I said I would come the following year.

Thus I spent three weeks in Ireland with Em. Em knew the range of fieldwork I was interested in: healing, small and large pilgrimage centers, holy wells, graves, and the people's spiritual world. Most importantly, I was able to visit the woman whom Em had recommended.

One morning I threaded my way down the tiny road to her house, a narrow road with a grass strip in the middle. On this kind of road if a driver meets another car she has to back up and find a field gate entry so both may pass. This road took me to Croine's gate. When I parked and climbed out all I could see was a mass of flowers: red ramblers, speedwell, heal-all, monkshood, comfrey, valerian, and many other healing herbs, in a profuse tangle. The cottage was old and had not been prettied up. It was built of stone and whitewashed—a little house engorged with huge herbs, such as hemlock six feet high and tall cow parsley, with bog willows on each side.

I knocked at the door. It opened and a fine mature woman stood before me, intelligent and strong. Her mother had been an herbalist, and she herself gave healings by appointment.

Notes for this section begin on page 222.

She settled me down in her kitchen with some tea and soda bread. She was a true pink-cheeked, energetic Irishwoman. We began to talk about the countryside. "The ring forts up the hill from the house were the homes of my people," she said. "There were three rings for kings, two and one for commoners. 'Tis the old land of my ancestors, just here. When I walk on it, I can feel it in the ground with my feet—electricity. I know it because when I go further away, at a certain point I can't feel it." She gave a little shiver and looked at me meaningfully. Later we would talk much about the Celts, whom she loved and understood.

In our first wandering conversation she talked of the potato famine and how the people starved. At that time the British were shipping huge cargoes of wheat *out* of Ireland. The wheat had been grown by starving tenants and owned by English landlords.

I got angry. "And they talk about the atrocities of Ruanda and Serbia! The British haven't got a leg to stand on"—then shut up. Anger was no good.

Croine spoke with a rush of information, often questioning in tone and at the same time strongly and with authority. I could see her domain as in a sense enormous, continually filled with events. This land of hers, with its huge past, was a universe all of its own.

Talking of the land, we compared notes about the stalactite cavern at Aillwee in County Clare, a cave with a deep abyss.

"It made me feel strange," she said. "I felt the walls very close around me. There was that river above, and a lake below, and metal walkways. Suppose the walkways gave way! I said to my friend, 'Oh! I feel pressed.' It was the electricity there."

Indeed, when I think of that electricity, my own hair begins to tingle, and I sometimes shudder, like Croine. I was beginning to take more notice of these physical reactions. Shuddering and cold chills are good and ancient, inborn, physical recognition signs of something spiritual.

In another conversation I said to Croine, "You told me you do your healing with your thumbs."

"Yes. There was this woman who was run into by a shopping cart. She was a long time under the doctor's care, in bed. Nothing was any good. Her back—" Croine drew a picture on her lap "—was swollen on each side of the spine. There. I could 'see' the fluid in it. I had to get rid of it." She shook herself, remembering.

"Did you cut an incision?" I was thinking of African healing.

"No, no. I could feel something sticking out from the disk, so I put it back with my thumbs. Then I put my thumbs on the spongy stuff and the fluid was reabsorbed."

"Kind of dispersed?"

"Yes." This was just like other healings I had seen, like the time the Iñupiaq healer Claire worked on little Lee's knee and the water on the knee simply went away.

Croine continued, "That woman came in looking over seventy, and went out looking under fifty."

There was a knee case. "An athlete came to me, a runner. His body was twisted. I took a quick look at him. He had one leg bent inward a bit." She demonstrated with her right leg. "As he stood up I said to him, 'It's your kneecap.'"

"He said, 'The doctor never said anything about that.'"

"He'd been walking about with it dislocated. I took the kneecap in my hand to move it to the correct position. Then I 'saw' in my head things like two rough boulders grinding heavily against each other."

"It was terrible," Croine went on. "I almost lost my courage to touch that knee. I moved the kneecap a bit. 'Do you feel it?' I asked the man. 'Does that hurt?'"

"'Can't feel a thing,' he said. And I moved it to the right position. He had no pain at all."

I said, "Your mind kind of took the pain off him."

"Yes."

"Wonderful. I know. I recognize all you've been saying." I certainly did, having studied it and experienced it in Africa and Northern Alaska.

She looked at me gladly, and we laughed.

She went on, "After another visit to take away the knots in the tendons, he went on and won races again."

Croine's thumbs were like divining rods. They resembled two separate animals that arose from her lap at the least thing. When I looked at her hands I saw that each thumb grew from a heavily-fleshed root on her hand. They seemed awesomely muscular thumbs in the dim light of the room. She constantly made little actions with them. She said they guided her to where the trouble was in the body.

"When I do this," she pushed her thumbs forward, "and I've put them in the wrong position, they turn back toward me and won't go forward." She showed how the thumbs joined and crossed by her stomach. "When it's okay, out they go." This healing method was so different from that of Native Americans. There the native peoples use the whole hand, sometimes with trembling fingers, sometimes still, sometimes pressed deeply into the body as among the Iñupiat. Thumb divination was Celtic in origin.[2]

"It's like water divining," I said.

"Yes, and for finding things," she went straight on.

"A woman came to me and said, 'It's terrible, I've lost my wedding ring. It's very unlucky to lose one's wedding ring.'"

"'I'll come,' I said to the woman. She'd lost it along a path with long grass up on the side. 'This is where I was,' the woman said. The people had even marked out with sticks where she thought it must be.

"'You sure?' I said to the woman.

"'Yes.'

"I said, 'Maybe you don't really know, but you were up there a bit. I know it's not here.' I *knew* it wasn't where she said it was. I went a bit further up and happened to notice something shining. I didn't say anything because it might have been just yellow grass glinting in the sun. And then I saw it. It was the ring!" She shivered, shaking her skirt in front and looking at me in awe.

Hardly taking a breath, she went on with another story. It was set off by our looking at the old spinning wheel standing in her house. She said, "You can 'see' the person who used it."

"I was sent an article about a father and son who were healers. Before that time I had a vision. I saw a man, very distinctly, with one very long thin right arm and a long hand and fingers. Also a beard. His leg was turned in, and his trousers were wrinkled. His foot was also funny. It was months afterwards when I saw that article on healers in which the son described his father. It was my first read of it, months afterwards. The healer had this very long arm and hand, and that is how he healed. You see?" She regarded these previsionings with a kind of glad bewilderment.

Often her visions were connected with the land and were about the sacredness of objects. One day she was working by an old wall higher up the hill in the garden, digging. She looked up from her garden fork and saw a woman standing there, resting her outstretched arm on the wall. She was wearing a long brown dress made of shiny material, with pleats in front at the waist. On her head she wore an old-fashioned cap, and on her feet, shoes with Cuban heels. Croine thought she might have come up by the old road from the village, but how could she have walked all the way along the bad road wearing those Cuban heels? Why had she appeared just there, by the old wall?

Croine frequently sighted figures of people who used to live there. Late one night when she was not quite asleep and not quite awake [this sounds like a waking dream], she saw a boy quite distinctly, with a fresh face, looking to one side of her, not straight at her. Then she saw a man with very rough features, with a drawn face, wearing a skin hat and dark, dark clothes.

The next day, for some reason, she was digging in the side part of the yard when she found a child's jaw with teeth in it, then another jaw, an adult's, with the teeth knocked out. She wondered why the teeth should have been knocked out. Then she remembered her waking dream. The two people in it had been calling her. At this point in the story Croine shook her skirt in front like a proud girl.

I told her a story of having felt the presence of a dead friend in a church in Northern Alaska. She went on to tell me another story of having seen the dead.

"A man named Brady died," she said. "I wanted to phone the family and offer my sympathy. I managed to contact his sister, so that was something. I tried to find the man's number in the telephone directory, but there were so many Bradys. Was it O'Brady? Then I remembered the man's first name, John. There were many John Bradys but I knew the address and found the number.

"But as I sat with the phone in my hand before ringing, I looked up and saw a man in the doorway. I knew him; he was dressed better than when I used to meet him before. He looked fine, though pale, and cleaner than when I knew him. It was John Brady there, and at the same time he was lying in his coffin in the church. Will I be called crazy?"

A year later I took my daughter Rene to see Croine. Rene had a nasty ache in her upper back, near the shoulder blade. She had had it for about fourteen years, since the strain of breast-feeding her premature baby daughter. We asked Croine if she could help Rene. It was a sunny day so we went into the garden to the right side of the house. Croine sat Rene down on a garden chair and waited for a time. Then I watched while she got those two thumbs to work on Rene's back, scouring around the sore muscle on the right side. She pushed her nails hard against the muscle, digging in, from below upward, then down and outward. She seemed to haul the flesh up, again and again. Rene said afterward it felt very hot, not as if she were being scratched.

Croine worked on the muscle for less than ten minutes.

"The pain's gone," said Rene. (She has told me it has never come back.)

"That's my electricity," said Croine with her jaunty air of knowledge, grinning with delight. "You see, I can't do it if I'm busy. I need to quiet down, to feel my electricity." She shook her shoulders.

"The healing is different each time. I never know if it'll happen. I just get overwhelmed with the desire to heal, and it works. It comes into my hands and arms."

She stood there big and knowledgeable. She couldn't help but heal. "You cross your arms like this afterwards," and she did so.

Rene described the healing as a sense of "Zing!" going down through her whole body—yes, she said, it was a sense of electricity. "You're aware the body changes and passes on to a different state," she said.

At the time of my next visit I myself was in trouble with a bit of sciatica up my left leg and lower back, due to attempting the footwork of the ancient Irish dance. Croine's thumbs did their work again on my left lumbar vertebra; she found swelling there, and fluid.

"My hands are like X-rays," she said. She knew exactly where I was hurting. She started pushing with her thumbs—or I should say, her thumbs started pushing, since they were acting of their own volition.

"The pain's kind of moved off to the side," I said.

"That's the pain moving before the thumbs, that's what I call it," said Croine.

Her nails—they were long and sharp—dug in, and it hurt. She had told me it is not the nails that do the healing, but the pads of the thumbs.

My whole back became hot. "Your thumbs are very hot," I told her.

She was surprised. "I thought they were cold," she said, and felt them.

The ache in my back was becoming more shadowy, and I thought to myself, "We'll see."

Now Croine was saying, "I don't know really if it will get better. With Rene, my hands tingled up to the elbows, and my legs tingled afterward. With you, my hands tingled. Look, my arms are tingling now."

It did actually turn out all right. In a day or two the pain had gone altogether.

Here in Croine were all the traits of a woman gifted with psychic or spiritual powers. One may find similar individuals all over the world. They are nested as she is in their ancient culture, and radiate from it a kind of power that is treasured by those who have preserved it from ancient times.

So again, what is going on? Croine's living consciousness and the progression of events in her life demonstrate the wide field of spiritual powers of which any of us is capable. Some call it the collective unconscious. Perhaps one should call it "paths of consciousness between people and spirits that enable communitas, healing, and visions." I could see that, with regard to Croine's work of bodily divination and her bodily healing with the thumbs, we were beyond the Jungian limitations of working with the psyche only. Here was no mere collective unconscious of the mind at work, but a *bodily* awareness called "seeing" that can enable the spirit of the healer to jump into someone else's body, or sense invisible objects. So, it is in the world of matter, the world of the body, that these strange events occur.

Croine is the classic "wise woman" existing in 2001, reborn intact from way back, from 1600, 1200, 800, 800 BC, or earlier ages still, from the time when the use of spiritual power was an everyday affair. The ancient Celtic tales of Cúchulainn and the salmon leap coalesce in

Croine, the aproned woman of many simples and brews, threading her way through a century like any other, happy to exist to help people.

Meanwhile I had a question for my friend Em: what was happening at Knock Shrine after my absence of twenty-three years? In response she took me there, and it turned out to be an emotional visit, not to say an angry one.

As we approached from the Claremorris direction I saw a huge needle-sharp spike emerging from behind a hill. Then appeared bed-and-breakfast suburbs, and immediately the main street was upon us. Then the old church. Neither of us sighed. The church was almost hidden under the monstrous black cowl of an ultra-modern apparition-site Mass Center—and then—the basilica! (See figure 12.1.) What did we have here? An enormous putty-colored hexagonal cardboard box? A modernesque railroad station, say Penn Station, New York? A supermarket with an anomalous space needle on top, complete with a fast food carry-out service window in front? That turned out to be the window where the pope said Mass in 1979 for thousands of people outside. The whole conception didn't seem right. From what I was just seeing it was a shock, and from the spectacle of the gift shops behind the main street, I could understand why eight out of nine people told me Knock was commercialized.

People were approaching the cathedral-ceiling glass entrance to the Mass Center, so we entered too. We were in an entirely new church

Figure 12.1: Knock Basilica, County Mayo, Ireland in 2000 (photo by Edith Turner)

built onto the back of the old gable. Mass was about to begin, said without singing by a well-fed older priest. I saw a full congregation of the usual flat-faced middle-aged women with longing in their eyes, each body packed tight with prayer, the faces more or less wrinkled, all "gone" into prayer. They were still an injured-looking suffering people—strained, put-upon, ordinary folk.

My eyes wandered to the statuary. Now, my god, even the statuary was changed. The middle of the sanctuary was dominated by a dramatic lamb and altar in white, with a halo of modernesque angels darting around it. Huddled far to the left side, the nondominant side—stood three white marble figures, so white they were almost formless, like ghosts hanging there. The figures faced at an angle across the congregation, none concerned with it. Joseph was there on a plinth; and a minatory figure, not looking at us at all, wrapped like a mummy, was supposed to be Mary. My hair rose. Then there was John, somehow unconnected and unmemorable.

I remembered my holy picture of 1971, with the motherly figure almost central, big, facing everybody with her saints, making a row parallel to the back wall, and certainly *the* key figure in the apparition (see figure 7.2). Whatever had the church done to its one woman of note? I never caught her name mentioned once during the Mass that was in progress. It was usurpation.

Later, when I was in the shrine bookstore, since I was interested in the woman-question, I picked up the official brochure on the shrine and its meaning. On the front cover was a picture of the Mass Center lamb and altar, by themselves. The section on the meaning of the apparitions dealt first with the meaning of the lamb and altar and gave it at greatest length. The other figures were dealt with more shortly. At the end of the book, on the back cover, was a picture of the Mass Center marble figure of the Virgin.

"Look, they've put Our Lady at the back," I said to the woman assistant. "They've got the lamb and altar at the front."

"The lamb and altar were the principal figures in the vision," she told me authoritatively.

"It's wrong," I muttered. "The poor woman gets pushed to the back."

She flashed back, "We'll get there in time, though!" Apparently she had got my meaning.

Afterwards I asked myself, "What on earth are people getting told? The church has painted itself into a corner. I can feel something giving in the structure."

We went out and followed the crowd who were circumambulating the church counterclockwise just as in the 1970s, saying their rosaries. Having finally circled left, back, and past the glassed-in Mass Center again, they took a position by the new back outside wall of the sacristy on the right, where there seemed to be a framed square in the wall, like a picture. When I came closer I saw it was a neat display frame set with some of the stones from the original back gable where the apparition had first taken place. Every woman in this new pilgrimage crowd put her hand on these rocks and then to her face, staying there in pensive thought. This corresponded to the buttress-marking rite I had seen in 1972—the act constituted some kind of material connection with the original event.

Then we went into the old church, which was much the same as in 1972, and as restful, mercifully. I could pray a little bit in there.

On a second trip in 1996 with my daughter Rene we took the pilgrimage bus to Knock, along with a full bus load of pilgrims. The people began to say the rosary, all five decades of ten prayers each, then a pause, and then we said it again, then again.

Rene said to me, "These ordinary people are getting the point of prayer by *doing*, by the chanted words. The words are spoken in a flowing collective rote. To say the rosary with 'meaning' in every word would spoil it." She thought. "The occasion gets to be spirituality, by the rise and fall of voices, by the contentedness of the collectivity." I had been mentioning how contented people are when saying it. "They know the words, of course," she went on. "The words are like a well-worn garment. The effect is, we're in the mode of spirituality for that duration."

We all talked and joked a little between the mysteries; then the sound of voices in unison began again, while the bus rocked and roared, and the hedges gave way to naked stone walls and there were sheep in the fields, with fewer cattle. We were in the north, in County Mayo. Everyone became silent—like the apparitions—as we drew nearer the goal. The growing silence in the bus and the noticeable vagueness—even a kind of trance—were in keeping with the thinning veil between the living and the dead and the mystery of the shining tableau of the heavenly souls who had come to earth again at Knock.

After the Mass I observed a vast procession of people going along the walkways of the domain saying the rosary, sometimes in Irish. I joined them with my own rosary and contentedly walked and walked and spoke the prayer and spoke the prayer. It was just the one prayer being said. No one person seemed to be saying it, but instead, the whole body of people. I wished it would go on for ever.

The Irish have kept this faculty hanging loose, that is, the true sense of mantra. They have resisted the rationalizing Reformation and have often even sidestepped the more recent rationalizations of their own Catholic Church, while backing Christianity to the limit.

It was time to go. On the way back in the bus everyone began to sing, choosing the songs of each county through which we passed, Mayo, Galway, Clare, Limerick, and Cork, with occasional yells of pride from a native of one of them. The old'uns sang fine if a little out of tune. I grinned: we were thawing out. They liked us, we liked them. It was the classic pilgrimage communitas.

On the fourth visit to Knock, I had a long conversation with Father Mike Riordan, one of the priests in the list of those serving the shrine.

I waited in the shrine office, and when Father Riordan appeared he led me off to a sitting room and gave me a cup of tea. He was a young man in ordinary clothes, tall. I think the room we were in was the same in which Vic and I had met Father Horan in 1972, when he had marveled in a puzzled kind of way at the crowds. Why did they come? "It's their *simple faith*," he had told us in slow Irish wonder.

It was now twenty-five year later. I described my research to Father Riordan.

"I'm afraid you've come to the wrong person," he said. I wondered, would he think it of no avail to get entangled in some anthropological discussion of Knock?

"Wrong person?"

"No, no. It's just that I don't know enough to help you."

I said immediately, "Of course you know more than I do. I only come here occasionally, for a few hours. You're right *in* it." This was the old anthropologist/people differential. Who is the expert? How can an anthropologist be an expert when she wasn't born in the country and had only book-knowledge of it?

Nevertheless we had a good wandering conversation over our tea, and just as with Father Horan, it was about faith. I talked out my thoughts on faith, that faith *is* experience, it is as material as that, and is often continuous in an Irish person as far as I could see, a condition of the continual experience of resting in God. When people see an apparition, they know it, it is experience itself and it takes precedence. The "holding pattern," "signed-up" type of faith, exercised while not really seeing the point of anything, is a moral state of loyalty that has been derived from some experience in the past. This is what I was saying. Father Riordan was not too sure about the first part. He seemed to understand the holding pattern only too well.

I wanted to know something. "What's this 'thing' about Knock, do you think? What's the meaning of this place?"

"M-m-m. It's hard to express .... "

I was delighted with those words. They were a sign we were on to something.

I told him, "Look, I've discovered that that's what all really spiritual people say. What's at the center is the very thing they can't express." I was putting this lamely. It was basically about religious experience. Would he understand?

He thought a minute and came back with a neat phrase, "The experience of authority is given by the authority of experience." I jumped to it. He'd said it. All our passive experiences of temporal power (my own term for temporal power being "Power I") hide the point from us, which is "The Experience," itself, from "out there," whose authority is immediately recognizable. I thought, they've been discussing experience versus authority in the seminary—no doubt tempered by safeguards against phony experiences. Riordan's words of respect for experience differed, then, from the doctrine, "Church teaching comes first," a doctrine to which most clerics are supposed to adhere.

Father Riordan said, "But *I* don't get experiences at Knock. Only the people do [that "simple faith" statement again]. You see, my training has been intellectual. Two years of philosophy, four of theology. *Nothing*"—he spread his hands—"*Nothing* about religious experience."

"No pastoral parish-work training?"

"Nothing."

"No field experience?"

"No." He cupped his hands and closed them. "We were totally cut off from the world."

"Did you have a spiritual director?"

"Yes."

"Did he help?"

"Yes. But this was entirely separate from the intellectual side of it. The two sides never joined."

I found this fascinating—and tragic.

"Has this changed for the better now?"

"Well . . . a little bit. But there was no change then."

"I'm getting the impression that no priests ever have religious experiences. Just the people. Is that true?"

"Not quite. Some do."

It was clearly not the norm that they should have religious experiences. I wondered whether by far the majority of priests do what they do out of a moral conviction of what is good. I realized that what they had been taught was mental and not spiritual. And they mourn because they do not have any experiences. Maybe they think such experiences have to be visions of flights of angels and so on. I thought, "My god, they're worse than anthropologists!"

However, as Father Riordan saw it, priests do pick up—by rule of thumb—some kind of feel for pastoral work as they go along, once appointed.

"Did you yourself choose to serve to Knock?"

"No, by no means! Here by far the greater number of pilgrims are elderly women." His figure of a total of 1,500,000 pilgrims a year amazed me. One may calculate that *all* the middle-aged women of the Irish Republic come at least once a year. This tallied with my conversations with many elderly women in Ireland.

He said, "I can observe how the people feel."

"What do they say to you? How do they describe it?"

"Of course, it's silence over there," he pointed out of the window over the wall into the domain. "They sometimes tell me, 'I go to Knock in one frame of mind and I come out different. There's something—that I have—a knowledge—' They go to Knock sometimes over some trouble, and then they feel all right about it."

He went on speaking, in a kind of aphorism, "We priests must be careful we don't altogether take away the faith of the people." So he hoped the people's faith would survive what the priests told them. I felt warm toward Father Riordan.

"We have to respect subsidiarity," he said.

"What's that?"

It was an interesting principle with which he was familiar, a spiritual principle. Each level of what used to be called authority in the church needs to operate and be honored in its own right. The role of each higher level is to help the lower level, *not* to govern it.

"Wonderful. In other words, 'small is beautiful,'" I said. I knew it was the ordinary folk who were the real pals of Jesus. "It's the kingdom of heaven," I said and grinned.

"Yes," he said. "Something like that is the mysterious reversal of authority." The famous *servus servorum* principle, I thought. The pope is supposed to be the servant of the servants. But this is often not so in the church itself. I thought of Cardinal Ratzinger, living in a terrible mess of canon laws, under the illusion he was protecting the people from themselves. His was the sorrow of Dostoyevsky's Grand Inquisitor.

Generally, what I saw of the spirituality of Knock was shadowy and piecemeal, but it was there. It was too big to come at you as a unified spiritual force. There was nothing there if you didn't look at every human face who was present. If you did, you began to feel the presence of the lady.

I was getting there. It took even another trip, one I was able to make entirely alone, as a pilgrim, pure and simple. Nothing could have stopped me, that time in May 2000. It kind of forced itself upon me, even in spite of the considerable difficulties in making the journey.

When I arrived I didn't realize how fond I was of the awful place. I parked, crossed the street, and at once saw women walking around the old church counterclockwise saying the rosary. Inside the church among the praying women I looked long at a new picture on the right, showing the apparition scene. There was Mrs. Trench lying prostrate on short grass among puddles of rain, about three yards from the lady. Children were in this picture. Then I looked up at the "touch-me-not" stained-glass window over the gable, with the Magdalene and the "gardener," when Jesus said "touch me not." The window even showed Magdalene's pot of ointment by her side. I saw the noble intentions of this window, a reminder of Mrs. Trench's attempt to touch the Lady. I remembered looking at the window when Vic had been there, and I cried for the holy beings—as I sat there now with all the women around me as before, with the experience of great love and thankfulness in them—for holiness, natural holiness, even now making my heart quail with love.

I went out and walked around, saying my rosary. I came around past the new Mass center and nearly overshot the "stone picture" from the gable which the women used to touch. No one was touching it now, and it did not seem so polished as before. I touched it anyway, and continuing around, I went by the old corner where the buttress was, where the women used to touch the rock. The corner now consisted of new masonry hidden by yellow plaster. A sign said, "Pilgrims are directed to the Old Rock picture at the north-east wall." I touched the corner above the sign. At least that was where the old pilgrims like Bidgy had dug their rosaries deep in as far as the original stone.

I said to myself, "The church seemed to feel it had to move the pilgrims away from this place because the pilgrims might ruin the stones—and there was also the sense that pilgrims were also doing something on their own and should be stopped. Perhaps it was paganism. This was control for the sake of control. So now the pilgrims won't even use the stone picture. Just try artificially *making* them do anything."

I went into the church in time for the 5: p.m. Mass and sat in a pew on the right. I proceeded to sleep comfortably through much of the Mass—it was surely the sweetest place to sleep after my trials on the road with my stick-shift car, with driving on the left, with an attack of laryngitis, a hernia, the loss of a side mirror, broken eyeglasses, alternating thunderstorms, dazzling sun, and hail, and ending up with a nosebleed in the priest's rest room. Sitting in the pew I idly noted that the shelf in front of me was scratched on, marked, as we schoolgirls had done in church in 1929.

In my sleep I was vividly aware of the presence of one of the members of the sociology department at University College, Cork, a woman who sees eye to eye with what I am doing. Then I realized she wasn't there and that it was raining outside. I was awake. I glanced again at the old pew before me. How battered and worn the pews looked! I loved them. No one had replaced them. Father Riordan told me the authorities were at least leaving the old church exactly as it used to be. I looked at the scratches. These were crosses: there were crosses here and crosses there along the shelf, as with the old buttress, as on many a tomb in churchyards, all done with the metal crosses of people's rosary beads—this then was the material contact. I touched these cross marks myself, along their lines.

So the pilgrims' spontaneous urge had found expression in yet another place and was not to be put down after all. Father Riordan and I looked at each other afterwards and said: "Nothing will stop them." We grinned.

Now that I had some material laid out I could see many possible levels from which to view the strange apparitions of 1879.

One level is hate.

"I hate Knock," said a University College, Cork woman undergraduate. She was learning feminism, critical studies, Marxism, and deconstructionism. For her, Knock was the most retrograde, hegemonic, patriarchal power in the country, a force for pure destruction. The idea that I could be interested totally mystified her. She was oddly not unlike Mike Riordan, quite a good, generous person, but stumped.

As for the symbolic analysis approach, this verges upon psychoanalysis. The argument goes like this: at the time of the apparitions the country was in the grip of the famine. Just as children who are abused invent an imaginary playmate, so the people had invented a highly self-aggrandizing magical event. Then, as it succeeded and its fame grew, an entire symbolic apparatus with a strong national power-focus was attached to it.

The view as from an imaginary villainous church prelate might go like this: the apparitions were indeed done by trick lighting as at Ballinspittle, in this case with the primitive magic lantern of the time, engineered by a skillful Jesuit somewhere back of the lane. We should keep quiet about that. Or it may have been that the fifteen people were drunk and hallucinating. Nevertheless the church has quite rightly developed the pilgrimage, hoping to lead the people more strongly under the influence of the hierarchy of Rome and away from the temptations of Fenianism, home rule, and all that might develop the people's sense of independence and self-determination. Above all the pilgrimage would divert women from their own struggle for gender justice, and thus keep families and particularly children in line with the strict tenets of the church. Then as time went on and it seemed that too much attention was being paid to a woman figure—in other words there was a danger that she was being worshiped instead of God—it became necessary to literally shift the statues to make the male God central. (Sadly, the last part of this was true, the church did rewrite history.)

A gentler version is that the priests found the visionaries' stories genuinely moving, but had to take them on faith. Few of the priests or elite of the church had any vision or call of that kind. The miracles were unproven, but one was grateful for them. The priests' role was to service the pilgrimage and encourage the prayers.

The version from church conservatives comes through like those of many elderly priests: "Almighty God has given us these visions to warn us and for the protection of the family. They are real and have a big message for us. All should pray their rosaries constantly. Priests and people should trust and obey their bishops, who know better than they. Just remain steady in faith and God will bless you with happiness and confidence. Make no mistake: it is feminism, homosexuality, and abortion that is ruining the world. The Holy Father is right."

In anthropology on the other hand we see a policy of ignoring the phenomenon of Knock as being unsuitable for study, and tricky because one might become personally involved. It was somehow unclean.

Yet anthropology might have another picture. Anthropology's function is to present to the world, among much else, the world's own ritual systems, this one among many; and therefore, anthropology is less and less able to resist the rich reports that are coming in from far-flung places such as this about conscious live people in the midst of communications with spiritual beings of many kinds.

The view as from sociology might be that a study is needed that would prove by research and statistics once and for all that the cult is false, damaging to progress, and as Marx would say, opium for the mass of abused women who need to right their own wrongs. As for the level of a person writing like myself from personal experience, such accounts are open to the sociologists' criticism: they are "anecdotal." That is, anything personal from me, or the rare event of 1879 itself, would merely fall through a hole in the sieve of statistics.

What about my own "humble judgment"? It is not a judgment but a cry. I see the ordinary folk manipulated and messed about. Just let them be left, as Gerard Manley Hopkins pleaded for all things natural.

Figure 12.2: St Patrick's Purgatory, Station Island, Lough Derg, Ireland (photo in the possession of Edith Turner)

If the villagers said they saw a visionary mother, they did. If the critics themselves once experienced something they couldn't explain, they might be able to understand the Knock event and not pick on the poor.

In the summer of 1998 I went to Ireland again with my daughter Rene and granddaughter Rose, and on 7 July, a Tuesday, we drove to St. Patrick's Purgatory located in County Donegal, a large complex of buildings on Station Island in the middle of Lough Derg—one of the three great pilgrimage centers of Ireland (see figure 12.2).[3] This pilgrimage, whose main feature is austerity, is attended by fifteen thousand people a year, compared to Knock at 1,500,000. I had once gazed on Station Island from the shoreline of Lough Derg, but I knew I wouldn't be able to understand the pilgrimage until I went over the water to the shrine and made the rounds. Humility was the real issue and this was a bother to me. I couldn't help turning the trip into a research project, yet I couldn't humble myself *unless* I humbled myself.

Naturally I was doubting my capacity to endure the austerities practiced there. I would go, and I would see. Getting no food: that was okay, my stomach was playing up anyway. No sleep for forty hours, well, I was sure to cheat and take naps, but there it was. Being warm enough while going barefoot? We'd see. My granddaughter Rose, a beautiful active girl of fifteen, might be a great help.

Now we were actually on the water and the die was cast. Our boat drew up at Station Island in the middle of the lake and our twenty pilgrims stepped out. When we landed we saw the simple ancient scene

Figure 12.3: Pilgrims walking on the stones of the "beds" of old monks' cells, St. Patrick's Purgatory (photo in the possession of Edith Turner)

of "stations" being made on the "Beds." That is, barefoot people were treading carefully around the Beds, people in sports jackets and long pants, warmly dressed. My eyes were fixed on the Beds. They were small stone circles as illustrated in many old pictures and photographs, simply the low remains of the walls of monks' beehive cells with rocky paths around them (see figure 12.3). The people circling on the rocky paths were walking barefoot.

I saw the people's lips moving all the time in the given prayers, some of them with their arms holding the cross that stood in the middle of each circle, caressing the cross for love of Jesus—and for balance. I took off my shoes and socks. First I was supposed to enter the basilica. Just within the entranceway of the basilica lay an area of pavement that was icy cold to my bare feet, and I hurried over it to get inside. Inside the building it was by no means warm. I quickly said the prayers and came out to pray at the St. Patrick's Cross, which was a little low stone post graced with a winding Celtic pattern up its stem and topped with a small cross of iron. I always liked feisty old Saint Patrick. I had read in his Confessions[4] how he had had the experience of spirit incorporation, like many shamans. This spirit was none other than God, and he had noted it with puzzlement. "I felt God actually *inside* me!" The poem-prayer "*St. Patrick's Breastplate*" has the same statement written into it too, "Christ within me." Furthermore, Patrick had had the experience of being hag-ridden by a satanic being, a terror that he survived, as all victims can, with prayer. He was a real person.

Then to St. Bridget's Cross—honoring both Bridget the abbess, she who had in ancient times consecrated the Host like a male priest, and Bridget the pre-Christian goddess of milking, beer, and healing, who knows which? Here we stood with our backs to this ancient stone cross with its equal projections, newly brought to the island and set in a fresh wall. We were supposed to stretch our arms in the cross form of the figure and renounce the world, the flesh, and the devil. Ha, this was where I had to alter the words. I knew with all the strength of my seventy-seven years that most of the theology of the rite was wrong. I loved the world. The body—made of flesh—was totally wonderful, as is all of nature. Rene and Rose stood grinning at me as I said, "I accept the world and the flesh, and I renounce the devil." The cross at my back was something I loved. It told me there was at least one person who had given up the beloved body rather than be a leader in the style of the Pharisees or Romans.

We then made many circlings of the basilica reciting the rosary. By now a tearing wind had risen that was whipping long wales of foam across the lake. It was very cold and I buttoned up the hood of my light raincoat, holding the hood on with my hands.

We could at last go to the stone circles. Looking back, they were my favorite places, agony and all. The first circle was St. Bridget's Bed, with a wall about a foot high, around whose rim was a narrow circular path about nine inches wide consisting of very sharp and rough rocks on which we pilgrims were to walk with our bare feet. The wall had a gap facing out to the lake. This was the "door" to the tiny open-air enclosure. Within the wall lay a similar circular footpath, and inside that there was just room for a rough stone platform bearing a solid concrete block in which stood a plain black bronze cross about two and a half feet high, with Christ's body on it, black, with his out-stretched hands and crown of thorns rubbed shiny yellow. The sign above said, St. Bridget's Bed. When I came to the cross in my circling, I caressed the pitiful yellow crown of thorns as the others did.

I started walking in my bare feet on the rock path. The stones were truly sharp and I had trouble keeping my balance for fear of being cut. My feet hurt badly. I had to think about the prayers. They went through my head. I liked the first prayers, to the man ("Our Father") and the woman ("Hail Mary"). Most of the words of these two prayers were the utterances of the people concerned: Jesus, the angel Gabriel, and Mary's cousin Elizabeth. They were taken from real events. But the creed[5] has long since bothered me because it was con-structed later. For a start I don't "believe" any of this stuff, I "know," like Carl Jung—just a little. Spiritual things are a matter of *experience* for me, not dogma. So at the start of the creed, my own utterance, said under my breath, was simply said to the things under my eyes, the small grasses growing up between the stones: "I do know you, I know a little about you, you green leaves in front of me, all doing your own thing, able to photosynthesize, having developed your own power from long ago, having the urge to press through to a good living form. The creation is the creator."

For me the next part on Jesus went: "Also all the people here. Each of them is 'Jesus Christ our Lord, born of .... ' etc.'" There's no hier-archy, just the pilgrims at Lough Derg where the water laps beside us. Each of these people is Jesus"—I looked over at the stumbling figures and stumbled myself—"sons of the creation/creator, daughters.... These praying faces are right where they were destined to be, in prayer, in the condition of the godhead. Here." Then, continuing in the creed, "Yes, and I know a little bit about Jesus's own story under Pontius Pilate and so on, engaged in the suffering that was imposed by structure, by cruelty similar to, worse than the cruel Sisters of Mercy, by the narrow patriarchy of the church system, by governments, law, bigotry, and so on and so forth. Jesus crucified, not by the sins of these people here, whose release from purgatory by their very presence is a foregone conclusion, there accomplished before my eyes." I gazed my full.

I remembered the "Holy Spirit" section of the creed and added to it, "All the spirits, Jesus's, the whale's spirit on the North Slope, African ancestors, and the spirit that has so marvelously helped me. The initiative is with the spirits: 'You haven't chosen me, I've chosen you'— it's the same report all over the planet. And then, all the religions (by no means only 'the church'), and the rest of the list. The last ones are really true, not 'believed in,' but experienced—communitas and communion, the sacred object, bread. Thanks, dear ones! And, 'I look for the resurrection of the dead and reincarnation': most certainly."

It became a quick version, just this: creation; the people as an all-in-one-with-Jesus; spirit; all the religions. That way I did not belie myself, nor betray my loved friends in other religions. I began to remember those friends, and the list of people who had asked me to pray for them at Lough Derg. I brought them all into front focus as I said the necessary by-rote words under my breath. Suddenly my foot put weight on an agonizingly sharp rock and I fell. An old gentleman happened to be kneeling at the low wall entrance, and I shouted at him, "Look out!"—and fell right on top of him. To my surprise he was soft.

"Are you all right?" I gasped.

"Quite all right," he said.

"Thank goodness." People around me looked vaguely grateful and a little concerned. One pilgrim leaned over to me and said confidentially, "Sure and the attendants go out late at night and *sharpen* those rocks." I managed a smile.

I went on in pain. Everyone went on. Everyone was finding it difficult. I saw out of the corner of my eye a picture of struggling, patient humanity, the mouths in motion, all the faces absorbed in the work of praying. It was perfect because it was entirely simple, it was what it was. The historic depth of time implicit in the actions also made the actions precious. At various times I blurrily saw the figures as they were five hundred years ago. And there I was too, struggling along with them five hundred years ago, as I was now. It was, in that blur, just the same; and in five hundred years into the future, there they were too, people bending over the rocks praying.

Never mind my thoughts. I wasn't looking where I was going and terribly stubbed my toe. "Oouuch!" I collapsed for a moment in agony, while blood oozed out. The blood rather pleased me—but not for long. After another two minutes I stubbed the same toe in the same place and *howled*. Shortly after that I stubbed it again.

When all the six circles were done, we went to the water's edge where we saw kneeling-stones. Standing and kneeling, we said many prayers. Ripples were coming in; reeds stood nearby; other islands could be seen further out; and far away all around lay the hills.

Then again to St. Patrick's funny little cross, and after that, one was supposed to say prayers for the pope's intentions inside the basilica; but I prayed for women priests, which were not the pope's intentions. This pilgrimage for me was real.

Afterwards I was able to go where they provided dry toast, and ate some. All of us pilgrims chatted, and it appeared that many of them made the pilgrimage every year. People liked my efforts to somehow make the pilgrimage.

When we went in for Mass the priests entered the basilica. The first thing they announced was that the doors of the basilica had been locked—we were locked inside. This was another symbolic act—and a real act as well, a reminder of the days before 1600 when the penitential chamber was a low cave with a ceiling only four feet high, made of branches with a sod cover. In it the pilgrims were "imprisoned," as they called it, for twenty-four hours. Some of them actually died inside. This was their willing experience of purgatory, a place of suffering and doubled-over prayer. There exists at Todi in Umbria a medieval fresco showing this mound in cross-section,[6] with seven cells inside for the seven deadly sins, with devils in each cell torturing the souls of the penitents. Saint Patrick in his bishop's miter is seen in the vent-like entrance at the top, poking down the hole with his stick to keep the prisoners in. Down on the far right is the exit—like the magma exit of a smelting furnace—out of which can be seen emerging the purged souls, dressed in white, hopeful, free, and happy. And there, bending in welcome to caress them, is the lady herself.

So that was the reason we were locked in for the period of the Mass—to keep the tradition. Here, however, it was not a matter of, "I'll punish you if you don't love," but paradoxically, "You want to go to the purgatory because of love, because so many things have hurt you in the past. Those objects there in front of you, the crude crucifix, the grim faces, the locked doors, the hint of monsters, the pilgrims tottering as if they were dying, they are the worst this religion can do, there in front of you. They are a reenactment of your troubles." Rene my daughter told me afterwards that much that went on in her life at that time was worse than this purgatory.

The next exercise was the exposition of the sacrament in the basilica. The basilica was cold to the feet: I was in for a long night in which I wasn't supposed to sleep at all. Rose my granddaughter sneaked in a small quilt from her backpack in the hostel. Now we heard that the hostel where our things were left would be locked too, although there were conflicting accounts about this.

The stations inside the basilica began, during which we walked around inside saying the same prayers as outside. But somehow it wasn't as good, I wasn't as warm. The floor was smoother underfoot, but colder. When we had made one set of stations another set began. It was beginning to rain. We went out for a break and came back. Time passed in the same way—around and around and around, doing the stations. I was saying the prayers as a mantra, as advised in so many words in the priest's announcement. And here the Lough Derg thing began to work. I found it so, walking along at 1 a.m., following someone else in the circling procession, cold, tired, dropping everything else from my mind but the task of keeping my bare feet moving after the bare feet in front. I now had the sense of being a monk in a line of monks, of being one body with them; all were going forward too, endlessly saying the prayer. We pilgrims occupied—*were taking occupation of*—the basilica like this, filling it to the walls.

I put my hands in my light raincoat pockets to keep them warm and pushed them together in front as if they were folded, as if in a monk's robe. On. On. On. I was happy.

It was later still. Sometimes the ritual had us sitting down in the pews and saying certain prayers there. This is when from time to time I began to have an idea I was somewhere else. A scene would descend, hiding the one in front. What it was I don't know, a kind of wash of gray with people in it. One is familiar with such things in the form of waking dreams.

When I went to the resting room after one of the stations, the wind was screeching through the broken windows at what must have been 38 degrees, and I *could not* get warm sitting there with Rene and Rose. Rose tucked the quilt over my feet. My feet were kind of alive from the walking but as I sat I began to chill. Exactly six months before, on January 7, I had had my gallbladder removed after it had produced stones as big as marbles and had inflamed my liver. I had not been eating very well since then. Here at Lough Derg I was wearing warm underclothing, but it wasn't doing enough for me, nor did my long underwear help much under my flimsy dress pants. I had my raincoat on with the hood up and my hands in my pockets, but cold was all the time coming up from below.

I put my bare feet near Rose's. This did not warm me, because I found that her own feet were icy cold, colder than mine—like ice. When I realized this, I was alarmed. My granddaughter's feet were like ice! So I put my feet over hers in a vain attempt to give her what heat I had. At this point the cold spread remorselessly right up my body.

Suddenly I felt pain in my midriff and abdomen—a feeling that my insides were going rotten. My head sank and I felt faint. I got up, frightened, and told Rene, "I'm not very well."

She looked as if she had been rather expecting this. We just stood there. I sat down again. Immediately the pain returned: my stomach was rotting. Was it an infection of the scar from the spreading cold? This can't happen and you live.

I stood up and we gathered around. What should we do? "Actually," I said, "I don't think I'd better go on with the pilgrimage. This'll happen again. It's my feet. I can't make it."

It was bitter facing it. I said, "I'll go to the hostel and get into bed and warm up. Then perhaps we'd better leave in the morning."

"Hostel?" Rene said. "It's locked. I know it. I went around earlier and the door was locked and there was a man outside preventing anyone from getting in."

"What! You did?" And I started to move off to try for myself.

"There's the first-aid room," she said.

"No no no. I don't want that." I could look after my own troubles. First aid? No. I walked off in the direction of the hostel.

"Mom, mom, it's useless. They won't let you in."

I sighed, really needing *something*.

I went along with Rene in the raging wind, rain, darkness, and extreme cold, suffering from the soles of my bare feet up. Rene stopped, not at the hostel further on as I hoped, but at the lighted door of the first-aid room.

"No no," I said. She went inside regardless.

She came out again to the door and I saw her finger imperiously beckoning me in—like a dog, Rose said, laughing. And like a dog I trotted in, swearing to myself. Talk about humiliation.

The woman in charge—one of the sisters, I discovered—looked a little annoyed at being woken up. I described my pain.

"Sit down, will ye," she said, looking more kind.

"I can't. I'll feel faint if I sit down. I don't mind dying—" and I thought a minute—"but I've got responsibilities." It would be an awful nuisance for the others if I died, and I did have work to do of a sort. Dying wouldn't do just then. So the nurse took me down the passage to a room with a bed, a *bed*! Rene and Rose and I trooped inside. I didn't dare take off any clothes, begrudging the slightest loss of body heat. Big woolen blankets lay ready and I sank into them, my stomach signaling its pain. The door opened and in came the nurse with a rubber hot water bottle. Warmth!

Quick, my toes, my stomach, more blankets, gratitude all around! My family of two stayed with me, thank god, and after a second Rose jumped up on the bed and got in beside me. This time I passed her the hot water bottle, and we both had a bit of it. Rene laughed.

My fear of death began to leave me as the warmth made itself known, though the pain was still there. It took about half an hour for me to feel the pain lessen somewhat and the cold diminish. Very gradually my body warmed, and finally I was warm all over. I had missed the next station in the basilica because it was about 3:30 a.m. Rose slept a little. Rene, leaning on us two, slept a bit too. Even so I tried to stay awake to keep the vigil. At 4:45 the others roused. "We're going to the five o'clock stations," they said.

I was impressed. "Great. I just know I can't—it's that floor!" I was still feeling wrong inside.

"No no, don't you do it. We'll come back." And they did, after I had slept, willy-nilly. They told me about the 6:30 morning mass, how after a sermon that was about love, the priest had spent half an hour reprimanding the pilgrims for smoking cigarettes around the walkways.

This was 1998, not the Middle Ages, so we decided to curtail the visit, and that all of us would leave next morning, July 8, Wednesday, by the 9:45 a.m. boat.

We had indeed felt the liminality, the apartness, of the shrine at Lough Derg: on an island, in a lake, built on, but with water lapping at the end of every building. Everywhere one sees the choppy angry water trying to chop us into shaman pieces, the strong wind trying to tear off my raincoat hood. The very location in Ireland was liminal because it was far in the north of the republic in Donegal, in a land of sheep, bog, and simplicity. How could it have been 38 degrees, when it was early July? Even Ballyshannon on the coast was warmer. This dip in the hills has a fearsome character: the wind—and something else that is bad—focuses on the lake, which was wielding foam in those long, long wales like stripes from a whip. I couldn't get over the anger of the waves. This used to be the "Red Lake" in pre-Christian times, the lake of the dragon, a lake frightening in its negation of things. St. Patrick was said to have driven out the dragon, as he drove out the snakes. Nowadays the buildings on the tiny Station Island look like fortresses, some of them sitting on artificial foundations of huge rocks, grimly determined to be there. The place is an outpost against the devil, against the dragon of the red lake. Thus, it is a substitution shrine like so many. But this shrine was not a substitution for an older spiritual religion. The lake undeniably had been a bad place. We did get a sense of the devil, as the Knight Owen did in the Middle Ages, even a sense of his nightmares. Then the faint sense of something else. It was the Beds, beautiful, magical, peopled with myriads of souls from way back, and we had come to know the union of souls in the middle of the night. So Saint Patrick, maybe, as the scholars warned us, had come with his stick. Maybe he did turn the island with its cave into a curious hell, but one that leads through its bottom exit into purgation and heaven.

Thinking about it afterward, what do I see? A fair land. But how does it come about that it's "fair"? I say it again, it's precious ... most completely precious.

Is it just the old dogma of heaven at the end of purgatory? No. This woman, me, praying, had a sense of more. You felt an "attraction vortex" that pulled you; this vortex is felt by the Beds. It makes you feel ... full of wonder. Tears start from your eyes. It's the cold wind, and the souls—"What are these, that shine from afar?" and as in the Book of Revelation, "dressed in white." That's it. "For ever and for ever, are clothed in robes of white."

I was one of those souls. I went on, into the face of my weakness, right into it, to encounter it face to face. Which I did. The purgatory simply and directly showed me my limits and made me fail, and I accept that this was where the matter stood.

Notes

1. Further aspects of my Irish research of the 1990s are recorded in Edith Turner, *The Ancient and the Holy: The Roots and Flower of Irish Spirit Experience* (manuscript, n.d.).
2. Compare:
   By the pricking of my thumbs,
   Something wicked this way comes.
   [Shakespeare, *Macbeth*, act 4, sc. 1, lines 44–45.]
3. For much history of the pilgrimage see Shane Leslie, *St. Patrick's Purgatory* (London, 1932).
4. Patrick, Saint, *Confessions* (Dublin, 1924 [5th century?]).

5. *The Apostles' Creed*

   I believe in God, the Father almighty, creator of heaven and earth.
   I believe in Jesus Christ, his only Son, our Lord.
   He was conceived by the power of the Holy Spirit and born of the Virgin Mary,
   He suffered under Pontius Pilate, was crucified, died, and was buried.
   He descended to the dead.
   On the third day he rose again.
   He ascended into heaven, and is seated at the right hand of the Father.
   He will come again to judge the living and the dead.
   I believe in the Holy Spirit, the Holy Catholic Church, the communion of
   saints, the forgiveness of sins, the resurrection of the body, and the life
   everlasting. Amen.

   —c. 400, sixth century, eleventh century

6. Medieval picture attributed to Jacopo di Mino del Pellicciaio, 134[6] fresco,
   Purgatory with St. Patrick (at the convent of St. Francis, Todi, Umbria, Italy).

13

A SMALL SPIRITUAL GROUP
Cloud Nine

I remember a flashback to 1986 when my son Bob said to me, "Mom, you could join the Holy Comforter choir." He sang in his own church choir in Bethesda.

"I dunno. I might not get on with the choir director."

"You might."

I had been accustomed to sit somewhere near the back at the Holy Comforter, glad to be there at Mass at all. I was nervous about being religious because anthropology was supposed to be a science, yet events had given me to understand that spirits were real. During that period, the early 1980s, I often suffered from acid stomach. Grindal and Stoller sent me their pieces on spirit experience. I wrote down my own experiences in Ihamba, which I entitled, *Experiencing Ritual*. I often looked back to 1958, the time when I joined the church, the time of my early "sighting" of the grail. This "badger," Edith Brocklesby Turner, that smelly *muskelidae* beast, wouldn't give up. The line had come out of the cave wall at Kahona Village and that was that.

I did join the church choir, and became hooked on the music. I found that the choir director, whom I will call Lisa, was very good at her calling. She was large in person, and was often inspired. Some people did not like her, so just to be awkward, I did. This was me being Edie-ish again. Lisa was wafting us all the way up to the heavens with her inspiration—it was music that she composed herself that she gave us. At our practices we laughed excitedly, got high on religion, and blended our voices to the topmost rafters of the church until we had an idea we really were up there with the angels. We prepared

---

Notes for this section can be found on page 233.

a program for Christmas that was so beautiful it was out of this world, complete with Rachmaninoff and the bells of the Kremlin, and low heart-rendingly pitiful music about the poor. Never had I been in a choir that sang so sweetly.

But as things turned out, Lisa had to leave. After that I went to the Church of the Incarnation located nearer my house, and I sat in a pew right at the back where the light was dim. The music was not as good as it had been at the Holy Comforter. After a time I shifted to the choir area in that church and sat as close to the singers as I could, so that if I wanted to sing, nobody would turn around and stare at me, as members of the congregation were in the habit of doing at anyone who sang out loud. So I sat behind the choir and sang along with them, and nobody noticed. This little detail of my change of church and my seating in it had consequences later.

Privately I called this new church, the Church of the Reincarnation. This was not only in order to be naughty but because I had a sneaking suspicion that human reincarnation really did take place, and because I always felt quite at home with the miracle of transubstantiation. To me the consecration was a genuine spirit-into-flesh happening, a re-fleshing, a reincarnation of a spirit.

Also for me communion was perfect, *perfect*, and, like many other great rites throughout the world, it was a supreme act of communitas. All religions were true, none of them was "mother" to the others. All were "supernatural"—a term viewed with disapproval in those days. Actually, for me, all was *also* natural, and still is: God, miracles, shamanism, spirits, science, the whole continuum—real, thick, powerful, there inside the process of creation, all of it creating the creation, all one, all alive with spirit.

At Incarnation I sat behind the choir and sang. Andy in the choir became a friend of mine. He was busy writing a PhD dissertation on Thomas Merton, before and after his conversion. Andy asked me to join the choir, which I did. I found the members were good old arch-liberals just as in the choir of the Holy Comforter, and that this choir also did a lot of laughing in church. Furthermore nearly all of us supported the ordination of women priests.

It so happened in 1994 that I was asked to work with a Loyola University group of Christian sociology researchers on the growing phenomenon of small Christian groups. The project made me curious. Now that I belonged to the Church of the Incarnation I thought I might do research there. In April 1995 I asked the parish priest at Incarnation if there were any small Christian groups attached to the parish.

"Yes, there's one," he said, looking kindly at me, sort of concerned. He named it. I will call it Small Group.

"The women have their meeting in the Sunday School room," he said. "On Tuesdays at 9:30."

"Thanks." I could do research again.

I went along and found the women amiable and doing a little praying, such as "Come Holy Spirit." That done, they got on with the real work—which consisted of feminist-type encounter-group discussions, along with real live spirituality rather in the style of my own search for spirituality. What was that spirituality? It seemed to be found in curious answers to prayer, the sudden coming of communitas, and so on. We laughed a great deal, and sometimes cried in sympathy with one of our number, as heartbroken as she was. I got to love those characters in the Small Group and brought cookies to add to their muffins and coffee.

This was from April to June 1995. Soon I forgot about doing formal field research aimed to determine the social composition and interactions of the Small Group in Charlottesville. It was from this group that I found out where to go next on my roundabout journey.

After a time my friends let drop that an initiation ritual was in the offing. I hadn't realized that an initiation was in order in the Small Group. The initiation was simply known as "the weekend," in an understated sort of way.

To tell the tale I have to be discreet and leave out some secret elements. But I am recording the main event that took place, because it changed my life.

The weekend was held in a retreat camp in the mountains. All of us were women. We were a flamingly feminist group, mainly consisting of very motivated teachers, health professionals, mothers of families, and one or two artists. Most of the choir had made their weekends already and were enlisted to help.

Our initiators constituted themselves as our spiritual helpers and group leaders. They chose an active woman out of their number to be organizer of affairs. When we arrived at the retreat camp with sleeping bags and luggage the spiritual helpers took our bags and showed us our cabins—where I noticed a flower on each bunk. We were asked not to speak much, to be quiet. At that, a lot of people began to feel cut off, some a little sarcastic—and we were put to work to write down what we thought in a private letter "to Jesus." My letter was sarcastic all right. The set-up looked a bit too holy. It's true I liked being given flowers. Still.

I took a long time going to sleep because everything was a negative blank.

Next day at the camp breakfast, which we ate at long plastic-covered tables, we learned a doggerel song with a good tune which we immediately picked up from our guitar player, and then we belted it out ourselves. Somehow we fell straight into communitas. We were all in the same odd circumstance of not knowing what was going to happen. We ate a lot and talked a lot.

The helpers, every day of that long weekend, told us various stories about their own poor little lives—danger from flood, being divorced from a drunk, a child with a disability, being fired from a job—I got the impression they'd been dying to tell someone, and I hoped that somewhere along the line we ourselves would get to talk too, because we'd all had odd and lurid lives. I certainly had. What was happening was that the helpers were getting behind us and giving us a leg up into this comradeship. Nothing seemed as heavy as we thought. The magical effect of support, actual hefty support from a group that was creating something spiritual, was getting under way. These helpers were united in—in creating some kind of element, ether, or medium, through which our own feelings could pass. One thing was certain: everyone present seemed to have been through some kind of hell and nobody was "better" than anyone else.

We had religious services at the chapel and to our surprise we found that everyone was singing the songs as loudly as she possibly could, belting them out—rare in American life. The music broke the shell of our individuality and we passed into one another right there in the flowing notes—and all this hidden in the far mountains.

What next took place was a manifestation of the support that the outside community was giving us—with a puzzling element of the miraculous about it. Each of us received a bright-colored bag full of letters. Letters? Each woman took her bag and sat down outside under her own tree far away from the others. Friends, and total strangers as well, had written all these letters wishing us a marvelous "experience" (sic), letters written in all kinds of individually-chosen words. It was weird how they hit the mark. As we read, each of us cried separately. We had begun to "get" this "experience."

We came back together and did posters at our tables; we talked like mad. We invented a skit, and someone did a deadly imitation of the bishop. One curious episode was not planned by anyone. We went to the chapel for what is nowadays called the sacrament of reconciliation, the ritual that used to be called "confession." Nowadays one sits in a room with the priest and more or less has a chat. This could be useful if one actually received spiritual direction, but it hasn't turned out like that, nor can a woman get a chance to talk to a woman. This has become an almost insuperable snag.

All the forty women were there for confession. It appears the priest, a man of about forty-five, had distributed little printed cards with long lists of sins on them, to remind one what one's sins were. Liz, who had acted the pseudo "bishop" in the skit, and I were sitting next to each other. We all liked Liz.

Liz was reading the little card. She looked uneasy.

"I can't do this," she said. She frowned. Tears began. "And I was going to make my first confession for twenty years." She was biting her lip. "I did hope. ... " Her head sank.

"What's this card say?" I said. "Let's look."

I read it. "Oho," I said. "What a loathsome card! No one will go for that. Masturbation, that's not a sin. Kissing! My God. Where did that little man get this card from? He goes in for this sort of thing because he's celibate! He must be sick. Look, there's 'necking.' No sin at all. What's the matter with the guy? And down here it says 'gloom.'" I laughed.

Just then our chief organizer, Mary, came around, a great tough liberal lady whom I love. Liz held up the card. All the other women were goggling at their cards.

"Where'd you get that?" snapped Mary.

"The Father Confessor passed them around," said Liz.

"He did? This should never have been given out," said Mary, and she rapidly went around the circle collecting up all the cards, hoping that they hadn't already made too many of her beloved women feel like Liz.

It came to my turn in the confessional room. I looked back at my friends. I was easily the eldest; I could take this little forty-five-year-old boy. These lascivious, depraved, criminal health professionals, these fiendish mothers and teachers needed a angry old woman like me to defend them.

I went in.

"I'm going to be up front with you," I said to the dog-collared smooch-haired slightly fat-faced person in front of me. "You should never have put this card around. These women are actually angels. They are working 1000 percent all their lives for the good. You have no idea. You have no business :. "

"They are in sin," he said. "Many are taking the Eucharist who have not confessed. The numbers who take communion when they are in sin are very many. I am here to teach them."

"Not these women. They're not in sin." I knew their lives.

Then he said, "You're in denial."

Aha! I'd got him. "*You* are creating iatrogenic disease." I translated for him in case he hadn't heard of it. "These are the troubles caused, *caused* by doctors, psychiatrists, and *priests*! Misery, the suppression of joy, fear— "

That stopped him.

"Okay." I said. "Here's my confession. I've committed the sin of gloom. That's it," and I said the words of the confession. I sat there.

He very rapidly gave me absolution and got rid of me as quickly as he could. I marched out of there grinning to the remaining women. "You'll be okay," I said. We weekenders had a fine time for the rest of our stay.

On the last night, when we unsuspectingly entered the wooden dining shack, all the tables were laid out with fine linen and silverware, with wineglasses and grapes and cheeses and dainties and flowers. It was the Agape, the love feast; and there at the wide center table at the end, as in the MASH scene[1], appeared the communion vessels of gold, and the priest standing to serve us—it was awesome, it was somehow the original last supper, a situation of "paramount reality," as Rory Turner describes it, an "actuality," as Michael Harner and I named such things. After all my troubles and anger and conflicts, the feast was there:

Love bade me welcome: yet my soul drew back,
     Guilty of dust and sin.
But quick-eyed Love, observing me grow slack
     From my first entrance in,
Drew nearer to me, sweetly questioning
     If I lacked anything.

"A guest," I answered, "worthy to be here":
     Love said, "You shall be he."
"I, the unkind, ungrateful? Ah, my dear,
     I cannot look on thee."
Love took me by the hand, and smiling did reply,
     "Who made the eyes but I?"

"Truth, Lord, but I have marred them; let my shame
     Go where it doth deserve."
"And know you not," says Love, "who bore the blame?"
     "My dear, then I will serve."
"You must sit down," says Love, "And taste my meat."
     So I did sit and eat.

That was how George Herbert put it in 1633.[2]

After we had partaken of communion and drunk and eaten all the goodies, the accordions were brought out; we danced the Macarena and made wicked jokes.

Next day we looked again at our original letters to Jesus and saw the difference between our feelings, before and after that bit of experience. How could we have doubted? We wrote another letter and ritually burned the first one.

Then before leaving we were taken—in some state of secrecy—down to the chapel. We entered, and it was jam full of a huge crowd of supporters—old initiated types, men and women, who rose to their feet and cheered and yelled to see us. It was the Last Day, the return celebration of this rite of passage. I thought of the Ndembu circumcision boys on their return after three months of seclusion, mounted on the shoulders of their guardians and brought back at a run into the village circle by a secret way: the reunions, the dancing, the celebration. Here at the Small Group it was the same. Here, each of the novices stood up and said a piece—just as each of the boys who were newly made men took a turn at dancing up to the chief with a knife—and at each sentence that we got out, those fellers in the big crowd stood up and cheered again. By now I was walking on air and goggling. When it was my turn, I said exactly what I was experiencing. "'Thy kingdom come,' right? It's come! *This is* the Kingdom of Heaven."

These words of ours were the initiation event itself, and after that the larger membership of the Small Group took us to their bosoms. In another six months I helped to do the same thing for a later bunch of candidates, the men this time, and it felt good. Those men were crying. The sense of something out there is now around me all the time, and no way do I want to shake it off. Some have kept the sense for twelve years.

I was in awe of the instinct that created this classic rite of passage. The major phases of Van Gennep's analysis were there: Separation, Liminal Seclusion, and the Return. In the separation phase, the first experience was one of being driven for an hour to a strange place in the heart of the mountains, and we felt the classic sense of humiliation, equivalent to the traditional rites of stripping the body and cleansing. I felt I was nobody at all, even estranged from Jesus whom I happened to love. Then we entered the phase of unfamiliar events, surprises, material happenings that were not to be explained. The stories the helpers told brought us into an amazed unity—we'd all been through the mill. We *knew*. Furthermore, the music made us one. The skit blew all the dirt that had fallen off us into fantastic garbage that could be swept away. The Agape feast telescoped time back to the sacred event of the Last Supper and forward to the table of heaven. The new letter we wrote at the end was like a change of name; the old name or personality had gone and the new one was in place, irreversibly. Then at the end the rite of return brought us back together with the wider community, a community consisting of many people we knew who were taking us to their bosoms as sweet comrades forever. We went home dazzled with the knowledge.

When one realizes that the Ndembu women's initiation, far away in Africa, also meant as much to the young women of the tribe, then one can begin to understand how the whole Ndembu community loved and longed for the next one, and why it was that the little girls voluntarily and assiduously practiced the dances and longed for their own celebration to come.[3] Celebration is of this order—in every religion. This one was fully existential to me. *I was initiated*. And at the same time I was delighted to find such a rich example of a rite of passage here on my doorstep in Virginia. I knew it was one of the major pearls of that kind to be found anywhere in the world, a list that included the Apache girls' initiation, the Ndembu girls' initiation, the Burmese boy monk's initiation with hair shaving and seclusion period, the Bangla Desh wedding, the Nepalese shaman's personal initiatory experience, and others, all conceptions of genius.[4]

In 2000 I described the Small Group initiation in greater detail in a paper on the ontological matrix of spirituality, but the passage was rejected by the editor as unscientific and therefore as unsuitable material for an academic publication. The piece was not an attempt to convert people but to give the sense of a true rite of passage. It seems to me that the consistent suppression of such material deletes many phenomena in our society out of the record, phenomena that do in fact have deep effects. It appears that anthropologists are free to describe initiations and personal experiences of magic in Africa, but not anything so moving and close to home as this "weekend." Is this not a choice made by an elite, making academia the arbiter of reality and denying value to the experiences of ordinary people? Orson Scott Card, a noted science fiction writer and a Mormon (which I am not), has recently attacked such narrowness. In the following passage Card is discussing science fiction and religion. I now realize that what he is saying applies equally to anthropology. Card protests the prejudice against religion in literature. I do so in the case of religion in anthropology.

> If you read most science fiction you wouldn't have a clue that religion played a part in anyone's life. Most sci-fi characters are utterly untouched by religion, by ritual: *except* when religious rituals or faith are used to show how benighted or depraved or primitive a particular group or individual is. This is actually right in line with contemporary American literary fiction, so it isn't just because of a pro-science bias on the part of the writers. Yet this is so contrary to reality and betrays such a profound ignorance on the part of the writers that it should betray to most people a rather uncomfortable fact: American writers tend not to be in tune with America. Or, to put it another way, religious Americans and literary Americans have, consciously or not, separated themselves almost completely. Religious people who are becoming writers get the idea: that it's faintly embarrassing to present religion as a matter-of-fact part of life. Writers who would otherwise vigorously resist any attempt at censorship rigorously remove from their work anything that might suggest that they

harbor some sympathy for a particular religion or faith. I was determined
to undermine the fashionably hostile stereotypes that mark American fiction whenever it *does* include religion.[5]

After reading this I wanted to add my weight to the task of reopen-
ing the heavy door that has been barred to the experience of religion
in serious philosophy, anthropology, many aspects of religious studies, and the study of the psyche. What, then, of the Small Group? It
gave me, immediately and directly, the knowledge and vivid experience of a spirit power sizzing under my fingers like the power in an
old-time overhead trolley bus arm that brings the power down into
the trolley engine. Very like that. The material is embarrassing?
Pseudo? Not good material? To me it is first-class material, existential,
solid as rock, on all fours with Wordsworth's Presences and shamanism and African spirit rituals and the Dreaming of the Aborigines and
Black Elk and the best in anthropology. Why on earth taboo it from
polite society?

What stands out about the Small Group initiation is its well-practiced social effectiveness, the effect of deliberate support, the effect of
a *group* of people in prayer, in love, not in a social milieu such as in
competitive business that one might call "social I." This was social II,
where the souls of a group of people are at one. What is the nature of
the thing called "support," alias communitas, alias "social II," that
actual phenomenon of change of consciousness, differing from the
usual understanding of the term "change of consciousness" in that it
can be experienced by a plurality of people at once? Here was an element of ritual that was going to need more attention.

My path at this point did not seem so much a path as the job of trying to lay together (perhaps like laying the paving stones of a path)
the characteristics of spirit events so as to arrive at a recognizable
object, the spiritual human being, found in whatever culture or in
whatever competitive religion. I had ventured into all sorts of paths
already and saw how they wound around and under each other and
even into the inside of me. The winding was the way it had always
been with me. About the complexity I encountered, I felt its richness
gave an even greater material rootedness to this spirit process going
on across humanity.

Notes

1. As in the classic film, MASH, about a medical unit in the Korean War, showing a kindly but spoofed "Last Supper" scene put on by the crew for the sake of a tormented fellow worker.
2. George Herbert, "Love (III)," in *The Norton Anthology of Poetry*, eds. Allison et al. (New York, 1975b [1633]), 300.
3. Edith Turner, *The Spirit and the Drum*, 58-81.
4. Claire Farrer, *Living Life's Circle* (Albuquerque, NM, 1991), 128-183; Lena Fruzzetti, *The Gift of a Virgin* (New Brunswick, NJ, 1982, Bangla Desh wedding); and Larry Peters, *Ecstasy and Healing in Nepal* (Malibu, CA, 1981, Nepalese shaman initiation).
5. Orson Scott Card, *Cruel Miracles* (New York, 1990), 10-11, 14.

14
UP FRONT AND ARGUING
The Spiritual Direction Institute

The Small Group steered me into an important territory of thought that furthered my explorations on the spirit front. Some of the Small Group people had been through a training in an organization called the Spiritual Direction Institute, the SDI.

"It's just the thing for you," said Mary. "Father Chet teaches it."

"Not that old priest who gives a plain run-of-the-mill homily? Hm." I was puzzled because he seemed just—ordinary.

"You've got him wrong. You've no idea. He's not like that, he's great." I respected Mary's opinion because she was a real thinker.

"The only thing," Mary added. "You have to write an autobiography of twenty-five pages to be accepted in the course."

He'd never take me, I thought, me with my Communist past and penchant for native religions. All right, I'd give it him. I'll tell all. I did, and was accepted.

Now I found myself with 60 others undergoing something like "the Small Group to the power of 2." Father Chet worked us, he drew each student out to speak; we seemed to find each other to be fascinating and gifted.

However, I was concerned with the name "Spiritual Direction." At first I wondered, is one person ever able to direct the spiritual life of another? Such a thing smacks of the Inquisition, or at least of the Jesuits: one suspects that it involves mind control. Some of the books for the course did indeed have the tone of some benevolent religious psychologist who would draw you through the dark night of the soul, through a hedge backwards, as it were. And it would be good for you.

Notes for this section can be found on page 255.

All would be well if you did so and so and so and so. Some books, owing to the very subject matter, "spirituality," set off blazing flashes of clarity and were rather exciting. One psychologist, Ira Progoff,[1] concluded his book by portraying his patient Carl as a really great visionary, far beyond the spirituality of the psychologist himself. It must have felt the same to Van Gogh's psychiatrist when he tried to treat the genius who was so far above him.

The core of the spirituality course was the practicum, the *practicing* of giving spiritual direction. Two people sat facing each other in the middle of the circle of students, one as "director" and the other as "directee." To begin with, the "director" prayed for a blessing on the success of the direction process. Then the "directee" began on her main trouble in life and the apparent impossibility of doing anything about it. She was clearly irritated with some protagonist, who turned out to be a daughter who wouldn't go to Mass.

At this I privately got irritated. "To hell with the wretched bigoted grumbler," I said to myself. "And see, the daughter must be thinking, 'to hell with her' too. That's how Christianity gets the stinking bad name it's got."

This was where, curiously, the practicum started to turn around and became altogether reversed. The directee became the director and now as director she suddenly realized what was needed, all on her own.

"I know," the bigot was saying. "I'm going to simply show her love, none of that teaching stuff."

The original director was listening open-mouthed—she had never seen this sort of thing happen before and didn't expect it. Something or other had gone over, without command or authority, to the person with the problem—it just floated over. Watching this, I kind of *saw* or felt the spirit pass into the picture—I saw it arrive.

Here we have seen two ritual reversals on one page, the patient Carl who is greater than the psychologist, and the directee who knows better than the director. This "Spiritual Direction," then, is no Jesuit inquisition. After that I leaned forward in the practicum to catch every word.

I saw the same kind of result in each practicum session when the sympathetic opening words of the director released the stress and tension of the directee in an atmosphere of unconditional love. The directee had been longing for a chance to clear up some deep trouble or other. The circumstances were blessed beforehand and the spirit prayed for, and here the spirit came around us, strengthening us. Then the directee began to think and wonder, and found there was indeed a good path to take—and took it. Almost always the means was unconditional love, being one's true self, never arguing or using the power of the rules—in a manner very like the way the Dene Tha Indians respect one another.

This was where the practice of reconciliation—that is, confession—came in. As I watched I could see how much better this practicum was than the confessional system. It came home to me that it was this, what I was watching, that would develop into the real reconciliation style of the twenty-first century, becoming—along with sex, music, and the encounter with the divine—one of the great means of connection between human beings. It would also obviate the anomaly of men hearing women's confessions. It was warmly and fruitfully humanistic, and poles apart from the rules of the Vatican and Cardinal Ratzinger and the Machiavellian rationalism of the hierarchy.

Nevertheless within that hierarchy Father Chet had been made Monsignor. Why, I couldn't imagine. For when the course got under way I found we were in the hands of what one could only term a shaman of religion, a master, a wizard, a Merlin—dealing in practiced gestures with a language miles above our heads. My ears belatedly pricked up. I edged forward more. I became entirely hooked.

The man was eighty-three, white-haired, slightly jaunty, a born professor of wizardry, learned in Carl Jung and in sure-fire spiritual discernment. He had a voice deceptively simple—that was it—a voice promising in its forward tilt some very interesting things coming up next. We were to be trained. We wanted that. "Chet" was what we called him among ourselves. His full title was Monsignor Chester Michael, the former spiritual director of the Bishop of Richmond.[2] He lived in a shack on the Blue Ridge Mountains and climbed a thousand-foot mountain every morning. He was eighty-three and I was then only seventy-six.

I had a vital fact to report: communitas reigned in that class. It already contained a large proportion of Small Group members. Many of us therefore knew each other and knew a little of the ungraspable, unthinkable liberalism of unconditional love.

Here was a complete turnaround from the legalisms and suppressions of what was considered to be the Catholic church and still is, in its unliberated sector. I was witnessing something which was likely to undermine the whole authority of the male law enforcement system of the church, because those at the SDI were at least half women, and all of us, not only I myself, twigged that the training would enable us to hear confessions. It is the system of confessions and the power it has claimed, the "power of Peter"—"whatever you bind on earth shall be bound in heaven, and whatever you loose on earth shall be loosed in heaven"—that has built the structure, the canon law, and the worldly power of the church.[3] I was thinking that whatever we do we have to detach this worldly power from those words, and it will be a difficult task, because the church has made Christianity un-Christian. We can *never* erect worldly power on the words as we have been doing.

> Doff sorry pride,
> For ever love go by—

as Vic used to say.

Chet was trying to teach us charity and tolerance for each other. He did have some teaching tools. One was a chart of one's advancement in the spiritual life, showing levels of advancement 1 - 8. I remember level one as being that of the Latin-American peasant: Catholic, but only just; obeying the church's dictums without knowing anything about them; wedded to the social structures; "superstitious." Level two was characterized by those in small parishes, unadvanced: for instance, in Brazil, those who revere religious objects such as relics and go on pilgrimages. Then came level three, consisting of the regular devout Catholic in the church pews in America, cradle Catholics taught by nuns, and I reckon there are still 40 percent of them around. These are the ones who changed to the vernacular at Vatican II because the Pope told them to; good people. Obedience is everything with them, and a strong "in-group, out-group" attitude to the Roman Catholic Church. Here Father Chet told us that today, in order to be consecrated, bishops have to make a solemn vow to deny absolution to those who use contraceptives and practice abortion. They also have to vow to oppose the ordination of women. Bishops are appointed from above. How many brilliant ones must have refused the "honor" of a bishopric under those conditions?

But ... what about level four, when light breaks on those unfortunate people? They and their children can't see any sense in all the rubbish. The children prefer the horror movies that don't entail a moral code and other such nuisances. But the parents struggle on, in doubt, while continuing to attend church. I could see that here is the dawn of individualism in religion. Their conversion consists of knowing oneself as a solitary conscious individual in one's unique relation to God. It is this sort of light that breaks at this level; the Small Group may help them, and I see the Group as a lifeline back to the community sense of the "primitive village," a sense that would be lost without it. The idea of unconditional love dawns, and love is the way out from being under the control of the third level.

And in the fifth and sixth levels, a person may suffer severe "doubts"—what I now call "soul loss," for—let's face it—that is what "the dark night of the soul" entails, *soul loss*—not, in my view, ordained by God. Then the person may shake herself free of the little, iron, ingrown parish controls and gossip and, as I remember from Vic and from Chekhov's great saying, proceed to "squeeze the slave soul out of oneself day by day and wake up one morning a free artist." This kind of person will recognize the spiritual quality of all peoples on earth and will not be bound by the thinking and laws of the local parish.

I was fascinated by Chet's categories and embroidered on them in my mind. What about the sweet saintly woman sitting next to me, whose eyes showed she was living in a steady world of angelic experience and had always called that experience "the faith"? I know this woman. This is exactly how it is: it's like sitting next to a scented rose; one is in happy awe all the time. But here she was, being groomed to be a future confessor—and—*priest*. She was destined to be better trained than most priests. This training too she absorbed obediently; while the light in her eyes grew. She came to be my best friend.

Others were making similar leaps into freedom and love, even to level five, and were happy to exist in the world of beautiful guitar singing and holy communion. But the next levels. ... The next levels don't deteriorate as in Shakespeare's seven stages, but rise to a considerable discovery, that of the world of spiritual psychology, of poetry, and of the Bible and its strange steps, the Bible's own gold threading through its own bloody and unthinkable—and wicked—violence and intolerance, toward an outcome of a group of friends who learned at last how to get rid of the domination of other people's systems and act from the heart. Here on this level, in our own era, we have Martin Luther King and Gandhi; and at eight, Jesus. These were killed for what they believed in because one was supposed to obey only some racist authority or military conqueror. One wonders. "Roman" is supposed to be an admirable thing. I think, when writing this, that "Roman" is an entirely vicious category.

Chet was talking about level five. "These are our SDI types," said Chet. "You should be here," he said to us, marking the spot on his blackboard chart.

"I'm a 'level one,'" I said—suddenly "doing an Edie" again after seventy years.

Chet looked over at me pityingly, unbelievingly.

"Yes," I insisted. "I'm superstitious, too. The peasants really did see visions of Our Lady. They're closer to the soil. They spend their lives in real community. I don't think they're low in rank. I'd be glad to be in their company." I reckoned that visions were sometimes shown to people who were deeply in the middle of things, people in situations of poverty and distress. People with advanced minds often weren't open to visions.

This interruption of mine wasn't according to the class plan. However, interruptions were not forbidden. The others gave me covert looks and wondered how much of an anthropologist I really was (see figures 14.1 and 14.2). Anthropology was supposed to be a social science, wasn't it? For me, anthropology was often as hidebound as the Vatican in its own way.

Figure 14.1: Doctor of Humanities at Wooster College, with son Fred Turner (photo in the possession of Edith Turner)

Figure 14.2: Doctor of Humane Letters at Kenyon College, with Wendy Singer (photo in the possession of Edith Turner)

I laughed and looked quaint and peasant-like. Chet gave me a puzzled look and we passed on to stage six.

Level six was often the stage of a conversion. Vic had gone through this level after a sudden opening up in his exploration of religion—then the conversion in 1958. My conversion was without the immense reading of a scholar, a conversion from nil upwards and back to one. For me, the Small Group was of the "six" kind.

Then came the level of great enrichment of religion in every part of a person, seven, the saint, in blissful, humble union with God and humanity. This could be someone acting self-sacrificially. None of our popes were in this category. Jesus was in it, St. Francis was in it, people like the Protestant Bonhoeffer were. I would have said, Shakespeare, and I know he was a fiction-play writer, but he was in many ways the greatest humanist the world has ever known.

No popes were mentioned. Someone raised her hand. "What level is Pope John Paul at?"

"Level three," said Chet.

The class looked at each other. "You mean, he hasn't risen from the level of pure obedience?" someone said.

"No. He's not so far along as many of you."

Chet was right. You could see the results emanating out of the papacy, in the continual suppression of anything physical, especially where it concerned women's gifts, her fully human and as yet unexploited spiritual gifts. It was in the papacy that this backwardness remained, and did not seem to have been caused by the state of the wider church at any level. The anomaly was due to the appointments system of the hierarchy: nondemocratic, elitist in the extreme. In self-justification the Vatican continued to argue that the Holy Ghost Himself made the appointments, not the men concerned, and that democracy would only bring the church down to the level of dirty politics. To the level of the dear old parish members, did they mean? To the level of the women who made pilgrimage to Knock Shrine in Ireland? They were to be out of it? Did they sin more than the priesthood?—a pretty question. So my mind ran. I was now warming to what Chet was saying, and was content to add my own private proviso about the peasants and let it go at that. It was hard, I felt, for a priest to know what it was like to be a peasant. As for me, I had liked milking cows and had lived almost like Africans in African villages.

The unity of us students was achieved by dint of prayer of the kind already mentioned in an earlier chapter and by dint of round-robins when we'd tell of something odd and spiritual that happened to us, strange events verging on synchronicities. Again, it was like the Dene Tha Indians and their mutual understanding of the high importance of receptivity to stories of spiritual events. The unity appeared in the excitement of all of us students when contemplating a new Catholic church, "inverted," governed not by law but by subsidiarity, the inversion of authority for which we had all been secretly hoping. We took voluminous notes and got out library books, amazed at the changes advocated by many theologians. We were reading all the time, and heard talk of psychic energy, much on archetypes, and some on feminism. I heard some feminists advise women to sit out the dying male priests and then walk into their jobs, while other feminists merely want to live at peace altogether and let things be. "All right"— I felt about this last idea: "Shall we get out our knitting?" *NO!* We can get on with our task and grow big and active through it all, and our size will push those guys aside painlessly.

Some of the authors of the books laughed at the ordinary folks' experience with angels and also at their consciousness of the power of sacred objects. Kennedy,[4] one of those authors, calls the experiences only *metaphors* for the goodness in people, and denies they amount to anything more than that. Other authors have put aside the Resurrection and such irrationalities, kindly attributing to them the psychological meaning of liberation. I wrote my book reports on behalf of visionaries, on behalf of those who said they had actually seen the

Resurrection—because I myself had seen a spirit form and felt the benevolent presence of the dead.

Now there are droves of such nice-minded religious-rationalist-psychologists, and indeed, their influence had produced a whole generation of brainwashed children who, as a result, are never likely to be visited by a spirit. And yet I know that a great number of people are truly fascinated, for example, by shamanism and are not particularly impressed by the new elite theologians. There is of course a loving side even to the theologians, those who are not always eager to correct the benighted visionary, a side which is itself imbued with its own kind of visionary love, eager to nourish the growth of love and peace and nonviolence between people.

The reading I had to do broke into my anthropological thinking again and again. Meanwhile Chet was busy teaching us "The Types." When I first read Chet's syllabus for the year, I saw that it included the "Myer-Briggs Type Indicator," and later, "The Enneagram." I flinched. What kind of pseudo-psychologizing mumbo-jumbo was this MBTI stuff, trying to fit that extraordinary being, the human, into slots someone else had thought up, someone who obviously fancied herself as a great student of human nature? No. I might even have to give up the course.

I still don't like to talk about the MBTI because I was in a rage when I took the test, and deliberately put down the wildest answers in the multiple-answer list. As a result I was classed as having little judgment and no thought. So I haven't dealt with the testing here. What I really think Chet was getting at was fair enough: some people are different in type from oneself, and are not beyond the pale just for that reason; on the contrary, they can be recognized for the good they do within the given character with which they are endowed. This notion is not fundamentally different from that of anthropology, which scans the entire globe with its different cultures, gaining an understanding of the way people act as within the style of the society concerned. Theoretically this is called the "culture and personality" school of anthropology, which later developed into "relativism." The ethic of anthropology has always been global. In its generous aspect the ethic shows anthropology to be greater than religion as religion now stands, still narrow and ethnocentric.

So Chet as a Christian was interested in the forgiving aspect of typology. What then were the types indicated on the Enneagram? I couldn't help being inquisitive.

He told us.

Type 1	The perfectionist
2	The servant
3	Person obsessed with order
4	Artist
5	Scholar
6	Conformer
7	Good time guy
8	Boss
9	Laid-back person

Everyone in the class thought I must be number Five, the scholar, since I had taken an MA degree and taught at the university.

"Me? In an ivory tower like Five? A recluse? No way!" I took a look at the "artist" category. It could include writers. The main thing the artist tells herself is "I am special, unique." Okay, I've said so much in this book already, talking about the strangely directed path of my life. But this "artist" type is unreliable and never finishes anything. I knew artistic people of that kind and had always urged them to get on and finish their work. I thought I did finish things. Judging from my list of publications I did. But that was because I had developed a lot of the Three in me for the sake of survival: Three, the person obsessed with order.

Chet broke in on our musings. "Everyone spotted their type?" he asked cheerfully. We mumbled various numbers. Then he said, "I'm the boss type, number Eight, the Hitler type." He laughed shamelessly.

"Chet!" we exclaimed, seeing his point a little. The funny thing was, he could lead us against leadership. Fine. Jesus was like that.

We were beginning to have fun. My angelic friend with the smile, so obedient, was—self-confessed—the servant. The woman who had insisted her daughter go to Mass was the perfectionist and there it was, she couldn't help it. St. Francis turned out to be a Seven, the fun guy, the troubadour of God, sort of in love. The pope and all his ilk were the conformers, scared to move, the types whom Mary Douglas the anthropologist would have called the witchcraft-obsessed ones, keeping their group intact against the howling wilderness of the enemy outside, afraid of things that puncture the system and might poison it. Mary Douglas had a typology of her own. I could see that according to her system the Vatican was "high group" and "high grid," obsessed with both correctness *and* levels of status. This Enneagram stuff might be interesting.

No one in America seemed to be "laid-back," they were all too busy. I pictured Californians of twenty years ago in their Jacuzzis, laid back in the steaming waters. But now? One or two of our members confessed guiltily to being laid-back, but were now obviously resolving to work harder on that sin. Then we discovered that the laid-back one could also be a meditator, even a mystic. Ah, that was different. Maybe my son Alex, the Buddhist, was a Nine, and had suffered as a kid because I had "pushed" him, or at least had tacitly criticized him for lack of get-up-and-go. Now I could see more about the person he really was. What had I been doing to him all this time? I'm sorry. There was also that wonderful laid-back character, the Dalai Lama; and I also thought of Alex's son Joshua. Maybe he was the only one of my grandchildren who had experienced anything really religious, and boy, was he happy with it!

Another trick up Chet's sleeve was to put people of the same type together at the same table, and get them to compare notes. I was put with artists and got on with them a treat. In the SDI, somehow the ambiance was kindly to artists, to inquirers, to anybody, for that matter. So that instead of my general feeling about the Enneagram system—that all it could do was thrust complicated square pegs into complicated round holes—I now felt, okay, there exists an even wider ground for forgiveness of just about anybody if you know more about what they're really like—just like anthropology at its best, with its deep knowledge and laid-back view of every and any culture.

Which brought us on to discernment. A spiritual director had to be trained in discernment. Chet with his passion for lists of items, like myself, had identified fifteen forms of discernment. I had long been interested in this faculty since I knew it was necessary for the understanding of several shadowy or hidden matters that I had encountered in anthropology. The matters about which Chet was concerned were often situations of dilemma when you didn't know which of two courses of action to take. One of his methods of discernment was simply "tossing up for it" between the two alternatives. Another interesting one was praying to God for a sign, as in making a divinatory proposition or consulting an oracle—even hitting on a course of action this way: "If it thrills you when you think about it, it's right." Father Chet said, "That works!" Another is the simple matter of consulting one's spouse. If both agree, it's the right answer.

On top of the list came prayer; then, leaving the matter overnight; then opening a Bible at random and reading the top line. There were more subtle methods: asking a wise person, for instance. It seems that negative capability has to come into play. Something "out there" can see into the problem better than we can. When one hands the problem over to that someone (not necessarily a Christian deity), after a few minutes everything becomes clear. It seems that when it's no longer your problem the pressure is off you and you are twice as strong and perceptive. These two, the brain plus the spirit, if they are left to do their combined work, do a lot of the untangling of dilemmas for you.

I myself had seen some curious examples of discernment in action. In 1985 when I watched Singleton tracing the path of the wandering tooth in the body of Meru, his Ihamba patient in Zambia, I could tell that a gift for discernment was in operation.[5] His discernment included the timing of his capture of the evil thing, marking the moment when Meru was sufficiently "down" and her body was willing to let go of the thing. He was helped by his ancestor spirits. Vic Turner noted the same thing in the Ihamba doctor, Ihembi, in 1953. However rationalist Vic's analysis appeared to be, much of what Vic saw and described was spiritual.

Good holistic healers have to employ such discernment. Crione's thumbs were the organs of discernment in her case. The hands of Claire in the Arctic just *"knew"*—as she said—the condition of the body under her hands. Some people can discern ley lines, or see auras. It is said that only men over forty can discern the meaning of the sacred book *The Zohar*. When I studied the arcane pages of *The Book of Kells* I strained to understand them, and realized that only a gift of discernment, probably now lost, might unveil the mystery. Also in the strange ritual of folk Christianity called "speaking with tongues," there are people who are able to "understand" what the speakers are saying. They can "discern" it.

The word "discernment" covers all kinds of divination, including Ndembu basket divination. Even tea leaf readers, tarot card consultants, palmistry fortune-tellers, and astrologers can come under this category—for good fortune-tellers do exist.

I hungrily absorbed this part of Chet's course and found myself reinforced in my knowledge of the craft of discernment and enlightened about its importance in spirituality. The power that guides discernment is most certainly spiritual—like that of Singleton's ancestors.

During the course we were given a fair education in Biblical studies, in which we discovered that the book of Genesis had been written by four persons, and that some of the stories in that book conflict. We also realized that the New Testament gospels from which we have taken our texts were written down from 64 AD onwards. Matthew's version, said Chet, was distinctly anti-Semitic, because Matthew's own faction had suffered very greatly from the Jews at the fall of Jerusalem in 70. This was obviously why I had had so much trouble reading the gospels as I had been advised to do after Vic died, supposedly for my comfort. I had found much of them rife with cruelty and prejudice, and had to stick to science fiction for my bedtime reading, with an occasional "great book."

During Biblical studies with Chet I got the impression that student priests had been told in seminary that because of the gap in time between that of Jesus and of the writing of the gospels no one knows for sure exactly what happened. Historians state there is no proof Jesus existed, except for an on-the-spot but chilly reference by the pro-Roman Jewish historian Josephus. Priests are left with that. This dilemma resembles the one arising from the work of textual scholars in Judaism, who claim that *The Zohar* could not possibly have been written by Bar Yohai in the second century—therefore millions of Sephardic and Hasidic Jews were wrong in their claim.

In the Christian case, the "careful rational judgment of the experts" has clearly got under the skin of the priests. I now see the priests are running on their emergency levels of faith, levels that were so plentiful in the days of the doctrine of the true "word of God." Now, who knows? A new doctrine, that the events were "metaphoric"—given to us of course by God, has been helping the priests, and sometimes appears in sermons. But I have often been thinking that actual religious experience, not the rational judgment of the experts, would help the priests enormously if they would but let it happen. If they could have classes to unlearn some of the rationalism and respect for experts, and take classes in experience, then the fun would begin.

But let's see how Chet became so inspired. He is a Jungian. We found that a study of Carl Jung's idea of the Self[6] was the next part of our course. Chet first drew a Freudian "ego" on the blackboard, with the dominant ego like a knob in the center, the superego on top of it, clearly invented by the punishing parents, and below, the id with its ravening desires. The fact that this concept of the person used to be a landmark and a liberation in its time is astonishing to us now in 2005. At least we know now that the idea of the scientific dominant ego has done great harm to the world, because its unconnected individualistic rationality has fallen easy prey to utilitarianism and has permitted much exploitation and destruction of the ecosphere. To the extent that we are aware of the failings of the Freudian concept, we feel we have made progress. We do have a more sensitive environmentally conscious world.

Chet then drew a terrific Jungian "Self" on the blackboard, and handed Xeroxed copies of it around the class.

It showed the knob of the ego topping an inverted cone, with an area of the "personal unconscious" just below it. The rest of the cone extended below to a locus, the Jungian Self with a capital S, which was dipped into a wide circle of "the collective unconscious, the infinity of God himself," as Chet put it. "That is God," he said.

I played about with the diagram, making it look like a Polynesian atoll, with small things made of coral poking above the sea level: islands of consciousness. There were many of them. I was making the

pattern *social*, not individual. These were the egos with their psychology; while below, a huge spreading base occupied most of the page
and continued to the edge, and it would have spread beyond if there
had been room. The beyond was to everywhere, stretching to everybody else; the universe was all coral, as it were. Yet I had left out the
"Self" and had to think again. I marked each different Self on the
lower end of each "person-cone," each one dipping into the nutri-
ment, each like a knob, unitary, wet with enormously strong power
and purpose when connected with all the others—and canceling itself
out when not flowing with love, the circulating medium. The whole
system—taking it that every human being was like that diagram with
the universal under-base that connects—this was what Chet saw. I
could imagine it as a great coral field, or a mushroom field with
mushrooms rising from a universal mycelium, or as mosses, or even
the skin on the palm of one's hand complete with its all-over sensitiveness, or—some great concourse of people underwater holding
arms, all with their heads sticking out. That was the nearest.

The conscious self is the island; the collective unconscious is all the
region below the consciousness line.

"*Self*," as I said, did not seem the right word. But one may have to
give honor to the concept and use it for now.

There are one or two mysteries about the diagram that one would
not find in an undersea world—except on a medieval map. For there
are signs around the place: "Here Be Monsters." These are areas of
shadow, what one might call the unconscious of the unconscious. Our
under-unconscious is complicated; it's sometimes scary—yet it is also
connected with the rest. The nature of that general undersea world, in
light and shadow, is fully alive and by no means altogether "unconscious," because it sends up echoes and reminders and associations
and ideas all the time. It's a kind of aquarium, pullulating with life.
Where do the ideas come from? We recognize an oddity here: the
ideas don't come from oneself, and often not by word of mouth from
other people.

"I've got an idea." This comes to *me*, not from another person, but
it came *to* me from elsewhere. Is there an "ideas" god tucked in the
unconscious somewhere? Angels are supposed to give "messages,"
not ideas. Maybe the ancients meant "ideas." Is the collective unconscious a land where ideas come into being like babies, from some kind
of flash that takes place from time to time, a flash that is as fruitfully
engendering as the original sparking of a life form, or like the sex act
and maybe as blissful?

This then is the collective unconscious, and always, somewhere
hidden inside it, exists the feared shadow that pops up in dreams as

something threatening and bad. Yet the good Jung was right. The threatening entity comes up in dreams because you haven't addressed it, you fear the growling dog instead of becoming introduced to it with the proper dog courtesies. In the dream, or after the dream, you have to stop running away, you have to turn around and say to the somewhat terrifying appearance, "What do you want?"

I had rather a disturbing dream of a wounded mouse. It wasn't good.

When I addressed the mouse, it said, "Stop wounding me. Look, *you* are wounded."

"Me?"

"Yes. Be quiet. You go on too much. You can heal yourself. Don't keep the wound open. You are a healthy person."

"Oh.... I see."

I was starting to think about how the collective unconscious worked, and what it could or would do. Father Chet called it God because it could take priority, it could command the person. It was the provider of intuitions, the source of a kind of telepathy, of healing, of a sense of tremendous well-being, the medium of discernment through material veils, the source of all the varieties of love, of the gift of power. The way to it was through negative capability—for the religious that would mean humility and selfless prayer. That is, you don't dive headfirst into that ocean merely to get in contact with yourself, you lose yourself to *become the Self of others* through your very roots.

I couldn't understand how I could have missed all this in my studies of ritual and symbol. As soon as I grasped the Jungian soul, the knowledge entered the papers I was writing: it was my DNA answer, Rosetta stone, square root of minus one, the catalyst by means of which everything begins to work and make sense, my electrolytic energy. I gained a very much better understanding of soul loss and the rituals of restoring the fleeing soul.

Having taught us the craft of discernment and the Jungian mystery, Chet proceeded to give us a practical class on dialoguing with the dead or with enemies, using the method of Ira Progoff. Dialoging with the dead? Here we were, sorcerers' apprentices, wizard's students, ensconced, that particular weekend, in a Moravian retreat center called Camp Bethel in the Blue Ridge mountains of Virginia. This stage in the course needs some anchoring down; so to practicalities. We were to get out our plain old notebooks, which was a comfort. I was used to writing in notebooks, having done much anthropological fieldwork. Now I was in the true participatory fieldwork situation, not being a person of a different color or language from those I was with, being there because I had a natural calling to be there. I was happy and excited the same way they all were.

Chet said, "Center down."

Most of us knew what that meant from the popular meditation classes of our era.

"Put yourself in the presence of the Holy Spirit. This is the collective unconscious."

We were quiet.

"You're wanting to talk to someone you've needed to talk to for a long time. It could be a living person. It could be a dead person. Be quiet, let it come. Just write down what comes. This is a dialogue. So you talk to that person. Remember what I said about the Shadow. If you talk to it, it will *tell* you why you've been dreaming about it, why it's chasing you, what it wants. Write down your words and write down its words. Now, make the contact. Don't worry if there's nothing at first. Just try again."

He played some soft music and we began to relax. It was nice just to be all together and quiet like that. For myself I had it in mind to "dialogue" with my mother with whom I had quarreled so badly, as I have told. She died in 1960. It was now 1999.

I poised my pen over the paper. This is the dialogue I found myself writing. The words came of themselves.

E. Mummy, I have to be a child again to do this. I've almost forgotten the language.
M. ... What do you want?
E. I dunno quite. You *are* my mother, after all. I'm now seventy-six; I recognize a lot of you in myself.
M. I am with the Lord Jesus Christ. (*This was over-pious, I thought.*)
E. You said Grandpa would come back from heaven—no, I mean, he'd be teaching little children in heaven, ones who had died young. May I ask, are you doing that?
M. ...
E. (*I'm thinking I'm being too distant, rationalistic, level-headed.*)
M. I loved you, Edie.
E. I think I know that. I turned from you a lot.
M. Why did you do it? I was only human. How could I like your doing that?
E. Yes. *I'm* human. I know.
M. I love you still.
E. That's funny. You know, you could do a lot for me.
M. ... If it be the Lord's will—though I'm tired of doing things for people. You yourself, go ahead, do things for old people, *for* me. I'd feel all right, then.
E. Is this imaginary?
M. ...
E. I'll chance it that it isn't. Are you there?
M. I'm with George [*Daddy*].
E. I hardly dare see it. Is he driving a car?

M. You have no idea, have you?
E. … I cry for you.
M. …
E. I did you the honor of crying for you for three months when you sent
me to boarding school at the age of eight.
M. Couldn't you take it? You were strong, as your brother Bob told you.
E. … M-m-m-m. … Look, I forgive you for that, you didn't realize what
you were doing.
M. I forgive you too—for all your meanness.

So my Anglican mother seemed to have somehow turned up when
invited that way, giving a vague sense that she was wearing a black hat
and carrying a Bible. My reading of the piece aloud brought quite a
laugh among the other SDI students, and at the end of the weekend old
Chet said the dialoging was the most spiritual event he had known.

I cannot say that I understand it, but among that crowd of people
at the workshop in May 1999 my mother sprang onto paper with her
genuine voice. And what she said was to do with old people. At that
point I vividly felt some other memory hanging around, that I had
been with, or had been helping, some particular old person, but I
couldn't remember who.

I felt I had come home again, and that all my researches from the
outside in had landed me once more inside of the culture. The process
was becoming almost routine, a part of the regular natural history of
how things were. But it never ceased to show an unexpected path,
whose end I still don't know. That's all right. The experience of being
an anthropologist and at the same time right *in* the culture is mad-
dening to many anthropologists, but I was getting pretty comfortable
with it after all these decades and I find it good to be able to speak
about how comfortable it could be.

Having somehow made us holy sorcerers, Chet brought us back to
earth with a bump. This time he faced us with politics. Politics? For
me it was odd to come back to politics after a gap of forty years, a gap
in which I had been chasing after ritual and symbol rather than politics all over the globe. It wasn't that we students of Chet entered
active politics in this part of the course, would that we had. But we
received some hitherto unfamiliar instructions. They are encapsulat-
ed in the book *Engaging the Powers*, by Walter Wink.[7] The book turns
out to be a how-to volume on Christian active politics, a method ener-
gized by the use of some interesting retranslations of passages of the
New Testament. It is about war, about the oppression of the poor by
big business, about racism, chicanery, and the like. Walter Wink has
got in front of the world and drawn aside the curtain, exposing the
deceiving Wizard of Oz for what he is, none other than the old indus-

trial/military complex, as the good old hippies used to call it. Wink's answer is not to confront violence with violence. He recognizes that there have been circles of companions such as Gandhi's followers who were not taken in. I have seen my Buddhist son Alex, my sweet Alyosha as in *The Brothers Karamazov*, say "Blessings on you" to a thug who threatened him in a poor district of New York City. I will never forget that example. The Walter Wink book teaches the same thing. Puzzle your opponent by being a human being with him. Love the poor fellow, infected and invaded as he is with a horrible philosophy, a Satan (possibly more visible than Wink dares to say, a type of being well-known to Africans who are the experts on bad spirits).

On the large scale—which Wink knows full well has to be addressed—the whole system has become too much for us. Capitalists believe that without private enterprise there will be no progress, only dictatorship. The Harvard Business School therefore teaches hard ruthless methods of moneymaking. The resulting pyramidical system of business is ironically very like the Constantine church system—with no notion of unalienable rights, no notion of a voting system that is not run by money, no idea of true self-determination. The arguments for the capitalist system itself are much the same as for business. Now, how to leaven *that* concrete lump? The book describes how to humanize mammon, mammon itself, and that is through the courage that comes with the cross.

The first part gives a brilliant retranslation of much of the gospels, exposing what is behind the mysterious word "mammon." I had always thought mammon meant various low dives down in the city where they gambled and drank and did dirty business deals. But no, it is temporal power in any of its forms, especially in governments. It is the world domination system in all its forms. The book appeals to us not to always believe our rulers are right. Because the ego has been entangled with thousands of tendrils from the alienating system of domination, the process of dying to one's conditioning is never fully over. One can see the domination system awkwardly sticking out in the phrase, "you cannot serve God and mammon [the domination system]."

This got me thinking again of the battles I and my sister Helen used to wage with our parents in the 1930s about our then rulers in England, the conservative party. But at that time I had little idea what communion, community, and communitas were. I didn't see the communitas that flourished in front of my face in the form of the unity between all of us eight brothers and sisters in our games. Later I understood that it had been there. Eventually I recognized communitas in Africa during our researches, in the ritual singing, in the intention to heal. The Africans did know what it was. White clay was their symbol for it. Wink showed what communitas was—though he showed it in politics: how to resist nonviolently and knowingly, which is possible if the resister has won courage from her training in good political knowledge and nonviolent resistance, developed with a group of supporting and experienced friends. Wink's prime example was Rosa Parks in Montgomery, Alabama, sitting in front in the bus in disobedience to the color bar regulations of the American South.

The book takes the step that has been implicit in liberation theology for two or three decades—it is telling us that unless we move now to activate the already existing kingdom of God, the kingdom of God simply won't be born. Meanwhile we have seen despair and depression among many of our intelligent youth, especially widespread among those in academia in the humanities and social sciences. Their depression goes hand in hand with agnosticism and a kind of helpless positivism, fed by a horror of all Christianity from Vatican Catholicism to Bible fundamentalism and, among graduate students, fed by scorn of the New Age. Better dead than under the thumb of a commanding male God or inveigled into the New Age. These depressed folk have never experienced the miracles of the Holy Spirit or the mysteries of nonmedical healing.

In the Stone Chapel Hall adjoining the Church of the Incarnation at Charlottesville there is a mosaic on the inner back door, of Christ in gold and orange, with a long solemn face as in El Greco's pictures, holding his cross as if it were part of him. On occasion he seems to move right into whatever is going on in the hall, gliding right into and through it and through everything in the hall without being stopped by anything. This is somehow the idea I got from the Wink book: Jesus, nonviolent, not punishing us for our own good, not "teaching" the Serbs with "redemptive violence"—bombs—"for their own good," but walking on through, cradling his pathetic cross, white-faced and afraid, infiltrating into all Powers and Dominations, coming right on, unstoppable, *through* them and out the other side. His rising again is implicit in his own death, on through anything the Powers could do to him, and in this there is an enormous lesson for history.

The Powers don't always listen—they somehow become mad, and an entire vision of true community is at stake. The poor little community around Jesus was horribly frightened by the Powers, that is by the violence of the Romans and the Jewish hierarchy. In fact Peter was ready to deny that the whole thing had ever come up. Later, Peter lectured in terrible language in his epistles and was still a pain in the neck. But the humanistic message of Christianity did not get lost. It took time, through nonviolent visionaries throughout the centuries—

the Copts, Francis, Blake, Wilberforce, Gandhi, the Berremans, Mandela—for the religion to begin to mature. Wink lists seven pages (244-251) of collective actions without violence that have indeed overcome evil with good; with good, *not* by means of violence.

What is the scene today? Early in the twentieth century the communists in Russia acted—as they thought—to bring about a just community, using what they thought were good means commonly employed by governments—that is, the institution of more just laws, backed by what they felt would have to be applied, a redemptive "force," which, they said was the "midwife of progress," alias violence, to push the laws through against the immense power of old money and authority. The communists—and I remember it well—felt themselves blessed with a great philosophy, materialism. And it's a curious truth that if we lose sight of materialism and become wholly "spiritual" we are lost, hating our mother, as it were, the source of all "mater"-ial.

In Russia the twentieth century edifice of communist law, that "just" law, has become shattered, and Russia has become a victim of the Mafia. On three occasions, in 1988, 1993, and 1999, I was in Russia and saw something of the wreck of socialism, and encountered the brave and cheerful irony and feeling of defeat in all good people, their vulnerability and openness—like open wounds—to greedy lawless business and the Mafia. It was worse than sad, because in truth it had been communitas rather than communism that they had wanted. And it's gone. I saw in a corner of the Square of the Revolution in Moscow Russian Orthodox priests singing and praying in a tiny domed temple; it was beautiful, but it was small compensation for the old vision of comradeship. Elsewhere, the corpses of other socialist countries have been fed upon by the terrible breed of dictators that we have been seeing at this era, Saddam, Milosevek, and the ruler of Myanmar, those who like Stalin grew to actually love force and violence.

Reading Wink's book, I hoped that somehow people in America could build true human justice with neither shibboleths nor dogma nor cruelty nor "redemptive" punishment, but with the unparalleled happiness of communitas. I remembered the communitas at my Small Group weekend and later while working for those at a weekend the following year. This experience does happen. You sing at your work.

I hoped and hoped we could build a sisterdom (not kingdom) on earth, with never a hint of any kind of violence whatever. We could agree to pay taxes happily for all the big needs of national organization, but not for violence. We're nowhere near to alignment with the Great Spirit who is in fact present, working away, and has been sending us Desmond Tutus, Dalai Lamas, Mother Teresas, Mandelas,

Oscar Romeros. We don't know how these star-saints were produced (they have been called "constellated individuals," with something about them certainly not limited to the material sphere). Like many others I see something of that kind of breakthrough even in the early works of Karl Marx if you carefully subtract his "redemptive violence." He taught us to go back to "thing-mysticism" (which for me includes our bodies, and takes in the similar Eskimo idea that everything has a spirit). And he reminded us of what was clearly communitas and our alienation from it. But he didn't reckon with bureaucracy, the cancer of too much power. Meanwhile, parallel to that, all of the world knew perfectly well—however corrupt the churches and temples were—that a spirit power was available, through Jesus, Buddha, Gandhi, and many others. Huge populations knew they had spirit help. True nonviolent people of any religion can even now blow the whistle on injustice, and even if the whistle-blower is sacked or crucified for it, we will have heard the whistle.

I asked myself, does this plan for politics seem futile? A candle is better than no light. A group I know, the Industrial Areas Foundation,[8] works with churches to carry out a nonviolent humanistic policy involving a multi-church application of will, backed by their congregations. Their leaders listen to both sides in the disputes between the poor and the authorities. In these meetings one can treat the enemy as a friend. It's quite odd. I made friends with an enemy in that fashion. Love has a habit of growing, like vegetation.

Going back to the SDI course, at our last meeting the students got together and turned a side room into a chapel, where Chet appeared in his clerical robes with a knowing lightsome look in his eyes. He took holy oil—called chrism—and beckoned each of the students forward one by one, getting us to put our hands out, palms up. With a prayer he anointed the palms. My angelic friend sitting at my side was surprised. She whispered, "But they only anoint the palms when they're ordaining a priest."

I looked at her. "What—?" We both gazed at our palms. Priests? I remembered how Chet had said we SDI graduates were receiving a better training than priests and the religious. I could hardly breathe.

Now my palms burn often, in a hurry to get the writing done.

Notes

1. Ira Progoff, *The Symbolic and the Real* (New York, 1963).
2. See Chester Michael and Marie Norrisey, *Prayer and Temperament* (Charlottesville, VA, 1991).
3. Matthew 16:19.
4. Eugene Kennedy, *Tomorrow's Catholics* (New York: 1988).
5. See chapter 10 above.
6. Carl Jung, *Two Essays in Analytic Psychology* (New York, 1928).
7. Walter Wink, *Engaging the Powers* (Minneapolis, MN, 1992).
8. See Edward Chambers, *Roots for Radicals* (New York, 2003).

15

UNKNOWN REALMS

At last I tried to gather together all the hints of spirituality I had been noticing, in order to bring them into focus and see if I could recognize exactly where I was, on this long lumbering trip of mine.

I have felt all along that such an effort should include the spirituality of many ordinary people in America, for instance, those in the Small Christian Group and those whom I met at the Charlottesville healers' group such as the man with the divining rods and the man with the pictures of the soul, and people in New Age Christianity or New Age Hinduism, or in any religion. No one takes these Tims and Margarets and Lizzies and Indras seriously. They are either "holy women," to be avoided at all costs, or New Age "weirdoes and airheads," dead set on doing something that can't be done, like combining Native American religion and Hinduism.

But the spiritual experiences that these Americans encounter were originally encountered by native peoples from the earliest ages right up to the present, and the experiences are certainly not limited to the Native American Lakotas, the Hindus, or Christians. They were given to my friend Manyosa at Mukanza in Zambia who actually went into trance, Claire the Iñupiat healer, the Japanese drummer with whom I went on a bus trip, Mae de Santo Porphyria who was an African-Brazilian spirit leader, and many more. These also are the sisters of my New Age friends in America. A consideration of the experiences of all peoples, especially our own local spirituality, has clearly not been completed; it merits careful and sympathetic attention.

I have been continually seeking a way to encompass all of these, native and Western, that would show the body-soul-mind at its most alive and operating; some kind of trick that would serve to shift the whole discipline of anthropology over (drag it as with a mouse) to where it actually belongs, and drop it into the window of living beings themselves.

The anthropologist Colin Turnbull said, "What is needed is a technique of participation that demands *total involvement* of our whole being. Indeed it is perhaps only when we truly and fully participate … that we find this essentially subjective approach to be in no way incompatible with the more conventional rational, objective, scientific approach. On the contrary, they complement each other and that complementarity is an absolute requirement if we are to come to any full understanding of the social process … it provides a wealth of data that could never be acquired by any other means."[1] He had been speaking of the tranced singing of pygmies in the Ituri forest.

Thus the anthropologist would be able to recognize consciousness as sometimes able to sustain time-warp, space-warp, people-warp, the magic moment, and "THE experience." When a good anthropologist like Clifford Geertz writes down these moments, we see immortal ethnography, as in the Balinese cockfight[2] when in a humble but historic moment both natives and anthropologists were hunted down by the police for being present at an illicit sport. The Geertzes experienced a rush of communitas with the people at that moment, and after they had all escaped they laughed together. The Balinese were friendly from then on. Or when we seem to be watching Lévi-Strauss[3] watching the Bororo of the South American rain forest skillfully plaiting their strands and interweaving bird feathers, lost in the flow of attention. We look through the anthropologist's eyes. We can *see* what he saw.

So in the field, when daring to make this total involvement—this "something added" that goes far beyond, as Turnbull put it, anthropologists are striking levels they never plumbed before. We are in that world of the unknown. For instance, I was in the world of the unknown when I sat at the Ihamba ritual in Zambia, then started forward to clap with all my soul at the climax—and saw it happen, *saw* the bad entity leave the suffering woman. Now what are we talking about? Yet we are in the world of people, just as anywhere else. The first step to materializing the unknown seems to be to allow oneself to "get it," if one can. Then—to think.

The Unknown

We are dealing with anomaly and we try to recognize this thing that has no name. I have been attempting to draw a map of that land in very rough sketches—trying the outside lines of the shape daringly, outlines to show what is within, to catch the nature of what we sense dimly inside in order to suggest the unknown there. Religious people find themselves doing this, often gracefully in poetry, hinting at beauty; and it is the principle behind the patterns on some Arabian prayer mats, which show a plain empty space, a lacuna, in the middle, a space where one bows one's head to earth and worships the inconceivably great Allah. But the mat is gorgeously adorned around the rim of the empty space, the shape of the rim betraying the shape within. The splendid art is a mere sketch of the deep unsayable feelings.

Some pointers have arisen to indicate this unknown. It seems to have something to do with the collective unconscious. One could just as well call the collective unconscious the "collective nonordinary consciousness," referring to something happening to various people in rituals, people who are not out for the count, unconscious in that sense, but who are on a different level and can communicate with one another. This still needs much in the way of exploration.[4]

For a long time I have been on the lookout for hints of the unknown. For example, the phone rings; I've just been thinking about so-and-so, and it's her. Simple. I get healed by the young Eskimo woman in Point Hope. That sort of thing is not supposed to happen, but regularly does.

In what world does this sort of thing take place? In some "spiritual" world? That's not quite it. I did not feel particularly "spiritual" or holy when the Eskimo woman healed my headache, just wretched until she did it, that's all. At the Ihamba, I was excited and thrilled to see the entity come out of the patient, but it was with a gang of Africans; no one was meditating or anything, just bellowing out songs and drumming. They were busy "getting" something and they knew it.

Turnbull in the Ituri forest suddenly clicked into it when he heard the pygmy singers, when he *saw* it all, the unity. Others have described similar times, unexpected ones, and called them the greatest experience of their lives. I note them nowadays with nodding familiarity. I wake up in the middle of the night having had a dream about a long and beautiful estuary of water. There has to be something one can say about all this.[5]

I've tried playing with an idea. What is it that can explain these things? Let's see. We need Occam's razor, the rule of parsimony. (I couldn't find it in me to go out of my way to invent complicated explanations involving the social construction of reality and hallucination, just in order to avoid what was in plain sight: the nonlogical.) First, we know that human beings continually communicate with one another and naturally follow familiar channels and styles of communication, using certain kinds of connective tissue, as it were. One might see that around and part and parcel with all this connective tissue floods an impalpable element like blood plasma that carries—just as the air carries our voices—unspoken thoughts from person to person, body language and state of mind, love, the shaman's powers, the witch's lethal act. The development of awareness of it is like that of the myelin sheath for the nerve that enables the impulse to run along better. But this is something that responds to spirit power, not mere biological promptings.

The element gradually becomes more easily recognized. It is the ambiance in which the halo shines and which the angels inhabit; people you meet can put their hand near your hand or above your head and feel the tingling, and you can feel theirs. It's a kind of integument, clothing itself around people, providing a natural imperceptible connection between person and person—a tent, as the Iñupiat Clem said, talking about our tents set up on the ice while whaling: "When things are right, our friendship covers all of us like a tent." But among people with a sense of resentment the integument sometimes gets scarily sick, as in Germany in Hitler's time—like a horrible deadly peritonitis, a virulent infection in what should provide connection and oneness.

One might see the possibility of a reservoir of power somewhere—and classically the power is not "owned" by the person who appears to have it, it comes through him or her. People know it very well when it comes into consciousness. Victor Turner called it communitas—that is, the condition of a group in which the impalpable power operates, the condition of all being at one. It seems to be where healing takes place, where the burden is lifted, as my son Rory put it. It is God to Monsignor Chet Michael. Yes, for him, Jung's collective unconscious was God; at first it puzzled me greatly.

Here we have just seen an odd leap occurring—when Chet said the collective unconscious was God. Not the place where God was, but God. This is precisely the ambiguity I was facing, and it is precisely the world of non-logic we are in. Old Chet puts his head on one side and looks quizzical when he says it, and rather pleased. As for me, familiar with so many of the multitudinous forms of power, spirit, and ambiance, I know it is useless to try classifying and categorizing and clearing up the ambiguities in all these, because each is right in its own context. Each shades into each. Understanding is a matter of direct perception at the time, innocent of categorization and ordinary reasoning. But it is understanding.

So then the collective unconscious is a major property of the human being. We realize that anthropologists have had a good instinct in following their investigations across the whole planet, because there does seem to exist one big leading principle of humankind in all the pores of every human being. We are all connected. We are all gifted with this collective unconscious, whatever people want to call it. It is somehow the Holy Spirit, and many spirits. *It* has the initiative, not you—just as the whale, for the Iñupiat, has the initiative and will come to a good person, and just as the shaman's spirit helper takes the initiative to call a person to the shamanic life. The Iñupiat Eskimos are quite clear that spirit animals desire humans to be spiritual and are trying to teach them this by offering their bodies. Human spirit teachers exist too, and ancestors. A person could get reprimanded by an autonomous spirit like that, as I was by my shaman spirit teacher in 1987.

Mary Watkins in *Waking Dreams*[6] also has the same odd idea. The forms that come up in waking dreams just before you wake up—figures she calls "imaginals"—have a mysterious independent existence and produce events and pictures outside the experience of the dreamer, and also have a will of their own, purposes for you. Here we have yet another path for the soul, through dreams. The psychologist Ira Progoff says of the psyche that it is "a directive principle and its contents are not contents as such. They are not things *within* the psyche. They are aspects of a moving principle, like images and sparks from a large fire that start fires ... [they are] derivations of the directive process ... in motion, never fixed, in flow."[7] And like Jung he says, "The concept of psychic reality leads to more than intellectual knowledge, it leads to dimensions of reality that reach beyond the individual."[8]

Is then the collective unconscious, as well as being God, a shared power—*and* a reservoir? The Celtic vision of the steaming cauldron has been used as a metaphor for it. Another feature is the curious state of consciousness that simply *allows* the unconscious to flower, called by Keats "negative capability." The same thing was well put by Kenneth Clark, commenting on William Blake's picture of a crawling werewolf, a picture that first remained

> in Blake's mind, unallocated, unfulfilled. Then suddenly he recognized what the vision was—it was Urizen's most degraded victim, Nebuchadnezzar.... For the student of visionary art, the interesting fact is that an image comes first and takes up residence in the mind long before the artist has any notion why it is there or what it means. Whether visions come from some great *reservoir* [my italics] of symbolic images which are eternally there (and if one examines the recurrence of images in history this proposition is not quite as crazy as it sounds) or whether they are due to buried memories, their obsessive power over an artist's mind, and their clear, compulsive emergence in his work depends on a mental condition that can come and go.[9]

Here is a hint that "an image comes ... and takes up residence in the mind," implying that the image or whatever it is has taken the initiative and in a sense has autonomy. And at the same time Clark hints at a reservoir being the source of visions, and also that what is in them can recur. Clark as an art scholar may have put this better than the psychologist Jung. Again, Wordsworth the poet in the passage cited in chapter 1 talks about a kind of fertilizing sea:

Ye Presences of Nature in the sky
And on the earth! Ye Visions of the hills!
And Souls of lonely places!
... ye, through many a year
Haunting me thus among my boyish sports,
On caves and trees, upon the woods and hills,
... Work like a sea?[10]

People have had experiences that they connect with the beauty of a place. They are overcome with a sense of awe, a sense of holiness in a certain ambiance. Material places, I think, have a power, and perhaps this is because material things are involved in that very reservoir connecting all peoples' collective unconscious, which is a region of great discovery.

It is also from this reservoir that ideas break the surface. For instance, you can't remember the exact word that's on the tip of your tongue, and when you don't think about it, there it is. You leave a problem overnight or until after dinner and the darn thing solves itself. You're with a group of people and they come up with the answer you've been seeking for in vain. It's as if *you* had told them the answer, too. It's weird. This isn't done by willed action, nor by some kinds of disciplined meditation. In my case meditation comes over me; I am no good at inducing it. Something out there lifts me away from the mundane focus, and I'm off.

You sing in a group and it really takes. You blend your voices in song, and get cold chills. The sports game goes just right. All kinds of situations manifest it. It is the "flowing" described by Csikszentmihalyi, that magical happy experience when you know you're "doing it right," perfectly.[11] And when a big group "gets it right" and knows it, and is happy with it, there has taken place an enormous natural focusing such as could produce heaven on earth. I think the great cathedrals of Europe were produced like that, and Stonehenge, and the Avebury Rings. The Black Pagoda too.

In a way this spiritual consciousness is the same as the Hindu idea of *man* (*manas* in Sanskrit), meaning: "mind-that-is-also-the-feelings,-the-heart,-and-the-soul," something which is not confined to the brain but which exists as a collective consciousness that may be pooled as one "soul-mind," escaping its confines in the brain and body of single persons, so that, for instance, a group of people can feel themselves to be soul-mates. This may not be just a "nice feeling," but could be an actual fact. It is over this "ether," seen as fluid, that healing flows, sometimes even like a jolt of electricity, as I experienced it in 1996. The following account tells the story.

It was on 20 November in San Francisco at the American Anthropological Association annual meetings. I was in my hotel bedroom at the Hilton when I contracted the most severe giddiness attack, which turned into vomiting. Pam Frese, my erstwhile colleague and now my roommate, tenderly gave me assistance but it was of no avail. All night the trouble became worse so that I could hardly lift up my head without the room swimming around. I was going to miss the sessions. Was it lack of salt in the diet-conscious Hilton food? I'd had attacks of salt deprivation before. But pretzels did no good. All morning I lay there in misery. A little after noon Pam burst into the room. She was excited about something.

"Edie, I met that man called—was it Daar An?"

"Whoozat? Charlie Chan? What's—"

"Look, I told him you were sick. He laid his hands on me—he's just an ordinary white guy, he was on your panel yesterday. Okay, and he said, 'When you get to Edie, you put your hands on *her*, right?' And so I came. I don't know what this is all about, but here goes."

I reared up miserably and Pam put her hands on my head and shoulders.

Then she yelped. "Look, look at my arms!" Pam was wearing short sleeves and all along her arms you could see goose bumps pricking up everywhere. "It feels funny!"

And at that moment I felt whatever it was also up my own back, like a super cold chill, going right up my spine and over the top of my head. I can feel it now—these were no ordinary goose bumps. It felt like turning inside out. We stared at each other.

I said, "Pam, I feel quite all right! The dizziness has gone. Who is that guy?" She told me, but I have to be discreet about his name.

I was delighted. Pam said, "Look, you have a rest. I'm going off to hear Roy Wagner's paper."

"Wait, I'm coming with you." I put on my clothes, feeling perfectly okay, and we went off to Roy's paper.

So "healing" was invading the halls of academe.

Up to that time I thought healers were just being metaphorical when they talked about "energy" healing. I am sorry and I have changed my tune. There *is* energy healing.

I asked myself, how important is this? It would seem to be some kind of data, at the very least—something impinging itself on our discipline; and I had an idea it was not good etiquette to ignore it. It would not be good methodology in anthropology to ignore it, not to say it would be rude and ungracious. I asked around a little and I found I was not alone in having these experiences.

As regards group healing, it seems the group that does the healing may include persons in the past. As I saw in 1985, Ndembu healers will utter the names of their healer ancestors, six steps back, calling them up to be there with them when they go out to gather the herbs. It seems the ancestors instruct them how to proceed. It is a curious idea—that some difficult thing we are trying to do may be backed by a dead ancestor whose past experience may thus be written into the act. I no longer think this is impossible. Anthony Appiah, the Ghanaian scholar, told me that when he came to lecture at the University of Virginia he was aware that his ancestors were with him on the stage as he spoke. I was not aware of them at the time, but he was.

On one occasion in 1993, I myself was aware of two tending spirits of that kind. I had got lost on the streets of Miami, considerably scared by that dangerous city and unable to find my conference center. Walking along the sidewalk I became aware that my long-dead mother-in-law (a spiritualist) and my old friend who had recently died (she and I had promised each other some kind of communication after death) were walking one on each side of me. I couldn't see them, but I quite distinctly felt them to be there. Now that I knew a little bit about such things I was rather delighted, and greeted them in my mind. All seemed very nice and chummy. At the end of the street they glanced over the other side—or my glance fell to the other side—and when I looked back they were no longer there. I went over where they indicated and immediately found the conference center.

The experience I had of the two spirit presences was quite vivid. I was aware of what it was like before they were there—then aware that they were there—and then that they were not there.

Sometimes such entities decide, for reasons known only to themselves, to come to a suffering community and give it a huge leg up, as in the apparitions of the mother spirit woman, "Our Lady," in Mexico, Ireland, Poland, Cairo, and many locations among the poor, also in the form of Kwanyin, the woman Bodhisattva in Buddhist regions, and in the form of the goddess Shakti in India. Also, I couldn't help feeling when reading Chapman's *Homer* that Athena did actually appear to Ulysses in his dark moment before his return to Ithaca.

Different kinds of ritual show it. Looking back, I see that what Vic Turner and I saw happening in the betwixt-and-between periods of rites of passage, puberty ceremonies, and initiations, happen in a spirit-laden "liminal" region where the normal does not apply. It is a kind of crack between the worlds,[12] like the looking glass world of Alice, where animals and chessmen speak—and reprimand the visitor. By now the liminal is becoming recognized, even though it is hard to put it into logical terms.

More examples have been coming to me, and they are about ethereal beings. Various witnesses report them. It seems that that this "spirit"—this "consciousness-extended-beyond-the-body-and-existing-in-a-mysterious-fluid-sea"—might persist beyond a lifetime, being beyond the body. I reckon it is what we see in ghosts, and in the entity I saw in Ihamba. Souls are somehow still individuals in this state, yet with far more fluid powers than in ordinary bodies. In a variety of cultures people say they receive support and communication from their spirits, and also they say that some spirit beings are dangerous.

This fluidity of the soul appears to be the condition or sphere in which reincarnation takes place, the in-between world after death where souls take the paths where they have to go. In Native American thought[13] they seem to get siphoned off here and there, to heaven and simultaneously to a grandchild, even to several descendants or while the giver is not yet dead—in all kinds of directions. The matter defies our logic altogether. We "grope," and "get inklings" of it, "intimations," as Wordsworth put it—that is our kind of language about it. And that is why one hears so many people say, "You can't put it into words," "It's hard to describe." It is when one is most in the dark that one is coming to it—which is how negative capability works.

Jungian psychology has been urging our generation to accept not only what seems positive in their deeper levels but, as Chet taught us, what looks scary, because the collective unconscious is also where the "Shadow" dwells, deep inside the soul, as in Arjuna's famous vision of Krishna when the god appears as a terrible demon with teeth and skulls. This kind of being may make itself known in dreams. The Shadow is what one is almost totally unconscious of and *is* the devil if one does not see what it is. It may have a form that is unmentionable, demonic, obscene. And yet it is oddly fruitful and should not be sanitized or drugged away. It is one's Self, and needs to be confronted and supplied with what it is really demanding. When I went on the pilgrimage to the island in Lough Derg (the "Red Dragon" lake), at the shrine of St. Patrick's Purgatory, I suffered considerably from cold. I had to renounce the devil at the Cross of St. Bridget. There came a thirty-nine-degree wind across the lake, creating streaks of foam in long lines everywhere beside us, right up to our naked feet. That devil wants you to be unhappy, he feeds on your unhappiness. What I needed to do was to tempt him to be happy and to rejoice with him after it was over in a warm bed and blankets.

From this vision of the Self I inferred that the "Self," though also an individual, seems to have its foot reaching into all soul-stuff everywhere; thus I glimpsed the idea that it is staggeringly limitless. The psychologist Anthony Stevens said this individual is truly great because it is in fact the two-million-year-old human being within us, and knowledge of it is the *satori* experience of Buddhism.[14] It is our sharing of a common soul.

Jung and also Stevens use the name "Anthropos" for this ancient being—it is the universe, the earth, or Gaia itself, in a sense: it is Leonardo's outstretched naked human figure, existing in a small drawing, almost mathematical in Leonardo's age of humanism, yet able to resonate with the whole planet. The figure of Anthropos remains as mysterious as the collective unconscious itself. The two are one. Philosophers and mystics have tried to get their minds around the mystery. What we learn from the concept is that we live in a process world, not organized in a pyramid of absolute power separated by levels.[15] Paracelsus said that "heaven is a human being and a human being is heaven, and all humanity together is one heaven, and heaven is nothing but one person."[16]

"Anthropos" could be human, an animal (in the Native American vision), or a natural object (as with the *kami* gods in the Japanese vision of the cosmos). We learn from Buddhism and from our regular astronomy that the cosmos is in process, a working entity, seen in various scales from different perspectives. The Buddhist view of the cosmology runs like this: whatever creates is also created, and the process of creating and being created goes on simultaneously without beginning or end. Furthermore the creating takes place in intimate connection with everything else, and by means of everything else. This is known as the concept of dependent origination, or interdependent co-origination. One might compare this insight with that of Henri Bergson's "creative evolution," a vision of the natural condition of things, somewhat different from Teilhard's alpha and omega system which implies a single directing power. Dependent origination could perfectly well include transcendent gods, animal spirits, the world of the dead, the impulsion that urges one personally to find a path, "the force that through the green fuse drives the flower" of Dylan Thomas,[17] all of them.

What was this idea, rich in archaic lore, that resonated with what I was pondering in my mind? We do not always live in the great reservoir of power I described, and this tallies with our awareness of the slenderness of the life path of this Self, the fragility of the power.

In another view of this being, it seems we can "switch in" to connection with it, as at those times when ideas think us and we don't think them. It is what the unblocked collective unconscious can see. The anthropologist Barbara Myerhoff wrote of the power of the dream as "the dropping into the unconscious that precedes understanding and generates what is not-yet-born."[18]

Even in a minor way, this being is found in connection with the sense one has of one's soul going out to the grandeur of the universe—a dim sense of unity with it. Again one asks, why not go beyond the vague feeling and grab on to the sense, which is trying to tell us something. As I saw earlier, Wordsworth had actual and vivid experiences of the Presences of nature.

William Blake also had a sense of this "fecund sea of fertile spirits" that one feels in the collective non-ordinary consciousness. In his case the figures bore the shape of the huge archetypal characters Albion and Los. They were strongly personal to him. With Blake that world opens up to the soul of the artist, whom we now can see as a modern heroic figure gifted with a kind of spiritual-genetic endowment—or as the scientist of the soul, the apocalyptic architect of the new universe. Blake said, "And was Jerusalem builded here, Among these dark satanic mills?"—the cotton mills of the industrial revolution.[19]

Various other visionaries have attempted to describe the power they have seen in the form of human or animal figures. The Iñupiat creation story shows something of the same figure. The Native American Raven—interestingly enough a member of the animal kingdom—seems to be that "one person" to whom Paracelsus refers. Raven, the Iñupiat creator figure, discovered the whole world and pulled it up out of the sea with his harpoon while he was paddling in his kayak on the endless northern ocean. It was the whale that he pulled up, it was the point of land at Ivakuk, it was the woman, it was the shaman, it was the world.[20] There is no contradiction in this kind of thinking, it is true in the collective unconscious. "It works," as the Iñupiat healer woman said.

There is ambiguity at every step and it is fitting. Logic is not the tool for this material. In one aspect I see the ambiguity as power, a kind of "ether" or communicating medium, and/or a reservoir. And/or it can be found in the "flowing" experience in focused enterprises (ritual or sport or the arts and all endeavors). These are states, conditions, or elements.

And/or it is the inner person, a primordial person the size of the universe, God, the shamanic helper spirit of the Iñupiat and of many other cultures, a beloved remembered ancestor spirit, one that takes the initiative, one that may come in dreams as the Shadow, at the same time being the Self, or may come in apparitions as a female being, mother of the creator with what that implies, or a string of healing ancestors—all of them persons, which contrasts with the idea of "One God, King Omnipotent." Here, also, a recognition of the soul jumps into being, the soul of a dead person who visits us after death, the curious sense that one has lived before and will live again, the intimations of a glory beyond death. The Christian attempt to state the ambiguities by the word "trinity" is a brave one, but is fearfully simplified in face of the multitudinous strings of meanings that exist.

All these various phenomena dwell in the bloodstream of the collective unconscious, "the collective psyche," which appears to be always in operation, just as both sides of our brain are in operation at every turn. The thing seems to be an endowment with which we were born. Humanity in varying contexts has a strong idea that such thinking is true. Where Jung wins out is because he follows what he actually feels, not any given theological system featuring a supreme being who issues a list of rules. We too get a strong sense of the power or its absence. Anthropologists sometimes find such power anomalous but it persistently turns up in their fieldwork.

A good example of the power was experienced by the anthropologist Henry Stephen Sharp, who revealed how the Chipewyan sense their land, the northern Canadian tundra. Steve himself married into the tribe. By long acclimatization he was able to internalize a sense of mystical participation with the land:

> [the people's] awareness of its beauty and of its bounties. It is a pervasive aspect of the sense of place held by a people living in an active sensory and aesthetic interaction with their world.[21]
>
> They exist in a constant communication with the living beings surrounding them, a communication intensified by an order of magnitude every time they move more than few hundred feet away from their camps. Their universe is animate and filled with sound. The ice sings to those who travel upon it, the snow has its own songs to reflect its temperature and moisture content, the ground underfoot speaks with the passage of animate beings, and the muskegs protest the intrusion of a footfall. The plants, the lakes, the streams, the wind, and the animals, sometimes even the rocks and the earth itself, engage in constant communication with those who choose to listen.[22]

This is the natural state of affairs. It is part of Sharp's "before-and-after" account of this experience of awareness, first, this passage on the people's own habitual feel for the land, and then the change when a party of Royal Mounted Canadian Police arrive, having mistakenly suspected conflict and criminal assault. Sharp describes how the old

awareness winks out, replaced by the cold shadowy dull world the
police brought with them.

> I was suddenly struck by waves of disorientation. The entire world in
> which I was standing ... became out of alignment.... The rich and fecund
> landscape was noticeably dryer and harsher.... Grays predominated
> where had been rich dark green. The very colors of the world had
> bleached. Fewer birds were singing, their singing was thinner, as though
> most of the overtones were absent. What had been a background sym-
> phony was now an unorchestrated and disjointed series of individual per-
> formances. A presence that had been there was no longer there.[23]

In Sharp's article one learns the sense of the ordinary blessedness of a
community in tune with the interdependency of the ongoing creation—and then the other condition, also described by Wordsworth:

> At length the man perceives it die away
> And fade into the light of common day.[24]

Wordsworth knew of this membrane between the visionary and the
banal; Stephen Sharp did; the ancient Yaqui of Mexico also did, knowing full well they had lost the flower-and-animal world of their pre-
colonial past.

The documentation I have quoted of the change in the tundra has
the nature of an actuality. In connection with all these experiences I
found the collective unconscious a useful concept, recognizable and
palpable, and even when I merely describe *around* it—which is what I
have been doing and all I can do—it appears to set off affirmation.

The Social

What is still missing is a wealth of experiences everybody has which
do not seem to count because the experiences are so much fun. Their
specialness consists of what anthropologists can sometimes see but
psychologists cannot—the social, the *we*, plural, the *people* who participate together in the experience.

I realized that in just about all my experiences, in all the directions
in which I was wandering, it was not just "me experiencing on my
own." When I climbed Croagh Patrick in Ireland, there were thousands in the rain behind me, in front of me, beside me, and sometimes seeming to echo inside me. So I was experiencing something
social. But I came to realize that most people in America avoid "the
social," being adamantly determined to keep their hard-won individuality. They have learned a horror of social pressure, of old-time

prejudice, and so forth; this prejudice is also documented in anthropology. But some anthropologists are trying to write about *communities* of souls, those that experience a change in collective non-ordinary consciousness, or about the occasions when a number of people get into flow together in a collective enterprise. This occurs, of course, in team sports.

I often find myself on a path where people are crowding along too. But the ordinary word "social" seems to bring to mind something artificial, forced, and constructed: social organization. Communitas, though, can be felt. It is that sense of union with others which is a large part of the aim of ritual and a major concern of religion. The religions call it charity, compassion, generosity, or humanitarianism, even the sacred communion—and it is a different kind of "social," it is that "social II" I have mentioned. Anthropologists have lately been dealing intimately with ritual and changes of consciousness and have actually been operating *inside* these states. They find them different from what they expected.

In those great spirit occasions that I came across on my life path—either personally or through the accounts of others—the details of their support system could be traced. The work of support and back up, fervently provided by the community, was a strong and emotional power.

I remember how at my girls' boarding school we played a game in which about five of us would get in a circle around one girl in the middle. I think it was called "flying." First, all the five put their hands on top of the center girl's head and pressed her head down hard, using all their weight, until she was crouching. Then each of us put a finger under her armpit and quite easily raised her up high above our heads, where she hung for a minute before she came toppling down. In Africa much later I saw the Ndembu girls do this, and have heard from various other women how they did it too when girls.[25] No one quite knows why it happens. But it does. The factor of group is paramount. First your companions all literally bring you low, then very easily they propel you upwards, shooting you up in an uncanny fashion.

Yet another, much richer example begs attention. Every year in Tibet a great ritual is held in Llasa, described by Ter Ellingson.[26] It is the coming of the Tibetan State Oracle, the occasion when a Buddhist monk who is also a shaman goes into trance, receives the god, and then is burdened with an immensely heavy crown. He bursts from his monastery holding a bow and arrow; he is now receiving and giving enormous psychic power. The crowd presses forward to throw him white scarves, even braving his arrow.

How is this done? Very early in the morning, inside the monastery, drumming starts up and the monks gather around the man who will give himself in this way. High above the altar is a picture of three dark gods in their palace surrounded by a great mandala. Down at the foot of the picture are depicted the monks, their hands folded in worship; one can see their drums and cymbals on each side, and their cones of rice in front on the altar. At the same time, the monks themselves in actuality are standing in person surrounding the oracle man, and beside them are the rice cones and drums. The drums are playing, producing an unforgettable slow, rising, hastening, and thundering sound, right up to a climax; then another wave of drumbeats gathers force and rises, and fades away. These are the times when the god falls into the world (I've known this in the Mass). All present steeple their hands and focus intently on the god who is now present—again, just as my spirit helpers were present in Miami. The oracle monk finds that he is abandoning himself to their presence. Now he finds one word he has to say, a mantra. At once the god and his heart become joined by a ray of light that fuses the two identities "like water flowing into water." At this moment all the monks feel the strong waves of blessing. The effect even passes to the assembled crowd outside and it changes many people's lives. One more great towering burst of sound, and trance overcomes the Oracle. From that time on, the monk remembers nothing.

Now the assistants array the monk in the god's robes and place a mirror on his chest, which gives him humility and detachment from the world. This mirror is itself a kind of membrane, marking where divinity begins. On the monk's head they place the enormous, conical, ornate crown weighing fifty pounds. They steady his head for a moment, then in his trance his muscles grow and he can support the crown. Nevertheless his face is humble and accepting, listening, like a servant, for he has become an oracle. They put a bow and arrow in his hand. The drums bellow. The gates open, and he goes out to meet the crowd.

The special consciousness of the Oracle has combined with the special kind of consciousness possessing the other monks, and it passes to the crowd outside. Hundreds and thousands of people have been assembling in the predawn darkness before the induction ritual began. All of them have been catching a sense of the religious energy and have heard the drumming emerging from the monastery. The god has been entering them too, through the music.

Now, when the Oracle emerges, the crowd becomes frenzied. Men, women, and children charge forward, reaching for contact with the Oracle, trying to present him with white greeting scarves, or simply throwing the scarves at him, oblivious of everything, even of the danger from the arrow. Ellingson relates that even his video camera seemed drawn forward to receive a shot of the event. He had to shoot the scene with one arm holding the camera, and one arm and one leg wrapped around a tree, and he had all he could do to keep from being swept away by the crowd.

There was one spirit going through all the throng. The Oracle had allowed his own consciousness to recede so that he could be the instrument for the whole assembly to feel the god. Now there could be an invisible presence on earth.

As for me, reading this, I could see it was not an intellectual matter, and it pointed me in a new direction.

The Ndembu singers and drummers in Africa gather around with a focused purpose, to cure the woman afflicted with a spirit. The sick woman endures bloodletting, is encouraged to tell her nastiest grudges, falls, then becomes the center of an extraordinary sense of social release—and out pops the trouble. The tiny pygmies take Turnbull into the forest far away from village, food, and business, and they all open their throats in song. This band merges as they sing: Turnbull sees them at it and feels that strong thing, something "far beyond sound, another mode of perception"—a different consciousness again.[27] This social group has become one, as "social II." Then in another continent, in the private world of the Dene Tha, a people careful not to spill their precious talk with those who don't receive it, storytelling is like the nature of an electric current which needs two poles.[28] You simply can't talk unless the others are connected too— unless they also *know*. If they are in it, the story is about the returning soul, messages from the dead, second sight. The tribe and its religion become the community of experiencers. Those who do the supporting are essential to the process and enable the messages to go through. It is also consciously created in the Small Group initiation, and in the girl's initiation among the Ndembu—both at the behest of the spirits.

Thus one begins to perceive something of the *social* in the realm of different levels of consciousness. We know it may be called "bonding." Sick Hitler used that idea. It is the good form that is so welcome. "We may say we're very happy," to quote the African medicine man, Singleton—the power is obviously courted by human beings. It is from this power that healing flows.

Jung's collective unconscious, on the other hand, was what an *individual* experiences from a culture, the experiencer being a lone individual who made links with archaic symbols as from the position of that individual. However, what I saw coming across in the truly social rituals was what all may experience together—a very different thing.

So there are times when people are all one. The predisposition for that oneness and the different ways such a capacity develops in a human being begin to look like an instinct, like fatherhood and motherhood, like a tiny baby's arm moving out, not to grab but to make a communitas signal, a fact that the neurobiologist Trevarthen has determined.[29] We need this odd thing, communitas, to process life. A world purged of it would die, just as a baby whom nobody touches dies. The shape of the unknown I am trying to sketch looks much more like the immanent presence of spirit in every part of the universe, at work like the sun producing oxygen in leaves. We breathe it all the time.

Notes

1. Colin Turnbull, "Liminality: A Synthesis of Subjective and Objective Experience," in *By Means of Performance*, eds. Richard Schechner and Willa Appel (New York, 1988), 50-81.
2. Clifford Geertz, "Deep Play: Notes on the Balinese Cockfight," in *The Interpretation of Culture*, by Clifford Geertz (New York, 1971), 412-453.
3. Claude Levi-Strauss, *Triste Tropique* (New York, 1997).
4. The delay in discussion of a collective unconscious shared by many people probably exists because, although the word "collective" is employed, the theory as it comes to us from Jung is based on the experience of an individual, not of a group of people, much less a group of souls. I myself came to recognize the idea of "groups of souls" only after long delay, such was the prevalence of the Jungian individualistic perspective.
5. The dream took place in about 2000. On 20 December, 2004, I walked beside the very estuary I had seen in the dream. It was the Firth of Forth, near Edinburgh, and I was with Colwyn Trevarthen the neurobiologist.
6. Mary Watkins, *Waking Dreams* (Dallas, TX, 1984).
7. Progoff, *The Symbolic and the Real*, 102-103.
8. Progoff, *The Symbolic and the Real*, 108.
9. Kenneth Clark, *The Romantic Rebellion: Romantic Versus Classic Art* (Don Mills, Ontario, 1975).
10. William Wordsworth, "The Prelude, Book I," in *The Norton Anthology of Poetry*, eds. Alexander Allison et al. (New York, 1975 [1798-1800]), 586.
11. Mihali Csikszentmihalyi. *Flow: The Psychology of Optimal Experience* (New York, 1990).
12. Jay Ruby, ed. *A Crack in the Mirror* (Philadelphia, 1982).
13. See Antonia Mills, "Scientific and Participant Validation of Rebirth: Similarities, Differences, and Is There a Bridge?" Paper read in the panel "The Spirit Hypothesis" at the Annual Meetings of the American Anthropological Association (Philadelphia, 1998).
14. Anthony Stevens, *Archetypes: A Natural History of the Self* (New York, 1982), 24.

15. Since my stay among the Iñupiat I have often pondered the mistake of Western Christians in basing their metaphor of God on that of a king. The use of such a metaphor merely shows the effect of the age of the barbaric kingdoms, in which power first gained by force and violence was used to exact obedience from all subjects, along with the application of enforced punishment if obedience were not rendered, resulting in all the fears and guilts that have afflicted Christianity ever since. The barbaric structure of Christianity therefore grew to be like this: God on top of a pyramid, Man (male) on the middle level, and animals and the lower creation under Man's feet, at the bottom base. We have environmental disaster deriving from this idea. Whereas the Inuit picture is a circle, showing cosmological cycling, with humans, animals, all things in existence, as being spiritual and passing one into the other ceaselessly (see Ann Fienup-Riordan on the Yupik Southern Eskimos in *The Nelson Island Eskimo* (Anchorage, 1983)). People with this kind of view of the creation show respect for the environment.

16. Quoted in Larry Dossey, *Recovering the Soul* (New York, 1989), 228.

17. Dylan Thomas, "The Force That through the Green Fuse Drives the Flower," in *The Norton Anthology of Poetry*, eds. Allison et al. (New York, 1975 [1934]), 1162.

18. Barbara Myerhoff, "Pilgrimage to Meron," in *Creativity/Anthropology*, eds. Smadar Lavie et al. (Ithaca, NY, 1993), 213-214.

19. William Blake, "And did those feet in ancient times," in *The Poetry and Prose of William Blake*, ed. David Erdman (Garden City, NY, 1970 [1804]), 95.

20. Edith Turner, *The Hands Feel It: Healing and Spirit Presence among a Northern Alaskan People.* (DeKalb, IL, 1996), 238-239n4.

21. Henry Stephen Sharp, "Experiencing Meaning." *Anthropology and Humanism* 21, no 2 (1996):183.

22. Sharp, "Experiencing Meaning," 182.

23. Sharp, "Experiencing Meaning," 173.

24. Wordsworth, "Intimations," 602.

25. See also Elizabeth Tucker, "Levitation and Trance Sessions at Preadolescent Girls' Slumber Parties," in *The Masks of Play*, eds. Brian Sutton-Smith and Diana Kell-Byrne (New York, 1984), 119-124.

26. The account is paraphrased from Ter Ellingson, "The Arrow and the Mirror: Interactive Consciousness, Ethnography, and the Tibetan State Oracle's Trance," *Anthropology and Humanism*, 23, no. 1 (1998):51-76.

27. Turnbull, "Liminality: A Synthesis of Subjective and Objective Experience," in *By Means of Performance*, eds. Richard Schechner and Willa Appel (New York, 1988), 56.

28. See Jean-Guy Goulet, "Ways of Knowing: Towards a Narrative Ethnography of the Dene Tha," *Journal of Anthropological Research* 50, no. 2 (1994):113-139.

29. Colwyn Trevarthen, "Neurological Development and the Growth of Psychological Functions," in *Developmental Psychology and Society*, ed. J. Sants (London, 1980), 46-95.

16
ELY

When I first saw the cathedral after so many years, as we slowly approached it along a winding road through gradually rising fields, all my dreams came back to me as if I had dreamed them yesterday.

Sometimes I used to view the cathedral in a spirit of disbelief. It seemed Anglican and dry, with a sense that its tide had receded. It was disenchanted, belonging to Wordsworth's "common day," disinfected, a rose without scent, empty. Now, however, in telling this story, the cathedral has given me its scent again—the fume of the big coke stove and the scent of the dry stone columns, eternal again, benevolent; it has come back to me, the huge beloved enclosed space, altogether alive.

What were those dreams? I used to have them often. I experienced another set of them in May before I left for England, after poring through pictures of the cathedral.[1] At the beginning of the dream I saw Ely before me as in ancient times. I was slowly traveling past four or five huge sacred buildings built of stone, one in particular which was a rectangle of stone facing me, enormous, finely decorated, with pinnacles along the sides; it had no tower. Then I had a dream of being *inside* the structure of the cathedral building itself, high in the roof somehow, looking through the rafters to a convent section walled off behind an extended part of the west end. I had never seen a convent there before—or had I? It was puzzling. Then once again I was outside seeing the series of buildings one after the other, all of them old. (None of these existed in ordinary reality, anywhere.) The dream changed and I was passing along Ely High Street, seeing a kind of coalescence of all the old sacred buildings—of all kinds of old build-

---

Notes for this section can be found on page 283.

ings from all the streets of England—as if they were all actually "the same place, the same building" in an odd way. I accepted that this was so. I saw other arches and entries, but this one strange building, the multiple of all the buildings, was distinct.

I regarded the coalescence dream as a gathering-together in the form of pictures. The land, as we saw it coming up from the west, had power. But the power of the buildings was absolute. I saw soul raised on stone, carved, huge, connected with my soul; constructed, spirit by spirit, stone on stone, absolute, as stone is.

So it was that on the first day, while we were driving along the winding road toward Ely, my eyes followed the cathedral's changing orientation. Now we saw it from the side, its four features lengthened out: tall tower, nave, lantern tower, choir—it had been a very familiar icon (see figure 16.1). At a turn in the road the tower faced us head-on and the huge "lantern" appeared behind it, becoming larger and larger (figure 16.2). It was a great being, *approaching us* as we approached it; now you could see it like a huge beast, its claws outspread. Those were the transepts. The fact that I was just one person seeing it this way wasn't the point. Its power, message, came to me, through me, simply WAS. Even these are the wrong words. The cathedral said, "All things are in connection with me whether you see it or not."

Figure 16.1: Ely cathedral from the river showing the old warehouses (photo by Edith Turner)

Figure 16.2: Ely cathedral, back view showing the lantern tower behind (photo in the possession of Edith Turner)

We drove through town and found our bed-and-breakfast room located above a bookstore on Fore Hill. A book celebration was in progress. The book they were celebrating was about St. Etheldreda, the saint who in 673 AD founded Ely Cathedral (her saint's day had just taken place that June 23, 1999). The dean of Ely was present; also the author of the book, a man who was living in a new house on the site of my old home on St. Mary's Street; then there was the wife of Tony Fletcher who was guide to the cathedral; a woman architect who found some Saxon remains out at Prickwillow Road; the daughter of Sergeant Wall who used to know my father, Dr. George Davis; Mrs. Burgoyne who ran the bookstore and was our landlady; also about thirty middle-aged Ely people. I was surprised at all this. I had not met the Ely intelligentsia since I had left town in 1939, and then I had not been in any position to talk to them. The dean and the author made speeches and Mrs. Burgoyne poured wine. I chatted a lot. After the book-fest I suddenly decided to go and see old Daphne Murfitt, who always sends me Christmas cards and talks about her old dog. I knew her address, 19 Deacons Lane.

It was sunny outside. I had to walk a long way, past where the old movie theater used to be, along pavements where youths now passed with Walkman radios and earphones, then down beside the sports-ground chestnut trees and past an endless series of small row houses.

When I arrived at number 19 I knocked, but had to go to the back alley to get an answer. Daphne Murfitt had been listening to Beethoven on her miniature radio and didn't hear the knocking. She was girlish, fanciful, slender, and a full sixty-two years old. She had not been a maid at 62 St. Mary's Street like my friend Daisy Tucker but remembered Dr. Davis.

The room had linoleum on the floor, two old armchairs, one straight chair (Daphne stood a long time at first), a very small table, the six-inch radio, and that was it. There was nothing else in the room but a lot of space. I asked if I could sit down because I had walked a long way wondering if I'd find her, all down Deacons Lane by those summer evening chestnuts past the row houses, with the sports ground wall on the left. Yet it had been a kind of sacred walk, magical. I sat down.

She said she had a cat and dog, who were not there but "getting trained." I liked her. She was rather guarded. She had a sister, both sisters having been adopted to an aunt. Many people seem to experience this. She was very lonely: "The neighbors are no good."

"Why?" She and I agreed that all the young people of Ely were materialistic, kitschy, "into cars," and the women talked in baby voices. We were in a bad era which showed up the shallowness of the young, while middle-aged people were just like the previous generation of middle-aged people. They were nothing special.

On leaving I gave her £30. After all, she possessed almost nothing.

Writing in 2005, the visit to Daphne is still magical. I think it was the linoleum, the emptiness of the room. It reminded me of little Lee's house in Ivakuk, Alaska, only poorer, and it was magical because I was under the power of a predictive waking dream concerning Mummy and old people, the same odd feeling I experienced in the dialogue with the dead, recorded in chapter 14. The chestnut trees and my tiredness came into it—imponderables. A poem might say it. The power was Ely, breathing everywhere. "Ely." It makes me shiver.

Next morning early, at 6:15, I walked alone down sunny Fore Hill to the river and along beside it to Ely High Bridge, past endless brand-new marinas with their brand-new houseboats. Mrs. Porlack's house was still there, in its place on the left of the road just before you come to the river. She gained her wealth from her husband's brewery and warehousing. She's gone, and so is all her selfishness in refusing evacuees in 1940, and her spoiled lapdog that would eat only fresh liver—as I witnessed once by our front door during a visit of hers, during the German bombing. I remember that I looked jealously at the dog. As for us, we had been on rationing.

But this was now 1999. I went past the inlet where Appleyard's boathouse used to be, where old Mr. Appleyard used to put out varnished rowing boats with plush cushions, letting them bob on the river. We would pay two and six and row down the river. The boathouse was gone, but the tiny inlet over which it used to sit was still there. A posh pub stood beside the inlet now. I even remembered the old basket-maker's shed, full of exciting baskets piled up to the roof. But that shed is no more. I walked alongside trees on what used to be the towpath, now widened for vacationers. At the end I turned left and crossed Ely High Bridge, which I still admired as a grand engineering feat of girders and ornamental rails, quite unique. Now, traffic was streaking over the bridge, daring all kinds of accidents, early in the morning. Even so I paused and looked out along the river just as I used to do—then crossed to the further bank to look for the stile on the right. The hedge was there, different, and bigger than ever. The stile seemed changed and consisted of an arrangement of boards. Yes, the track across the cow field still faintly showed among the high grasses and the dew of June, precisely in the spot where Roly the dog ran obediently with guilty ears between the cows in 1926. The bathing place far away on the opposite side of the river had gone. Coming back to the middle of the bridge I could see two swans, and bushes where the sheds had been. It was the river, the field, and the path that I remembered; the unbelievable richness of the black soil in tilled fields as far as the eye could see, the fens; me on the bridge looking at the river and the field and the path in the clear morning sun, seeing the old bathing place and the dog, now gone; knowing my memory standing in me like a conquering angel, invested in me there, in wonder and awareness and acceptance, held by the diaphanous angel—which was only light and memory. Now, writing later and remembering June 25, I saw again the two swans owning the place up the river a mile away, white and visible in the blue summer morning. It was the straightness of the river—for it had actually been bodily moved and straightened by the Dutch to bring it nearer the town—the river's accuracy, its compelling green and blue perspective, that pointed far away, pointed me far back to the older memory. I remembered my brother, Charlie, dead in World War II, and I quailed with bursting emotion, with homesickness. I heard the cheerful humble speech of the people. The women were even childlike, kind, speaking in diphthong vowels, cleaving close to the revered ordinary; Daphne, the poor woman of Deacons Lane, listening to Beethoven. That was ordinary.

On June 25, 1999 it was a blue, blue morning as it always was. Not a cloud. I watched.

It was from this blessedness that I used to be afraid I would be "sent away"—the threat I was given as a child, a threat twice realized.

I had for years been strung between fear of being sent away and great love of such things as rhododendrons and the smell of warm sand and a hint of the sea. *Now* I have a deep desire to work, sing, anything, with others, in full consciousness, as I do in the choir with the altos. Just that.

In the afternoon I went with my daughter Rene to the cathedral. We entered the Galilee porch, created in 1215 with Moorish onion-dome arches—a style brought straight from the Crusades in Galilee; then forward along the cool pavement and immediately through the main portals into the dim nave. At once I found myself walking on a maze, set in dark and light smooth flagstones on the floor. Now I really was at home. When I was a kid I used to run that maze, fascinated with it. Now, much later, I knew it as the maze of the life path, and I trod it gradually, forth and back, forth and back—"he who would find truth, about and about must go" as the metaphysical poet put it—and I finished up as always, in the center. Then, as always, I craned back my head and looked way upwards, a hundred feet above—and there was Christ, as always, in his colored painting, looking down at us from a ceiling midway up the tower.

The maze under my feet was saying the same thing as "*saa na g'hai bike hozho*," which is the Navajo great salute to the universe: "The beauty that goes back and forth and back and forth forever and ever." It means "process in ecstasy." You'd think they'd never come together, that Navajo utterance and the Ely Cathedral maze, but I *saw* them together, I *spoke* the words, and *walked* the maze. I looked up at the unbelievable height and saw poor old Christ in his bright royal robes. The painters had put him up there; the last shall be first, after all.

We entered, as always, deep in awe, lost in the scent of stone and oak; bowing our heads under great heights. Who—but *who* made this cathedral? What great unthinkable band of people in communitas, like all the choirs of angels, laid hand with hand on chisel and stone, and lifted and placed and finished the columns, in a mystery that has never faded. The cathedral was built on that particular hill brow, side by side with the ancient rise on which the pre-Christian ancients made their mound, the one called Cherry Hill—in order that the land could give birth to that on which it insisted.

These men, by means of strong horses and boats, had hauled eight sixty-foot oaks, each a yard thick, from faraway Barnack near Stamford. Tony Fletcher the guide told us this in his cheerful Saxon accent, now the ordinary cockney East Anglian accent. He told us about it as we gathered on the floor of the octagon, which was the huge space under the lantern tower where tourists and kids wandered. Rene and I listened, along with two photographers from New

Zealand. The eight pillars in their far-spread stations rose around us. There was no music to be heard then, but I had heard the singers many times, sweetening their high tones to mingle with the fan-vaulted sweetness far above—among vaulting that gathers sound in with its fingers, its hands touching each other around the lantern-top, holding together in a vast ring like hovering angels over nothing, high above us all.

Now we are listening to Tony's account of the building of the first tower in the 1300s, and he is telling it as if he had been there himself. The first tower was as tall as the main tower is now. The first tower was intended to rise from the crossing place of the nave and the two transepts. The builders dug down to bedrock to create the foundations of the pillars. They found rock and went ahead. They proceeded to erect the tower on four pillars, closely-spaced, and they burdened them with many hundreds of feet of stone and thousands of tons in weight. However, no one knew at the time that the rock they had originally discovered continued down for only eighteen feet. It was not bedrock at all, because below the apparent bedrock lay *sand*, treacherous sand. They built the tower though, having no geological probes. It stood for a year or two and held as best it could. Then, in 1322.... Could anyone picture the night it crashed? No.... Yet the mind provides the sound. I can hear it. They heard it in the next county.

Then a goldsmith from Walsingham in Norfolk, Alan by name, came to the place. He was a man who knew about jewels, eight-sided crystals. He knew about stress, about strength, about materials, and he was hired to build a new tower. Did he make a model of the new replacement beforehand? Tony led us to an iron model on the left, an object constructed in the nineteenth century. It was a neat perfect web of iron bars about five feet high, the skeleton of the lantern tower. Now we could understand the octagon and the lantern tower. Eight stone pillars, not four, were chosen by Alan, spread far apart so that there would not be too much downward pressure on any small area. Alan wanted to suspend a tower shaped like a lantern far above, balanced over the much wider octagonal space that was guarded by the stone pillars. Somehow the lantern would be held aloft in a mysterious web of forces.

I could hardly look upon the model, I was so much in awe. I was dressing the model in my mind with the tower's flesh, the decorated stone, the eight flag turrets you could see from the outside, gaily painted in silver with caps; the sprigged pinnacles around them. They used to hang bells inside the lantern tower but the monks found the bells might shake the whole structure to ruins. I made a penciled sketch of the iron model, but the model itself was much stouter and stronger than my drawing. The stress-and-strain calculations were meticulous, back and forth, angle and stanchion, brace and counter-brace, the entire way around the eight sides, to hold that stone aerie like a flying boat suspended above *nothing*. This was like St. James's marble coffin flying to Compostella in Spain, or Pohjola's daughter high in the air, weaving at her loom in the *Kalevala*—a scene twinkling with Sibelius's music, or like Kehuq's vision of the Iñupiat flying boat with shamans in it. Impossibilities.

I was looking at the iron model, and on and off I glanced up at the far lantern tower with its eight angel pictures and eight daylight lantern windows hundreds of feet above, looking at them out of the corner of my eye. What I was looking at were concrete completed facts.

Tony led us up winding stone staircases until we emerged between the inner and outer walls of the lantern tower. Here we saw a huge private web of oaken "statements of momenta," hefty limbs fanned out and braced and locked together. We went up more stairs to a place even higher, where Tony took us behind the walls of the lantern itself and let us open the angel panels from within to look down on the floor far below. I felt a gout of vertigo. I moved away and opened the next window-door. It seemed we were standing on a terrific over-hang. I moved more softly then and didn't jump around. I peered out once more and found I could see the stone vaulting spreading away to the side *beneath* me, *under* my feet; I was walking a plank, a diving board, and there was nothing in front of me or below me. This was—crazy! But real. All was balanced and true; far across the gulf was the other side of the lantern. Four sides extending from my left and four sides extending from my right met opposite me and held, clutched in an immovable circle. We were safe. And above, the eight sunny win-dows of the lantern rose, topped by a ceiling from which a painted Christ seemed to burst through a hole from another dimension, sur-rounded by angels.

This work outshone all the modern concrete cantilevers of our pre-sent-day architectural geniuses. Alan de Walsingham, praise! And praise for all the city of masons and holy workers that centered on Ely, centering on it just as Alan's angled oaken ribs centered on the eight kings of the forest that had been hauled up there on the original scaf-folding, then had been bonded together so that they would stand over nothing, anchored upright by stress and pull, forever in a heavenly miracle (see figure 16.3). Tony Fletcher stood us in front of those great oaks themselves as they stood upright, enshrined in strength, their heavy weight standing over nothing, each clutched into place from the side; they smelled of oak, peppery. Rene leaned forward and smelled them too. Some of the eight had had to be replaced. They themselves,

Figure 16.3: Oaken beams anchored to the eight upright oaks of the Ely Cathedral lantern tower (photo in the possession of Edith Turner)

those huge trunks, had been hewn until they too were octagon-sided, humble, invisible, they and their brothers doing the job for seven centuries, long estranged from the sunny forest. "*Oho mitakwi asn*" as the Lakota say. They are all our relations, those oaks. Thank you.

Tony took us outside onto the leads, the very roof of the octagon, where eight huge buttresses muscled themselves against the tower preventing the widening of the web from within. We could now see the sprigged pinnacles close to us, and above, the eight flag turrets, gaily painted in silver and topped with caps. Concealed beneath the silver paint were the great oaks.

In the sunshine we could see Ely spread below. I peered around until I spotted the place where I was born. Then I walked over the leads to Tony and told him about my father.

"I remembers him all roight, when I wos a littl'un. Yore dad!" We wrung each others' hands and smiled hugely.

"That's the sycamore I climbed as a kid," I said. "See? That big one. All of us eight kids used to climb it, and when we got to the top we thought we were nearer the cathedral." Tony and I grinned at each other. "We weren't, were we?"

Note

1. For instance in Michael Higgins's *Ely Cathedral* (Andover, UK, 1993.

BIBLIOGRAPHY

Angell, Norman. 1913. *The Great Illusion*. London: Putman.

Augustine of Hippo, St. 1950 [427]. *The City of God*. New York: Modern Library.

Bergson, Henry. 1931. *Creative Evolution*. New York: Holt.

Bernard of Cluny, St. 1989 [12th century]. "Jerusalem the golden." From *De Contemptu Mundi*. Tr. J.M. Neale. In Kevin Mayhew, ed. No. 273. Bury St. Edmunds, UK: Kevin Mayhew.

Bible, The. Psalms 16, 19, 23, 29, 31, 34, 40, 42, 139.

Blake, William (1757-1827). 1970. *The Poetry and Prose of William Blake*, edited by David Erdman. Garden City,NY: Doubleday.

_____ 1970 [1804]. "And did those feet in ancient times." In *The Poetry and Prose of William Blake*, edited by David Erdman. Pp. 94-95. Garden City, NY: Doubleday.

_____ 1991 [1804]. "I will give you the end of a golden string. " In *Jerusalem: The Emanation of the Giant Albion. The Illuminated Books, Volume I*. Ed. with introduction and notes by Morton D. Paley. P. 77. Princeton, NJ: William Blake Trust/Princeton University Press.

Cadhain, Liam. 1945. *Cnoc Muire in Picture and Story*. Dublin: Frederick Press.

Card, Orson Scott. 1990. *Cruel Miracles*. New York: Tom Doherty Associates.

Chambers, Edward. 2003. *Roots for Radicals: Organizing for Power, Action, and Justice*. Foreword by Studs Terkel. New York: Continuum.

Clark, Kenneth. 1975. *The Romantic Rebellion: Romantic Versus Classic Art*. Don Mills, Ontario: Longmans.

Colson, Elizabeth. 1971. *The Social Consequences of Resettlement: The Impact of the Kariba Resettlement upon the Gwembe Tonga*. Manchester, UK: Manchester University Press.

Csikszentmihalyi, Mihali. 1990. *Flow: The Psychology of Optimal Experience*. New York: Harper and Row.

Dakowski, Bruce, video recording. 1990. *Strange Beliefs* (Evans-Pritchard among the Azande). Princeton, NJ: Films for the Humanities.

Dante Aligheiri. 1965 [1321]. *The Divine Comedy*. Cambridge, MA: Harvard University Press.

Del Pellicciaio, Jacopo di Mino (attributed to). 134[6]. Fresco: Purgatory with St. Patrick. At Todi, Umbria, Italy. Convent of St. Francis.

Deren, Maya. 1953. *Divine Horsemen: The Living Gods of Haiti*. London: Thames and Hudson.

Desjarlais, Robert. 1992. *Body and Emotion*. Philadelphia: University of Pennsylvania Press.

Donne, John. 1975 [1633]. "Holy Sonnets 7." In *The Norton Anthology of Poetry*, eds. Alexander Allison, Caesar Blake, Arthur Carr, Arthur Eastman, and Hubert English, Jr. P. 249. New York: Norton.

Doré, Gustav. Illustration to Dante's *Inferno*. "The Violent Tortured in the Rain of Fire." http://dante.ilt.columbia.edu/new/images/index.htnl

Dossey, Larry. 1989. *Recovering the Soul: A Scientific and Spiritual Search*. New York: Bantam.

Driver, Tom. 1991.*The Magic of Ritual*. San Francisco: HarperCollins.

Durkheim, Emile. 1965 [1915]. *The Elementary Forms of the Religious Life*. New York: Free Press.

Eliade, Mircea. 1964. *Shamanism: Archaic Techniques of Ecstasy*. Princeton, NJ: Princeton University Press.

Ellingson, Ter. 1998. "The Arrow and the Mirror: Interactive Consciousness, Ethnography, and the Tibetan State Oracle's Trance." *Anthropology and Humanism* 23(1):51-76.

Evans-Pritchard, E.E.
_____ 1976 [1937]. *Witchcraft, Oracles, and Magic among the Azande*. Oxford: Clarendon.

Farrer, Claire. 1991. *Living Life's Circle: Mescalero Apache Cosmovision*. Albuqerque, NM: University of New Mexico Press.

Favret-Saada, Jeanne. 1980. *Deadly Words: Witchcraft in the Bocage*. Cambridge: Cambridge University Press.

Fienup-Riordan, Ann.1983. *The Nelson Island Eskimo*. Anchorage: Alaska Pacific University Press.
_____ 1994. *Boundaries and Passages: Rule and Ritual in Yup'ik Eskimo Oral Tradition*. Norman, OK: University of Oklahoma Press.

Forde, Daryll. 1950. *Habitat, Economy, and Society*. London: Methuen.

Fortes, Meyer. 1945. *The Dynamics of Clanship among the Tallensi*. London: Oxford University Press.
_____ 1949. *The Web of Kinship among the Tallensi*. London: Oxford University Press.

Fortes, Meyer and Edward E. Evans-Pritchard, eds. 1940. *African Political Systems*. London: Oxford University Press.

Foulks, E.F. 1972. *The Arctic Hysterias of the Alaskan Eskimo*. Washington: American Anthropological Association.

Fruzzetti, Lina. 1982. *The Gift of a Virgin: Women, Marriage, and Ritual in a Bengali Society*. New Brunswick, NJ: Rutgers University Press.

Gaffney, Patrick. 2000. "Fire from Heaven." In *The Nature and Function of Rituals*. Ruth-Inge Heinze, ed. Pp. 151-178. Westport, CT: Bergin and Garvey.

Geertz, Clifford. 1971. "Deep Play: Notes on the Balinese Cockfight." In *The Interpretation of Cultures*, by Clifford Geertz. Pp. 412-453. New York: Norton.

Gennep, Arnold van. 1960 [1909]. *The Rites of Passage*. London: Routledge and Kegan Paul.

Girard, René. 1977. *Violence and the Sacred*. Baltimore: Johns Hopkins University Press.

Gluckman, Max. 1941. *The Economy of the Central Barotse Plain*. Manchester, UK: Manchester University Press.

Goodman, Paul. 1960. *Communitas: Means of Livelihood and Ways of Life*. New York: Vintage.

Goulet, Jean-Guy. 1994. "Ways of Knowing: Towards a Narrative Ethnography of the Dene Tha." *Journal of Anthropological Research* 50(2):113-139.

Harner, Michael. 1968. "The Sound of Rushing Water." *Natural History* 77(6):28-33.
_____ 1972. *The Jivaro: People of the Sacred Waterfall*. Garden City, NY: Doubleday.

_____ 1980. *The Way of the Shaman: A Guide to Power and Healing*. San Francisco: Harper and Row.

Herbert, George. 1975a [1633]. "Prayer (I)." In *The Norton Anthology of Poetry*, eds. Alexander Allison, Caesar Blake, Arthur Carr, Arthur Eastman, and Hubert English, Jr. P. 287. New York: Norton.

_____ 1975b [1633] "Love (III)." In *The Norton Anthology of Poetry*, eds. Alexander Allison, Caesar Blake, Arthur Carr, Arthur Eastman, and Hubert English, Jr. P. 300. New York: Norton.

Higgins, Michael. 1993. *Ely Cathedral*. Andover: Pitkin Pictorials.

Hopkins, Gerard Manley. 1975 [1877]. "God's Grandeur. " In *The Norton Anthology of Poetry*, eds. Alexander Allison, Caesar Blake, Arthur Carr, Arthur Eastman, and Hubert English Jr. Pp. 899-900. New York: Norton.

Howard, Albert. 1946. *Soil and Health*. London: Industrial Christian Fellowship.

Hufford, David. 1982 *The Terror that Comes in the Night: An Experience-Centered Study of Supernatural Assault Traditions*. Philadelphia: University of Pennsylvania Press.

Hulse, Gould. n.d. Talk. "Soul and Reincarnation." *Alternatives*, Healers' Group, Charlottesville, 1980. Gould Hulse, 1 Stone St., Staten Island, NY 10304; (718) 4471436.

Hunt, Eva. 1977. *The Transformation of the Hummingbird*. Ithaca, NY: Cornell University Press.

Jackson, Michael. 1989. *Paths Toward a Clearing: Radical Empiricism and Ethnographic Inquiry*. Bloomington, IN: Indiana University Press.

James, William. 1958 [1902]. *The Varieties of Religious Experience*. New York: Mentor. New American Library.

Jeans, James. 1930. *The Mysterious Universe*. Cambridge: Cambridge University Press.

Jung, Carl. 1928. *Two Essays in Analytical Psychology*. New York: Dodd and Mead.

Junod, Henri A. 1962. *The Life of a South African Tribe. Volume II: Mental Life*. New York: University Books.

Kelsey, Morton. 1991. *Companion on the Inner Way: The Art of Spiritual Guidance*. New York: Crossroad.

Kennedy, Eugene. 1988. *Tomorrow's Catholics: The Two Cultures of American Catholicism*. New York: Harper and Row.

Kierkegaard, Søren. 1954 [1843]. *Fear and Trembling*. Garden City, NY: Doubleday.

King, Franklin Hiram. 1911. *Farmers of Forty Centuries: Permanent Agriculture in China, Korea, and Japan*. New York: Harcourt, Brace, and Company.

Leslie, Shane. 1932. *St. Patrick's Purgatory*. London: Burns, Oates, and Washbourne.

Lessing, Doris. 1995. *Under My Skin: Volume One of my Autobiography*. London: Flamingo.

Lewis-Williams, David. 1990. *Discovering South African Rock Art*. Cape Town: D. Philip.

Levi-Strauss, Claude. 1997. *Triste Tropique*. New York: Modern Library.

Lex, Barbara. 1979. "The Neurobiology of Ritual Trance. " In Eugene D'Aquili, Charles Laughlin, and John McManus, eds. *The Spectrum of Ritual*. Pp. 117-151. New York: Columbia University Press.

Maslow, Abraham. 1964. *Religions, Values, and Peak Experiences*. Columbus, OH: Ohio State University Press.

Mead, Margaret. 1928. *Coming of Age in Samoa*. New York: Armed Services.

_____ 1930. *Growing Up in New Guinea*. New York: Morrow.

Michael, Chester, and Marie Norrisey 1991. *Prayer and Temperament*. Charlottesville, VA: Open Door.

Mills, Antonia. 1998. "Scientific and Participant Validation of Rebirth: Similarities, Differences, and Is There a Bridge?" Paper read at the Annual Meetings of the

American Anthropological Association, Philadelphia, in the panel, "The Spirit Hypothesis."

Moody, Raymond A. 1976. *Life After Life: The Investigation of a Phenomenon: Survival of Bodily Death*. New York: Bantam.

Myerhoff, Barbara. 1974. *Peyote Hunt: The Sacred Journey of the Huichol Indians*. Ithaca, NY: Cornell University Press.

_____ 1993. "Pilgrimage to Meron: Inner and Outer Peregrinations." In *Creativity/Anthropology*. Smadar Lavie, Kirin Narayan, and Renato Rosaldo, eds. Pp. 212-222. Ithaca, NY: Cornell University Press.

Neihardt, John. 1932. *Black Elk Speaks: Being the Life Story of a Holy Man of the Oglala Sioux*. As told through John G. Neihardt. New York: Morrow.

Nietzsche, Friedrich. 1932. *Thus Spake Zarathustra*. London: Allen and Unwin.

Otto, Rudolf. 1928. *The Idea of the Holy*. London: Oxford University Press.

Patrick, Saint. 1924 [5th century?]. *Confessions*. Dublin: Irish Messenger.

Peters, Larry. 1981. *Ecstasy and Healing in Nepal: An Ethnopsychiatric Study of Tamany Shamanism*. Malibu CA: Undena.

Progoff, Ira. 1963. *The Symbolic and the Real*. New York: McGraw Hill.

_____ 1975. *At a Journal Workshop*. New York: Dialogue House Library.

Radcliffe-Brown, Alfred. R. 1922. *The Andaman Islanders*. Cambridge: Cambridge University Press.

Rappaport, Roy. 1999. *Ritual and Religion in the Making of Humanity*. Cambridge: Cambridge University Press.

Reinhardt, Douglas. 1988. "With His Stripes We Are Healed: White Pentecostals and Faith Healing. In *Diversities of Gifts: Field Studies in Southern Religion*. Ruel Tyson Jr., James Peacock, and Daniel Patterson, eds. Pp. 126-142. Urbana, IL: University of Illinois Press.

Richards, Audrey. 1982 [1956]. *Chisungu: A Girl's Initiation Ceremony among the Bemba of Zambia*. London: Tavistock.

Ruby, Jay, ed. 1982 *A Crack in the Mirror*. Philadelphia: University of Pennsylvania Press.

Sharp, Stephen. 1996. "Experiencing Meaning." *Anthropology and Humanism* 21(2):171-186.

Shaw, Bernard. 1929. *The Intelligent Woman's Guide to Socialism and Capitalism*. London: Constable.

_____ 1931. *Complete Plays*. London: Constable.

Shelley, Percy Bysshe. 1975 [1820a]. "Ode to the West Wind." In *The Norton Anthology of Poetry*, eds. Alexander Allison, Caesar Blake, Arthur Carr, Arthur Eastman, and Hubert English Jr. Pp. 669-671. New York: Norton.

_____ 1975 [1820b]. "The Cloud." In *The Norton Anthology of Poetry*, eds. Alexander Allison, Caesar Blake, Arthur Carr, Arthur Eastman, and Hubert English Jr. Pp. 671-672. New York: Norton.

Sholem, Gershom. 1965. *On the Kabbalah and its Symbolism*. London: Routledge and Kegan Paul.

Spicer, Edward. 1980. *The Yaquis: A Cultural History*. Tucson: University of Arizona Press.

Stalin, Joseph. 1939. *The History of the Communist Party of the Soviet Union (Bolsheviks)*. New York: International Publishers.

Stevens, Anthony. 1982. *Archetypes: A Natural History of the Self*. New York: Morrow.

Stoller, Paul. 1984. "Eye, Mind, and Word in Anthropology." *L'Homme* 24(3-4):91-114.

Teilhard de Chardin, Pierre. 1961. *The Phenomenon of Man*. New York: Harper.

Thomas, Dylan. 1975 [1934]. "The Force that through the Green Fuse Drives the Flower." In *The Norton Anthology of Poetry*, eds. Alexander Allison, Caesar Blake, Arthur Carr, Arthur Eastman, and Hubert English Jr. P. 1162. New York: Norton.

Trevarthen, Colwen. 1980. "Neurological Development and the Growth of Psychological Functions." In *Developmental Psychology and Society*. J. Sants, ed. Pp. 46-95. London: Macmillan.

Tucker, Elizabeth. 1984. "Levitation and Trance Sessions at Preadolescent Girls' Slumber Parties." In *The Masks of Play*. Brian Sutton-Smith and Diana Kelly-Byrne, eds. Pp. 119- 124. New York: Leisure Press.

Turnbull, Colin. 1990. "Liminality: A Synthesis of Subjective and Objective Experience." In *By Means of Performance*. Richard Schechner and Willa Appel, eds. Pp. 50-81. New York: Cambridge University Press.

Turner, Edith. 1985. Prologue. In *On the Edge of the Bush: Anthropology as Experience*, by Victor Turner. Pp. 1-15. Tucson: University of Arizona Press.

_____ 1986. "Philip Kabwita, Ghost Doctor: The Ndembu in 1985." *The Drama Review* 30(4):4-35.

_____ 1987. *The Spirit and the Drum*. Tucson, AZ: University of Arizona Press.

_____ 1989a. "The Yaqui Deer Dance at Pascua Pueblo," in *By Means of Performance*. Richard Schechner and Willa Appel, eds. Pp. 82-95. New York: Cambridge University Press.

_____ 1992. *Experiencing Ritual: A New Interpretation of African Healing*. Philadelphia: Pennsylvania University Press.

_____ 1993. "Rabbi Shimon Bar Yohai: The Creative Persona and his Pilgrimage." In *Creativity/Anthropology*, ed. Smadar Lavie, Kirin Narayan, and Renato Rosaldo. Ithaca: Cornell University Press.

_____ 1995. "Changes in the Status of Senior Women Anthropologists after Feminist Revision," paper presented in the invited session, Society for Feminist Anthropology, entitled *Through a Gendered Looking Glass: Women Doing Ethnography, Before and After 1974*, American Anthropological Association Annual Meetings, Washington, November.

_____ 1996. *The Hands Feel It: Healing and Spirit Presence among a Northern Alaskan People*. DeKalb, IL: Northern Illinois University Press.

_____ 1997. "There are No Peripheries to Humanity: Northern Alaska Nuclear Dumping and the Iñupiat's Search for Redress." *Anthropology and Humanism* 22(1):95-110.

_____ 2004. "Taking Seriously the Nature of Religious Healing in America." In *Religious Healing in America*. Susan Sered and Linda Barnes, eds. Pp. 387-404. New York: Oxford University Press.

N.d. *The Ancient and the Holy: The Roots and Flower of Irish Spirit Experience*. Manuscript.

Turner, Victor. 1957. *Schism and Continuity in an African Society: A Study of Ndembu Village Life*. Manchester: Manchester University Press.

_____ 1962. *Chihamba the White Spirit: A Ritual Drama of the Ndembu*. Rhodes-Livingstone Papers 33. Manchester, UK: Manchester University Press.

_____ 1967. *The Forest of Symbols: Aspects of Ndembu Ritual*. Ithaca NY: Cornell University Press.

_____ 1968. *The Drums of Affliction: A Study of Religious Processes among the Ndembu of Zambia*. Oxford: Clarendon.

_____ 1974. *Dramas, Fields, and Metaphors*. Ithaca, NY: Cornell University Press.

_____ 1975. *Revelation and Divination*. Ithaca, NY: Cornell University Press.

_____ 1985. *On the Edge of the Bush: Anthropology as Experience*. Tucson: University of Arizona Press.

Turner, Victor and Edward Bruner, eds. 1986. *The Anthropology of Experience*. Urbana: University of Illinois Press.

Turner, Victor, and Edith Turner. 1978. *Image and Pilgrimage in Christian Culture: Anthropological Perspectives*. New York: Columbia University Press.

Wagner, Roy. 1986. *Symbols That Stand for Themselves*. Chicago: University of Chicago Press.

Walsh, Michael. 1959. *The Apparition at Knock: A Survey of Facts and Evidence*. Tuam, Ireland: St. Jarlath's College.

Watkins, Mary. 1984. *Waking Dreams*. Dallas, TX: Spring Publications.

Werbner, Richard. 1996. *Tears of the Dead: The Social Biography of an African Family*. Edinburgh: Edinburgh University Press.

Whiting, W. 1989 [1825-1878]. "Eternal Father, strong to save." In *Hymns Old and New*. Kevin Mayhew, ed. No. 127. Bury St. Edmunds, UK: Kevin Mayhew.

Wink, Walter. 1992. *Engaging the Powers: Discernment and Resistance in a World of Domination*. Minneapolis: Fortress Press.

Wordsworth, William. 1975 [1798]. "Lines Composed a Few Miles above Tintern Abbey." In *The Norton Anthology of Poetry*, eds. Alexander Allison, Caesar Blake, Arthur Carr, Arthur Eastman, and Hubert English Jr. Pp. 577-580. New York: Norton.

_____ 1975 [1798-1800]. "The Prelude, Book I." In *The Norton Anthology of Poetry*, eds. Alexander Allison, Caesar Blake, Arthur Carr, Arthur Eastman, and Hubert English Jr. Pp. 582-588. New York: Norton.

_____ 1975 [1798-1802]. "Ode: Intimations of Immortality from Recollections of Early Childhood." In *The Norton Anthology of Poetry*, eds. Alexander Allison, Caesar Blake, Arthur Carr, Arthur Eastman, and Hubert English Jr. Pp. 601-605. New York: Norton.

Zohar: The Book of Enlightenment. 1983 [2nd Century CE by Rabbi Simon Bar Yohai; 1286 by Moses de Lyon]. Tr. Daniel Chana Matt. New York: Paulist Press.

INDEX